S0-CFZ-939

COMMUNICATING ACROSS CULTURES AT WORK

Communicating across Cultures at Work

Second Edition

MAUREEN GUIRDHAM

Ichor Books
An Imprint of
Purdue University Press
West Lafayette, Indianna

© Maureen Guirdham 2005

First published 1999 as *Communicating across Cultures*
Second edition 2005

Published in North America under license from
Palgrave Macmillan Ltd,
Houndmills Basingstoke, Hampshire, RG21 6XS, United Kingdom.

ISBN-13: 978-1-55753-410-1
ISBN-10: 1-55753-410-1

This book is printed on paper suitable for recycling and made from fully managed and sustained forest sources.

A catalog record for this book is available from the Library of Congress.

Printed and bound in China

For Damon and Oliver

Contents

List of Figures and Tables

Preface

The intention in this new edition of *Communicating across Cultures* is to retain and improve the features of the first edition that were most valued by its users, while adding new dimensions that were not previously covered. The practical focus of the chapters on how to communicate interculturally and how to function internationally has been retained; so has the breadth of diversity covered, so that ethnic, gender, age, social class and religious subcultures are covered and not just national cultures. The book also continues to rely heavily on published research for its main conclusions, while many illustrations are drawn from the author's own research and from current news reports.

The structure has been improved by a division into Parts which make clearer the distinction between those chapters focused on culture and its impact on communication, those focused on intercultural communication and those which are extensions and applications of the earlier chapters. Other improvements include integrating intercultural communication theories more thoroughly with their practical implications, a closer focus on European examples and research, so that the book complements American texts with their emphasis on US and Far Eastern examples, and the inclusion of more cases and worked examples.

One new dimension of this edition is the coverage of work activities in Chapter 8. Cultural differences in selection interviewing, negotiating, mediating, working in groups and teams, leadership and management, and working in international alliances lead to the need to conduct these activities appropriately in intercultural settings. Another new element is the inclusion of questions and exercises at the end of each chapter.

A NOTE ON TERMINOLOGY

References in the text to cultures and subcultures as distinct concepts use the terms without brackets. To cover the combined concepts the terms (sub)culture and (sub)cultural are generally used; however, when referring to communication and interactions between members of different groups, I prefer the term 'intercultural', to avoid the clumsiness of 'inter(sub)cultural'. To refer to members of groups other than a communicator's own, I generally use the terminology, which is gradually becoming current, of 'different others', and to capture the quality of their difference, 'otherness'. However, certain intercultural communication theories use the term 'strangers' instead of 'different others' and where that is so, the author's original terminology is retained. Again, I generally use the term 'interpersonal' to mean 'between people' or 'face-to-face'. However, in some writings on intercultural communication 'interpersonal' is used in contrast to 'intergroup' and 'intercultural', in the sense that an encounter, even between only two people, may occur on an intergroup, intercultural or interpersonal level. Again, in these cases I follow the terminology of the writer but try to make the difference clear.

Labels for societal groups are always problematic – the subject is discussed in the section on inclusive language in Chapter 6. The term 'minority' is often used not literally, but defined as a group in a subordinate position irrespective of relative size; for example it can be applied to women in Britain or Black people in South Africa, both of whom are numeric majorities. This usage can be sensitive because of its indirect reference to subordinate status, but in the absence of any other accepted general term and because it is adopted by the UK Commission for Racial Equality, it is the usage of this book.

USING THIS BOOK

As far as possible, this book is based on research material. Because the field, though rapidly developing, is still a young one, this necessarily limits its coverage. Nevertheless, it has proved possible to cover adequately most topics needed for an understanding of cross-cultural and intercultural communication and to provide guidance on applying these understandings at work. The underpinnings of cultural theory, psychology, social psychology, communication studies, interactive behaviour are touched on, but readings such as those given in Further Reading are needed for full comprehension.

Each of the eight chapters contains an introduction and summary as well as the core sections. The questions and exercises offer a range of learning opportunities, including case analyses, group discussions, role plays and self-completion questionnaires. Appendix C shows how to score and interpret these questionnaires.

The boxes in the text provide illustrative material. Many are based on the author's own interviews. Some are referred to in the text; others are not, allowing readers to interpret them for themselves.

Acknowledgements

I would like to thank all those who helped my research with contributions and interviews, with especial mention of Frances Truscott. Thanks also to the reviewers whose comments on the first edition and the proposal for this one were invaluable and to friends, including Jinnu Gao and Alan Woodcock, who helped edit.

Table 3.4 Reprinted from Orbe, M.P. (1998) 'From the standpoint(s) of traditionally muted groups: explicating a co-cultural communication theoretical model', *Communication Theory*, **8**(1): 1–26, by permission of Oxford University Press.

Table 4.1 Reprinted from Schwartz, S.H., 'Universals in value content and structure: theoretical advances and empirical tests in 20 countries', *Advances in Experimental Social Psychology*, **25**: 1–26 (Copyright 1992), with permission from Elsevier.

Table 6.1 Reprinted from Orbe, M.P. (1998) 'From the standpoint(s) of traditionally muted groups: explicating a co-cultural communication theoretical model', *Communication Theory*, **8**(1): 1–26, by permission of Oxford University Press.

part one

Culture and Communication at Work

chapter one

Communication and Diversity at Work

This book is about culture, subculture and the impact of these on how people at work communicate with one another. It is also about (sub)cultural differences and how to overcome the obstacles to communication that these may create. This knowledge leads to understanding how to communicate effectively with people from different backgrounds. (It should not, however, be thought that culture is the only important influence on communication. Many other factors influence it and both hinder and facilitate intercultural communication.)

Modern societies and organisations are composed of people who differ widely in terms of nationality, ethnicity, gender, sexual orientation, age, education, social class or level of (dis)ability – in other words, in terms of their demographic profile or social background. The countries of world regions (such as Europe) are becoming integrated, their markets and workforces diverse and their organisations international. At work, therefore, individuals are now likely to interact with a highly diverse range of people as colleagues, subordinates, managers, clients, patients, customers, students, professional advisers and other service providers, sales representatives and other interface workers. More people than ever before now interact with 'different others' in these varying roles. (Different others are people whose demographic profile or social background is different from an individual's own.) Their communication in such interactions, especially face-to-face, is the subject of this book.

Part I of the book analyses diversity at work, cultures, subcultures and cultural and subcultural similarities and differences in how we communicate. This chapter (Chapter 1) has two main purposes: to substantiate the claim that intercultural communication at work is of great and growing importance and to begin describing the context in which such communication takes place. Some of the material in this chapter serves both purposes. For instance, facts about the size and employment position of different societal groups demonstrate the amount and range of intercultural encounters that must be happening. These facts are also relevant to the beliefs, attitudes and so to the communication behaviours of the participants. Admittedly, there is a problem with this last point: it is people's perceptions that influence their beliefs and attitudes, rather than any 'objective' facts, and in individual cases the two may diverge quite widely. Nevertheless the facts are useful as an overall foundation for understanding how interlocutors view the intercultural social world of work. Appendix A gives more detail on the facts.

A discussion of discrimination and harassment at work is included in this chapter because there is clear evidence that these are part of the everyday realities of working life for some groups and so an essential part of the context. Descriptions of organisational diversity policies and practices are also included here because they significantly affect the climate for intercultural interactions at work, especially among colleagues.

The last quarter century of cross-cultural research has firmly established that there are differences in the ways that members of different societal groups behave, both in private life and at work. Chapter 2 sets out to increase readers' understanding of what culture means. Approaches that emphasise communication and cultural identity are particularly important for this book. Chapter 2 also analyses cultures and cultural differences, using a range of models. Many of these models are taxonomies based on underlying factors, such as values; others are based on communication itself, such as Hall's 'high-context/low-context' distinction. Later sections discuss certain conceptual issues, including whether cultural concepts can be generalised to subcultural groups and whether and how cultures change. A final section considers the impact of culture and cultural difference at work.

Chapters 3 and 4 cover face-to-face communication at work and the effects of (sub)cultural difference. The subject of human communication is a huge one and radical selection has been necessary for this book: it has been done by selecting those elements of general communication which differ between cultures, such as the concept of 'politeness', and those which feed directly in to intercultural communication, such as 'elaborated and restricted codes'. Chapter 3 deals with analyses of overt communication behaviour at an individual level; Chapter 4 expands the analysis into the psychological factors and processes affecting behaviour.

Part II of the book is about intercultural communication at work. Chapter 5 presents the argument that intercultural communication is problematic in particular ways. It describes the wide range of barriers that apply. It both deals with 'universal' factors, such as stereotyping and prejudice, and builds on the analyses of Chapters 2, 3 and 4, by showing how (sub)cultural differences also impede intercultural communication. Chapter 6 is concerned with how intercultural communication can be made more effective. Its coverage ranges from inclusive language to the practical application of a number of intercultural communication theories. Attention is paid to behaviours and traits such as tolerance for ambiguity, mindfulness and self-monitoring. There is discussion of the underlying motivations, goals, emotions and cognitions as well as the processes of intercultural encounters.

Part III consists of applications and extensions of the understanding of (sub)cultural difference and intercultural communication. Chapter 7 deals with the different situation that arises when the work context is that of a culture other than the individual's own. Sojourners and people on international assignments need additional skills and new attitudes to work effectively in a foreign culture. Chapter 8 discusses cultural differences in and effective intercultural communication for interviewing, selection interviewing, negotiating, conflict resolution (mediating), leadership/managing, international project management and working in international alliances. Because of its focus on specific applications, this chapter has a different structure from those of the other chapters in the book. Figure 1.1 shows the structure of this book in a diagram.

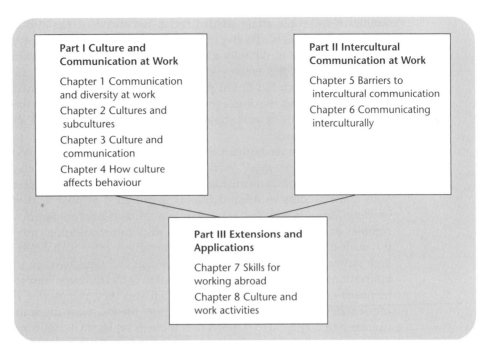

Part I Culture and Communication at Work

Chapter 1 Communication and diversity at work

Chapter 2 Cultures and subcultures

Chapter 3 Culture and communication

Chapter 4 How culture affects behaviour

Part II Intercultural Communication at Work

Chapter 5 Barriers to intercultural communication

Chapter 6 Communicating interculturally

Part III Extensions and Applications

Chapter 7 Skills for working abroad

Chapter 8 Culture and work activities

Figure 1.1   *The structure of this book*

1.1   THE IMPORTANCE OF WORK COMMUNICATION

The significance of any activity at work can be 'measured' by the amount of time employees spend at it, and by its impact on how effectively and efficiently the work is carried out, on job satisfaction and career success for individuals, and on profits or other measures of results for organisations. By all these measures, it is likely that communication is the most important work activity, especially in modern, service-oriented, team-based organisations. Communication has been described as a revolutionary discovery,[1] energised by technological development, increasing global literacy, and 'the philosophies of progressivism and pragmatism, which stimulated a desire to improve society through widespread social change'.[2] In the world of work and organisation, many writers now acknowledge the central role of communication and there is a large literature devoted to it.[3] The new recognition that in order to compete modern organisations need to tap the creativity, expertise and know-how of all their employees places a premium on interpersonal communication. There is considerable evidence that both individual achievement in organisations and organisational effectiveness are closely related to the communication abilities of staff. Research in a large insurance company and two other organisations showed that persuasive ability was a relatively strong predictor of performance appraisal ratings, job level and upward mobility.[4] Another study investigated the link between communication abilities and organisational achievement among 394 employees of three south-east US organisations – a State-owned not-for-profit retail store, a state human services agency and a private mail-order company (from which came 203 participants). This research established that communication abilities and achievement are closely linked for both men and women. The researchers concluded, 'The results lend additional support to the claim that these abilities help people attain desired social outcomes.'[5] It has also been shown that small business owners who give directions and control to their employees in a 'person-centred' way – that is, skillfully adjust their instructions and feedback to the characteristics of the individual employee – are perceived more positively as leaders by their employees. Research has linked person-centred communication by doctors to health outcomes, including the degree to which patients comply with 'doctors' orders'.[6] There is a developing body of work showing that teacher communication methods influence student empowerment.[7]

Communication can be defined as the 'collective and interactive process of generating and interpreting messages'.[8] Work communication is essential for co-ordinating activities; co-ordination is fundamental to organisation. Work communication also leads to both understanding or misunderstanding and good or poor work relationships. All communication is complex; work communication is less complex in some ways, more complex in others. Focus on tasks reduces work communication complexity; however, it is made more complex by continuous interaction, often with different others, by the high stakes often involved for both individuals and organisations, by the conflicting motivations of participants and by the need to work in groups. New technologies have increased communication opportunities but also their complexity. For instance, call centre staff in Asia, responding to callers from the UK, must adjust to time-of-day differences and may need to respond to comments on local UK concerns such as politics. Again, staff who need to send frequent emails to colleagues or customers in another continent can experience difficulty if they have never visited and have no first-hand knowledge of local conditions. Appendix B describes some effects of technological mediation on interpersonal communication.

> Effective communication at work is crucial and often difficult.

1.2 CULTURAL DIFFERENCES AND COMMUNICATION AT WORK

From about 1960, fairness concerns and pressure from minority groups led many countries to pass equal opportunities legislation. It became unlawful to discriminate in employment against people on the grounds of their 'race' (ethnicity) or gender. Over subsequent years, the coverage and demands of this kind of legislation gradually expanded. However, traditional equal opportunities approaches came to be criticised for denying differences. 'Equal rights necessarily came to mean we are all the same.'[9] A more recent trend has been towards valuing diversity, which means 'viewing people as having equal rights while being different'. Valuing diversity in the workplace 'is about recognising, valuing, and managing people's differences and about sharing power and communicating'. Workplace diversity focuses on 'empowering people of all kinds to develop and contribute their own unique talents to solving our business problems', rather than having employees 'give up their own ethnic, gender, or individual identities to be successful'. Heightened concern with diversity stems not only from the growing presence of women and minorities in the work force, but also from modern organisational strategies that require more interaction among employees of different functional backgrounds. The effects on performance were and still are unclear. Studies have found both positive and negative effects of workforce diversity on performance. Some have shown that group diversity both enhances and diminishes task performance. The negative effects may result from poor management of diversity. Even

Box 1.1

The departmental managers of Motorola in Malaysia 'looked like a visionary's ideal of multicultural co-operation. Chinese, Malay, Indian, black, yellow, pale brown Christian, Buddhist, Muslim, Hindu. The racial diversity was the result of being advised by the Malaysia government to play an active role in restructuring the ethnic composition of the company.

"We were told to hire a number of Malay people. ... Chinese, Indians, just like your affirmative action in the U.S.", one of them said.'

Source: Greider, W. (1997) *One World, Ready or Not: The Manic Logic of Global Capitalism,* New York: Simon and Schuster

though working with diversity is intrinsically more demanding, good management of diversity can enhance overall performance.[10]

Recently, the need to adapt for cultural difference has become a major concern of general management, marketing and human resource management. One reason is the increasing globalisation of business. Another is the demonstration by researchers that cultural differences within modern societies are profound and significantly affect how people behave. These differences are not disappearing, even though in superficial ways some aspects of life are becoming more similar.

The importance of culture for international business and the problems managers have in dealing with it have been summarised as follows:

As markets globalize, the need for standardization in organizational design, systems and procedures increases. Yet managers are also under pressure to adapt their organization to the local characteristics of the market, the legislation, the fiscal regime, the socio-political system and the cultural system. ...

Culture still seems like a luxury item to most managers ... . In fact, culture pervades and radiates meanings into every aspect of the enterprise.[11]

The following are some 'aspects of the enterprise' affected by culture:

- Cultural differences are known to affect people's purchasing behaviour, and therefore the most effective ways of marketing to them. For instance, Scandinavian countries have much faster take-off rates for adopting new technical products, such as DVD recorders or third generation mobile phones, than those of the big European economies such as Germany and Britain. Scandinavian countries also adopt new products twice as fast as Mediterranean countries. Culture is considered more significant than economics in these differences.[12] An 11-country study found that cultural variables influence the focus of consumers' product information search activities.[13] With spreading globalisation, more organisations must take these kinds of difference into account.

- In service economies, such as those of many European countries, business success depends on effective interactions and communications between people. 'Delivering service products requires employees with well-developed interpersonal skills; cultural similarity between the service provider and the customer may improve the effectiveness of service delivery and the perceived quality of service.'[14]

Several studies have found that race and gender affect interactions between employees and customers in service businesses. Organisations may better understand and meet customers' needs in ethnic and international markets if they not only have a diverse workforce but also 'listen' to its diverse contributions.

■ Diversity in domestic organisations is a growing concern, 'as more and more minorities are brought into domestic work forces.'[15] Tung argued that there are important similarities, as well as differences, in managing diversity in international and national contexts. There is a need, however, for more emphasis on the domestic issue rather than the international one.[16] In a later presentation, Tung explained why:

[First] due to the localization policies of most host countries and the rising costs of expatriation, there will be a decrease in the number of expatriates. In comparison, the problem of managing intra-national diversity is definitely increasing in size and magnitude ...; [second] ... expatriates involved in managing cross-national diversity do so on a short-term basis (2 to 3 years). In contrast, in light of the changing demographics of the ... workforce, those involved in managing intra-national diversity are expected to have a long-term (permanent) commitment to such policies and practices.[17]

■ There is also concern with 'capturing individual capabilities and motivating the entire organisation to respond to the demands of the environment'. Earlier, companies were mainly concerned with strategy; organisational structures were designed to support strategy. Companies believed that by changing their structure they automatically changed the 'shared norms, values and beliefs that shape the way individual managers think and act'.[18] Because these assumptions of managerial responsiveness were false, many organisations were incapable of carrying out the sophisticated strategies they developed, as Box 1.2 illustrates.

Recognising the constraints placed on strategy implementation by individuals' limitations has brought a shift in organisational priorities; there is a new emphasis on individual capabilities and motivations as key factors for implementing strategy. Growth, development and prosperity are seen to depend on developing a

---

Box 1.2

'We (the Human Resource Department) have done an audit of the top 250 staff, and found, much as we expected, that the company does not have the capabilities it needs. We found that, even if all the other factors like marketing and finance were in place, we would still trip up because there is no way we could resource the strategies that the company is dreaming up. For instance, there's a target for 50 per cent of our business to come from international markets. ... You could count on the fingers of one hand the number of people in this company who could carry out an international assignment. And we don't have the lead time to buy in the expertise, even if it were out there, which it isn't because this is an industry-wide problem – the few people who have the experience are highly marketable and volatile – more likely to set themselves up in competition than stay with us.

Another example – they've planned to do international telemarketing (we already do some domestically). There's been no real thought about how to resource this. Most of them think that if we recruit some school leavers with GCSE [elementary] French, we'll be able to telemarket in France!'

Source: Interview with a UK Human Resource Manager in an insurance company; author's research

creative, consultative culture in which individuals can contribute fully. Human capital is often regarded as the strategic resource of the future;[19] the role of managers has been changing from directing to facilitating, coaching and counseling.[20] Organisations are 'trying to build into their very structure' the capacity for individual learning and development.[21]

■ Interpersonal communication, which, as Section 1.1 showed, is vital for modern work effectiveness, is also the aspect of work where the impact of cultural difference is arguably most direct and experienced by most people. In the words of Khoo:

It is simply not enough for us to know how and why people differ culturally. We also need to know to what extent such differences can be generalized across situations, and especially to interactions with culturally different individuals. The need for a more global understanding of people, organizations, attitudes, norms, group processes, values and ways of operating can be enhanced by examining how people interact and transact, both among themselves as well as with culturally different individuals.[22]

Although these remarks were addressed to intercultural researchers in particular, there seems no reason to doubt that they also apply to anyone concerned with cultural difference and its impact on work and organisations. There is clear evidence that organisations should value skilled interpersonal communication. For instance, trust in both top management and an immediate supervisor is strongly related to the amount of information received by organisational members.[23] In turn, perceived organisational effectiveness is strongly related to trust in management. This finding remains significant across diverse organisations, industries and geographic locations. As a 1996 literature search reported, 'Communicated knowledge is viewed as probably the single most important source of competitive advantage into the 21st Century.' Since competitive advantage yields above normal financial performance,[24] it follows that there is a strong positive relationship between effective and efficient communication and financial performance.[25]

Parallel to, and as important as, the needs of managers for intercultural communication skills are the needs of the large numbers of service providers who interact directly with an increasingly diverse public. For example, health care organisations face demographic shifts in the patients served and their families. Ulrey and Amason found that cultural sensitivity and effective intercultural communication, besides helping patients, personally benefit health care providers by reducing their stress. Effective intercultural communication and cultural sensitivity were found to be related. Health care providers' levels of intercultural anxiety also were found to correlate with effective intercultural communication.[26]

Figure 1.2 summarises these influences on the increased importance of intercultural communication at work. Communication at work may, however, be one of the more problematic consequences of diversity. Though diversity is 'an asset to be valued rather than a problem to be solved, … communication can be seen to work best when people are similar, or at least on a similar wavelength'[27]; '… it should be clear that communication works better the more participants share assumptions and knowledge about the world.'[28] Research has indicated that people behave differently when they are interacting with others whom they perceive as culturally dissimilar: they ask more questions, but self-disclose less; they seek out information about dissimilarities instead of information about similarities. They are less willing to draw inferences about the attributes of people from other cultures. The researcher's conclusion is that 'people know how to

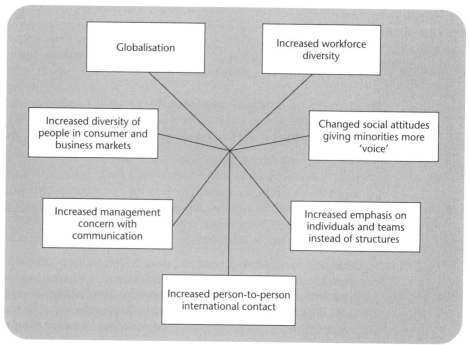

Figure 1.2   *Factors increasing the importance of intercultural communication at work*

Box 1.3

A woman Council officer responsible for parks met with a local Residents' Group representative. The representative was young, male and from an ethnic minority. His Group had been petitioning the Council to double the resources for patrolling and clearing up in their local park, claiming that drug users' needles were often left lying about. From the start, he seemed intemperately angry to the officer. He stood too close, looked intently in her eyes and spoke loudly. Gradually she responded by getting angry too. It ended in a shouting match.

Based on: Author's research

---

get to know other people from the same culture but not from different cultures'.[29] The findings suggest that people experience intercultural contact as different, even difficult, and attempt to handle it differently. Grimes and Richard even argue that whether cultural diversity is advantageous or detrimental for organisations depends on how organisation members communicate.[30]

For professionals, other service providers and interface workers training in how to deal with people appropriately is gradually being introduced; similarly, equal opportunities awareness training is now widespread. However, most of the interpersonal skills training being provided gives little help in adjusting to the different values, attitudes and motives of different individuals; and most of the equal opportunities awareness training omits any serious treatment of communication. It is true that adaptation at the individual level can only be achieved through sensitivity, active listening and gaining feedback; nevertheless, awareness of cultural and subcultural difference and knowledge of how to communicate with different others is an important underpinning for such adaptation. This raises a number of questions. One is what we mean by diversity, or, rather, which aspects of diversity are relevant. The emphasis in diversity studies to date has been on demographic diversity.[31] This term usually refers to nationality, ethnicity, gender, age and so on. There is some agreement that demographic factors are important primarily for their effects on psychological factors, such as values, beliefs and attitudes and thus on behaviour, especially communication behaviour. Arguing that researchers should examine other facets of diversity in addition to demographic background traits, Dansby and Knouse pointed out that in a group dynamics study, as the time that group members worked together increased the effects of surface-level diversity (demographic and physical differences) decreased, whereas those of deep-level diversity (attitudes, beliefs and values) increased.[32]

Another question concerns how the work context affects intercultural communication. 'Work context' refers to the fact that colleagues usually share an understanding of tasks and technical knowledge; also that their communication is influenced by their work roles and by the organisational culture. Does this work context obliterate or eliminate differences in communication and behaviour resulting from differences in backgrounds? Is it the case that: 'When social behaviour is regulated by other, less diffuse social roles, as it is in organizational settings, behaviour … primarily reflect(s) the influence of these other roles and therefore lose(s) much of its … stereotypical character'? The author who posed this question answered it in the negative from her own research findings on leadership styles:

> Nevertheless, women's leadership styles were more democratic than men's even in organization settings. This sex difference may reflect underlying differences in female and male personality or skills (e.g. women's superior social skills) or subtle differences in the status of women and men who occupy the same organizational role.[33]

While, clearly, there are task and organisational constraints on differences in behaviour at work, the evidence that will emerge in this book confirms that such differences still obtain, are significant and need to be taken into account more than they are currently. The core competencies required of both domestic and international managers in the twenty-first century have been identified as an 'ability to balance the conflicting demands of global integration versus local responsiveness; an ability to work in teams comprised of peoples from multiple functions/disciplines, different companies, and diverse industry backgrounds; an ability to manage and/or work with peoples from diverse racial/ethnic backgrounds'.[34] These three competencies all depend on intercultural communication skills and all assume that cultural differences remain potent despite the work setting.

This point is reinforced by a second: how people communicate at work generally reflects the preferred style of one cultural or subcultural group. In Western societies, with some exceptions (such as BodyShop) the dominant style is that of the individualist, monochronic, universalistic male. In other societies, other modes prevail: in Hong Kong Chinese businesses, for instance, people tend to express themselves less explicitly than is usual in Western businesses. There is evidence that work and organisational effectiveness can be enhanced if more diverse communication modes operate, allowing entry and influence to the diverse values, attitudes and ideas of the diverse populations now involved. Third, large numbers of people interface with the public in the course of their work. As the behaviour of their clients, patients, students or customers may not be greatly affected by the task setting, the social and cultural influences on their co-interactors' behaviour are still likely to be paramount and need to be understood.

> Globalisation of both marketing and production, plus the increasing diversity of domestic workforces, markets and populations mean that few organisations or individuals at work can afford to ignore cultural difference. A new emphasis on the individual and on teamwork has reinforced these pressures. In Europe there has been a shift from concern with equal opportunities to a concern with diversity. For individuals to be effective at work in diverse organisations and societies or internationally, they need to be able to communicate interculturally. The work context does not suppress differences so far as to eliminate this need. Such communication is difficult but achievable through awareness and skills development.

1.3 DIVERSITY AT WORK

Most twenty-first century workforces will be diverse – that is, they will consist of people from many different national and ethnic backgrounds, be composed of women to nearly the same degree as men and include more people with disabilities. They will reflect legal recognition that people are entitled to differing sexual orientations, religious affiliations and family structures. The extension of working age limits and the cumulative effects of the open labour market will also expand the diversity of people at work. In Europe, substantially increased legal rights instituted by the European Union (EU) will increase the visibility and voice of minority groups, who will be found more often in positions of power and influence.

For most people the diversity of the people they meet through work – as patients, students, pupils and their parents, clients, customers, suppliers, advisers, accountants, bankers and lawyers – is already wider than that among their colleagues alone and is growing. For business executives and managers, for instance, the diversity of the backgrounds of their contacts will increase even faster than the rate at which it increases among colleagues, owing to globalisation. For the caring professions, because people are living longer and, as they age, need more medical and support services, mainly young or middle aged nurses, doctors and care workers are dealing with more and more elderly or very elderly people; women live longer than men and so are disproportionately served by doctors who are still predominantly male; members of ethnic minorities have a higher birth rate and so use more maternity services; and so on. The purpose of this section is to show the context of communication at work in terms of diversity. It begins by discussing the position of national and ethnic minorities, then that of the female minority, and then those of other groups.

Nationality and ethnicity

Nationality, as the term is used here, is decided by a person's national status, which is a legal relationship involving allegiance on the part of an individual and (usually) protection on the part of the state. This usage distinguishes nationality from ethnicity, since a nation may be composed of many ethnic groups but of course only one nationality. However, the importance of nationality itself to how people behave and so to its impact on work communication is far from clear. In terms of culture, the concept of nation is rather vague, because while some nations are predominantly mono-ethnic, others are multi-ethnic. In these countries, many peoples contribute to the creation of a national culture's symbols, meanings and norms.

An ethnic unit is 'a population whose members believe that in some sense they share common descent and a common cultural heritage or tradition, and who are so regarded by others'.[35] Another definition of ethnic identity reflects a similar idea: it is 'identification with and perceived acceptance into a group with shared heritage and culture'.[36] Minority ethnic groups share a sense of heritage, history and origin from an area outside or preceding the creation of their present nation-state; they often also share a language or dialect. Ethnicity is situational; it is possible to be simultaneously English, British and European, stressing these identities more or less strongly in different aspects of everyday life. Similarly, a person might identify as Gujarati, Indian, Hindu, East African, Asian or British depending on the situation, his or her immediate objectives and the responses and behaviour of others.

One indicator of the growth in the significance of national and ethnic differences for communication at work is the increase in the volume of international trade, since doing business internationally obviously requires international contact and communication. By value indexed at 100 in 1990, world exports of merchandise increased from 2 in 1950 to 183 in 2000, dipping to 175 in 2001. Europe shared in this growth. Western Europe's merchandise exports grew by an average annual 5.9 per cent over the period 1995 to 2000, only falling back by 1 per cent in 2001; merchandise exports of Central and Eastern Europe, the Baltic states and CIS grew by an average annual 8.4 per cent between 1995 and 2001, despite a dip in 1999. A second indicator is the growth of the stock of foreign population living in a country or region. In Europe, this grew steadily over the period to 1997, reaching a figure of 21 million, mainly in Western Europe; the accession of 10 countries to the European Community in the early 2000s can be expected to increase this figure further. According to the Council of Europe, the latest statistics indicate that total numbers of foreign residents are still growing in most Western European countries but that the overall rate of increase in numbers has declined significantly since the early 1990s. The pattern in Central and Eastern Europe is somewhat different. Data for the early 1990s are not available for most countries but figures for the three years 1994–97 suggest not only a decline in rate of increase but in several countries an actual decrease in foreign resident populations.

The stock of ethnic minorities in a population is a third factor affecting the level of intercultural communication. There are obstacles to obtaining statistics on ethnic minorities in some European countries, including the widespread belief that international law and/or the domestic legislation of some countries prohibit the gathering and maintenance of ethnic statistics. There is also the obstacle of the widespread fear, among racial minorities and others, that – regardless of their legal status – ethnic statistics will be misused to the detriment of minorities, and/or that the very effort to gather statistics on the basis of ethnicity reinforces negative racial stereotypes. Where figures are available, they indicate that the ethnic majority population ranges from 58 per cent (Flemings in Belgium) to 98 per cent (Greeks in Greece). In between are Finland (93 per cent Finnish), Germany (92 per cent German), Austria (88 per cent German) and the UK (82 per cent English). Table A.1 in Appendix A gives breakdowns for minority populations for most European countries.

Labour market participation and employment rates help indicate the extent of intercultural communication with colleagues and members of other work organisations. Less data is available for this area; thus this section can only show the situation in two countries, the UK and the Netherlands, recognising that they may not represent the situation elsewhere. In the UK in 2001, employment rates for White men were around 80 per cent, the median for Asian men was 64 per cent, and for Black men it was 61 per cent. Among White women of working age the employment rate was 71 per cent, the median for Asian women was 38 per cent, and for Black women it was 57 per cent. These figures partly reflect cultural tendencies in some ethnic groups, especially for women to be full-time housewives, partly the tendency for some groups to be self-employed and partly different unemployment rates.[37] There is a slightly greater concentration of ethnic minority employees (and the self-employed) in the service sector in comparison with Whites (74 per cent against 68 per cent). They are particularly strongly represented in wholesaling, retailing and the motor trades (in the private sector) and in health and social work (in the public sector). Eighty-five per cent of ethnic minority women and 71 per cent of men work in the service sector. Successive studies have shown that persons of minority ethnic origin in the UK are at a consistently higher risk of unemployment than are White people,[38] employed in less-skilled jobs, at lower job levels, and concentrated in particular industrial sectors, although obtaining qualifications benefits members of these groups. White males continue to predominate as managers. Much lower proportions of ethnic minority males are classified as 'managerial'. The difference between White and ethnic minority females in management is much less, mainly because White females are also under-represented as managers. The managerial gender gap, at nine percentage points, is especially marked among White women; at the supervisory level, it is actually reversed among Black and Indian employees. More details on the UK employment of ethnic minorities are given in Appendix A.

In Holland, while it is clear that the Turkish, Moroccan, Surinamese and Antillean minorities suffer labour market disadvantages in comparison with the Dutch, it is also clear that their relative position is improving and that in Holland members of these groups are very likely to be met with in a work context. Appendix A includes labour market participation, employment and unemployment figures for the different ethnic groups in the Netherlands.

Gender

Gender differences continue to have growing significance for communication at work. Gender has been defined as: 'patterned, socially produced distinctions between female and male. ... Gender is not something that people are ... rather for the individual and the collective, it is daily accomplished'.[39] The term gender therefore refers to a society's

---

Box 1.4

Officially, Britain has five main ethnic categories: white, mixed, black, Asian and other. ... It is all voluntary; you can describe yourself as you like.

At one of Britain's main black information outfits, Blink, the editor, Don de Silva, is of Sri Lankan origin. 'Black is a generic term and includes all ethnic minorities,' he says. That includes Jews.

The muddle reflects history: now outnumbered, blacks were once the biggest immigrant grouping. ... some groups campaigning against prejudice come under it [the label 'Black'], others march beside it. And other categories are just as tricky: if you think it is hard defining what 'black' means, just try pinning down the meaning of 'European'.

Source: *The Economist*, 20 September 2003, p. 37

beliefs about the differences between the sexes and its rules for appropriate behaviour for males and females.

In Europe as a whole, women outnumber men by 105 to 100 (1995) compared with a slight advantage in men's favour worldwide (98.6 women for 100 men). The role of women in the European labour market continued to become more important between 1996 and 2000, as it had over the decade 1985–95. Of the working age population, the proportion of women in employment in the EU rose in those five years from 50.2 per cent to 54 per cent.[40] All 15 countries, except Germany, where the figure remained static at 46.1 per cent, experienced an increase – a dramatic one in countries as different as Denmark (50.2 per cent to 71.6 per cent) and Spain (32.3 per cent to 40.3 per cent). In the countries which were candidates for EU membership in 2000 and for which data are available, the median figure for women of working age employed in that year was 54.3 per cent, a figure close to the EU average, though the range is much smaller than in the EU countries.[41] Table 1.1 shows the figures for both sets of countries for the year 2000.

Despite their high and (in the EU) growing participation in European labour markets, women face 'harsh realities'. They are more likely to be unemployed, in part-time work (which is generally less secure, less protected, less well paid and more lacking in benefits than full-time work), and more likely to be in service sector jobs than in better-paid work in manufacturing. As a result of these and other factors, women are disproportionately represented among the low paid. Again, while women managers 'appear to have achieved parity in salaries', when differences in productivity, behavioural factors and age are controlled for, it is clear that 'gender plays a significant role in salary determination'.[42]

Overall, in the year 2000, women in the 15 countries of the EU were 38 per cent more likely to be unemployed than men (9.7 per cent against 7.0 per cent), despite the greater tendency of women not to register when they lose their jobs. The ratio was highest in countries with high unemployment, like Spain and Greece, where women

Table 1.1   *Employment rate of women as per cent of population of women aged 15–64, year 2000*

Western European country	Womens' employment rate per cent	Eastern European country	Womens' employment rate per cent
Denmark	71.6	Romania	59
Sweden	71	Lithuania	58.3
United Kingdom	64.6	Slovenia	58.3
Finland	64.4	Estonia	57.1
Netherlands	63.7	Czech Republic	56.8
Portugal	60.3	Latvia	54.3
Austria	59.4	Cyprus	52.5
Belgium	57.9	Slovakia	52.3
France	55.3	Hungary	49.4
Ireland	54	Poland	49.3
Luxembourg	50.3	Bulgaria	47.2
Germany	46.1		
Greece	40.9		
Spain	40.3		
Italy	39.6		

Source: Eurostat: Key Employment Indicators 2000

were 2.1 and 2.3 times as likely to be unemployed as men. In contrast, in the UK and Sweden, two relatively low unemployment countries, unemployment for women was lower than for men. In contrast to the EU countries, however, the gender gap for 11 candidate countries was small; in fact, in seven out of the eleven it was reversed, with men more likely to be unemployed than women, despite higher overall unemployment rates. The median women's unemployment rate for these countries was 11.6 per cent. Women in all 15 EU countries were much more likely than men to be in part-time employment. As a proportion of total employment for women in 2000, part-time work ranged from 7.4 per cent in Greece to over 70 per cent in the Netherlands, with an average figure for the 15 countries of 33 per cent, against 6.2 per cent for men. Gender segregation in employment in the EU was very marked, with 82.5 per cent working in services and only 14 per cent in industry; in the candidate countries, though still high, the median difference was considerably lower, at 68.5 per cent in services and 22 per cent in industry.

Among 13 EU countries, the proportion of people paid less than 60 per cent of the median wage who are women ranges from 59 per cent in Greece up to 86 per cent in France, with a median figure of 78 per cent. Even those women in full-time employment comparable to men's suffer a pay gap, though in the EU it is a diminishing one. Of 12 EU countries, median women's pay in 1995 was 85 per cent of men's, but had risen to 88 per cent by 1997, representing a quite rapid improvement. On pay, women in ten candidate countries were doing less well, with the median figure in the year 2000 standing at 79 per cent.

However, the marked skewing of female employment away from industry and towards services, which is so notable a feature of Western European countries (73 per cent in 1994), is less marked in the former Communist countries of Europe (48 per cent), where women also have a higher share in professional categories such as professional and technical, administration and management and sales force (see Table A.4, Appendix A).

The supply of women qualified for jobs in management, or in executive, administrative and managerial occupations continues to increase as more women accumulate work experience and complete management and professional education programmes. However, although women have made progress in obtaining managerial jobs, their median weekly earnings continue to be well below those of male managers. Furthermore, the statistics still paint a discouraging picture of Europe in terms of seniority and power at work and in society generally. There are only six countries

Box 1.5

Hymowitz and Weissman, who originated the term 'glass ceiling', wrote, 'the biggest obstacle women face is also the most intangible: men at the top feel uncomfortable beside them.'[a]

'Talking about the glass ceiling and the maternal wall irritates me. They're gone. ... It's a woman's world now. It's a time of great change ... and we're faster at, and better at, dealing with that.'[b]

Sources: (a) Hymowitz, C. and Weissman, M. (1997) *A History of Women in America*, London: Bantam Books (b) Sunita Gloster, head of worldwide business development at Lowe and Partners advertising agency, quoted in *The Observer* magazine, 14 December 2003, p. 21

Box 1.6

'My boss is a woman; she's terrifically good at the job, but she would never have got it, because a long career break to raise her family meant she didn't have the same length of experience as a man. However, the corporation had a jobs quota for women, so she got the job, and she's shown that she's fully competent. Of course, she has to work about sixty hours a week – but so do I.'

Based on: Interview with a UK broadcaster, author's research

where more than 25 per cent of directors and senior managers are women (Bulgaria, Finland, Germany, Hungary, Norway and Sweden).

Younger people

Despite a major decline in the numbers of young people in Europe, EU-wide unemployment of people under 25 was 21.3 per cent in 1997, substantially above the average of 11 per cent; in the UK in 2001, people aged 16–24 in all ethnic groups for which figures are available were substantially more likely to be unemployed than those aged 25–64. These facts point to a serious disadvantage for young people; however, the predominant cause is less likely to be discrimination than labour market rigidities: the difficulty for younger people is to gain entry. Most job opportunities arise only as the total number of jobs expands or as natural wastage creates vacancies. People in the age group 25 to 49 tend to have a degree of tenure in the jobs they occupy.

Older people

Employment rates among workers over 50 years old vary considerably across the EU, ranging from 69.4 per cent in Sweden to 27 per cent in Belgium. Reforms are still needed to keep older people in the labour market – the Stockholm European Council, held in March 2001, set a target of increasing the employment rate of older workers to 50 per cent by 2010.[43]

People with disabilities

Persons with physical, sensory or mental impairments that can make performing an everyday task more difficult are defined as having disabilities. Most disabilities are not 'handicaps' in the sense of making people unable to work and take part in community life on an equal footing with others. This includes severe disabilities such as being confined to a wheelchair. Often it is only the fact that an environment is not adapted – there are no wheelchair ramps or lifts – that makes full participation difficult for people with such impairments. A qualified person with a disability is someone who, with or without reasonable adjustment by the employer, can perform the essential function of the employment position that s/he holds or desires.

In the EU, the proportion of people with disabilities varies between 9.3 per cent and 15.2 per cent by country, averaging about 12 per cent. Disability increases with age in a rising curve. People with disabilities are a significant part of the workforce. In the UK, for instance, where there are over six million people who are registered as disabled

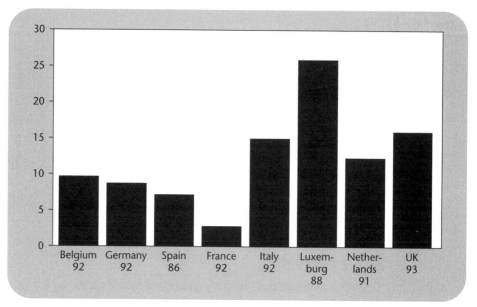

Figure 1.3   *People with disabilities looking for work as a percentage of all jobseekers – various years*

(12 per cent of the population), nearly 1.5 million people with disabilities are employed full time; a further 600,000 or more work part time. Despite this, 'in general disabled persons are over-represented in the total unemployed population. The percentage of disabled persons unemployed is in fact generally higher than 10 per cent of all unemployed persons, although their percentage of working age in the total population varies between 6 per cent and 8 per cent'.[44] Figure 1.3 shows the percentage of unemployed people with disabilities in various European countries.

Homosexuals

Estimates for the numbers of male homosexuals and lesbians are, for obvious reasons, unreliable: the figures quoted for the EU range from 2 per cent to 10 per cent. Anecdotal evidence suggests that homosexuals often attain seniority at work more rapidly than the majority population; this is sometimes attributed to their greater commitment, owing to the demands of family life being lower for them than for heterosexuals. Despite instances of persistent discrimination, such as the armed forces and some churches, the European workplace in general is now perhaps not a prime problem area for homosexuals as a group.

Religious groups

Appendix A includes a country-by-country breakdown of European and other countries by self-reported religious affiliation. In Western Europe, about 10 per cent of people (38 million) attend Christian churches regularly and a further 26 per cent are occasional churchgoers; in Europe as a whole, 40 per cent are Catholic and 11 per cent are Protestant. In Western Europe active adherents of Islam are about 10 million (2.5 per cent of the population), with a further 46 million between Eastern Europe, Turkey and Russia. There are about 4 million adherents of the Jewish faith in Western and Eastern Europe combined, and approximately 1.5 million Hindus and 0.5 million Sikhs. Persons professing atheism, scepticism, disbelief, or irreligion, including antireligious (opposed to all religion) numbered 23.5 million in 1996.

No figures are available for labour market participation or employment by religious group, but it is likely that cultural values reduce participation by some groups (Moslem women). Lack of accommodation to religious needs, such as Moslems' needs to worship five times a day or the need of Jews to be home by sunset on Fridays, distorts the employment pattern towards self-employment or part-time working.

Social class, education and other differences

Social class is one dimension on which Western European societies became less diverse during the last quarter of the twentieth century, with the growth of a large category of 'intermediate' and other non-manual workers and a decrease in the percentage of all manual workers, especially the unskilled. These changes were largely a result of the decline of manufacturing and heavy industry. These trends are set to continue, reinforced by government policies that see an increase in the educational and technical skill levels of the population as essential to international competitiveness. Final educational level is undeniably a major source of difference between individuals in the workplace. There is, for instance, a considerable amount of initial job segregation of graduates, eighteen-year-old school leavers with higher level school qualifications (such as A-Level) sixteen-year-old school leavers with qualifications and those who leave school at the earliest legal date without qualifications. In this respect, the UK, for instance, is still elitist, despite recent changes, compared with some international competitors, such as USA or South Korea, where about 70 per cent of the population receive university-level qualifications.

Other educational/professional differences also create significant differences between groups of people at work. Examples include subject specialisation (especially science versus arts), independent versus state-maintained schooling (because of its perceived implications for social class) and professional training (vide the problems created by legal jargon, 'academese' and civil-servant-speak.)

> This section, together with Appendix A, has shown that, numerically, both the population at large and the workforce in the UK, EU and Europe as a whole are diverse and are continuing to become more so. This implies a significant increase in the amount, and therefore the importance, of inter-group (intercultural) face-to-face communication at work. It has also shown that despite an improvement in their societal position, minorities' earnings, employment rates and career prospects are still below those of the majority groups in most of Europe; these facts are part of the context of intercultural communication at work. The next section turns to another aspect of that context: discrimination and harassment.

1.4 DISCRIMINATION AND HARASSMENT

Discrimination and harassment are a widespread part of the context of work communication. All minority groups, including people with disabilities, religious minorities, homosexuals and older people as well as ethnic minorities and women, are affected by prejudice and discrimination both at work and in society more generally. A wide range of people – not just women – is affected by harassment. Understanding and knowing about this is essential background for communicating across barriers created by difference. Without such understanding and knowledge, there can be no possibility of the awareness of sensitive issues, which, as Chapter 6 will show, is vital. Of course, the actual relevant variables are 'perceived' rather than 'actual' prejudice and discrimination and a section such as this, which deals with 'actuals', can only heighten consciousness rather than provide the needed information, which will have to be obtained face-to-face, person by person. Nevertheless, consciousness-raising is an important part of the process of improving intercultural communication effectiveness.

In modern usage the term 'prejudice' usually refers to an irrationally unfavourable or hostile attitude towards the members of another group. Discrimination is any situation in which a group or individual is treated unfavourably on the basis of arbitrary grounds, especially prejudice. Discrimination is a manifestation of prejudice that is often institutionalised and pervasive throughout an organisation. Discrimination seriously reduces minority groups' chances of obtaining employment, equal earnings and promotion. Discrimination is part of the context within which intercultural communication takes place and so is treated in this chapter; prejudice is a direct barrier to communication and is covered in Chapter 5.

Statements from the US State Department Report on Human Rights for 2001 describe some of the discriminatory problems in different European countries. For instance, on France, they wrote:

> The law prohibits sex-based job discrimination and sexual harassment in the workplace; however, these laws have not been fully implemented. Women's rights groups have criticised the scope of the law as narrow and the fines and compensatory damages as often modest. For example, the law limits sexual harassment claims to circumstances where there is a supervisor–subordinate relationship but fails to address harassment by colleagues or a hostile work environment.
>
> The law requires that women receive equal pay for equal work, but this requirement often is not implemented in practice.

On Germany:

> The Basic Law provides for the freedom of religion, and the Government generally respects this right in practice; however, there is some discrimination against minority religions.
>
> Scientologists reported employment difficulties, and, in the state of Bavaria, applicants for state civil service positions must complete questionnaires detailing any relationship they may have with Scientology.
>
> Resident foreigners and minority groups continued to voice credible concerns about societal and job-related discrimination. Unemployment affects foreigners disproportionately, although at times this was due in part to inadequate language skills or nontransferable professional qualifications of the job seekers.

On Greece:

> The Constitution provides for equality before the law irrespective of nationality, race, language, religious or political belief; however, government respect for these rights was inconsistent in practice.
>
> The rate of employment of Muslims in the public sector and in state-owned industries and corporations is much lower than the Muslim percentage of the population. Muslims in Thrace claim that they are hired only for lower level, part-time work.

The General Confederation of Greek Workers (GSEE) women's section reports that sexual harassment is a widespread phenomenon, but that women are discouraged from filing charges against perpetrators by family members and coworkers since they believe they might be socially stigmatized.

The law provides for equal pay for equal work; however, the National Statistical Service's latest data, for the fourth quarter of 1998, show that women's salaries in manufacturing were 71 per cent of those of men in comparable positions; in retail sales, women's salaries were 88 per cent of those of men in comparable positions.

On Spain:

The Constitution provides for equal rights for all citizens, and discrimination on the basis of sex, race, ethnicity, nationality, disability, ideology, or religious beliefs is illegal; however, social discrimination against Roma and immigrants is a problem.

The law prohibits sexual harassment in the workplace, but very few cases have been brought to trial under this law. Police received 364 sexual harassment complaints during the year. Although prohibited by law, discrimination in the workplace and in hiring practices persisted. A 1998 study of 100 labor union contracts revealed that 38 contracts failed to use gender-neutral language, 22 employed gender-specific job titles resulting in the imposition of discriminatory wage differentials (i.e., the salary of a male secretary, 'secretario,' was 13 per cent higher than that of a 'secretaria' in one food processing industry contract), and only 17 addressed the problem of sexual harassment.

On Poland:

The Romani community, numbering around 30,000, faced disproportionately high unemployment and was hit harder by economic changes and restructuring than were ethnic Poles, according to its leaders. Societal discrimination against Roma is commonplace, and some local officials discriminate against Roma in the provision of social services. Romani leaders complained of widespread discrimination in employment, housing, banking, the justice system, the media, and education.

It should be noted that these countries have been selected at random: there is no suggestion that they are either better or worse than others in Europe. To counterbalance these negative comments, the US State Department Report on Human Rights for 2001 on all the above countries also contains positive statements on discrimination levels or trends. For instance, on France:

There is no discrimination against persons with disabilities in employment, education, or in the provision of other state services.

On Germany:

There were no reports that women were victims of sexual harassment. ... if factors such as differences in age, qualification, occupational position, structure of employment or seniority are taken into consideration, women usually are not discriminated against in terms of equal pay for equal work, although they are underrepresented in well paid managerial positions.

The Basic Law specifically prohibits discrimination against persons with disabilities, and there were no reports of discrimination against persons with disabilities in employment, education, or in the provision of other state services.

On Greece:

> In the civil service, 5 per cent of administrative staff and 80 per cent of telephone operator positions are reserved for persons with disabilities. Recent legislation mandates the hiring of persons with disabilities in the public sector from a priority list. They are exempt from the civil service exam, and some have been appointed to important positions in the civil service. There is no societal discrimination against persons with disabilities.

On Spain:

> There were no reports of discrimination against persons with disabilities in employment, education, or the provision of other state services. The Government subsidizes companies that employ persons with mental or physical disabilities. The Government mandates that all businesses that employ more than 50 persons either hire such persons for at least 2 per cent of their workforce or subcontract a portion of their work to special centers that employ them.

On Poland:

> The Constitution states that 'no one shall be discriminated against in political, social, or economic life for any reason whatsoever', and the Government attempts to ensure that these provisions are observed.
>
> There is no discrimination against persons with disabilities in employment, education, or in the provision of other state services. There were approximately 5.5 million persons with disabilities in the country by year's end, and the number is expected to reach 6 million by the year 2010. In 2000 the Central Bureau of Statistics (GUS) reported that 17 per cent of persons with disabilities able to work are unemployed, roughly equivalent to the national unemployment rate. Advocacy groups have claimed that the percentage is much higher.

Thus, the overall picture is a mixed one: discrimination persists everywhere in Europe, though in some places more than others and in different countries is directed mainly against different groups. In most cases, the situation is improving, though only slowly. The rest of this section examines the position of various minority groups in more detail, particularly with reference to the UK.

Ethnic minorities

One problem affecting ethnic minorities has been indirect discrimination: selection criteria are applied equally to everyone but disproportionately affect members of particular groups. 'Many of the ordinary, routine aspects of the recruitment market and the labour market may give rise to indirect discrimination – for example, the notion that candidates must "fit in". If selectors hold stereotypes of minority ethnic groups which mean they do not "fit in", indirect discrimination follows.'[45] Changing work patterns only add to this – Asian women workers are recognised as loyal, hardworking and uncomplaining; but new labour demands are for flexibility, ability to exercise initiative and responsibility for checking one's own work. There is often an assumption that just because Asian women workers are the former, they cannot be the latter.

Recent race regulations in the UK give a definition of indirect discrimination on grounds of race or ethnic or national origin as occurring when a person, X, applies to another person, Y, a provision, criterion or practice which X applies to everyone; and the provision, criterion or practice puts (or would put) people from Y's race or ethnic or national origin at a particular disadvantage; and the provision, criterion or practice puts Y at a disadvantage; and X cannot show that the provision, criterion or practice is a proportionate means of achieving a legitimate aim.

Examples of provisions, criteria or practices which might be indirectly discriminatory include the following: 'A firm's policy of filling senior management positions internally, from a pool of senior and middle managers, most of whom are white'; 'A word-of-mouth recruitment policy in a firm where the majority of the workforce are Asian'; service provisions such as 'A bank requires applicants for a loan to be registered on the electoral roll, so that it can carry out credit checks. This may discriminate indirectly against non-citizens who are not eligible to vote'; 'if the proportion of qualifying people from an ethnic minority group who receive meals-on-wheels (a service provided by the local government) is smaller than persons who are not of that racial group'; 'if the proportion of potholes in the road filled in an ethnic minority area is lower than that in a non-ethnic minority area'. Indirect discrimination can arise through lack of monitoring, rather than intention. Organisations must not rely on phone-ins. (These regulations implement the Race Relations Act 1976 (Amendment) Regulations 2003.)

Women

Recent evidence for direct discrimination against women is less explicit than that for discrimination against some ethnic groups, although the statistical story told in Section 1.2, combined with the evidence of women's suitability for modern employment and management, are strong pointers. In addition, there are undoubtedly sectors, such as the insurance industry, where prejudice and discrimination are overt. Indirect discrimination may, though, currently be having more damaging effects on women at work. Indirect discrimination ranges from the lack of family-friendly policies in many organisations to the gendering of organisations.

'Family-friendly policies' is the term for the provision of childcare (and eldercare) resources and facilities, such as workplace nurseries, part-time, flexi-time, work-at-home, job sharing, compressed work weeks, extended lunch breaks and maternity and parenting leave. However, many European employers, including very large employers of women, provide few if any of these benefits. Even where they exist, their value is limited. First, there is a widespread belief that the use of leaves and flexible working arrangements involves sacrificing career advancement, at least in the short term, and perhaps permanently. Second, it has been shown that an individual's immediate supervisor or manager affects how much work–family conflict individuals experience, and whether they fear negative effects at work from using family-friendly policies. Attitudes of such supervisors and managers are key and may often be unsupportive. A study in an insurance business found that supervisors often sent 'mixed messages' about work and family when implementing family-friendly policies amidst organisational constraints such as frequent deadlines and a team-based culture. These constraints often called for supervisors to make 'judgement calls' about work–family programme implementation, which they made while at the same time trying not to set a precedent they might regret. Third, research has shown that family-friendly resources are more likely to be available to senior and non-minority staff, which means they may actually reinforce the glass ceiling.[46]

Organisational gendering refers to the existence and persistence of a male-dominant organisational culture and climate that occur through four distinct but inter-related processes:

1. The construction of gender divisions, with men almost always in the highest positions of organisational power,
2. The construction of symbols and images that explain, express or reinforce those divisions, such as language, dress and media image,
3. The gendered components of individual identity and presentation of self, and
4. The demands for 'gender-appropriate' behaviour and attitudes.[47]

One explanation for the gendering of organisations is that 'the suppression of sexuality is one of the first tasks the bureaucracy sets itself'.[48] This suppression occurs in order to try to control the interferences and disruptions to the 'ideal functioning of the organisation' caused by sexuality, procreation and emotions. There is a view that women working in bureaucracies will alter them in a significant way, but others argue that it is more likely that women will become co-opted – that is, will function like men in order to operate effectively at senior levels.[49]

Despite their progress in the last 30 years of the twentieth century, women as a group are still comparatively in low power positions at work. In the words of Colwill, 'The lack of women in management is an issue, not of education and training, but of power. Time, patience and women's self-improvement do not appear to be the solution. The solution, in fact, is similar to the problem: power.'[50]

People with disabilities

Until the second half of the twentieth century, it was rarely recognised that, apart from their specific impairment, people with disabilities have the same needs, abilities and interests as the mainstream population. For many people with disabilities, the greatest handicap has been the image of them as a 'breed apart' who have often been pitied, ignored or placed in institutions that offered mere custodial care.[51]

This situation has improved. People with disabilities are, as a previous section showed, a significant part of the active workforce. Despite this, they continue to face discrimination. A 2002-study found that most UK employers are aware of governing legislation, most give positive statements of intent to meet their legal obligations, but that little use is made of government schemes to promote and assist employment of disabled people.[52] Organisations are often frightened of the cost of employing people with disabilities. However, a US analysis of more than 10,000 disabled employees showed that 31 per cent of their hirings required no added cost for special training or facilities, 50 per cent were under $50 and 69 per cent cost less than $500. Only 1 per cent cost over $5,000. Studies show that building a new facility that is accessible adds only one half of 1 per cent to the building's cost.

Another UK study found significant differences in the levels of satisfaction with their working conditions between men and women with disabilities. Only 43 per cent of men with a long-term illness or disability affecting their daily lives were extremely, very or fairly satisfied with physical working conditions, hours of work and amount of variety, and a slightly higher 50 per cent with relationships with management; only 29 per cent were satisfied with departmental management and attention paid to suggestions. In contrast, 85 per cent, 87 per cent and 82 per cent respectively of women with disabilities were extremely, very or fairly satisfied with physical working conditions, hours of work and amount of variety, 81 per cent with relationships with management, and 64 per cent with departmental management and 67 per cent with attention paid to suggestions.[53] It is not clear whether these differences are due to different treatment of men and women with disabilities or other causes.

Older people

Ageism, a term originating in about 1970, is discrimination against people, usually older people, on the grounds of their age. Ageism has been blamed for being a cause why people age poorly in Western society. Discrimination directed against older people leads to higher redundancy rates among older employees and difficulty for anyone over 50, or in some cases 40, in obtaining employment following redundancy. Age prejudice is largely a problem of individualist Western cultures – in collectivist cultures elderly people are usually highly respected and their contribution is acknowledged. Fear of growing old among the young and middle-aged is a powerful factor in ageism. Age discrimination affects women particularly, as it reduces career prospects for women returning to work after childrearing.

Homosexuals

There is a global shift towards reducing prejudice and discrimination against homosexuals. There are four factors promoting this favourable change: scientific evidence of homosexuality as innate, an around-the-world development of a middle-class, a category into which many gays fall, democratisation – democratic societies are more permissive – and the use of the Internet for global information-sharing and resistance to oppression.[54] Despite such favourable trends, there are many persisting bastions of discrimination against homosexuals, including religious institutions and armed forces.

Religious groups

Some of the discrimination affecting 'minority groups' is so accepted that even liberal members of the dominant (sub)culture are barely aware of it. For instance, many European societies provide a double bind for people from religious backgrounds other than the dominant Christian one, so far as accommodating their religious practices is concerned. The working week is built around the practice of Sunday worship, even though in some countries the majority of the population takes no active part, while the secular tone means that organisations and individual managers often underestimate the priority which people from religious backgrounds give to having time free for worship. For Moslems, being able to attend a mosque on Fridays, for Hindus time free for festivals and ceremonials, for Jews being home before sunset on Fridays are considerations which they are often forced to trade off against earnings or career.

A report from the UK Department of Trade and Industry stated in 2001, 'We have no direct information on the extent of employment discrimination on the grounds of religion or belief. In most workplaces, religion is not an issue of dispute. The British Social Attitudes Survey (2001) found that only 2 per cent of the British public believed that employers discriminated against job applicants a lot on grounds of religion or belief. This contrasts with about 10 per cent on grounds of sexual orientation and around 20 per cent on grounds of race. We assume that about 2 per cent (roughly 92,000) of those who could possibly be affected may have experienced any form of discrimination.'

In France, Germany and Italy, statutes ban discrimination on the grounds of religion as well as ethnicity, gender and so on. Until the enactment of legislation

Box 1.7

'Four [UK] government departments were named by the Commission for Racial Equality [CRE] yesterday as suffering from "snowy peak syndrome": they have no one from an ethnic minority in their senior ranks. ... the results of a survey by the CRE ... show that nearly a third of Britain's 43,000 public bodies have yet to implement their new race equality duties. [The Race Relations Amendment Act 2001 requires them to set diversity goals.] The overall average of ethnic minority staff across 20 Whitehall departments was 9.7% but among senior civil servants it dropped to 2.8%.'[a]

A study found 'strong and consistent' evidence of positive discrimination by Chief Executive Officers [CEO] and boards of directors in favour of people demographically similar to themselves. In firms in which CEOs are powerful, new directors are likely to be demographically similar to the firm's incumbent CEO. When the boards of directors are more powerful than the CEO, new directors resemble the existing board, rather than the CEO. The study also found that the more similar demographically the CEO and the board, the higher the CEO's compensation contract.[b]

Sources: (a) 'Equality bypasses Whitehall mandarins', *The Guardian*, 4 July 2003, p. 5
(b) Westphal, J.D. and Zajac, E.J. (1995) 'Who shall govern? CEO board power, demographic similarity and new director selection', *Administrative Science Quarterly*, 40: 59–73

required by the European Communities Council Directive 2000, there was no equivalent legislation to ban discrimination on the basis of religion in Britain, except in Northern Ireland, where the amended Fair Employment Act (1989), in addition to banning discrimination, requires all employers of over ten people to report annually on the religious composition of their workforce and to review it at least every three years. Noncompliance can bring heavy penalties. The Act was a response to the evident imbalance in employment opportunities for Catholics in the province.

Within organisations, in addition to the consequences of direct discrimination, harassment and bullying, there may be glass ceilings and walls. These limit how far members of minorities may be promoted, segregate people into separate spheres and create status differences. In general, glass ceilings and walls reflect the conditions of the wider society. Writers on race comment on 'the silencing of the importance of race in organisations',[55] and ask, 'why so much attention [has] been given to race and ethnicity outside of organisations and why so little inside'.[56] Feminist writers argue that organisations are gendered, embedding the values, attitudes and norms of one gender, usually the male. It is possible to view gender and other classifications as something organisations 'do', rather than as a natural attribute of people. In some organisations, the relations between men and women doing similar 'male' jobs are defined by practices based on a 'symbolic' order which places women below men in the hierarchy. The result is rules and rituals which create and recreate ambiguity in the expectations of how women workers should behave.[57]

In addition to glass ceilings, organisations may contain 'glass walls', or job segregation, which keep women and minority men out of some functional areas (e.g., manufacturing) and locked into others (e.g., human resource management). Usually, the areas from which minorities are excluded are the ones most likely to lead to the top of the organisations; they may even be those where experience is essential to get there. For example, in a multinational company a woman or ethnic minority man may be less likely than members of the majority group to get an overseas posting, but international experience may be a requirement for a job at Board level; or, in an industrial marketing company, where a period of experience as sales representatives is regarded as basic for promotion above a certain level, women graduate trainees may not be allowed to gain such experience – theoretically, for their protection. A UK study found that senior posts to which women were promoted tended to be 'dangerous': those where the risks of failure were higher.[58]

As significant a problem for intercultural work communication as blatant discrimination is now caused by 'micro-inequities', which can occur wherever people are perceived as different. These include Caucasians in a Japanese-owned company, African Americans in a white firm, women in a traditionally male environment, Jews and Moslems in a traditionally Protestant environment. Micro-inequities 'include exclusion from informal peer support, networking, and mentoring; restricted information and a lack of feedback from supervisors and coworkers; inadequate or inaccurate performance appraisals by supervisors or work groups; and inequitable delegation of tasks. ... One of the main things blacks complained about ... was the withholding of information by white supervisors. Time and time again, they recounted how ... their counterparts were given the whole picture.' Blacks are given jobs to 'prove their competence'; Whites are given learning experiences. Because they often encounter stereotypes, Blacks tend to be more aware than Whites of how others may perceive and evaluate their behaviours. This perception may inhibit open communication within a variety of formal contexts (e.g., team meetings, job interviews, sales consultations, etc.). It has been shown that members of stigmatised groups are less likely to report an experience as discriminatory in the presence of a member of a non-stigmatised group than privately.[59] Racial dynamics also affect mentoring activities, often inhibiting authentic collaboration in cross-racial relationships.[60] Gender discrimination, too, is now often created and sustained more by communication micropractices than by overt discrimination. Women interviewed by Hatcher, particularly those from the financial institutions, spoke eloquently of the ways in which they are excluded from organisational life.[61] The topics of conversation, including the omissions such as parenting responsibilities, the styles of communication, the policing of female sexuality through the repression of involvement in banter, or the turning of the male gaze onto female bodies through innuendo and game-playing, all contribute to the performance of gender in organisations.

Harassment and workplace bullying

Dictionaries define harassment as 'vexing by repeated attacks'. US data suggest that 50 per cent of women will be harassed at some time in their working lives; consequences include job loss, decreased morale, absenteeism, decreased job satisfaction and damage to interpersonal relationships at work, as well as negative effects on psychological and physical health.[62] A European study found the incidence of experiencing workplace bullying to be equal for men and women at a reported 20 per cent of respondents, but for women it was more likely to be sexual harassment by co-workers and for men more likely to be bullying by supervisors as well as co-workers. Poor social climate were significant predictors for both genders and both experienced feelings of stress, poor mental health and lowered job satisfaction as a consequence.[63] Danish research indicates that it is not necessarily the quantity of the negative acts that cause the change in behaviour but the fact of being exposed to such acts at all.[64] In Britain, few differences were found for the experience of self-reported bullying between workers, supervisors, middle or senior managers. Workers and supervisors were more frequently exposed to negative acts, such as derogatory or exclusionary behaviour, than managers, who more often reported exposure to extreme work pressure. Women managers, however, were subjected to negative acts.[65] Research in a large telecommunications call centre showed that employees used the term 'bullying' to describe difficult work situations, which they saw as imposed by the organisation, as well as the oppressive behaviour of individuals. The authors commented, 'This additional narrative brings issues of power and politics in organisations to the fore.'[66]

Definitions of what constitutes sexual harassment depend on gender, with women consistently defining more experiences as harassing than men. The differences in definition create comparability problems for studies of harassment incidence; however, there seems little doubt that it is widespread in the workplace. Research into the problem of sexual harassment has tended to focus on harassment that occurs within overt power relationships, for example, bosses and employees, teachers and students, doctors and patients, lawyers and clients. However, sexual harassment often occurs between peers – persons whose relationship is not based on an overt power or status differential. One study found that sexual harassment was pervasive both in terms of the numbers of females and males who had been victims/targets of peer sexual harassment, the relationship of the harassers to their victims, the settings in which harassment occurred, and the verbal and nonverbal behaviours communicated.[67]

Many feminists regard sexual harassment as a patriarchal control strategy used by men to keep women 'in their place': men are seen as intentionally or unintentionally reducing women employees to sexualised beings. In addition, feminists assert, men often subscribe to a 'male sexual drive discourse' in which their sexuality is treated as 'incontinent', 'out of their own control' and essentially biologically driven. The psychodynamics of sexual harassment maintain an unequal power structure between the sexes, forcing women to comply with traditional sex roles. The findings from an Australian study suggest that organisational culture and environment influence respondents' attitudes to sexually harassing behaviour.[68]

> Direct and indirect discrimination, harassment and bullying are still part of the context of work for many people from minority groups and so are likely to affect their attitudes and communication behaviours. Micro-inequities may be more common than blatant discrimination. However, as the next section shows, in Europe new legislation is aimed at eliminating forms of discrimination, such as age discrimination, which have previously been permitted.

1.5 THE CHANGING LEGAL FRAMEWORK IN EUROPE

A major attempt is being made in Europe to establish a general framework for equal treatment in employment and vocational training. A European Communities Council Directive requires member states to regulate to prohibit discrimination in employment and vocational training on grounds of ethnicity, gender, sexual orientation, disability, age, religion or belief. The Directive has the following prohibitions:

- It prohibits both direct and indirect discrimination, though there is a loophole allowing for indirect discrimination if it can be justified.
- It prohibits harassment.
- It prohibits instructions to discriminate.
- It permits exceptions for public security and other specified reasons.

The Directive applies in relation to access to employment, employment conditions, access to self-employment and occupation, vocational guidance, vocational training and membership of workers' (or other professional) organisations.

The Directive permits exceptions where a characteristic is a 'genuine occupational requirement' (GOR) for a job, places an obligation on employers to take appropriate measures to meet the needs of disabled persons and permits the justification of some differences of treatment on grounds of age. 'Positive action' measures, which prevent or compensate for disadvantages, are permitted. Member states may maintain a higher level of protection than the Directive requires, but may not justify a reduction in the level of protection by reference to the Directive. Member states are required to ensure:

■ That procedures are available for individuals to enforce the Directive's obligations.
■ That procedures are also available in relation to discrimination that takes place after the relevant relationship has ended.
■ That organisations with a legitimate interest may engage in proceedings on behalf of or in support of a complainant.

The burden of proof falls on the respondent to a complaint, once the complainant has established facts leading to a presumption that discrimination has taken place. Member states are required to provide protection for persons who suffer victimisation as a result of a complaint of discrimination. (Exceptions for Northern Ireland are permitted in relation to police and teachers.) Member states are required to provide for effective sanctions to enforce obligations under the Directive, and to report to the Commission by December 2005 (and every five years thereafter) on the application of the Directive.

The new Directive reflects at least some of the changes required by changing societal expectations in the twenty-first century. Specifically, these changes are that the frontiers of equality law are expanding to cover disability, sexual orientation, religion and age, and that whereas the early aim was to achieve a 'colour blind', gender-neutral world, now the aim is for a merit-based world and for diversity. Current thinking is

Box 1.8

Up to 1999 Germany restricted citizenship to people with 'blood' ancestry despite using large numbers of 'gastworkers', especially Turks, to fill jobs that Germans could not or would not do. From 1999 on, though, Germany extended immigrants' citizenship rights and, in Spring 2000, allocated 20,000 'green cards' to be handed out to foreign IT specialists with relatively little bureaucratic fuss. By September 2002, only 12,000 of these green cards had been taken up. 'But the companies which have taken up the card have largely approved. In one recent survey of new media firms with green card employees, over half say they expect higher revenues this year, despite the sluggish economy. In another (disputed) survey cited by the Federal Labour Office, businesses claim that each job secured by the card has create two to three additional hirings, mainly Germans. Rather than taking jobs, proponents argue, the green card creates them.'

Source: Fessenden, H. (2002) 'Special Report: immigration in Germany', *Prospect*, September: 38–41

that legal positions should be based on four platforms:

1. Redressing disadvantage (equality of results).
2. Promoting respect for dignity (which has whatever content people choose to give it); the EU human rights legislation attacks stigma, stereotyping and denigration.
3. Affirming community identities (change is needed in the public 'space', not in the individual).
4. Facilitating full participation in society.

Early attempts to achieve equality through law consisted of banning direct discrimination (for instance, skin colour was to be irrelevant in appointing 'alike' people); this was found to be a flawed paradigm. There is difficulty in establishing what counts as alike. (For instance, it could be argued that if women are seen as irrational, they are intrinsically unlike men.) These early attempts led to a requirement that minority groups conform to a white male norm of behaviour. This showed that equal treatment can entrench inequality – it led to indirect discrimination. Instead there was a need to equalise the starting points. The later view is that authorities and employers should equip people to be able to use their opportunities and that business demands should be screened for fairness. In the UK, in the 1980s and 1990s, legal opinion began to reflect the business case for equality and diversity, so that, for instance, in some cases, diversity might justify giving preference to a minority member. (Although it can be argued that the law has a limited capacity to protect individuals who suffer subtle discrimination, such as excluding minority members from information networks, it can also be argued that the law has an educative function and that it can place positive duties on employers to support minorities.)

There is a growing tendency to criticise the multicultural assumptions on which legislation such as the above is based. Some of this criticism originates with the people affected, as the following statements illustrate:

■ Asian male, 20: 'It's those bhangra bands and television geeks like Sayyid Jaffrey. I say I am British Asian and internationalist. Don't throw me your pitiful multicultchis.'
■ Muslim female, 20: 'I am proud British Muslim. I am close to my community and they are really proud that I am training to be a doctor. I would never give up that heritage. I feel I have nothing in common with all this multicultural stuff.'
■ Black female, 20: 'I don't know. I am proud to be the child of an immigrant who came from Trinidad. But I am not an African Caribbean. I am Black British, with very radical ideas about what that means. It means thinking that you have a fundamental right to demand your place. Not beg for it like older generations. ... I hate that soppy nothing multicultural business. I have nothing in common with the Asian or white cultures.'

The author of this research concluded, 'For many of these young Britons, the idea of multiculturalism ... is old-fashioned, incomplete, static and divisive. It simply cannot explain or describe the complexity of what has happened to British society. ... While multiculturalism intended to enhance the status and opportunities of new Britons, members of so-called ethnic minorities have felt boxed in and constrained by the outdated assumptions it seems to make about who they are, what they want out of life and how we all fit together. ... The key tool of multiculturalism is seen as monitoring the ethnic background of the workforce. In fact, for many, multiculturalism has become the view that fairness to any group means ascribing an ethnic identity to each person, and then seeking to monitor all areas of life to check how far they reflect the percentages of different black and Asian communities.'[69]

In Europe, the legal framework supporting equal opportunities and diversity has been strengthened by an EU Directive which all member countries must embody in national law. Its coverage in terms of types of difference and disadvantage is wide and it is aimed at bringing into being a merit-based world. However, the principle of multiculturalism that underlies the legal framework is under attack from some of the people it is intended to benefit.

1.6 ORGANISATIONAL GOALS, POLICIES, CULTURES AND CLIMATES

Organisations and their managers are generally highly conscious of the disadvantages of diversity. They are aware of the difficulties involved in reaching agreement, standardising procedures and working in parallel on aspects of a project when individuals from a range of cultural or subcultural backgrounds are involved. For many organisations the cost of diversity is highly visible. It includes obeying equal opportunities law and the negative reactions to diversity in the workplace by some employees. Indeed, the main diversity goal of many organisations might be described as to minimise the costs diversity entails. In other companies, 'Diversity programs are not usually seen as critical to the survival of the company, even though statements are made about markets and bottom lines. No one in the organisation is likely to lose his or her job if they don't "value" diversity the way they could if the production of goods and the selling of goods and services are not improved. Thus, diversity can be seen as a discretionary activity to be postponed when more pressing situations are faced.'[70]

Organisations often omit to notice the benefits of diversity. These benefits are of two kinds: the first kind has been defined as affecting divergent activities. These are those activities where creativity is required, which range from generating strategies to writing advertising copy, from developing new products to improving systems. When people of different ethnic, national, gender, religious, sexual orientation, social class and specialist backgrounds share perspectives and approaches, it helps ferment ideas, while the tests applied by such a cross-section help filter out the good ideas from the bad. Diversity also helps guard against the dangers of over-conformity and groupthink, which are real perils in organisations. The second kind of benefits of diversity in organisations is that it gives them an increased capacity for dealing with the inescapable diversity that exists in the environment, for domestic and international organisations alike, in markets, user groups and publics, and, for international organisations, in governments.

A study of the success of nine organisations confirms that companies benefit from valuing 'diverse cultural modes of being and interacting', where 'all cultural voices … participate fully in setting goals and making decisions'. Managers in these companies have assessed cultural biases and devised new ways for people to work together. These include extensive cultural awareness training at all levels, from entry employees to senior staff; analysis of interpersonal communication and interactive styles; active support groups to share issues and to mentor all employees; increased assistance to parents in the form of daycare and flexible leave; and bias-free hiring, evaluating, and promoting. Historically, organisational theory has emphasised hierarchical structure, competition, division of labour, and leadership. Yet in the long run, such organisations curb productivity because workers 'who assimilate are denied the ability to express their genuine selves in the workplace. ... People who must spend significant amounts of energy coping with an alien environment have less energy left to do their jobs'.[71] Thus, marginalised groups are 'destined to failure and productivity decreases'.

Corporate goals and policies in managing diversity

These can include obeying the law, ethical conduct, the business case, building learning communities, meeting the needs of diverse user populations and attaining global competitive advantage.

Obeying the law

As this chapter has shown, there is in Europe an extensive legal framework governing the treatment of minorities, and those laws have teeth. Despite that, the position of minorities in regard to work in many of those same countries is by no means acceptable, pointing to the fact that organisations in many cases are evading the law. However, for the majority of organisations, obeying the law is a basic rule. The legal prohibitions of discrimination against minorities have therefore undoubtedly been a major influence on the improving position of minorities in employment. It has often been argued that ending discrimination will only come with a change of attitudes, not by legal means, but there are numerous examples of legal changes ultimately affecting people's attitudes. This happens particularly in democracies, where matters are publicly debated and receive considerable media exposure before they become law, and where people recognise that principles embodied in law usually have majority support.

Ethical conduct

A growing number of organisations are actively committed to operating ethically. For example, Duke Energy claims that its commitment to business integrity is constant, links this to a supplier diversity policy and to requiring ethical business practices from its suppliers.[72] Not all organisations share this commitment. For example, until its actions provoked an outcry, Shell International had a statement of principles drafted in the 1970s that ran: 'Shell shall not be influenced by those pressure groups that would have corporations make or withhold investment not on commercial criteria but in order to influence the course or pattern of political society. The latter is the role of citizens and governments, not business organizations.' However, there is undoubtedly a marked trend towards organisations adopting ethical principles, which are often embodied in mission statements. It has been described as an 'ethical boom'. Organisations adopting such principles are likely to make active support for equal opportunities a platform of their ethical conduct. Even in these organisations, however, the hidden presumption often is that the moral values of the social majority will prevail, and that individuals who adhere to other values will adjust. For example, most UK organisations would make no commitment to supplying food prepared in ways that are acceptable to people of Jewish or Islamic faith. These minorities among employees are simply expected to make their own arrangements for eating according to their religion.

The business case

Many organisations need more tangible reasons than ethical principles for embracing diversity, as the following extract from a letter published in a newspaper shows:

> The moral imperative is hardly foremost in the minds of those companies struggling to survive – and there is legislation in place to deal with that issue. Therefore the working group set up ... to improve equal opportunities in the [construction] industry has focused on the business case, because it is the most persuasive and constructive argument for change ... To survive, the construction industry must change to attract and retain the best people for the job. The benefits will be for men, women, the industry and the clients it serves.[73]

For many organisations, a strong business case argument for actively supporting equal opportunities is that it positively affects the motivations of staff. This applies both to existing staff and to potential staff. Many organisations believe that developing appropriate multicultural provision will affect how far employees identify with the organisation and feel loyal to it, with all the accompanying advantages of improved attendance, motivation and self-discipline. Research shows that diversity does improve productivity, probably because, when people have social rights, they feel valued, which makes them try harder. Job advertisements that carry the statement, 'X is an equal opportunities employer' generally attract a greater number and higher calibre of applicants than those that do not. This is particularly true of younger staff, whom many companies are especially eager to attract. A second business case argument is that existing staff, who represent a major fixed cost for most organisations, constitute a resource or capacity. Increasingly, organisations are recognising that under-using that capacity because of discriminatory barriers is inefficient, just as under-using any other resource is.

Some companies are very conscious of the need to be diverse, have strong programmes supporting diversity and reflect that diversity in their public face. A Human Resources Manager for a television company, interviewed by the author, said, 'We believe that it is in the best interests of the company to recruit, select, promote and train on merit. We aim to operate within the spirit as well as the letter of the law on Equal Opportunities. We have numerous positive action schemes, which we do not see as positive discrimination; they are designed to create a level playing field. We have a commitment to creating a comfortable culture/atmosphere for workers in this organisation. The community we serve (our viewers) contains a high level of ethnic minorities. We have both to have a work force that reflects that and to reflect it in our programmes.'[74]

Two other companies also supply examples of initiatives that promote diversity. Procter and Gamble's initiative includes:

■ Addressing important advancement issues for women on a yearly planning basis,
■ Making managers accountable for working with and managing diversity and incorporating it in their performance reviews,
■ Ensuring ongoing communication between managers and staff about the goals and initiatives of the programme, and
■ Emphasising measuring, reporting and following up on outcomes in terms of retention, job satisfaction and perceptions of organisational support.

Chevron Corporation's business plans at all levels include diversity programmes such as discussions on:

- Perceiving cultural differences,
- Understanding the unspoken rules of the organisation,
- Creating an environment in which individuals can fully utilise their talents to benefit the company, and
- Smoothing over cultural and professional differences.

'Effective diversity training reflects the values of the organization and the individuals in that organization. Therefore, it is not surprising to find diversity training initiatives differing, sometimes significantly, from organization to organization.'[75]

Building learning communities

Some organisations now aim to become 'learning organizations.'[76] This means that they try to ensure that learning from organisational experience and learning about environmental change are embedded in the structures, processes and culture of the organisation. The goal is a continuous transfer of understanding and knowledge from individuals to groups, openness to the outside world and a capacity for renewing the organisation. Within the context of the goal of being a learning organisation, diversity acquires an intrinsic value; people from different backgrounds, whether those are technical, educational, social, ethnic or gender-based, are attuned to different aspects of the environment. By providing the mechanisms for them to pool and transfer the information they gain through this attuning, the organisation can tap into a much larger and wider range of environmental information.

Meeting the needs of diverse user populations and attaining global competitive advantage

In earlier sections of this chapter, the diversity of the population of the UK, EU and Europe were briefly described. All these people of differing nationalities, ethnicities, genders, sexual orientations, levels of physical and mental ability, religions and age groups are potential users of services or are in the market for products. From libraries to confectionery manufacturers, hospitals to house builders, the users and consumers of services and products are highly diverse. With diversity comes diversity of needs and wants. Public service providers such as libraries, hospitals, schools, government and local authority agencies and many charities can only fulfill their role properly if they meet the needs of these diverse user groups. Marketing, for commercial organisations, implies 'meeting consumer needs profitably'. Some companies target their products at niche markets (such as hair detensioners), while more than half the market for 'universal' products come from 'minority' groups. In some cases, the main form of adaptation for market diversity is in the product advertising: confectionery count lines may appeal to individuals from many cultures. For other companies, a more fundamental adaptation is needed for diverse markets: media, for instance, is an industry with a particular need to understand and reflect its market (audience), because its product is so visible and explicit that it can easily offend large sections of its market.

In many organisations, however, diversity is treated as the province of the human resources department; the marketing department is not involved. This can result in neglecting the diversity of their users and consumers with adverse effects on profits or consumer satisfaction. A spokesperson for the UK charity 'Disability Action' said,

'I don't think businesses realise the buying power of people with disabilities, which is about £50 million.'[77] Marketing campaigns can offend customers from particular groups, by, for instance, depicting women car buyers as interested only in colour and style. Equally offensive to some user groups, such as ethnic minorities, is their invisibility in advertisements.

Organisational cultures

Organisational cultures can be analysed in a variety of ways, such as externally versus internally driven and as task- or people-focused. Hofstede identified six dimensions closely related to his concepts of culture and also significant for the likely impact of the culture on diversity within the organisation. The six are:

1. Process-oriented versus results-oriented cultures. Process-oriented work cultures emphasise technical and bureacratic routines; results-oriented cultures focus on outcomes. Because results-oriented cultures can tolerate a range of approaches, provided the results are satisfactory, they may well support diversity better.
2. Job-oriented versus employee-oriented cultures. Organisations with employee-oriented cultures assume a broader responsibility for employees' well-being than those with job-oriented cultures. Obviously, in organisations with a diverse work-force, an employee-oriented culture is more likely to ensure that all individuals have opportunities for advancement.
3. Professional versus parochial cultures. This distinction corresponds to an older one between individuals with a cosmopolitan outlook and those with a local outlook. A parochial organisational culture is likely to be linked with a degree of xenophobia or distrust of outsiders. Such distrust can make diversity costly because of the amount that existing employees must adapt.
4. Open system versus closed system cultures. Here the reference is to how openly the organisation communicates both internally and externally, and to how easily it admits outsiders and newcomers. Hofstede found that the Danish organisations studied were more open than the Dutch. This was the only difference found between organisational cultures in the two countries. Closed systems cultures are likely to be less accessible to minorities than open systems as well as less capable of benefiting from the increased sensitivity to the environment which diversity makes possible.
5. Tightly versus loosely controlled cultures. The difference here concerns the degree of formality and punctuality required of staff. Whether an organisation's culture is tightly or loosely controlled is partly a function of its technology – banks, for example, are more tightly controlled than advertising agencies – but some variation occurs within the same technology. Loosely controlled systems are better able to tolerate the behavioural differences which come with diversity; tightly controlled systems require all individuals to conform to a single model.
6. Pragmatic versus normative cultures. Pragmatic cultures have flexible ways of dealing with the environment, especially customers; normative cultures do not. The distinction reflects the organisation's degree of customer orientation. Since flexibility is both a necessary condition for and an outcome of diversity, pragmatic cultures are better adapted to benefit from it.[78]

In most organisations, at present, one culture is dominant. In the UK organisation Bodyshop, the dominant culture is that of white liberal women, which favours 'feminine' values, such as care for the environment and the support of equal opportunities.

This is exceptional, however: the pervasiveness of the masculine culture in most Western organisations has been noted by a number of researchers: the expectations of this workplace culture are masculine heterosexual. These expectations create difficulties for gay people as well as for heterosexual women. This culture is reinforced through joking, which often has a focus round three rules of sexuality (1) the ideal, typical, real man (2) definitions of males as not-female and (3) the normality of heterosexuality. Men's continuing domination of the most powerful positions in most organisations results in a widespread emphasis on power and control over people, resources, environments and events as the only path to corporate success; worse, in the late-twentieth century, in many organisations abrasiveness and macho approaches like working extremely long hours came to be valued for themselves. While the end of the 1990s saw the pendulum swing to some degree against this, performance evaluations in many British and North American companies continued to be heavily based on personal power and control.[79]

Organisations with a strong dominant culture force those from the 'minority' cultures (who may or may not be in a numerical minority) to adjust their behaviour to accommodate it. Worse, they may not even be able to admit to having values which conflict with those of the dominant group. This not only creates stressful internal conflict for those individuals, but sets up a climate in which creativity is hampered, because too many points of view are inhibited thus ruling out the conditions favourable to creativity. Such a climate may also be one in which the damage done by groupthink (or lack of challenge to majority views) can most readily occur.

> Corporate goals in relation to diversity range from evading legal requirements such as Equal Opportunities laws to fully embracing the benefits of diversity in every sphere. Moreover, multiple goals and various diversity policies can be overlapping and mutually reinforcing. The goals, policies and culture of the organisation or organisations for which communicators work create a climate which will impact strongly on their communication and which they need to take into account.

1.7 SUMMARY

This chapter provides evidence of the growing significance of intercultural communication at work, resulting from demographic and social change, increased international trade and workforce participation by minority groups. It also bears witness to the continuing disadvantages of some groups, which must be understood by all intercultural communicators as present in the thoughts, emotions and attitudes of those with whom they interact. However, an increasingly diversity-oriented legal framework in Europe and adoption of diversity goals and policies in more organisations give hope for a better environment for intercultural communication at work.

QUESTIONS AND EXERCISES

1. Discuss the relative importance of the factors given in the text as contributing to the increased significance of intercultural communication at work.
2. 'People know how to get to know other people from the same culture but not from different cultures.' Does this statement explain why people behave differently when communicating with culturally different others? Give your reasons.
3. What does 'diversity' mean to you?
4. Give an example to show the effects on communication of surface-level and deep-level culture.

5. What might be influencing the actions of the participants in the confrontation described in Box 1.3? What behaviours might improve their communication?

6. Discuss the questions raised by the following newspaper report. For instance, should 'next year's funding' of institutions like orchestras depend on diversity compliance? Is the promotion of diversity 'social engineering'? Should public money be used to compel institutions to practise diversity? How can diversity be practised in a way that is compatible with situations where, as in the case of orchestras, there is a shortage of qualified minority people available?

Lebrecht (2003), describing a symposium called 'Cultural Diversity and the Classic Music Industry', organised by the Association of British Orchestras (ABO) and attended by representatives of all major orchestras, wrote, 'As things stand in British arts, only an autist would dare to profess disinterest [sic] in diversity. ... ACE (the Arts Council of England [a funding body]) aims to make cultural diversity "central to all that it undertakes." ACE sent no fewer than 10 observers to a room holding 160. An awful lot of next year's funding must hinge on diversity compliance. ... The ABO ... was waving a white flag of acceptance that art must, for the time being, take second place to social engineering.'

Source: Lebrecht, N. (2003) 'How the pc brigade is destroying our orchestras: British musicians are the latest group to come under pressure for not engaging with ethnic minorities. But it's not really their fault', *Evening Standard*, 8 October 2003, p. 41

7. The dictionary definition of 'race' is 'group of persons or animals or plants connected by common descent'. How does this differ from the definitions of ethnicity given in this book?

8. In this text, the term 'ethnicity' is used rather than the term 'race'. What explanation may account for this?

9. The text gives a number of indicators of the importance and growth of intercultural communication at work in Europe. What are these? What others might be used if data was available?

10. The text makes no distinction among the different types of diversity – national, ethnic, gender, disability, age, religion, sexual orientation, educational level, social class – in terms of their importance for work and work communication. Should it? Give reasons.

11. Discuss the contention that disability is 'context-dependent'. What kinds of beliefs do people have about disability? How do these beliefs influence communication with people who have disabilities?

12. Give examples to clarify the distinction between prejudice, discrimination and harassment.

13. Discuss the extent to which an organisation known to you is 'gendered'.

14. Discuss the contention that sexual harassment is a patriarchal control strategy used by men to keep women 'in their place'.

15. The European Communities Council Directive intended to establish a general framework for equal treatment in employment and vocational training permits 'positive action' measures, which prevent or compensate for disadvantages. Positive action, especially positive discrimination, is controversial. Discuss its advantages and disadvantages.

16. The early aim of equality law was to achieve a 'colour blind', gender-neutral world. Give reasons that would explain why that aim has changed.

17. Currently, the aim of equality law is to support a merit-based world and diversity. How effective would you expect to be the four platforms on which, it is suggested, law with these aims should be based?

18. Assess the criticisms of multiculturalism given in the text. Is there an alternative?

19. The text gives two categories of benefits that diversity brings to organisations. What are they and are there others?

20. How would you describe the culture of the organisation in which you work (or study)?

NOTES AND REFERENCES

1. Barnett Pearce, W. (1979) *Communication and the Human Condition*, Carbondale, IL: Southern Illinois University Press.
2. Delia, J.G. (1987) 'Communication research: a history', in Berger C.R. and Chaffee, S.H. (eds) *Communication Science*, Newbury Park, CA: Sage.
3. See, for instance, Allen, M.W., Gotcher, M.M. and Seibert, J.H. (1993) 'A decade of organizational communication research', in Deetz S. (ed.) *Communication Yearbook*, **16**: 252–330.
4. Sypher, B.D. and Zorn, T.E. (1986) 'Communication abilities and upward mobility: a longitudinal investigation', *Human Communication Research*, **12**: 420–31.
5. Zorn, M.T. and Violanti, M.T. (1996) 'Communication abilities and individual achievement in organisations', *Management Communication Quarterly*, **10**(2): 139–67.
6. Kline, S.L. and Ceropski, J.M. (1984) 'Person-centred communication in medical practice', in Wood, J.T. and Phillips, G.M. (eds) *Human Decision-Making*, Carbondale, IL: Southern Illinois University Press.
7. Frymier, A.B., Shulman, G.M. and Houser, M. (1996) 'The development of a learner empowerment measure', *Communication Education*, **45**: 181–99.
8. Stohl, C. (1995) *Organizational Communication: Connectedness in Action*, Thousand Oaks, CA: Sage.
9. All quotations in this paragraph are from: Schreiber, E.J. (1996) 'Muddles and huddles: facilitating a multicultural workforce through team management theory', *The Journal of Business Communication*, **33**: 459–73.
10. Pelled, L.H., Eisenhardt, K.M. and Xin, K.R. (1999) 'Exploring the black box: an analysis of work group diversity, conflict and performance', *Administrative Science Quarterly*, **44**: 1–28.
11. Trompenaars, F. (1993) *Riding the Waves of Culture*, London: Nicholas Brealey.
12. Tellis, G., Stremersch, S. and Yin, E. (2003) 'The international take-off of new products', Institute for Operations Research and the Management Sciences, quoted in *The Economist* 9 August 2003, p. 57.
13. Dawar, N., Parker, P.M. and Price, L.J. (1996) 'A cross-cultural study of interpersonal information exchange', *Journal of International Business Studies*, **27**(3): 497–516.
14. Triandis, H.C. (1994) 'Cross-cultural industrial and organizational psychology', in Triandis, H.C., Dunnette, M.D. and Hough, L. (eds) *Handbook of Industrial and Organizational Psychology, 2nd edn*, **4**: 103–72, Palo Alto, CA: Consulting Psychologists Press.
15. Ferraro, G.P. (1994) *The Cultural Dimension of International Business, 2nd edn*, Englewood Cliffs, NJ: Prentice-Hall.
16. Tung, R.L. (1993) 'Managing cross-national and intra-national diversity', *Human Resource Management*, **32**(2): 18–34.
17. Tung, R.L. (1996) 'Managing diversity for international competitiveness', Paper presented at David See-Chai Lam Centre for International Communication; Pacific Region Forum on Business and Management Communication, Simon Fraser University At Harbour Centre. URL: hoshi.cic.sfu.ca/forum/RTung96-12-23.html
18. Bartlett, C.A. and Ghoshal, S. (1989) *Managing Across Borders, The Transnational Solution*, Cambridge, MA: Harvard Business School Press.
19. Chalofsky, N.E. and Reinhart, C. (1988) *Effective Human Resource Development*, San Francisco: Jossey-Bass.
20. Naisbitt, J. and Aburdene, P. (1985) *Re-inventing the Corporation*, New York: Warner Books.
21. Savage, C.M. (1990) *5th Generation Management*, Bedford, MA: BARD Productions, Digital Press.
22. Khoo, G. (1994) 'The role of assumptions in intercultural research and consulting: Examining the interplay of culture and conflict at work', Paper given at David See-Chai Lam Centre for International Communication: Pacific Region Forum on Business and Management Communication, Simon Fraser University at Harbour Center. URL: hoshi.cic.sfu.ca/forum/
23. Ellis, K. and Shockley-Zalabak, P. (2001) 'Trust in top management and immediate supervisor: the relationship to satisfaction, perceived organizational effectiveness and information receiving', *Communication Quarterly*, **49**(4): 382–98.

24. Porter, M.E. (1990) *The Competitive Advantage of Nations*, New York: Free Press.
25. Meyer, G.D., Tucker, M.L. and Westerman, J.W. (1996) 'Organizational communication: development of internal strategic competitive advantage', *The Journal of Business Communication*, **33**(1): 51–69.
26. Ulrey, K.L. and Amason, P. (2001) 'Intercultural communication between patients and health care providers: an exploration of intercultural communication effectiveness, cultural sensitivity, stress and anxiety', *Health Communication*, **13**(4): 449–63.
27. Thompson, N. (2003) *Communication and Language: A Handbook of Theory and Practice*, Basingstoke: Palgrave Macmillan.
28. Scollon, R. (2000) *Intercultural Communication: A Discourse Approach*, New York: Blackwell, (p. 21).
29. Gudykunst, W.B. (1983) 'Similarities and differences in perceptions of initial intracultural and intercultural encounters: an exploratory investigation', *The Southern Speech Communication Journal*, **49**: 49–65.
30. Grimes, D.S. and Richard, O.C. (2003) 'Could communication form impact organizations' experience with diversity?' *The Journal of Business Communication*, **40**(1): 7–27.
31. Pelled, L.H. *et al.* (1999) op. cit.
32. Dansby, M.R. and Knouse, S.B. (1999) 'Percentage of work-group diversity and work-group effectiveness', *Journal of Psychology*, **133**: 486–95.
33. Wanous, J.P. (1977) 'Organizational entry: newcomers moving from outside to inside', *Psychological Bulletin*, **81**: 601–18.
34. Tung, R.L. (1996) op. cit.
35. Smith, M.G. (1986) 'Pluralism, race and ethnicity in selected African countries', in Rex J. and Mason, D. (eds) *Theories of Race and Ethnic Relations*, Cambridge: Cambridge University Press.
36. Collier, M.J. and Thomas, M. (1988) 'Cultural identity: an interpretive perspective' in Kim, Y.Y. and Gudykunst, W.B. (eds) *Theories in Intercultural Communication*, Newbury Park, CA: Sage.
37. Annual Local Area Labour Force Survey, 2001–02, UK Office for National Statistics.
38. Owen, D. (1993) *Country of Birth: Settlement Patterns*, University of Warwick Centre for Research in Ethnic Relations, National Ethnic Minority Data Archive, 1991, Census Statistical Paper no. 5.
39. Acker, J. (1992) 'Gendering organisational theory', in Mills, A.J. and Tancred, P. (eds) *Gendering Organisational Analysis*, London: Sage.
40. *Employment in Europe 2001*, European Commission.
41. Ibid.
42. Martin, L.R. and Morgan, S. (1995) 'Middle managers in banking: an investigation of gender differences in behaviour, demographics and productivity', *Quarterly Journal of Business and Economics*, **34**(1): 55–68.
43. European Statistical Office, URL: europa.eu.int/comm/eurostat/
44. Ibid.
45. Noon, M. (1993) 'Racial discrimination in speculative applications: evidence from the UK's top 100 firms', *Human Resource Management Journal*, **3**(4): 35–47.
46. Farley-Lucas, B.S. (2000) 'Communicating the (in)visibility of motherhood: Family talk and the ties to motherhood with/in the workplace', *Electronic Journal of Communication*, **10**. URL: http://www.cios.org/getfile/farley V10n3400
47. Acker, J. (1992) op. cit.
48. Burrell, G. (1984) 'Sex and organisational analysis', *Organization Studies*, **5**: 97–118.
49. Colgan, F. and Ledwith, S. (1996) 'Women as organisational change agents', in Colgan, F. and Ledwith, S. (eds) *Women in Organisations*, Basingstoke: Macmillan.
50. Colwill, N.L. (1995) 'Women in management: power and powerlessness', in Vinnicombe, S. and Colwill N.L. (eds) *The Essence of Women in Management*, Hemel Hempstead: Prentice Hall.
51. Bram, L.L. and Dickey, N.H. (1993) 'Disabled people', *Funk and Wagnalls Encyclopaedia*, Cleveland, OH: World Almanac Education.
52. Stevens, G.R. (2002) 'Employers' perceptions and practice in the employability of disabled people; a survey of companies in south east UK', *Disability and Society*, **17**(7): 779–96.

53. McLean, J. (2002) 'Employees with long term illnesses or disabilities in the UK social services workforce', *Disability and Society*, **18**(1): 51–70.
54. *The Economist*, 6 January 1996.
55. Nkomo S. (1992) 'The emperor has no clothes: rewriting "race" in organisations', *Academy of Management Review*, **17**: 487–513.
56. Alderfer, C.P. and Smith, K.K. (1988) 'Studying intergroup relations embedded in organisations', *Administrative Science Quarterly*, **27**: 5–65.
57. Gherardi, S. and Poggio, B. (2001) 'Creating and recreating gender order in organisations', *Journal of World Business*, **36**(3): 245–59.
58. The *Times*, 9 September 2004, p. 7.
59. Stangor, C. and Thompson, E.P. (2002) 'Needs for cognitive economy and self-enhancement as unique predictors of intergroup attitudes', *European Journal of Social Psychology*, **32**: 563–75.
60. Wanguri, D.M. (1996) 'Diversity, perceptions of equity and communicative openness in the workplace', *The Journal of Business Communication*, **33**: 443–57.
61. Hatcher, C. (2000) 'Making the visible invisible: constructing gender through organisational micropractices', *Electronic Journal of Communication*, **10**(1 and 2). URL: www.cios.org/www/tocs/AJC/0192.htm
62. Grimshaw, J. (1999) *Employment and Health: Psychosocial Stress in the Workplace*, London: The British Library.
63. Vartia, M. and Hyyti, J. (2002) 'Gender differences in workplace bullying among prison officers', *European Journal of Work and Organisational Psychology*, **111**: 113–26.
64. Hogh, A. and Dofradottir, A. (2001) 'Coping with bullying in the workplace', *European Journal of Work and Organisational Psychology*, **10**(4): 485–95.
65. Hoel, H., Cooper, C.L. and Faragher, B. (2001) 'The experience of bullying in Great Britain: the impact of organisational status', *European Journal of Work and Organisational Psychology*, **10**(4): 443–46.
66. Liefooghe, A.P.D. and MacKenzie Davey, K. (2001) 'Accounts of workplace bullying: the role of the organisation', *European Journal of Work and Organisational Psychology*, **10**(4): 375–92.
67. Ivy, D.K. and Hamlet, S. (1996) 'College students and sexual dynamics: two studies of peer sexual harassment', *Communication Education*, **45**: 149–66.
68. De Judicibus, M. and Mccabe, M.P. (2001) 'Blaming the target of sexual harassment: impact of gender role, sexist attitudes and work role', *Sex Roles: A Journal of Research*, **44**(7/8): 401–17.
69. Alibhai-Brown, Y. (2000) *After Multiculturalism*, London: The Foreign Policy Centre.
70. Muir, C. (1996) 'Workplace readiness for communicating diversity', *The Journal of Business Communication*, **33**: 475–84.
71. Schreiber, E.J. (1996) op. cit.
72. 'Minority suppliers must adopt proactive strategies to overcome tough economic times', *Black Enterprise*, **32**, November 2001.
73. From a letter to The Independent, 16 November 1995, from Sandi Rhys Jones, Chairwoman, Construction Industry Board.
74. Interview at Thames Television: author's research.
75. Arai, M., Wanca-Thibault, M. and Shockley-Zalabak, P. (2001) 'Communication theory and training approaches for multiculturally diverse organisations: have academics and practitioners missed the connection?' *Public Personnel Management*, **30**(4): 445–56.
76. Argyris, C. (1990) *Overcoming Organizational Defenses*. New York: Prentice Hall.
77. Channel 4 News, UK 3 October 2003.
78. Hofstede, G. (1981) *Cultures and Organizations: Software of the Mind*, London: Harper Collins.
79. Collinson, D.L. and Hearn, J. (1996) 'Breaking the silence; on men, masculinities and managements', in Collinson, D.L. and Hearn, J. (eds) *Men as Managers, Managers as Men: Critical Perspectives on Men, Masculinities and Managements*, London: Sage.

chapter two

Cultures and Subcultures

This chapter begins, in Section 2.1, with examples of work-related and organisational behaviours that may be influenced by culture. Section 2.2 gives an outline of some theories of culture to help explain what culture means. Particularly important for this book are those theories in which communication is central to culture. Section 2.3 describes four classifications or taxonomies of cultures based on 'values'. The descriptive content of these taxonomies help us identify cross-cultural similarities and differences. Section 2.4 discusses three other ways of analysing cultures – as users of high-context, low-context communication, as civilisations and as subjective cultures. Section 2.5 considers questions of how widely the concept of culture applies, and whether and how fast cultures are changing. A final section expands on the topic of how culture and cultural differences impact on work, this time drawing on concepts that have been introduced in the chapter. The section includes a discussion of organisational cultures and their effects on communication in diverse organisations. Figure 2.1 shows the questions discussed in the sections of this chapter.

It must be remembered in what follows that culture represents central tendencies. In general, individual members of a culture are likely to act consistently with these findings, but not everyone will do so.

2.1 CULTURES, WORK AND ORGANISATIONAL BEHAVIOUR

Culture has been credited with a strong influence on a society's economic prosperity.[1] Lee and Peterson argued that a society's propensity to generate independent, risk-taking, innovative, competitively aggressive and proactive entrepreneurs and firms depends on its cultural foundation. Culture strongly influences how entrepreneurial people are, though economic, political-legal and social factors (also influenced by culture) moderate the relationship.[2] Conflicting with this idea is the suggestion that the society best known for entrepreneurialism, the North American, may be highly risk averse. 'Experts seem to agree that Americans find it harder than most people to evaluate risks accurately. Lawsuits, labels on coffee cups ("Warning; the beverage you are about to enjoy is extremely hot"), even political pronouncements, all often suggest it is possible to avoid danger altogether.'[3]

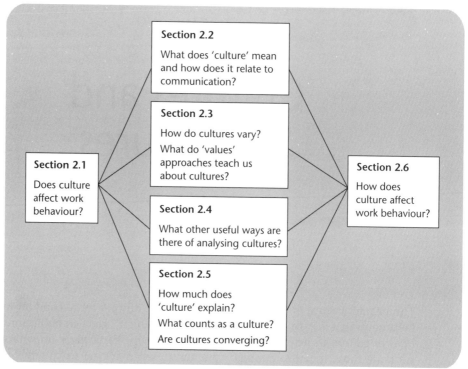

Figure 2.1 *The questions discussed in the sections of Chapter 2*

Cultural differences in risk assessment may lie behind the findings of a large-scale exploratory study that national business cultures within Europe affected acquirers' beliefs about how to proceed in cross-border mergers and acquisitions. Specifically, the study found that national cultural differences affected beliefs about the value of due diligence and professional advisers in the pre-acquisition phase. By influencing how an acquirer regards target companies, the researchers suggest, these differences may have important consequences for the negotiation of deals and the subsequent management of the acquired company.[4]

In marketing, cultural influences on consumers have long been recognised. When a company like the Danish producer of dairy products, MD Foods, markets cheese in Spain, the products which are accepted by the consumers in Spain are physically the same as the ones marketed in Denmark: there is no difference between the Havarti cheese which is sold in Spain and the Havarti sold in Denmark. However, the use to which the consumers put the cheese and the criteria by which they judge it are quite different. While the cheese in Denmark may be eaten on black bread accompanied by milk, the south Europeans eat it on white bread, as canapés, and take it with wine. 'To sum up, products are not just products: they become what they are as the result of their integration into particular contexts, i.e. by being creolized by the local socio-cultural and economic contexts.'[5]

Within organisations, culture affects behaviour at all levels. For instance, responses to Western management practices have shown that these practices can easily backfire in non-Western cultures. 'Some staff members grow cold and distant after receiving feedback on their work, and team members may clam up at meetings when asked for suggestions. A Western manager may view having subordinates participate in problem-solving to be a move towards making them feel valued, but an employee who has been taught deference to age, gender or title, might – out of respect – shy away from being honest or offering ideas, because offering suggestions to an elder or a boss might appear to them to be challenging authority. A time-conscious manager may wrongly see people whose cultures take a more relaxed view towards deadlines as being less committed to team goals, as well as less dependable, accountable and reliable. Another manager may be frustrated by an employee who nods in apparent understanding of a direction, then does not carry it out.'[6]

> National cultural differences have been linked to a range of economic, business and organisational concerns, including attitudes to risk, pre-acquisition information seeking, consumer acceptance of new products and workers' responses to management approaches.

2.2 AN OUTLINE OF CULTURAL THEORY

Culture represents an imperfectly shared system of interrelated understanding, shaped by its members' shared history and experiences. Individuals are rarely conscious of their culture, yet culture affects practically all aspects of the way the people of a group interact with each other or with outsiders. National boundaries are a convenient synonym for a culture. This framing of the concept is somewhat imprecise, however, since no nation is so pure that all of its members share a single dominant viewpoint. Nevertheless, members of a nation face a set of common experiences, themes and institutions that help

Box 2.1

'Pensions absorb 14 per cent of Italy's GDP, the highest share in any big European country. They thus siphon off cash that could be more productively used elsewhere. Yet, in a poll for *Il Messagero*, a Rome newspaper, only 25 per cent of those questioned would accept more than 'minor corrections'. Behind that response lie some deep-seated cultural attitudes. ... When asked by *Il Messagero*, only 28 per cent said they would take the money rather than opt for the deckchair. Italians may not be lazy; but they certainly have what economists call a high leisure preference.'[a]

'The idea of social equality is still as central for Germans as, say, personal liberty is for Americans.'[b]

'They may no longer lead in most areas, but Germans are world class in one: seeing the glass as half-empty, not half-full. In the small hours of December 15th, the Social Democrat-led government and the Christian Democratic opposition at last agreed to reforms that may be the most ambitious seen in post-war Germany. Yet the media were full of phrases such as "reformlet", "half-baked" and "a small step".'[c]

'The Governor of the Bank of England began an address to an assembly of bankers with these words: 'There are three kinds of economists, those who can count and those who can't.' A joke of this kind would be met with incomprehension by French listeners. It is not logical.'[d]

Sources: (a) *The Economist*, 11 October 2003, p. 4
(b) *The Economist*, 18 October 2003, p. 41
(c) *The Economist*, 20 December 2003, p. 55
(d) *The Economist*, 20 December 2003, p. 60

shape their values and ways of viewing the world. These shared experiences include geography, climate, economy, political system, racial mix, religious mix, media, language, educational system and so on. They result in a unique national character that is often more apparent to foreigners than to the nationals themselves.[7]

It is common to assume that demography and work behaviour are closely related. This has not been directly investigated.[8] In fact, there is some indirect contrary evidence. In China, unlike the West, researchers found, demographic variables such as age and gender had no direct effect on an individual's commitment to the organisation. Under the influence of traditional Chinese culture, including 'personalism' and 'guanxi' (connections), Chinese employees behaved differently from their Western counterparts.[9] Pelled pointed out that there are cultural differences in the significance of particular demographic factors; for instance, age and gender play especially significant roles in Mexican culture. In addition, some demographic categories vary cross-nationally: Mexican workplaces typically lack some of the ethnic categories present in US workforces (e.g., African American and Asian) while other ethnic distinctions (i.e., between Mestizo, Amerindian and White people) are important in the Latin American culture.[10] Other studies have shown that subgroups who vary in acculturation may have similar cultural values. A scale of cultural identity developed for Latino adolescents included cultural values such as *respeto* (respect for authority) and *feminismo* (attitudes towards traditional sex roles). However, those cultural values did not differentiate among subgroups of Latinos identified as Latino, American or bicultural.[11] Ofori-Dankwa and Julian (2000) argued that demographic diversity and value similarity (congruence) are not opposed but interact to determine how co-operative or competitive the relations between individuals and groups in an organisation will be.[12] In sum, at the individual level, we need psychological constructs, not only demographic categories, to integrate cultural processes in both psychological and structural terms.

There is a whole range of ways of defining culture, many of which provide complementary views of culture and psychological processes.[13] Table 2.1 briefly describes those that are drawn on in this chapter as underpinning for the study of cultural differences in communication.

Values as the basis of culture

A major part of cross-cultural research has sought to identify values or motivational goals that differentiate cultures. This emphasis on values is advocated by Rokeach, who wrote: 'The value concept, more than any other, should occupy a central position. ... able

Table 2.1   *Cultural theories*

Theoretical approach	Basis of explanation
Anthropological	Core values shared by communities explain variation in behaviours.
Ecological	Cultures are contexts; individuals and contexts are inter-related.
Structure-agency	Culture is social capital; core values interface with context and caste.
Ecocultural and sociocultural	Culture is a set of adaptive tools; similarities and differences across and within cultures are a function of dynamic interactions.
Social identity	Culture is a historically transmitted system of symbols, meanings and norms.
Cultural studies	Culture is about shared meanings.

to unify the apparently diverse interests of all the sciences concerned with human behavior.'[14] Within this approach, values are viewed as the criteria people use to select and justify actions and to evaluate people (including the self) and events.

> The ways that societal institutions (e.g., the family, education, economic, political, religious systems) function, their goals and their modes of operation, express cultural value priorities. For example, in societies where individual ambition and success are highly valued, the organisation of the economic and legal systems is likely to be competitive. In contrast, a cultural emphasis on group wellbeing is likely to be expressed in more cooperative economic and legal systems. Because cultural value priorities are shared, role incumbents in social institutions can draw on them to select socially appropriate behaviour and to justify their behavioural choices to others (e.g., to go to war, to fire employees).[15]

Section 2.3 describes values approaches in more depth.

Communication as the basis of culture

Over a number of years, approaches that place communication at the centre of culture have gained increasing acceptance. For instance Aldridge defined culture as follows:

> the shared system of symbolic knowledge and patterns of behavior, derived from speech communication, that human individuals carry to provide predictable internal and external psychological stability so as to prevent chaos among human individuals. We learn cultural codes for social life, role expectations, common definitions of situations, and social norms in order to provide predictability and survival of the human species. Human language (spoken and written) is the symbolic glue for human culture.[16]

A communication perspective emphasises process, interaction and meaning. Most communication theorists argue that people are not passive representatives of culture but regulators of a complex system, which they co-create during interaction.

For Kincaid *et al.*, communication is the work required to sustain a human group; it consists of the transfer of information among individuals, groups or cultures. Groups cluster together according to common beliefs, values and behaviour. Cultures are nothing more than common ways of thinking and acting, which develop because of relatively isolated within-group communication. Cultures differ from one another because there is less contact between cultures than within them. If everybody communicated with people outside their culture as much as they do with people within it, cultures would soon disappear.[17] Haslett held that culture and communication are acquired simultaneously: neither exists without the other. Culture by definition is a 'shared, consensual way of life and sharing and consensus are made possible only by communication'; in turn, humans communicate in a cultural environment that constrains the form and nature of communication. Through communication, members of a culture share a perspective or worldview, although members may not share that perspective equally or in every aspect of experience.[18]

According to Burke *et al.*, too, culture and communication are closely linked. Culture as communication is the process of creating and using shared meanings within a specific community and its history. This cultural approach to communication emphasises that people exist in a world of shared meanings, which they (usually) take for granted. Additionally, members of a culture continually participate in the production, maintenance and reproduction of a shared sense of what is real.[19,20] (Thus this cultural model of communication is based within the theories associated with the social construction of reality.) Human beings live in a world whose meaning they have produced through their own culture. This notion is reinforced by most theories of socialisation, which suggest that within modern societies certain activities and institutions, such as religions, families and schools, function to tell citizens or group members who they are and how they are to behave.

For scholars in the cultural studies tradition, such as Stuart Hall, culture is a process or set of practices which means that individuals function within a context of cultural assumptions as well as a network of social, political and economic factors. Culture is about 'shared meanings'. Meanings are produced and exchanged through language, which is the medium through which we 'make sense' of things. Meanings can only be shared through language. Thus, 'to say that two people belong to the same culture is to say that they interpret the world in roughly the same ways and can express themselves, their thoughts and feelings about the world, in ways which will be understood by each other'. This is not to deny that, within a culture, there may be different meanings, even for the same word or symbol, or that people within a culture may feel that they belong to different groups, have different identities or think different thoughts.[21] Culture is not only 'in the head'; it organises and regulates social lives. To communicate, people must speak the 'same language' – broadly, be able to use the same 'cultural codes'; they must interpret visual images, sounds, body language and facial expressions in broadly similar ways. They must also know how to translate their feelings and ideas into these various codes.[22]

Cultural studies treats discourses as ways of referring to or constructing knowledge about a particular topic or practice: they reflect the ideas and assumptions implicit in the communication of a group or society. For example, medical discourse refers to the ideas and assumptions associated with the medical world. While any one society includes multiple discourses, some discourses may be dominant in their influence and ability to shape what is defined as reality. This means that discourses have power relations embedded in them. For instance, the phrase 'doctor's orders' expresses the power exerted over patients by doctors based on their expertise and assumed beneficence.[23] Following this logic, culture can be defined as the way of life of a group or society including meanings, the transmission, communication and alteration of those meanings and the power relations which decide which meanings are accepted and which have more significance than others.

As an example of the practical application of the 'shared meaning' view of culture, it has been argued that 'brand personalities' are symbols and carriers of culture. Research found that Spanish brand personalities had some dimensions in common with North American (sincerity, excitement and sophistication) and others that differed – passion (Spanish) and competence and ruggedness (American). Japanese brand personalities shared sincerity, excitement, competence and sophistication with American, but also had the dimension of peacefulness.[24] Figure 2.2 shows the key ideas of the 'culture as communication' theorists described here.

Identities as the basis of culture

Communication and culture are seen as inextricably intertwined within another approach – cultural identity theory. A cultural identity is part of an individual's self-construal, or sense of selfhood. (Self-construals are explained further in Chapter 4.) It is the part that derives from a person's knowledge of his or her membership in a

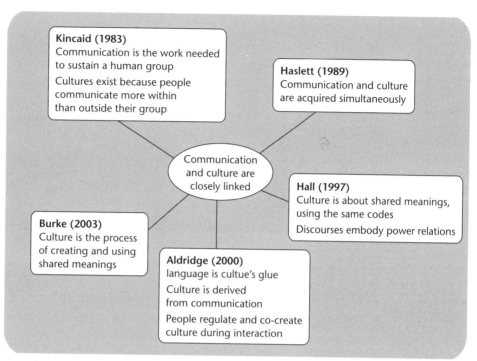

Figure 2.2 *Key ideas of culture – as – communication theorists*

cultural group (or groups), together with the value and emotional significance attached to that membership. A cultural identity is an aspect of social identity. That part of the self-construal not accounted for by social identity is personal identity. Within cultural identity theory, culture is defined as a historically transmitted system of symbols, meanings and norms. Symbols and meanings are what groups of people say, do, think and feel. To be a member of a group is to communicate with other members. This interpretation of culture is radically different from those approaches in which cultural status is determined mainly by birth rather than by subscribing to a system of symbols and meanings.

Core symbols are particularly important. For example, a core symbol for collectivist cultures, such as Mexico's, may be bondedness, whereas a core symbol for a more individualist culture, such as mainstream culture in the USA, may be individual accomplishment.[25] Meanings include metaphors, stories and myths. Norms are patterns of appropriate ways of communicating; attached to norms are prescriptions, proscriptions and social sanctions, while stories that are told often relate to norm violations and how they are punished. For example, the Biblical story of Sodom and Gomorrah refers to Hebrew norms against certain sexual practices; the folk tale of the fisherman who was granted three wishes but lost everything through asking for too much refers to a widespread norm against greed.

There are different types of culture corresponding to different types of groups which, according to cultural identity theorists, meet the requirements for being a culture. Cultural groups include corporations, support groups, national groups or civil rights groups; cultural groups are any such groups that are bounded (have restricted membership), have histories and are significant to individuals. Symbols and norms change over the lifetime of culture systems, but there is enough consistency in what is

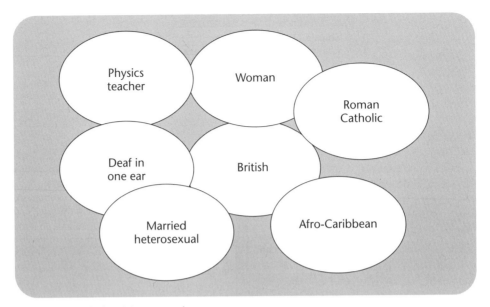

Figure 2.3   *An example of identities at work*

handed down to make it possible to define the boundaries between systems and distinguish members of one cultural system from those of another. This is why each individual has a range of cultures to which s/he belongs. Figure 2.3 shows an example to illustrate cultural identification theory.

Thus, for cultural identity theorists, national cultures are only one type among many. (This, of course, exposes the theory to the criticism that you end up with a 'culture of one'.) In fact, because many people contribute to the creation of a national culture's symbols, meanings and norms, national culture is diffuse. Ethnic cultural groups share a sense of heritage, history and origin from an area outside or preceding the creation of their present nation-state. Gender, profession, geographical area and organisation are other bases for cultural difference. The meanings and associations attributed to any category of people 'are a product of the enduring images and characteristics people have ascribed and assigned to men [sic] in groups over time'. For instance, masculinity can be defined as a social and symbolic construct. Based upon a survey of contemporary published research regarding masculinity, Chesebro and Fuse concluded that masculinity is now a construct that attributes ten traits to people viewed as masculine. These traits, it is suggested, overlap with, but are not identical with, those that would have been part of the construct of masculinity at other times. Cultural identities are enduring yet dynamic; for instance, the idea of what it means to be a woman changed considerably during the twentieth century, but the underlying idea of difference from men persisted.[26]

An identity to which people normally pay little attention becomes more important to them when, for instance, they meet for the first time with people whom they perceive to have a different cultural identity – for example, when they travel abroad. This point will be seen to have considerable importance in Chapter 6 when intercultural communication is considered.

> The cultural theories relevant to this book variously emphasise values, communication and identity.

2.3 THE VALUES APPROACH TO CULTURE

A major thrust of theorising and research into culture has been the attempt to identify similarities and differences among cultures in order to generate and test categories of cultures. This section describes some of the main results of these efforts, covering four taxonomies based on culture-level values and dimensions: Hofstede's, Boski's, Trompenaars' and Schwartz's. To the extent that some of these taxonomies claim to be comprehensive, they must be alternatives. Nevertheless, it is still not known which is most valid, so they may all be learnt from and usefully applied in appropriate ways.

Hofstede's culture-level values

In the late 1960s and early 1970s, Hofstede undertook the most comprehensive cross-cultural study to date, using questionnaire data from 80,000 IBM employees in 66 countries across seven occupations.[27] From this research Hofstede established four values which differ across cultures:

1. Individualism–Collectivism (I–C) is defined by the extent to which individuals' behaviours are influenced and prescribed by others: individualists prefer self-sufficiency while collectivists give more recognition to their interdependent roles and their obligations to their group. Studies of social categorisation and intergroup relations show that all people mentally 'group' others, using salient characteristics (i.e., those characteristics that are important to them. These range from family or work unit membership to demographic or other characteristics). The group that the categoriser feels similar to and identifies with is called the 'ingroup' and other groups are called 'outgroups'. People from all types of culture categorise others in this way, but the importance of the distinction is much greater for people from collectivist cultures. In individualist societies people primarily operate as individuals or as members of their immediate families, whereas collectivist societies are composed of tight networks in which people operate as members of ingroups and outgroups. They expect to look after other members of their ingroup in need and expect their ingroup to look after them. (Of course, even in individualist societies, there are rules and principles that reflect interconnectedness and serve to constrain an individual's pursuit of personal goals and outcomes. It is a matter of degree rather than kind.)[28] The I–C dimension is associated with how people relate

Box 2.2

Against the odds, Congolese students are learning about IT. When the students graduate, they find their skills in demand. ... Kinshasa University's e-learners are excited about their prospects, but realistic. Etiennette Mukwanga says she is proud to be learning something useful, despite all the hardships. Her ambition? The same as all the other students: 'To become someone who can support her father, mother, brothers and sisters.'[a]

When applying for something (planning consent, housing benefit) members of some ethnic minorities go in person, thinking that the relationship will ease their path.[b]

Sources: (a) *The Economist,* 5 July 2003, p. 54
(b) Statement by a local authority staff member, author's research

to one another. For people in collectivist cultures, the personal relationship prevails over the task, whereas the opposite is the case for those in individualist cultures. For scores on individualism, five of the top six countries researched by Hofstede are 'Anglo' countries – USA, Australia, Great Britain, Canada and New Zealand – with The Netherlands occupying position 5; five of the lowest in individualism (highest in collectivism) are South American and the sixth is Pakistan. Fourteen European countries cluster in the top 20 on individualism, none are in the lowest 18 and only three (Greece, Yugoslavia and Portugal) are in the middle group of 15 countries.

Although I–C may in fact represent a number of cultural factors rather than a single value, it is perhaps the most important as well as the most frequently cited cultural dimension.[29] It will often recur in this book.

2. Power distance (PD) is defined by the degree of separation between people of various social statuses or, to put it another way, the extent to which all members of a society, including the less powerful, expect and accept that power is distributed unequally. Low PD cultures endorse egalitarianism, high PD cultures endorse hierarchies. In high PD societies, relations between unequals are formal, often patron–client in format, information flow is formalised and restricted, and companies are organised in rigid vertical hierarchies. In low PD societies relations are open and informal, information flows are functional and unrestricted, and companies tend to have flat hierarchies and matrix organisations. Countries particularly high on PD are Malaysia, four South American countries and the Philippines; those particularly low on this variable are Austria, Israel, New Zealand, Ireland and the four Scandinavian countries. Eleven European countries are in the lowest 20 on PD, only three (Yugoslavia, France and Belgium) in the top 20.

3. Uncertainty Avoidance (UA) refers to the extent to which a culture prefers to avoid ambiguity and to the way in which it resolves uncertainty. High UA cultures prefer rules and set procedures to contain the uncertainty, low UA cultures tolerate greater ambiguity and prefer more flexibility in their responses. In high UA societies, families, groups and organisations tend to be closed to outsiders, to stress compliance and obedience, to punish error and non-conformity, and to reward conformity, loyalty and attention to detail. Low UA societies tend to accept

---

Box 2.3

If Eskimos have dozens of words for snow, Germans have as many for bureaucracy. As an example of ridiculous rules: a tailor (who) had to put up a sign saying 'fire extinguisher' next to (guess what) her fire extinguisher, to produce a thick folder with all regulations relevant to her business, to raise her work table by ten centimetres, to buy a special emergency kit, and to check if her only employee was allergic to nickel – at a cost of 400 euros.

Germany is, in short, one of the most rule-bound countries in the world.

The government has recently launched a 'masterplan for reducing bureaucracy'. It brought in a bill to do away with such workplace regulations as where to put light switches or the shape of rubbish bins.

Yet it will take years for Germany to match America and Britain. Germans may inveigh against bureaucrats, but they have a soft spot for state mollycoddling.

Source: The Economist, 11 October 2003, p. 46

Box 2.4

A Belgian research analyst who works for a UK research organisation in London, said, 'In my country only people with good qualifications in statistics or economics would be employed in this kind of work. As a result, they would be demanding about the quality of the data and statistics that they would agree to use, which might sometimes mean that they could not give the client companies the sort of information they need. Here, most researchers are arts graduates, with rather weak statistical backgrounds. As a result, they are flexible about data, and willing to provide client companies with answers to their questions, based, perhaps, on small samples. So long as the companies are aware of how the data are arrived at, that seems fine to me.'

Based on: Interview, author's research

outsiders at all levels, stress personal choice and decision-making, reward initiative, team-play and risk-taking. They also stress the development of analytical skills. In low UA cultures, values include a tolerance for deviance and innovative ideas. What is different is seen as curious, as opposed to dangerous. Therefore, in low UA cultures, innovations will be looked upon more favourably than in cultures with high UA.[30]

However, cultures with similar UA levels may devote different amounts of effort and attention to reducing uncertainty by imposing laws, rules and regulations. 'Although Germany ranks in the middle of Hofstede's scale, the author himself gives many examples about the German inclination for orderliness; expressions like Befehl ist Befehl ("a command is a command") or Ordnung muß sein ("there must be order") are well known internationally.'[31]

Two Southern European countries (Greece and Portugal) and two South American (Guatemala and Uruguay) are highest on UA, while those lowest in this characteristic are four small nations (Singapore, Jamaica, Hong Kong and Ireland) and two Scandinavian countries. European countries differ more on uncertainty avoidance than on individualism–collectivism or power distance: six are in the highest 20 countries, seven in the next 20 and four in the lowest 13.

4. Masculinity/Femininity (MAS) defines quality of life issues. High MAS cultures endorse assertiveness, competition and aggressive success; low MAS cultures prefer modesty, compromise and co-operative success. In high MAS societies people tend to believe that matters of material comfort, social privilege, access to power and influence, status and prestige, and ability to consume are related to ability and that any individual who wants these benefits of society can have them. This also means they believe that people who do not have the ability, or the character, cannot and should not have them, since they are essentially a reward for hard work and success. High MAS societies tend to reward financial and material achievements with preferential social prestige and status, and to attribute strong character and spiritual values to such high achievers.

In some low MAS societies, living in material comfort and having a high standard of living are believed to be matters of birth, luck or destiny. In some other low MAS societies, material comfort and lifestyle are considered less an indication of a person's character and value than their religious devotion, their social conscience, their intellectual or artistic abilities, their stature as a wise elder, or (and this probably applies in Scandinavia) their rights as a fellow member of a caring society.

On the MAS variable, Japan is significantly higher than any other nation while Austria, Venezuela, Italy and Switzerland are in positions two to five; four Northern European countries are highest on the 'feminine' end of the dimension. European countries polarise on MAS, with seven countries in the top 20, nine in the bottom 20 and only one (Belgium) in the middle group.

MAS was the only dimension on which Hofstede found significant differences between men and women, though, even then, not consistently. In the most 'feminine' countries, there was no real difference but in the most 'masculine' countries, men scored 50 per cent higher than women on MAS, and correspondingly for the countries in between. It was because this was the only dimension on which men and women differed that Hofstede labelled it 'masculine'/'feminine'; nevertheless, because sexism can be read into these labels, some writers have renamed its poles 'Achievement' and 'Relational' orientations.

Later, Hofstede identified a fifth cultural value – long-term or short-term time orientation: willingness to postpone 'payback' and satisfaction against wanting or needing quick returns and rewards. In the context of international joint ventures, it has been shown, the effect of long- or short-term orientation is stronger than that of any of the other dimensions of culture.[32]

Hofstede found that national culture explained half the variance in employees' attitudes and behaviours.[33] Hofstede (1993) found that although the original six European Community (EC) countries had a degree of homogeneity around individualism (with only 26 per cent of the variation seen across the worldwide samples) and power distance (with only 35 percent of the variance), the European Union (EU) of (at the time) 12 countries or a broader set of 18 European countries 'explodes' into massive cultural diversity. 'Nowhere on earth does such variation exist in such a small geographical space.'[34] 'Eighty-six percent of worldwide variance on uncertainty avoidance, 82 percent of variance on masculinity–femininity, 73 percent of variance on individualism–collectivism, and 70 percent of variance across power distance is found in Europe.'[35]

Hofstede's (1993) definition and analyses of culture are not intended to be rigid categorisations of behaviour or people: the culture of a country – or any other category of people – is not a combination of properties of the 'average citizen' or 'modal personality'. One person from a culture may react in one way (such as feeling nervous), another from the same culture in another way (such as wanting rules to be respected); these would both be manifestations of a common cultural tendency to avoid uncertainty. In addition, such reactions need not be found within the same persons or in all persons from the culture, but only statistically more often in the same society. Few people fall entirely into one or the other cultural pattern, but the tendency is there.

Hofstede's work has been both supported and refuted by replication, although the majority of replications support the existence of the values. Despite this support, the values are not all-inclusive and there are additional variables that can be used to explain the relationship between culture and, for instance, technological diffusion. Religion, gender equality, ethnocentrism and high- and low-context communication (explained in Section 2.4) are examples of national level variables that have been used to date.[36]

Boski's humanism/materialism values dimension

Boski argued that there are two 'axes' confounded in the concept of I–C: agency/self-direction–subjugation, and self-interest–social interest. Boski was particularly

Box 2.5

In Poland, life is regarded as too variable, multi-faceted and uncontrollable to be moulded by rigorous rules and restrictions. Polish culture thrives on a spontaneous, free-floating stream of life.

At the goal level, a broad spectrum of end-results will be considered as satisfying. ... The path of achievement is also planned in a sketchy way, so that many 'unforeseen' events will happen at any time, demanding emergency measures, interventions and extra efforts to be exerted before coming to the end. Plans and actions [are] ... in a constant flux; negotiated and renegotiated. ... concepts of 'work time', 'job-employment', 'social roles', 'traffic rules', etc. appear(ed) fuzzy.

Source: Boski, P. (2002) 'Interactions, research and history embedded in Polish culture: Humanism and uncertainty non-avoidance', in Lonner, W.J., Dinnel, D.L., Hayes, S.A. and Sattler, D.N. (eds) *Online Readings in Psychology and Culture* (unit 3, chapter 7), (http://www.wwu.edu/~culture), Center for Cross-Cultural Research, Western Washington University, Bellingham

concerned with 'humanism', as reflecting the predominant culture of countries such as Poland; its opposite pole is 'materialism'. Examples of measures of humanism–materialism are: 'Offering selfless sympathy and helpful hand, generosity – Always trying to tease out some profit or advantage' and 'Caring for life long friendships – Becoming a successful business person as life ideal'.[37]

The scale measuring these dimensions (the HUMAT scale), used in a number of studies from 1987 on, showed large differences at the culture-level of measurement between Poland and North America. Poles (residing in Warsaw), Polish immigrants (in Canada and in the USA), and Polish Canadians or Polish Americans of first and second generations rated Polish culture on the humanist side, while American culture was on the materialist side. Americans (residents of Florida) also rated their culture as materialist, and so did foreign students (at the University of North Florida). The differences were smaller at the personal level.

Research data have clearly shown that humanism–materialism also differentiates distinctly and predictably between socio-economic groups in Polish society. Among samples of five socio-economic groupings – labourers in private and social sectors, teachers, bank employees and city councillors (regional politicians) – the highest scores on humanism are earned by teachers and local community politicians; the lowest among people employed in banks. Research findings have also demonstrated that humanism–materialism is a different value set from collectivism–individualism. City councillors, with their highest scores in humanism, are also lowest in collectivism.

Trompenaars' relationships and attitudes taxonomy

For Trompenaars, culture was 'often intangible and difficult to define'.[38] However, Trompenaars, like earlier researchers, created a taxonomy (or classification) of cultures. Its analysis was derived partly from 15 years of training of managers, and more specifically from academic research. This used minimum samples of 100 people in each of 30 countries with similar backgrounds and occupations (75 per cent managers, 25 per cent general administrative staff) from a variety of multinational companies.

Trompenaars identified three main categories and eight sub-categories of cultural dimension. They are:

1. Relationships with people:
   - Universalism versus particularism.
   - Individualism versus collectivism.
   - Neutrality versus emotionalism.
   - Specificity versus diffuseness.
   - Achievement versus ascription.
2. Attitudes to time:
   - Future versus past orientation.
   - Polychronic versus monochronic time.
   - Time as a stream or a cycle.
3. Attitudes to the environment.

Universalism and particularism

These contrast a preference for drawing general principles versus a preference for the anecdotal or itemised. For example, where one person might say 'One of the characteristics of modern Western life is for married women with children to work,' another might say, 'It's a curious fact, but three of my friends – all married women with children – have got themselves jobs. There's Mrs. X running a playgroup, Mrs. Y working at the supermarket and Mrs. Z training to be a solicitor.' Much of the research into this cultural dimension has come from the USA, and is influenced by American cultural preferences. However, a British management writer, Handy, illustrated the principle from a personal experience:

> Particularist countries think that the relationship is more important than the contract and that a good deal requires no written contract – the particular people and the particular situation matter more than the universal rules. You can see that you could cause great offence if you got it wrong, as I once did myself, when I insisted on bringing in a lawyer to sign an agreement that my Chinese dealer had thought we had settled with a handshake over a cup of Chinese tea. That particular deal fell through. Or perhaps I should say that when I tried to apply my universal approach to that particular situation, it failed.[39]

Individualism and collectivism

Trompenaars defined this value dimension slightly differently from Hofstede (1981), as a conflict between what each of us wants as an individual and the interests of the group we belong to. Individualism is 'a prime orientation to the self', collectivism is a 'prime orientation to common goals and objectives'. For Trompenaars, writing in the early 1990s, the success of the 'Five Dragons' – Japan, Hong Kong, Singapore, South Korea and Taiwan – raised 'serious questions about both the success and the inevitability of individualism'.

Neutrality and emotionalism

This dimension is about the display of feeling, rather than the level or range of emotions experienced. Trompenaars considered that emotional display is a major

Box 2.6

'In the West we tend to separate work and play. In the mid-1990s I was training top managers of the oil and gas industry of one of the Central Asia' 'Stans. We were in an oil refinery's 'sanatorium', built for workers to have refreshing breaks. At lunchtime, having a siesta in the 45 degrees heat, after discussing corporate strategy in the morning, we were enticed out of our rooms by drumming and singing. Two of us from the UK (both women) ended up dancing traditional dances with the matron of the sanatorium and drummers and traditional stringed instruments playing. Our clients clapped and gave us money, which we gave to the band.

Thirty minutes later we were onto business strategy again. It was a great break.'

Source: Email from a financial expert, author's research

difference between cultures and argued, 'There is a tendency for those with norms of emotional neutrality to dismiss anger, delight or intensity in the workplace as "unprofessional".'

Specificity and diffuseness

This distinction is based on the concept of 'life spaces'. People have different senses of what is in the public and private domains of life and of how separate these different domains should be. For example, Swiss and Japanese people do not readily invite business contacts to their home; North Americans are much freer in this respect.

Achieved and ascribed status

This is a matter of the importance attached to what a person has done or is doing (what they have achieved through their own efforts) versus their position resulting from external factors. Trompenaars disputed the Western view that ascription is inferior to achievement, arguing that some ascriptions, such as age and experience, education and professional qualifications make good sense in predicting business performance.

Concepts of time

There are several ways in which concepts of time vary between cultures – time as a cycle or a sequence; past, present and future emphasis (the British emphasise the past, North Americans the future); time as a precious resource which must not be wasted versus a more leisurely approach. A major distinction is between monochronic and polychronic notions of activity: people from Anglo-Saxon cultures find their sense of order disrupted if work is not clock-regulated, if they are expected to do several things at a time or find others around them doing several things at once. For example, the British feel uncomfortable if they enter someone's office for an appointment, are waved to a seat and smiled at while the person they have come to see continues a telephone conversation, making notes. For an Argentinian, this would be quite normal and acceptable.

Concepts of the environment

Is the environment to be controlled or harmonised with?

Box 2.7

X is an internal auditor for an international company. His current assignment is to audit the travel department of the company's Italian subsidiary. The department has responsibility for organising and paying for all the travel and accommodation arrangements as well as visas for a staff of 35 international executives and sales representatives.

(1) X arrived at the time arranged but was kept waiting in an outer office for 25 minutes. When he entered, he looked somewhat pointedly at his watch. The manager of the department smiled broadly, saying, 'Ah, we have plenty of time, have we not? Would you care for a coffee?' X refused. (2) The manager, having shaken hands, moved closer to X, who felt uncomfortable and backed away. (3) X's discomfort was increased by the fact that the office seemed to be overcrowded with desks occupied by people to whom he was not introduced, while other people continuously came and went through a side door. (4) The conversation was several times interrupted by people asking the manager questions, to which he would intersperse his answers with his answers to X, who began to feel confused. The manager also often interrupted their discussion himself, to speak to a colleague about some unrelated matter, or to answer the telephone. He also seemed excited, jumping up to find a paper from his desk, and using emphatic gestures. However, X had expected the last of these: he'd heard about the Italians. (5) When they were seated, the manager asked him about his journey, and appeared to be really interested (possibly a professional interest, X thought). He asked about X's family, commented on the latest political happening in X's country and asked X about his political views. 'Next he'll be wanting to know what religion I am,' X thought. (6) X began by raising the two problem areas highlighted in his junior's preliminary audit report. One was complaints of late payment of travel expenses by expatriates working in the subsidiary; the other was numerous instances where rules had been infringed. (He did not beat about the bush in raising these matters, but came straight to the point.

Afterwards, he wondered if he had seemed impolite.) (7) He suggested they deal with them in that order; the travel department manager agreed, then jumped quickly to the rules question. (8) 'You know, some of these rules, they are not practical,' he said. 'They only make work for nothing. You will agree that your colleague found no instances of dishonesty or misappropriation of funds?' X agreed – none had been found, but 'Rules are rules,' he thought.

The following helps explain the behaviour of X's Italian colleague:

(1) It is said that punctuality in Milan means 20 minutes late, in Rome 30 minutes and in Naples 45 minutes. (It is also said that a red traffic light in Milan is an instruction, in Rome a request and in Naples a decoration.)

(2) Italians have a Mediterranean sense of distance comfort – closer than most North Europeans'.

(3) Italians' sense of privacy and of how compartmentalised different aspects of life should be is less restrictive than most North Europeans' – their culture is more diffuse than the more specific North European cultures.

(4) Italians' sense of time is polychronic – they expect to do more than one thing at a time and have others around them doing several things at once; this contrasts with the monochronic sense of time in some cultures.

(5) This experience also reflects Italy's diffuse culture. Matters are openly discussed which in some cultures would be irrelevant and private in a business context.

(6) It is likely that the Italian manager will find X's bluntness impolite, especially as it follows his earlier refusal of the coffee and determination to get right down to business.

(7) Following agendas and precise sequences of dealing with matters is not the Italian way.

(8) Italians frequently bend rules and interpret agreements flexibly; this does not mean they are dishonest, only that in grey areas they see flexibility as common sense.

Box 2.8

'As Americans, I think we often lose track of time, because we're too busy making money for a giant corporation, or defending "Big Business", or doing some other activity that will someday appear meaningless. In Europe, as I observed, things just move slower. People have more time for their lives, their families, and their selves. It's almost amazing to understand what people in our country are willing to give up for their job, and how the Europeans view that so vastly differently. ... One thing we seemed to find over and over again is that [in Europe] businesses are run on the schedules of the owners. When the owner of a business wants to eat lunch, he does so without thinking, even if that means closing his shop for an hour or two. Not only is this an accepted practice, it's conventional.'

Source: Required paper written to receive credit from the Haworth College of Business for Study Abroad Experience. URL: godzilla.hcob.wmich.edu/~s8rich/391.html

Schwartz's values approach

A different set of cultural values has emerged from the more recent work of Schwartz and his colleagues. Based on preceding anthropology, Schwartz *et al.* theorised that three basic issues confront societies:

1. To define the nature of the relation between the individual and the group,
2. To guarantee responsible behaviour that will preserve the social fabric, and
3. To decide the relation of humankind to the natural and social world.[40]

When a values survey was conducted among teachers and students in nearly 50 countries, Schwartz *et al.* found a set of culture-level values corresponding to these three concerns:

1. Embeddedness versus autonomy. This value is related to but not identical with earlier value concepts such as I–C and autonomy/conservatism, but also contrasts openness to change with maintaining the status quo.
2. Hierarchy versus egalitarianism. Again, despite a link to power distance, there is a key difference. Egalitarianism calls for people to recognise one another as moral equals who share basic interests as human beings – these elements are absent from low power distance.
3. Mastery versus harmony. Mastery is similar to masculinity but does not imply selfishness; harmony is related to uncertainty avoidance but does not imply an emphasis on controlling ambiguity.

A set of 44 country profiles suggested the existence of broad cultural groupings of nations. These are related to geographical proximity but are also based on other factors such as shared histories, religion, levels of development and contact with other cultures. The regions to which the countries in this sample were allocated are:

■ the Western European nations (high in autonomy, egalitarianism and mastery – except Italy, which is high in harmony);
■ the English speaking nations (high in mastery and autonomy, intermediate in hierarchy/egalitarianism); and
■ the Eastern European nations (high in harmony, conservatism, intermediate in hierarchy/egalitarianism).

Box 2.9

'In Italy, I wanted to start a CD shop. I found I had to first rent premises, then to apply for a permit. That would take six to nine months. All that time I would be paying rent but would not be allowed to trade, and I might not even get the permit in the end. I gave up. In London, I saw a shop to rent, took it, moved in some stock and started selling. Later, I had to register to pay taxes, but no permits were needed.'

Source: Interview with an Italian entrepreneur, author's research

Islamic countries (high in hierarchy, conservatism, intermediate in mastery/harmony), East Asian and sub-Saharan African countries form other groups. Thus empirical work based on Schwartz's theory has yielded meaningful transnational groupings, which may correspond closely to culture.

National cultures, differentiated according to Schwartz's values taxonomy, have an influence on organisational cultures and practices and therefore on individual employees' experience of, for instance, role stress. A comparison of 21 nations by Peterson *et al.* found that national differences in role stress were greater than role stress differences due to personal characteristics, such as gender, or organisational features, such as form of ownership.[41] A re-analysis of this data using Schwartz *et al.*'s cultural variables found the following:

- Managers in nations high on mastery and hierarchy but low on harmony, were more likely to report role overload. This may be the effect of their trying to 'change the world' and the overloading of subordinates being legitimated by superordinate (organisational) goals.
- Egalitarianism and intellectual autonomy had little effect on role ambiguity, although they might be expected to result from cultural willingness to change role definitions.
- Managers in nations high in hierarchy and low in harmony reported greater role conflict, though the correlation with mastery was not significant.[42]

(This re-analysis also found stronger relations with the Schwartz *et al.* cultural variables than the original research did with Hofstede's.) Sagiv and Schwartz, by re-analysing data from an earlier study of 12 nations, found the following:

- Managers in nations with cultures that emphasise harmony chose integrating rather than analysing solutions to managerial dilemmas.
- Managers in nations where embeddedness is emphasised chose pay systems that take into account the size of the employee's family, not just his or her work.
- Managers in nations where mastery and hierarchy are emphasised chose commitment to the organisation rather than commitment to a friend.[43]

Values surveys

The European Values Survey and the World Values Survey are major empirical studies based on a taxonomic approach. Surveys were undertaken in Western Europe in the late-1970s (published 1981), and both Western and Eastern Europe in 1990 and

2000–02. Some marked differences were found between Eastern European and Western European values. However, within both regions, different values and attitudes were variably interpreted and appreciated.[44] General values covered in the surveys include:

- Identity (whether primarily European, national or local)
- Patriotism
- Individualisation (sense of control over and satisfaction with one's life)
- Interpersonal trust
- Trust in institutions such as government and the civil service
- Tolerance (measured by willingness to live alongside foreigners or people of a different 'race')
- Solidarity with 'weaker' members of society, such as the elderly, people with disabilities and immigrants
- Environmental concerns
- Religious affiliation
- Moral standards
- The family, and
- The relative importance of work, religion and politics.

Work-related findings covered:

- Work ethos
- Instrumental and expressive work values, and
- Perceived instrumental and expressive work qualities.

The findings from the 2000–02 survey, some of which are described in Chapter 4, give a valuable picture of values and attitudes in different European countries.

Critiques of taxonomic approaches to culture

Treatments of culture such as those of Hofstede, Trompenaars and Schwartz *et al.*, which provide lists of shared background characteristics such as worldviews, values and behavioural characteristics, have been criticised for being over-simplified, static and lacking a basis for determining whether two cultures are different. Trompenaars' work also attracts the criticism that, while his variables are intended to be a continuum, only lip service is paid to this; in reality they are treated as dichotomous. For instance, he writes of 'the ascriptive culture', although 21 out of 39 countries in his research fall between 25 per cent and 33 per cent on this measure and of 'the achievement-oriented culture', although again 21 countries fall between 61 per cent and 70 per cent on this measure. Hofstede's work, though much admired and widely applied, has been criticised, primarily on two grounds: that it omits important values and that it is non-dynamic. The comment of Tayeb is typical of these criticisms: 'A country's culture is too vibrant and complex an entity to be simplified and described only in terms of these dimensions.'[45] According to Aldridge, 'Human culture is a problem formation and problem resolution process and uses higher order abstractions via speech communication to provide for change. It is possible, for example, to have a highly individualist culture, as defined by Hofstede, but miss the variations in individualist cultures around the globe which have differing core values that may enhance or limit second order change.'[46]

Other criticisms focus on the lack of explanatory power of dimensional and 'shared values' models. Kim, for instance, commented, 'When broad dimensions such as individualism–collectivism ... are invoked to account for cultural differences, it is uncertain exactly how or why these differences occur. The use of culture as a post hoc explanation of observed differences does little to help us understand the underlying causes of behavior.'[47] Collier and Thomas, too, criticised taxonomic conceptualisations because they do not supply answers to how many of the characteristics need to be different for there to be a cultural difference, because the fact that the characteristics vary in their impact on different cultures is ignored, and because such definitions may not capture the experience of the participants.[48]

There is a further problem in describing cultures as discrete entities. As de Munck put it, 'A theory of culture as a discrete entity (or as homogeneous) logically implies that every member of that culture is culturally more similar to each other than they are to any one member from any other culture. But this is obviously not so. This also leads to the confusion where culture is passive and one selects from it [known as hybridization theory], at the same time culture is active and shapes the individual.'[49] Hybridisation theory itself is illogical because if individuals select, then no two individuals are likely to select the same set of elements and everyone is going to belong to a culture (or group) of one. 'We might [also] argue that culture is a whole made out of parts such as class, religion, politics, economics, education and so forth and those similarities are limited to part similarities. But this Humpty Dumpty analogy of culture doesn't work, for if religion and the other subsystems shape individuals, then 'culture' is reduced to a category label that signals all these subsystems but has no function.' This critic concluded, 'The noun definition ignores and, in fact, hinders us from an analysis of the most constant and central aspects of culture – that it is a process and that it changes.' Unfortunately, de Munck was unable to propose a theory of culture that would satisfy his criteria, stating, 'At present I think we are not ready to develop a unified theory of culture, but we can develop many well-formed, midrange theories of culture that incorporate the core features: that it is shared, that it is located in the individual, and that it is learned. These features have many facets however, depending on the questions asked.'

Greenfield discussed the limitations of using Western-made research instruments in other cultures. She pointed out that it is not defensible to take a test to other cultures where respondents have different basic assumptions about values (e.g., Does the response to a question on values have the same importance in every culture?), knowledge (e.g., Are people in the various cultures equally likely to know something?), and communication (e.g., Does the context of the test item have the same meaning in all the cultures?).[50]

Four values-based approaches to analysing cultures have been described. These are Hofstede's, which distinguishes individualism–collectivism, power distance, uncertainty avoidance and masculinity/femininity as the primary cultural values; Boski's, which emphasises humanism-materialism; Trompenaars', which focuses on three primary values (relationships with people and attitudes to time and environment); and Schwartz's, which considers that there are three primary values, all related to but distinct from Hofstede's – these are embeddedness/autonomy, hierarchy/egalitarianism and mastery/harmony. Values surveys are also described here.

Taxonomic approaches such as these have been criticised, especially for their static nature. Culture, it is asserted, is dynamic and constantly being created through people's actions and communication. Such criticisms certainly have considerable force. Despite their limitations, though, taxonomic approaches have generated a large amount of empirical research and provided the most widespread increase in our awareness and understanding of cultural difference and its implications for work behaviour.

2.4 OTHER WAYS OF ANALYSING CULTURE

In addition to the values taxonomies, there are three other approaches to cultural analysis underpinning the rest of this book. These approaches respectively emphasise high-context, low-context communication, civilisations and subjective cultures.

High-context, low-context communication

Cultures can be analysed in terms of communication styles. Hall drew a distinction between high-context communication and low-context communication and used the distinction as the basis for differentiating cultures. In high-context cultures (HCCs), people rely heavily on the overall situation to interpret messages, so that spoken messages can be ambiguous or vague. In low-context cultures (LCCs), people rely more on the explicit verbal content of messages. Members of HCCs, like Japanese people, use nonverbal cues and information about a person's background to a greater extent than members of LCCs, like the British.

In a high-context culture, 'most of the information [to be communicated] is either in the physical context or internalized in the person, while very little is in the coded, explicit, transmitted part of the message.' In contrast, in a low-context society, 'the mass of the [communicated] information is vested in the explicit code.'[51] People in high-context cultures adopt a role-oriented style. Role-oriented communication emphasises the social roles that the participants hold. Different 'scripts' are used in different role relationships. Work meetings in Eastern countries, for instance, are usually very formal by Western standards. As a result, interactions in such meetings are impersonal and ritualistic. In contrast, people in low-context cultures use a personal style. A personal style emphasises personal identity over social position. Because role relationships and status differences are less important, communication is less formal and often more intimate.[52] Weldon and Ting-Toomey link conflict management behaviour to low- versus high-context communication style.[53,54]

Civilisations

Huntington, in 'The Clash of Civilizations', argued that a civilisation is a cultural entity – the broadest there is. Nations, regions, even villages are also cultural entities, but the most significant in the modern world is the civilisation.[55] Huntington identified eight civilisations. These are Western, Latin American, African, Islamic, Sinic, Hindu, Orthodox and Japanese. Unlike Hofstede, who saw language and religion as rather insignificant in cultural terms, Huntington saw them as 'the central elements of any culture or civilization'. Religion was seen as having grown in importance in recent decades. Both the psychological, emotional and social traumas of modernisation, which in many countries compressed into 50 years what in the West took 200, and the end of the Cold War led to religious revival.

Huntington distinguished consummatory cultures, such as Confucian and Islamic societies, from instrumental cultures, such as Japanese and Hindu societies. In consummatory cultures, means are closely linked to ends; equally, society, the state and authority are all part of a system pervaded by religion. In instrumental cultures, social, cultural and political institutions are more autonomous. Instrumental cultures are better able use Western technology to modernise and to bolster their existing culture. Japan, Singapore, Taiwan, Saudi Arabia, and, to a lesser degree, Iran have become

Box 2.10

'Islamic cultural activity in the European milieu is allowed only in so far as it does not effect any changes in the structures of society, and only to the extent that it does not allow for the emergence of an Islam-oriented political system. ...

The European community is not uniform, and we should learn from its political disparity, and the scope of its difference. ...

The European community is an open society, despite incidental crises. ...

Through constant media nourishment, the European community suffers from the fear of Islam. The reinforcement of the moral aspect of Muslims and the enrichment of their knowledge about the culture and history of the other, however, suffices to dispel numerous misconceptions conducive to such a fear. ...

European society is anxious about its future. Islam, with its dense population as well as the capacity of its faith to penetrate hearts, is considered as a threat.'

Source: Extract from 'Strategy of Islamic Cultural Action in the West', adopted at the Ninth Islamic Summit Conference held in Doha, State of Qatar, 2000

modern societies without becoming Western. 'Modernization, instead, strengthens those cultures and reduces the relative power of the West. In fundamental ways, the world is becoming more modern and less Western. ... European colonialism is over; American hegemony is receding. The erosion of Western culture follows, as indigenous, historically rooted mores, languages, beliefs, and institutions reassert themselves. As Western power declines, the ability of the West to impose Western concepts of human rights, liberalism and democracy on other civilizations also declines and so does the attractiveness of those values to other civilizations. ... This global process of indigenization is manifest broadly in the revivals of religion occurring in so many parts of the world and most notably in the cultural resurgence in Asian and Islamic countries generated in large part by their economic and demographic dynamism.' Religion, indigenous or imported, provides meaning and direction for the rising elites in modernising societies. ' "The attribution of value to a traditional religion", Ronald Dore noted, "is a claim to parity of respect asserted against 'dominant other' nations, and often, simultaneously and more proximately, against a local ruling class which has embraced the values and life-styles of those dominant other nations." ' The religious resurgence throughout the world is a reaction against secularism, moral relativism and self-indulgence, and a reaffirmation of the values of order, discipline, work, mutual help and human solidarity. The breakdown of order and of civil society creates vacuums that are filled by religious, often fundamentalist, groups.

Subjective culture

'Subjective culture' is an approach that focuses on psychological constructs, such as beliefs, attitudes and individuals' values, although it also includes a number of sociological factors, such as norms, roles and tasks. Triandis defined subjective culture as a society's 'characteristic way of perceiving its social environment'.[56] It 'consists of ideas about what has worked in the past and thus is worth transmitting to future generations. Language and economic, educational, political, legal, philosophical and religious systems are important elements of subjective culture. Ideas about aesthetics, and how people should live with others are also important elements. Most important are unstated assumptions, standard operating procedures, and habits of sampling information from the environment.' How people categorise the world is considered to reveal much about their subjective culture, partly because it shows what they value. An example is the Greek category of 'philotimos', which is possibly unique to that culture and, indeed, more prevalent in rural districts and islands of Greece than in cities. Its literal meaning is 'friend of honor' and it can be translated as 'a person who does very frequently what family and friends expect done'. Subjective culture theory distinguishes tight from loose cultures. In tight cultures, people are expected to behave precisely as specified by the culture's norms; in loose cultures, they have more latitude. Triandis pointed out, though, that a culture might be tight in some areas and loose in others. His example is that American culture is tight about passing bad cheques but loose about whom you choose as a room-mate.

Usefully, subjective culture incorporates an explanation for subcultures. They are considered to emerge 'because people share other elements, such as gender, physical type, neighbourhood, occupation, standard of living, resources, climates, and so on. For example, lawyers all over world share some elements of subjective culture. Japanese lawyers have a subculture that differs from other lawyers as well as general Japanese culture. A nation consists of thousands of cultures, but many of these cultures have common elements.'[57]

> The three approaches described in this section emphasise three different facets of culture. High-context, low-context communication differentiates according to communication style; Huntington's 'civilisations' approach is based on broad geographical and historical entities but treats religion and language as central; Triandis' subjective culture concept incorporates a large number of psychological and sociological constructs. For the most part, these approaches remain at the theoretical level, having received much less testing and research than the values approaches. Nevertheless, the concepts are empirically, if unscientifically, based and have plausibility and usefulness.

2.5 CONCEPTUAL ISSUES

Three important conceptual issues remain to be discussed – the questions of how explanatory and generalisable concepts of culture are and the question of whether cultures are converging.

How much does culture explain?

Given that any one individual is potentially a member of multiple cultural and subcultural groups, how can behaviours be identified with any one type of group? While researchers like Hofstede might answer that their samples controlled for factors other than the one they were investigating, that does not answer the point that in some cases the categories interact inextricably. Secondly, with so many factors influencing behaviour, including genetic, epigenetic, familial, local, social (such as the environment of a particular school or a particular set of friends) and individual experience, how can we know what behaviours to attribute to culture? As Hickson and Pugh pointed out, it may be hard to determine whether a 'highly personal, verbal practice of communication (*in an organisation*) is due to a culture that values person-to-person contact or to illiteracy among employees who could not read written instructions'. As these authors suggested, 'Perhaps it helps most to see the world as multi-causal, with many factors acting and interacting simultaneously. ... Whatever one's view, a sensitivity to the part likely to be played by societal cultures does aid understanding. Difficult though it may be to say exactly what that part is, the notion of culture is persistently useful and its manifestations are persistently recognizable.'[58]

How broadly can concepts of culture be applied?

There seems to be agreement that the term 'culture' can be applied to a much wider range of groupings than the national or ethnic. For example, Kim wrote, 'Culture is not viewed as limited to the life patterns of conventionally recognizable culture groups such as national, ethnic or racial. Instead it is viewed as potentially open to all levels of groups whose life patterns. ... influence individuals' behaviour.'[59] Hofstede wrote, 'The word culture is used here in the sense of the "collective programming of the mind" which distinguishes the members of one category of people from another. The "category of people" can be a nation, regional or ethnic group (national etc. culture), women versus men (gender culture), old versus young (generation culture) a social class, a profession or occupation (occupational culture) a type of business, a work organization or part of it (organizational culture) or even a family.'[60] However, Hofstede also considered that

> gender, generation and class cultures can only partly be classified by the four dimensions found for national cultures. This is because they are not *groups* but *categories* of people. Countries (and ethnic groups too) are integrated social systems. The four dimensions [individualism–collectivism, power distance, uncertainty avoidance and masculinity/femininity] apply to the basic problems of such systems. Categories like gender, generation or class are only parts of social systems and therefore not all dimensions apply to them. Gender, generation and class cultures should be described in their own terms, based on special studies of such cultures.

Surface culture differences are to be found in all types of grouping – age groups (e.g., the different ways pensioners and teenagers dress) religions (the Moslem shalwar kameez verus mini-skirts), genders (skirts versus trousers), occupations (the relative formality of most bankers' work clothes with the shirt-sleeve approach in the creative departments of advertising agencies). With deep culture, however, the case appears less clear. As Chapters 3 and 4 will show, research has found significant differences among genders, age groups, religious groups and so on in some communication behaviours and in some underlying values, attitudes, orientations and motivations. In Switzerland, empirically measurable differences in attitudes, openness to technical communication forms and ethnocentricity clearly correlate with the linguistically distinct cultures of the German-speaking and Latin areas. Widespread similarities have also been found, however, and in most cases it has not been demonstrated that the specific (subcultural) differences extend beyond broader cultural or civilisational boundaries. For example, the declining communicative abilities of people over the age of 65, noted in Chapter 3, may or may not extend to those collectivist countries where the elderly are revered. We simply do not know as yet.

In this book nationality, ethnicity and religion are regarded as full cultural divisions. Of these, only 'nationality' is generally accepted as 'culture'; 'ethnicity', where it does not correspond to nationality, has not been well researched so the interaction of the two variables is not understood; while, as noted earlier, there is disagreement over whether religion is a fundamental influence on culture. Despite this, on the grounds

Box 2.11

A guide published by the UK National Housing Federation and the Home Housing Trust in August 1998 recommended that architects and designers should take cultural, religious and social needs into account when creating housing for minority communities. The report's advice included the following:

- A private, sheltered outdoor space will be needed in some Bangladeshi, Indian and Pakistani households for sun-drying foods such as poppadums.
- A space for barbecueing should be provided in housing for Turks and Cypriots, for whom it is a popular social ritual.
- Orthodox Jewish people need the edge of the property clearly marked by, for instance, a high fence, as they are prohibited by their religion from carrying any object beyond the home's boundaries on the Sabbath.
- For some Vietnamese people it is important to have a pond, or, better still, a stream with a bridge, as water symbolises happiness.
- Bedroom design for Chinese people should take into account that some cannot have a bed facing any door, including that of a wardrobe; the colour white should be avoided in their homes.
- Niches and shelves are needed in homes for Buddhists, Confucians and Taoists who use them for shrines. In homes for Greek Orthodox people they are used for icons and candles.

that cultures must be marked by embedded shared values, nearly all the generalisations about cultural influences in this book apply to these three categories of groups. Therefore, a statement such as 'Culture implies a shared worldview and set of values which are largely held unconsciously because they were inculcated in childhood', would apply to most members (not all) of the same national, ethnic or religious groups.

The members of some other social categories, such as gender, social class or occupational groups, typically conform to many of the norms and values of their dominant culture, but they also have beliefs, attitudes, habits and forms of behaviour which deviate from those of others in their society. This reasoning leads them to be treated as subcultures. The statement 'Culture implies a shared worldview, etc.' in the paragraph above would not apply easily to gender groups. Women with different religious beliefs do not share a worldview; generally, men from Japan are positioned well apart on the I–C dimension from men from the USA, whereas Americans of both genders and all social classes are closer together. On the other hand, a statement such as 'Cultural differences lead to differences in communication styles' does apply to gender, social class and occupational groups: women communicate differently from men, working class people differently from upper class people, engineers from publishers (especially at work) across national, ethnic and religious boundaries. Overall, however, gender, social class, sexual orientation, age and educational, technical, professional and experiential background, though having a profound effect on the way people think and behave, do not meet the full criteria for cultures. For these societal subdivisions, some, but not all, generalisations about cultural influences will apply. Disability and sexual orientation are to some degree unknown. Some people with disabilities were born with them, and may have acquired particular worldviews and values as they grew up. Others will not have.

All these distinctions have fuzzy boundaries. There is substantial intra-group variation as well as intergroup difference. Not every Japanese person has a highly collectivist outlook; not every Muslim practises polygamy. The important point is to be aware of cultural and subcultural influences and how they may be affecting one's own and others' behaviour, while still remembering that individual variations due to differences in heredity, family, schooling and experience sometimes modify and outweigh those influences.

There is a view that groupings below the level of nation, such as those based on age, class, sex, education, ethnicity, religion, abilities, affection or sexual orientation, and other unifying elements should be termed co-cultures. 'The term co-culture is embraced over other terminology to signify the notion that no one culture ... is inherently superior (though it may be dominant) over other co-existing cultures. The intention is to avoid the negative or inferior connotations of past descriptions (i.e., *sub*culture) while acknowledging the great diversity of influential cultures that simultaneously exist.'[61] In this book, the term subculture will be retained, but it is not intended to connote inferiority, only that we are talking about a level of analysis below that of broad cultures.

Are cultures converging?

In the course of this chapter, some readers may have been wondering whether cultural differences are disappearing so fast that it is unnecessary to allow for them. People increasingly buy the same products, use the same labour-saving, transportation and communication devices, are entertained in the same way by television and music systems. Many now dress in Western-style clothes, live in Western-style houses, work at Western-style jobs and conduct many of their conversations in English. Does this mean that cultures are converging? Are people worldwide coming to share the same values, worldview, kinship system and social organisation? It is a question that a number of scholars and researchers have addressed. The answers vary. For instance, Pinker noted that the difference between two cultures generally correlates with how long ago they separated; this suggests that cultures evolve.[62] On the other hand, Aldridge pointed out, 'Each culture provides predictability, thus changing culture can be quite difficult unless the cultural value being changed has been demonstrated to be of less value or no longer useful to a particular group.'[63] Li and Karakowsky argued that national culture and cultural influences on businesses are not necessarily stable enduring characteristics. They can be altered, for instance, by consistent government

---

Box 2.12

Andrew Dalby, author of *A Dictionary of Languages* estimates that in 200 years the 5,000 languages that currently exist will be reduced to a mere 200. But only one will count. Unlike other, earlier world languages, English will never split off into distinct parallel forms, as the Romance languages evolved from Latin. For a new language to emerge requires a degree of cultural isolation, or at least independence, that

has become impossible. The world is simply too interconnected, by global technology and a global economy, to think in new words. Intrusive, restless English has made cultural privacy a thing of the past.

Source: Macintyre, B. (2003) 'A world of language, destroyed by vulgar Inglishe', *The Times of London*, 31 May, p. 26

policies. For example, in recent years, because of the effects of such policies, respect for authority, a traditional element in ethnic Chinese culture, has become less salient in both Hong Kong and Taiwan.[64] Single government policies may not lead to cultural change, however. For instance, the Singaporean government has been trying to encourage creativity and entrepreneurship, including export activity, for years, but uncertainty avoidance is actually increasing there. This is probably because the Singapore government's other policies are paternalistic, seeking to control many aspects of social life.

Several comparative studies of values in different European countries carried out over an extended period show evidence of both convergence and continuing difference.[65] (There appears to be little evidence of divergence.)

The case for convergence is that all European countries show the following:

■ The significance of religion as a source of moral obligation is decreasing.
■ Attitudes in favour of democratic political systems are stable.
■ People increasingly value having multiple social relations – with partners, friends and voluntary groups, instead of the old work–family axis.
■ People are coming to value work as much as leisure. (The educational explosion and the changing technological character of work are making it intrinsically valued, not just for the money it earns.)
■ General achievement orientation is growing; levels of 'individualisation' are increasing.
■ Social justice norms are becoming more important.
■ Values like 'peace', 'human rights' 'protection of the natural environment' and 'fighting poverty' which can be summarised as 'quality of life' values, are increasingly accepted, although in some countries there is also a backlash.

The case for continuing difference is based on the following:

■ Values are not converging in Western Europe. Although the trends point in the same direction in most countries, changes in values start from different bases and do not all take place at the same rate.
■ There is a north/south (Sweden, Denmark and UK / France, Italy and Spain) divide over cultural needs in work, organisations and society. For instance, in the south there is lower tolerance for uncertainty and therefore greater liking for hierarchy and bureaucracy; there is also less individualism and more collectivism.
■ There are culture clusters. These include an Anglo cluster (the UK and Netherlands); a Nordic cluster (Sweden, Denmark and Norway) marked by more 'feminine' values, such as a preference for caring for others and a clean environment over careers; a German cluster; and, finally, a Latin cluster where managers, for instance, are more likely to be seen as having a public role in the larger society and to be a business elite.[66]

If studies which focus on an area like Europe show evidence of both convergence and persisting difference, but not of divergence, what about the broader global picture? Hofstede's study provided little evidence of global convergence, but this was based on a comparison between points of time only four years apart – 1968 and 1972. However, Hofstede concluded, on more general grounds, 'There is very little evidence of international convergence over time, except an increase of individualism for countries that have become richer. Value differences between nations described by authors centuries ago are still present today, in spite of close contacts. For the next few hundred years, countries will remain culturally very diverse.'[67]

In business, cultural difference has been expressed as 'cultural distance', which can be measured and compared. Characteristics such as dominant religion, business language, form of government, economic development and levels of emigration indicate two countries' cultural distance from one another. Cultural distance between countries may be reduced by increased communication, geographical proximity (leading to more contact) and cultural attractiveness. For individuals, foreign experience and acculturation may also decrease cultural distance. For organisations, the presence of 'bicultural' individuals may have a bridging effect. A 1997 report on a study of international joint ventures found no decrease in the effect of cultural distance over the previous three decades and concluded that values are stable over time.[68] The concept of cultural distance has been criticized, however, because 'distance' is symmetrical, so that 'a Dutch firm investing in China is faced with the same cultural distance as a Chinese firm investing in the Netherlands. There is no support for such an assumption.'[69]

There are indications that ethnic, gender, sexual orientation and religious consciousness are increasing among some groups and that the claims for rights made by these groups are evidence of an increased cultural and subcultural awareness and sense of difference. In the USA, and to a lesser extent in Western Europe, the ideal of a pluralistic, multicultural society has largely replaced the old ideal of the melting pot. Minorities which seek to preserve and enhance their sense of a separate identity are now seen to have a strong moral case. In earlier times they were often seen by the majority as eccentric. There are backlashes, including among members of ethnic minorities themselves, as Chapter 1 noted, but these may be regarded as signs of a general acceptance of the multicultural ideal.

Box 2.13

America is a multicultural group with many ethnic groups, bound by a market economy and representing many cultures. (p. 74)

A Chinese cultural nationalism is … emerging, epitomized in the words of one Hong Kong leader in 1994: 'We Chinese feel nationalist which we never felt before. We are Chinese and feel proud in that.' In China itself in the early 1990s there developed 'a popular desire to return to what is authentically Chinese, which often is patriarchal, nativistic, and authoritarian. Democracy, in this historical re-emergence, is discredited, as is Leninism, as just another foreign imposition.' (p.106)

For East Asians, East Asian success is particularly the result of the East Asian cultural stress on the collectivity rather than the individual. (p. 108)

The Resurgence will also have shown that 'Islam is the solution' to the problems of morality, identity, meaning and faith, but not to the problems of social injustice, political repression, economic backwardness and military weakness. These failures could generate widespread disillusionment with political Islam, a reaction against it, and a search for alternative 'solutions' to these problems. (p. 121)

Source: Huntington, S. (1997) *The Clash Of Civilizations And The Remaking of World Order*, London: Simon & Schuster

> The term culture can usefully be applied in discussing ethnic and religious groups as well as nations; however, for other groups, such as those defined by gender, age, sexual orientation, social class, education and so on, the term 'subculture' may be more appropriate. Culture does change, but cultural and subcultural differences will continue to affect both the internal and external environments faced by most people at work.

2.6 THE IMPACT OF CULTURE AT WORK

Cultural values have a strong influence on the structures, processes and predominant managerial styles of organisations in different societies. For example, in a culture that is high on measures of uncertainty, formalisation and centralisation are prominent features of organisational structure, decision-making authority, responsibility and communication are distributed according to a hierarchical pattern, and the climate is reserved. In a low UA-culture, on the other hand, the structure is informal and decentralised, decision-making authority and all that goes with it is widely distributed and an open climate of discussion and bargaining prevails.

Not surprisingly, many descriptions of cultural difference at work have used Hofstede's values as their theoretical basis. For instance, countries high in UA showed the greatest increases in work centrality (the importance attached to work) among young people starting work. The smallest increases occurred in countries high in masculinity.[70] A survey of 82 French and 101 German product champions found that their effectiveness (ability to enlist top management support for an innovation project) and crucial characteristics (status and seniority) varied across national cultures.[71] Another study found that cultural values affected individuals' commitment to their organisation, supervisor and workgroup. High UA led to individuals feeling more committed to their relationship with all three; high PD led to them feeling a stronger sense that they *should* feel committed; high collectivism led to a stronger sense of commitment to their workgroup, though not necessarily to their supervisor or organisation.[72]

A review of the literature concerned with French, British and American work practices found a number of differences based on PD, UA, individualism and attitudes to time. French managers typically viewed organisations as a formal pyramid of differentiated levels of power, and thought that success stems from their ability to 'work the system' by managing power relationships effectively. Early attempts to transfer Management by Objectives (MBO) to France were unsuccessful because the idea of supervisor and subordinate jointly reaching decisions about the subordinate's performance was inconsistent with the importance of hierarchy in French organisations. In France, typically only the supervisor or manager has power, so MBO meant that subordinates were held responsible for goals without having the power to achieve those goals. Similarly, the ideas of matrix management are quite inconsistent with the way French managers view authority: 'How can someone take orders from two bosses?' In contrast, British managers hold a less hierarchical view of organisations; they see them primarily as a network of relationships between individuals who get things done by influencing each other through communication and negotiation. These differences are attributed to higher French cultural PD. Higher French UA is reflected in their being less willing to show trust, allow participation in decisions and share information than people from Anglo countries (British and Americans). French managers have been found to be preoccupied with absolute accuracy for all control indicators and less concerned about what the data implies. Schneider and DeMeyer found that the French, more than those from Anglo countries, view strategic issues as threats instead of as opportunities.[73] Lower levels of individualism in French culture may underlie findings that the French find it less important to be challenged while at work than members of Anglo cultures do. Finally, whereas Anglo countries view time as a valuable commodity ('time is money'), punctuality is expected, and deadlines are to be met, in contrast, Latin Europeans, including the French, are less inclined to abide by schedules.

Other descriptions of cultural difference at work have depended less on the Hofstede dimensions. These differences include the perceived nature of effectiveness, task versus relationships orientation, procedural versus distributive justice and employment relationships.

■ Across Europe, there are marked differences in the skills, qualities and competencies that are perceived to be central to performance and the consequent expectations of managers and the business systems in which they work. Assumptions about what makes a good manager are all influenced by national culture. For instance, 'While Anglo-Saxon managers emphasize the need for interpersonal skills and job visibility, being labelled "high potential" is the most important criterion for French managers (reflecting the elitist management development systems), and having a creative mind is the most important indicator for German managers.'[74]

■ There are also differences in task versus relationships orientation. Latin-European managers, including the French, have been found to be more focused on personal relationships than on tasks. However, a comparison of Nordic, Latin-European and Hungarian managers' management styles found the strongest task orientation in Latin Europe, whereas the most intense employee orientation was found in the Nordic countries. Latin-European managers scored lower on consideration 'as their cultures seem to support a more authoritarian manager who decides without any negotiation with his or her subordinates.'[75] Task behaviour in the study was further analysed, showing that Nordic managers emphasise planning and order, whereas Latin-European managers rely on goals, information and supervision behaviour. 'This seems to be indicative of the more authoritarian character of Latin-European managers, while Nordic managers plan more beforehand and communicate more with their subordinates.' In terms of employee orientation, Nordic managers were considerate. They relied on their subordinates, supported them, allowed them to make decisions and showed regard for them as individuals. Latin-European managers created 'an atmosphere free of conflict', probably by using direct supervision and clear rules and principles. Power seemed to be more centralised in Latin-European organisations. 'Managers have the knowledge and make the decisions. There are no negotiations and therefore there is a low conflict level in their organizations. Latin-European managers seem to have much more of the boss-oriented mentality in their organizations: the boss is the head of the organization and does not expect ideas and support from the lower levels.'[76]

■ There are cross-national differences in procedural and distributive justice. Procedural justice refers to the perceived fairness of policies and the procedures used for making decisions. Distributive justice is the perceived fairness of proportional differences in rewards in relation to the status and work contribution of those involved. Principles of procedural justice are similar across Europe. However, there are marked variations in distributive justice across Europe. Employees in Belgium, France, Greece, Portugal and Spain tend to prefer equality-based pay

Box 2.14

X was a newly appointed manager in an international Swedish engineering firm. X was not Swedish, unlike most of his subordinates. One came to see him in early March, (1) without an appointment. She opened with his first name, (2) then said, 'I need some time off – about two weeks, in June, to revise for my exams.' (3) Her tone, though polite, appeared to imply that the request was routine and would be granted automatically. X was surprised and pointed out that June was a peak workload period. It would be difficult for her to be spared. (4) Given her previous attitude, he expected her to argue back, but instead she said, 'That's a problem, I can see. How can we get round it?'

Intrigued by this unexpectedly co-operative approach, X suggested that he could re-arrange the unit's holiday schedule, so she could take some of her six weeks holiday in late May/early June – he would speak to Johann about swopping with her. She looked startled, (5) was quiet for a long time, (6) then said, 'Holiday schedules can only be re-arranged following extensive consultation and discussion among the whole team and with the agreement of all those affected.'

The responses of the subordinate in this manager–subordinate interaction may be explained as follows:

(1) Swedish culture is egalitarian (low in power distance), which is reflected in a lack of formality in forms of address within organisations. (However, as Box 3.3 shows, an increase in formality is occurring in other circumstances.)

(2) Swedish spoken style tends towards the direct or blunt, though not extremely.

(3) Workers' rights for time off in Sweden are more extensive than in some other countries.

(4) Swedish conversational rules encourage brainstorming and working things out co-operatively.

(5) Swedes are more comfortable with silence than some other people.

(6) Many decisions, which in some countries would be the prerogative of management, are taken by consensus in Sweden.

Based on: Author's research

policies that reward group-level effort and efficiency. In contrast, Danish, German, Irish and British employees prefer equitable pay policies. In many European organisations, it is expected that top pay levels should not exceed 12 to 15 times the average pay level. By comparison, in North American organisations, an individual deal may create multiples of over one hundred.

■ Employment relationships are typical for each country. Many practices that are valued and widely applied in the USA, the UK and Canada, are seen as far less important by Italy, Japan and Korea and positively devalued by France and Germany. These practices include pay systems that promote performance, wide spans of control that promote delayering, the eradication of specialised and directed work forces, reliance on flexible cross-functional teams, the promotion of employee empowerment and involvement, an emphasis on management development, the analysis of individual performance, reward for business productivity gains and the sharing of benefits, risks and costs with the workforce.[77]

The rest of this section will discuss some aspects of cultural differences in work practices and relations which depend on or impact on communication: work roles and norms, groupwork, manager/subordinate relations, management style and organisational cultures.

Work roles

Roles are extensively affected by cultural values: high power distance leads to steep hierarchies and narrow spans of control (and vice-versa for low PD); high uncertainty avoidance to strict adherence to job descriptions and formality (and vice-versa for low UA); individualism to an emphasis on personal responsibility; collectivism to an emphasis on group responsibility; high achievement orientation to prioritising task completion; high relationship orientation to concern with maintenance.

Norms

The link between norms and culture is also strongly marked, as shown in Table 2.2, because they exist to enforce values.

Groupwork

Behaviour during groupwork is also strongly influenced by culture, as Table 2.3 shows. However, while individualists are likely to behave in the same competitive way in most groups, collectivists will behave differently in different groups. In groups composed of their ingroup, co-operativeness will predominate; in those composed of their out-groups, they may be more inclined to compete or, in the case of conflict arising, to

Table 2.2 *Effects of cultural values on work norms*

Cultural values	Work norms
High power distance	Penalties for breaches apply more to lower members; higher ones are 'above the law'; norms are imposed by leaders rather than emerging by consensus.
High masculinity (achievement)	Adherence to norms is more enforced in more punitive ways than in feminine cultures.
High uncertainty avoidance	Norms are more rigid – there is less scope for different interpretations than in low uncertainty avoidance cultures.
High collectivism	Norms concerned with loyalty to the group are emphasised; there are different norms for ingroup versus outgroup members.

Table 2.3 *Effects of cultural values on groupwork*

Effect of	High/long	Low/short
Power distance	Difficulty in working in an unchaired or unsupervised group	Lack of deference to authority
Uncertainty avoidance	Preference for agendas and sticking to them, structured discussion, clear outcomes, minutes	Preference for informality
Masculine (achievement) values	Task orientation dominant	Maintenance orientation dominant
Individualism	Competitive atmosphere	Co-operative atmosphere
Time orientation	Exploration of all issues before seeking a decision	Sense of urgency, pressure for closure

'uncharacteristically' confront. Basic aspects of group performance, such as productivity and conformity, differ substantially by culture. In groups, people may tend to work less hard, partly because their effort is less likely to bring them personal reward than it is when they work independently. This tendency is known as social loafing. However, in China, Israel and Japan, social loafing is not only absent, but is significantly reversed. In studies in China and Israel, subjects who endorsed collectivist values worked harder in group settings than individually. This finding contrasts with the findings on social loafing found in Western societies. Again, a meta-analysis of 133 replications of the Asch conformity study (which found that people tend to agree with the judgement of a group even when it contradicts what they can see in front of them), found that conformity was even higher among those with high scores on Hofstede's collectivism value dimension. In some cultures, however, conformity processes may operate in a different manner. In Spain, researchers have found a higher incidence of 'perverse norms' than in Anglo countries. Perverse norms are norms that are agreed to exist but are rarely enforced. Within a system of perverse norms, authority figures may maintain control by determining when norms will be enforced and when they will not.[78]

Research has pointed to significant national differences in management roles and style. The cultural definition of a manager's role contributes to his or her structuring activities whether alone or with peers, and to the tendency to invite or disregard subordinates' input.[79] For instance, a general management survey on perceptions of national management style was given to 707 managers representing diverse industries from the USA (156), Indonesia (177), Malaysia (192) and Thailand (182). It found significant differences in formality of structures and controls, individual versus team development, employee involvement in setting goals and the appraisal process, intrinsic versus extrinsic rewards and frequency of feedback.[80]

In addition to these national differences, there are well-researched differences between women and men as managers. To a greater extent than men, Finnish studies have found, women tend to encourage their subordinates to use their abilities fully and to cut through bureaucratic red tape. They do this by facilitating informal contacts between leaders and workers, introducing new working methods and training, disseminating information and taking workers' views into consideration. Female supervisors' communication styles are perceived as placing more emphasis on interpersonal relations than those of male supervisors.[81] A meta-analysis by Eagly and Johnson of 370 studies compared men's and women's leadership styles and concluded, 'The strongest evidence ... for a sex difference in leadership style occurred on the tendency for women to adopt a more democratic or participative style and for men to adopt a more autocratic or directive style. ... 92 per cent of the available comparisons went in the direction of more democratic behaviour from women than men.'[82] This difference was attributed to womens' greater interpersonal skills and cognitive complexity.

Managerial beliefs

Culture and managerial beliefs have been linked since the early studies of Haire *et al*.[83] Their survey of 3,500 managers in 14 countries around the world found that about 28 per cent of the variance in managerial beliefs about participation and the capacity of their subordinates to participate effectively could be accounted for by nationality alone. The countries could be grouped, on the basis of the managers' responses, into four clusters: Nordic-European, Latin-European, Anglo-American and developing countries. A later study of Australian managers supported a cultural explanation of these findings by demonstrating the similarity of their leadership beliefs to those in the Anglo-American group.[84] Another study across 12 countries linked managers' goals, preferences for taking risks, pragmatism, interpersonal competence, effective intelligence, emotional stability, and leadership style to national cultures.[85] However, studies in Greece and five developing countries showed 'a low level of industrialization' to be such a potent explanatory variable as to offset the effects of cultural diversity. The researchers commented that national culture seems to have more explanatory power for mature industrialized countries.[86]

Organisational cultures

Research into the direct effects of national cultures on organisational cultures has produced conflicting results. An assessment of the cultures of an American, a Japanese and a Taiwanese bank, as well as an American bank operating in Taiwan, confirmed that organisational cultures differ as a result of the impact of national cultures on organisational culture.[87] On the other hand, a study in Saudi Arabia found that traditional values were more prevalent in governmental than business organisations. These traditional values included accepting nepotism, eschewing being rule-bound (bureaucratic) and not using performance-based criteria to evaluate employees. This government/business difference suggests that stakeholders, including employees, do not expect profit-oriented business organisations to reflect their national values.[88] In addition, Vertinsky *et al.* suggested that the norms on which organisational culture was based were subject to a process of globalisation that reduced cross-cultural and national differences. These authors, however, acknowledged that some norms of organisational design and management reflected national culture values and were resistant to change and convergence.[89]

Diversity and organisational cultures in combination affect work-based communication, conflict, creativity and productivity, a study found.

- Diverse co-workers in collectivist organisations communicated more by memos and less by face-to-face interaction compared with both non-diverse co-workers in collectivist organisations and diverse co-workers in individualist organisations. It seems that when people are more different from their co-workers they are more reluctant to interact in person. Unfortunately, sending memos may be less effective than face-to-face interactions for conveying information and resolving problems.
- No more conflict was found between demographically different than demographically similar co-workers. Also, in an organisational culture that emphasised collective goals, demographically different co-workers were more likely to find conflict beneficial. Workers in individualist cultures were more likely both to experience conflict (probably because their goals and values differed more from each other's) and to find it harmful.
- Dissimilar people in collectivist cultures had the highest creative output. This finding suggests that creativity emerges from the combination of (1) access to a larger set of novel ideas afforded by more diverse members and (2) trust that novel ideas will be used for the benefit of the collective.
- While similar people were significantly more productive in individualist than collectivist [organisational] cultures, dissimilar people were equally productive across the two cultures. They were also more productive than similar co-workers, though less likely to interact. This may be partly explained by whether the co-workers' interaction was task-related or social. Dissimilar co-workers may have focused more consistently on tasks, because they may have had fewer other topics in

common to discuss with one another. However, diverse people may have a wider variety of ideas to share and debate during their interaction, allowing them to realise greater returns for the time invested. Unfortunately, interaction among dissimilar people, while perhaps the most beneficial, also appears to be the most difficult to cultivate.[90]

The effect of national cultures on organisational cultures can make it difficult for organisational cultures to cross geographical boundaries. Individuals tend to select and to be selected by organisations with values similar to their own. 'Goodness of fit' with the organisational culture is important to an individual's commitment, satisfaction, productivity and longevity with an organisation. It may also affect attitudes to work communication. In Italy, it was found that people who do not agree with how success appears to be defined in the organisation (who may have a poor 'fit' with the organisational culture) are dissatisfied with their own ability to send messages to management, in contrast with those who agree with how success is defined.[91]

In this section, the impact of culture at work has been considered in terms of its effects on managerial attitudes, the perceived nature of effectiveness, task versus relationship orientation, performance criteria, procedural and distributive justice, employment relationships, work roles and norms, groupwork, manager/subordinate relations, management style and organisational cultures. Organisational cultures vary in their supportiveness or incompatibility with diversity. Those which are results-oriented, employee-oriented, professional, open, loosely controlled and pragmatic are more favourable than those which are process-oriented, job-oriented, parochial, closed, tightly controlled and normative. Research has not as yet clearly established how national cultures affect organisational cultures. However, the combination of the level of workforce diversity and the collectivism or individualism of the organisational culture does impact on communication, conflict, creativity and productivity.

2.7 SUMMARY

Differences in people's behaviour, including their communication behaviour, which may result from diversity, have been analysed in terms of culture. This chapter has described and analysed the elements and dimensions which are considered to be the core components of culture.

The chapter opened by identifying a range of business and organisational issues that have been shown to be affected by culture. It then outlined the three approaches to cultural theory relevant to this book – the values, communication and identity approaches. The next section described four values approaches, all of which provide taxonomies of cultural values. To varying but considerable degrees, these values are believed to influence taken-for-granted thinking processes. Hofstede, in a telling phrase, has called culture 'software of the mind'. Other approaches to culture described here include low-context/high-context communication, cultures as civilisations and the concept of subjective culture.

Conceptual issues that are discussed include the facts that cultures change (but deep cultures, unlike surface cultures, do not seem to be converging); which behaviours to attribute to culture and which to other influences is often unclear; and many important societal groups do not exhibit the predominating characteristics of cultures – those of shared values – and so must be regarded as subcultures. Despite these limitations, cultural concepts are significant and understanding of cultural difference is important: cultural differences are brought to work and affect people's behaviour there. To clarify this, the chapter returns to the subjects of culture and work, and discusses them in the light of the understandings of culture introduced in the chapter.

A particular benefit of understanding cultural difference is the point made by Trompenaars:

> Without awareness of the nature of the differences between cultures, we tend to measure others against our own cultural standards. An early and sometimes painful lesson is that all cultures have their own, perfectly consistent but different, logics.[92]

Cultural 'imprisonment' can lead to arrogance, cultural imperialism and an uncritical dependence on one way of thinking.

As a note of caution, it must be pointed out that acknowledgement of cultural difference should not be used, as it sometimes has been, to bring racism or other forms of prejudice in by stealth. There is a phenomenon known as 'new racism' which draws attention to cultural incompatibility. It confines racism to 'situations in which groups of people are hierarchically distinguished from one another on the basis of some notion of stock difference and where symbolic representations are mobilized which emphasize the social and cultural relevance of biologically rooted characteristics'.[93]

QUESTIONS AND EXERCISES

1. Discuss the cultural values that may be reflected in the examples in Boxes 2.1 to 2.4.
2. Which of the following are strongly influenced, influenced or not influenced by culture? Give reasons.

   - how people think
   - their loyalties
   - what they believe (e.g. religion, politics)
   - what they find moving (emotions)
   - how they behave (e.g. childrearing practices)
   - work motives
   - ambitions

3. Do you agree with Hofstede (1981) that religion is not a fundamental cultural value, or with Huntington, who considers it a central element of any culture? Give your reasons.
4. How might differences in cultural values explain the different experiences of the entrepreneur in Italy and London described in Box 2.9?
5. In the light of the material in this chapter on how cultural change is brought about, consider the following statements. Continue the discussion of how cultural change happens.

   - The traditional strong preference of Chinese people for boy children is being altered: 'After 15 years of state-managed family planning (supported by heavy fines and forced abortions for the rebels) many young people, male and female, now claim it does not matter to them whether their only child is a boy or a girl.' (*The Economist*, 10 January 1996)
   - 'Taiwan has become an industrialised economy. Social changes occur along with economic changes. Many modern symptoms such as crime (including economic

crime), divorce, labour unrest, political protests, illegal immigration, pollution, congestion, to name a few, have increased drastically in the past twenty years. A demand for a better quality of life, more leisure, recreation, education, and clean air and water have also increased rapidly. People's attitudes have changed as well. The important traditional values – authoritarian attitude, filial piety (respect for ancestors and parents), fatalism, male superiority, and conservatism (self-restraint and control) – have made way for modern values such as democratic attitudes, independence and self-reliance, progressiveness and optimism, equality of males and females and respect for personal feelings. However, filial piety is still very important.' (Matsu, B. and R.-S. Yeh (1992) 'Taiwan management communication practices: past, present and future', A summary of a presentation by Ryh-Song Yeh at the David Lam Centre for International Communication, Pacific Region Forum on Business and Management Communication, Simon Fraser University, Harbour Centre on January 23)

6. Would you categorise the following as high-context or low-context communication? Why?

   ■ 'There was also a note from Milly: "What have you been up to? You-know-who very pressing – not in any bad way. ... Seraphina's picture taken by press photographer. Is this fame? Go, bid the soldiers shoot." ' (Greene, G. *Our Man in Havana*)
   ■ '[To make computer chips] involves growing huge crystals of silicon, cutting them into circular wafers, subjecting each wafer to a series of chemical processes to carve microscopic circuits into its surface and then chopping the wafer up to produce dozens of identical chips' (*The Economist*, 5 December 1998, p. 132).

7. Explain the distinction between high-context and low-context cultures, with examples.
8. List three discourses (not including medical discourse, given in the text).
9. Draw an identity map for yourself, equivalent to the one in Figure 2.3. Compare your map with a colleague's and discuss the reasons for the differences.
10. Research in Germany (D), United Kingdom (UK) and France (F) found the following characteristics for organisations in those countries. Look up the findings of Hofstede's research for cultural values in the three countries, then discuss the extent to which the organisational characteristics shown may be related to the cultural values of the countries concerned.

	Low	Medium	High
Tallness of hierarchy	D	UK	F
Functional differentiation	D	UK	F
Share of white-collar employees	D	UK	F
Supervisory span of control	D	UK	F
Administrative and commercial personnel/workers	D	UK	F
Authority positions/workers	UK	D	F
Authority positions/white-collar workers	UK	F	D

Based on: Sorge, A. (1995) 'Cross-national differences in personnel and organization', Harzing, A.W. and Ruysseveldt, J.V. (eds) *International Human Resource Management*, London: Sage

11. Using the analytical base supplied in Section 2.6, examine manager/subordinate relations, predominant manager style, work roles, work norms and groupwork behaviour in an organisation known to you in order to determine what cultural values they imply.

12. Recent years have seen a trend for organisations to develop and emphasise their 'organisational culture' in order to unite their employees and co-ordinate their approaches at a deeper level than that achieved by plans and strategies. Discuss the implications of Chapter 2 for this process.

13. From *The Economist* 5 December 1998, p. 24: 'We live in increasingly intolerant times. Signs proliferate demanding no smoking, no spitting, no parking, even no walking. … Smoking, once prohibited in only a few train carriages or sections of aircraft, is now banned totally in many offices, on most public transport and even in many bars. Environmentalists have long demanded all sorts of bans on cars. Mobile telephones are the latest target: some trains, airline lounges, restaurants and even golf courses are being designated "no phone" areas.' Is this a culture shift?

14. In *The Language Instinct* (1994) p. 251, the linguist S. Pinker states that the difference between two cultures generally correlates with how long ago they separated. Find examples to support or refute this statement.

15. The following questions were used in research into cultural difference. What aspects of culture do you think they were trying to access?

   ■ You have just come from a secret meeting of a board of directors of a certain company. You have a close friend who will be ruined unless he can get out of the market before the board's decision becomes known. You happen to be having dinner at your friend's home this evening. What right does your friend have to expect you to tip him off?

   ■ Which of the following describes a company?
   (a) A system designed to perform functions and tasks in an efficient way: People are hired to fulfil these functions with the help of machines and other equipment. They are paid for the tasks they perform. *Or*
   (b) A group of people working together: The people have social relations with other people and with the organisation. The functioning is dependent on these relations.

   ■ Which of the following do you agree with?
   (a) A company should take into account the size of the employee's family. The company is responsible for the extra compensation per child.
   (b) An employee should be paid on the basis of the work he [sic] is doing for the company. Therefore, the company does not have to take into account the employee's family.

   Source: Hampden-Turner, C. and Trompenaars, A. (1993) *The Seven Cultures of Capitalism*, Garden City, NY: Doubleday

16. Is your country's culture low on Boski's Humanism dimension (i.e., high on Materialism)? Give your reasons.

17. Consider your own cultural identity in your relationship with a person from another culture (if possible a work colleague). How does your cultural identity impact on this relationship?

18. Describe some of the more important aspects of the subjective culture in your own society.

19. Which cultural values might be reflected in the European behaviours described in Box 2.8?

20. Ethnologist Donald Brown has given a list of over 50 characteristics and behaviours which are 'human universals' – that is, found in all cultures. Examples include sexual attraction, adornment of bodies and arrangement of hair, socialisation of children (including toilet training) by senior kin, punishment and the sense of right and wrong. In a group of four or five, if possible from different cultures, list as many other agreed human universals as possible.

21. Choose a colleague from a country other than your own. How much do you know about people from his or her country (hereinafter X)? Complete the following test and then discuss your answers with your colleague.

	True (T) or False (F)
In face-to-face communication, people from X stand closer together than people do from your own culture.	
People from X place a very high value on an individual's initiative and achievement.	
People from X value obedience to authority and typically will not disagree with someone in a higher position of power.	
When people from X communicate, they use words that are clear and direct, allowing for no ambiguities.	
People from X need formal rules, absolute truths and conformity.	
People from X tend to avoid conflict and competition and seek consensus.	
In X sex roles are highly differentiated.	
People from X tend to do one thing at a time. They take time commitments very seriously and adhere closely to plans.	
People from X have a high- (low-) touch culture.	
People from X commonly sympathise with the weak and believe that nurturing individuals is more important than material success.	

22. Working with a partner from a different cultural background (ethnic, national or religious), identify some core and peripheral values from your respective cultures. Discuss the reasons for and the implications of any differences in your lists.

23. Interview someone (several people) whose culture is different from your own on power distance, masculinity/femininity (achievement), uncertainty avoidance or individualism–collectivism. Discuss such matters as attitudes to work, spending and saving money, spending and using time, family, relationships and friends.

24. Complete the following questionnaire on your own culture.

People in my group (culture) generally tend to	Strongly agree	Agree	Neither agree nor disagree	Disagree	Strongly disagree
1. describe their experiences					
2. relate stories or anecdotes					
3. generalise					
4. give examples or particular instances when enunciating a principle					
5. speak in abstract terms					
6. feel personally responsible for their own success or failure					
7. have many friendships and relationships outside their families					
8. show emotion freely					
9. think showing emotion in the workplace is unprofessional					
10. talk about their feelings					
11. have most of their friendships from among their colleagues					
12. try to mix work and pleasure					
13. be respected for being wealthy					
14. think that people should be judged on their achievements alone					
15. believe in promotion by seniority					
16. think that time is money					
17. try always to be on time, even if it means risking offending someone by rushing them					
18. care about relaxation					
19. be more interested in the past than in the future					
20. think a lot about their future plans					

To interpret your scores on this questionnaire, see Appendix C

NOTES AND REFERENCES

1. Porter, M.E. (2000) 'Attitudes, values, beliefs and the microeconomics of prosperity', in Harrison, L.E. and Huntington, S.P. (eds) *Culture Matters*, New York: Basic Books.

2. Lee, S.M. and Peterson, S.J. (2000) 'Culture, entrepreneurial orientation, and global competitiveness', *Journal of World Business*, **35**(4): 401–16.

3. *The Economist* 19 October 2002, p. 55.

4. Angwina, D. (2001) 'Mergers and acquisitions across European borders: National perspectives on preacquisition, due diligence and the use of professional advisers', *Journal of World Business*, **36**(1): 32–57.

5. Kragh, S.U. (2000) 'Three perspectives on intercultural marketing', in Sorensen, O.J. and Arnold, E. (eds) *Marketing and Development Challenges*, Proceedings of the 7th International Conference on Marketing and Development, Ghana.

6. House, R. and Wright, N. (1999) 'Cross cultural research on organizational leadership: a critical analysis and a proposed theory'. URL: http://jonescenter.wharton.upenn.edu/papers/1999/wp99-03.pdf

7. Harpaz, I., Honig, B. and Coetsier, P. (2002) 'A cross-cultural longitudinal analysis of the meaning of work and the socialization process of career starters', *Journal of World Business*, **37**(4): 230–44.

8. Carroll, G.R. and Harrison, J.R. (1998) 'Organizational demography and culture: insights from a formal model and simulation', *Administrative Science Quarterly*, **43**: 637–67.

9. Chen, Z.X. and Francesco, A.M. (2000) 'Employee demography, organizational commitment, and turnover intentions in China: do cultural differences matter?', *Human Relations*, **53**(6): 869–87.

10. Pelled, L.H. (1996) 'Relational demography and perceptions of group conflict and performance: a field investigation', *International Journal of Conflict Management*, **7**: 230–46.

11. Phinney, J.S. (1996) 'When we talk about American ethnic groups, what do we mean?' *American Psychologist*, **51**(9): 918–27.

12. Ofori-Dankwa, J. and Lane, R.W. (2000) 'Four approaches to cultural diversity: implications for teaching at institutions of higher education', *Teaching in Higher Education* [Electronic database], **5**(4), Ipswich, MA: Academic Search Elite.

13. Cooper, C.R. (1998) 'Theories linking culture and psychology: universal and community-specific processes', *Annual Review of Psychology*, **49**: 559–84.

14. Rokeach, M. (1993) *The Nature of Human Values*, New York: Free Press.

15. Schwartz, S.H. (1999) 'Cultural value differences: Some implications for work', *Applied Psychology: An International Review*, **48**: 23–47.

16. Aldridge, M.G. (2002) 'What is the basis of American culture?' *Intercultural Communication*, 5 April. URL: http://www.immi.se/intercultural/

17. Kincaid, D.L., Yum, J.O. and Woelfel, J. (1983) 'The cultural convergence of Korean immigrants in Hawaii: an empirical test of a mathematical theory', *Quality and Quantity*, **18**: 59–78.

18. Haslett, B. (1989) 'Communication and language acquisition within a cultural context', in Ting-Toomey, S. and Korzenny, F. (eds) *Language, Communication and Culture: Current Directions*, Newbury Park, CA: Sage.

19. Burke, B.A. and Patterson-Pratt, J.R. (2002) 'Establishing understandings: teaching about culture in introductory television courses', *American Communication Journal*, **15**(2). URL: www.americancomm.org/~aca/acj/acj.html

20. Deetz, S. and Mumby, D.K. (1990) 'Power, discourse, and the workplace: reclaiming the critical tradition', *Communication Yearbook*, **13**: 18–47.

21. Hall, S. (1997) Introduction to *Representation: Cultural Representations and Signifying Practices*, Milton Keynes, UK: Open University.

22. Ibid., p. 4.

23. Foucault, M. (1982) 'The subject and power', in Dreyfus, H. and Rabinow, P. (eds), *Michel Foucault: Beyond Structuralism and Hermeneutics*, pp. 208–66. New York: Harvester Wheatsheaf.

24. Aaker, J.L., Benet-Martínez, V. and Garolera, J. (2001) 'Consumption symbols as carriers of culture: a study of Japanese and Spanish brand personality constructs', *Journal of Personality and Social Psychology*, **81**(3): 492–508.

25. Collier, M.J. and Thomas, M. (1988) 'Cultural identity and intercultural communication', in Gudykunst, W. and Ting-Toomey, S. (eds) *Culture and Interpersonal Communication*, Newbury Park, CA: Sage.

26. Chesebro, J.W. and Fuse, K. (2001) 'The development of a perceived masculinity scale', *Communication Quarterly*, **49**(3): 203–78.

27. Hofstede, G. (1981) *Cultures and Organizations: Software of the Mind*, London: Harper Collins.

28. Earley, P.C. and Gibson, C.B. (1998) 'Taking stock in our progress on individualism–collectivism: 100 years of solidarity and community', *Journal of Management*, **24**(3): 265–304.

29. Bazerman, M.H., Curhan, J.R., Moore, D.A. and Valley, K.L. (2000) 'Negotiation', *Annual Review of Psychology*, **51**: 279–314.

30. Maitland, C. (1998) 'Global diffusion of interactive networks: the impact of culture', *Electronic Journal of Communication*, **8**(3): URL: www.cios.org/www/ejc^8n398.htm

31. Boski, P. (2002) 'Interactions, research and history embedded in Polish culture: humanism and uncertainty non-avoidance', in Lonner, W.J., Dinnel, D.L., Hayes, S.A. and Sattler, D.N. (eds), *Online Readings in Psychology and Culture* (unit 3, chapter 7). URL: http://www.wwu.edu/~culture

32. Barkema, H.G. and Vermeulen, F. (1997) 'What differences in the cultural backgrounds of partners are detrimental for international joint ventures?', *Journal of International Business Studies*, **28**(4): 845–64.

33. Alkhazraji, K.M., Gardner, W.M. III, Martin, J.S. and Paolillo, J.G.P. (1997) 'The acculturation of immigrants to US organizations: the case of Muslim employees', *Management Communication Quarterly*, **11**(2): 217–65.

34. Hofstede, G. (1993) 'Cultural constraints in management theories', *Academy of Management Executive*, **7**(1): 81–94.

35. Sparrow, P.R. (1998) 'Reappraising psychological contracting: lessons for the field of human-resource development from cross-cultural and occupational psychology research', *International Studies of Management & Organization*, **28**(1): 30–63.

36. Maitland, C. (1998) op. cit.

37. Boski, P. (2002) op. cit.

38. Trompenaars, F. (1993) *Riding the Waves of Culture: Understanding Cultural Diversity in Business*, London: Nicholas Brealey.

39. Handy, C., Trompenaars, F. and Hampden Turner, C. (2000) 'The Handy guide to the gurus of management, Episode 13 – Fons Trompenaars and Charles Hampden Turner'. http://www.bbc.co.uk/worldservice/learningenglish/work/handy/transcripts/trompenaarsturner.pdf

40. Schwartz, S.H. (1999) op. cit.

41. Peterson, M.F., Smith, P.B., Akande, D., Ayestaran, S., Bochner, S., Callan, V. *et al.* (1995) 'Role conflict, ambiguity and overload by national culture: a 21 nation study', *Academy of Management Journal*, **38**: 429–52.

42. Sagiv, L. and Schwartz, S.H. (2000) 'A new look at national cultures: illustrative applications to role stress and managerial behavior', in Ashkanasy, N.N., Wilderom, C. and Peterson, M.F. (eds) *The Handbook of Organizational Culture and Climate*: pp. 417–36, Newbury Park, CA: Sage.

43. Ibid.

44. Halman, L. and Kerkhofs, J. (2001) The European values study: selected results. URL: www.romir.ru/eng/research/01_2001/european-values.htm

45. Tayeb, M.H. (1996) *The Management of a Multicultural Workforce*, England: John Wiley.

46. Aldridge, M.G. (2000) op. cit.

47. Kim, Y.Y. (1988) 'On theorizing intercultural communication', in Kim, Y.Y. and Gudykunst, W.B. (eds) *Theories in Intercultural Communication*, Newbury Park, CA: Sage.

48. Collier, M.J. and Thomas, M. (1988) op.cit.

49. de Munck, V. (2001) 'In the belly of the beast: two theories of culture and why they dominate the social sciences (Pt.2)', *Cross-cultural Psychology Bulletin*, **35**(3): 5–14.

50. Greenfield, P.M. (1997) 'You can't take it with you. Why ability assessments don't cross cultures', *American Psychologist*, (52): 1115–24.
51. Hall, E.T. (1976) *Beyond Culture*, NewYork: Doubleday.
52. Okabe, R. (1983) 'Cultural assumptions of East and West: Japan and the United States', in Gudykunst, W. (ed.) *Inter-cultural Communication Theory*, Beverley Hills, CA: Sage.
53. Weldon, E. (1997) 'Inter-cultural interaction and conflict management in US–Chinese joint ventures', in Stewart, S. (ed.) *Advances in Chinese Industrial Organization, Vol. 4*, Greenwich, CT: JAI Press.
54. Ting-Toomey, S. (1988) 'Intercultural conflict styles: a face-negotiation theory', in Kim, Y.Y. and Gudykunst, W.B. (eds) *Theories in Intercultural Communication*, Newbury Park, CA: Sage.
55. Huntington, S. (1997) *The Clash Of Civilizations And The Remaking of World Order*, London: Simon & Schuster.
56. Triandis, H.C. (2002) 'Subjective culture', in Lonner, W.J., Dinnel, D.L., Hayes, S.A. and Sattler, D.N. (eds) *Online Readings in Psychology and Culture* (unit 15, chapter 1). URL: http://www.wwu.edu/~culture
57. Triandis, 1972, pp. viii, 3.
58. Hickson, D.J. and Pugh, D. (1995) *Management Worldwide: The Impact of Societal Culture on Organizations around the Globe*, London: Penguin.
59. Kim, Y.Y. op. cit.
60. Hofstede, G. (1981) op. cit.
61. Orbe, M.P. (1998) 'From the standpoint(s) of traditionally muted groups: explicating a co-cultural communication theoretical model', *Communication Theory*, **8**(1): 1–26.
62. Pinker, S. (1994) *The Language Instinct*. London: Penguin, p. 251.
63. Aldridge, M.G. (2002) op. cit.
64. Li, J. and Karakowsky, L. (2002) 'Cultural malleability in an East Asian context: an illustration of the relationship between government policy, national culture and firm behavior', *Administration & Society*, **34**(2): 176–201.
65. van Dijk, J. (1990) 'Transnational management in an evolving European context', *European Management Journal*, **8**(4): 474–9.
66. European Values Survey. URL: www.ucd.ie/issda/dataset-info/evs.htm
67. Hofstede, G. (1981) op. cit.
68. Barkema, H.G. (1997) op. cit.
69. Shenkar, O. (2001) 'Cultural distance revisited: towards a more rigorous conceptualization and measurement of cultural differences', *Journal of International Business Studies*, **32**(3): 519–35.
70. Harpaz, I. (2002) op. cit.
71. Roure, L. (2001) 'Product champion characteristics in France and Germany', *Human Relations*, **54**(5): 663–82.
72. Clugston, M. (2000) 'The mediating effects of multidimensional commitment on job satisfaction and intent to leave', *Journal of Organizational Behavior*, **21**: 477–86.
73. Schneider, S.C. and De Meyer, A. (1991) 'Interpreting and responding to strategic issues: the impact of national culture', *Strategic Management Journal*, **12**: 307–20.
74. Sparrow, P.R. (1998) op. cit.
75. Arvonen, J. and Lindell, M. (1996) 'The Nordic management style in a European context', *International Studies of Management & Organization*, **26**(3): 73–93.
76. Ibid.
77. Sparrow, P.R. (1998) op. cit.
78. Fernandez Dols, J.P. (1992) 'Procesos escabrosos en psicologia social: el concepto de norma perverse', *Revue Psicologica Sociologica*, **7**: 243–5.
79. Ali, A.J. (1993) 'Decision-making style, individualism and attitudes toward risk of Arab executives', *International Studies of Management & Organization*, **23**(3): 53–74.
80. Vance, C.M., McClaine, S.R., Boje, D.M. and Stage, D. (1992) 'An examination of the transferability of traditional performance appraisal principles across cultural boundaries', *Management International Review*, **32**: 313–26.

81. Hanninen-Salmelin, E. and Petajanieme, T. (1994) 'Women managers: the case of Finland', in Adler, N.J. and Izraeli, D.N. (eds) *Competitive Frontiers*, Cambridge, MA: Basil Blackwell.
82. Eagly, A.H. and Johnson, B.T. (1990) 'Gender and leadership style: a meta-analysis', *Psychological Bulletin*, **108**(2): 233–56.
83. Haire, M., Ghiselli, E.E. and Porter, L.W. (1966) *Managerial Thinking: An International Study*. New York: Wiley.
84. Bass, B.M. (1981) 'Leadership in different cultures', in Bass, B.M. (ed.) *Stogdill's Handbook of Leadership*: pp. 522–49, New York: Free Press.
85. Kozan, M.K. (1993) 'Cultural and industrialization level influences on leadership attitudes for Turkish managers', *International Studies of Management & Organization*, **23**(3): 7–18.
86. Morley, D.D., Shockley-Zalabak, P. and Cesaria, R. (1997) 'Organizational communication and culture: a study of 10 Italian high-technology companies', *The Journal of Business Communication*, **34**: 252–66.
87. Lee, M. and Barnett, G.A. (1997) 'A symbols-and-meaning approach to the organizational cultures of banks in the United States, Japan and Taiwan', *Communication Research*, **24**(4): 394–412.
88. Al-Aiban, K.M. and Pearce, J.L. (1993) 'The influence of values on management practices: a test in Saudi Arabia and the United States', *International Studies of Management & Organization*, **23**(3): 32–52.
89. Vertinsky, I., Lee, K-H., Tse, D.K. and Wehrung, D.A. (1990) 'Organizational design and management norms: a comparative study of managers' perceptions in the People's Republic of China, Hong Kong and Canada', *Journal of Management*, **16**(4): 99–110.
90. Chatman, J.A. (1998) 'Being different yet feeling similar: the influence of demographic composition and organizational culture on work processes and outcomes', *Administrative Science Quarterly*, **43**: 749–80.
91. Hofstede, G. (1991) op. cit.
92. Trompenaars, F. (1993) op. cit.
93. Mason, D. (1995) *Race and Ethnicity in Modern Britain*, Oxford: Oxford University Press.

chapter three

Culture and Communication

There are certainly more similarities than differences between human beings from different groups, and this applies to their ways of communicating as much as to anything. Nevertheless, the differences are significant and do affect communication between people from different groups. Chapter 2 discussed ways of analysing how cultures differ and how these analyses can be applied to groups that differ by nationality, ethnicity, gender, age, (dis)ability, sexual orientation, education, social class or profession. In the next two chapters, the discussion is extended into how differences of background affect individuals' communication behaviour at work. Subcultural differences are considered alongside cultural differences. Chapter 3 concerns the overt behaviour of individuals; Chapter 4 looks at behavioural factors and processes underlying how we communicate. (The relation between Chapters 3 and 4 is shown in Figure 3.1.)

The chapter begins with a brief note on communication as a subject, encompassing definitions and the question of universals versus cultural specifics in communication. It takes the introduction given in Section 1.1 a stage further. Section 3.2 covers, broadly, some aspects of communication which may differ from (sub)culture to (sub)culture, in order to alert readers to recognise them when they occur. Section 3.3 gives more detail on what research has so far taught us about the communication differences and similarities of different cultures, ethnicities, genders and so on. Figure 3.2 shows the relationship of Sections 3.2 and 3.3 as a grid.

3.1 A BRIEF NOTE ON COMMUNICATION

One definition of communication would be 'message exchange between two or more participants which is characterised by the intentional, conscious (at some level of awareness) use of mutually intelligible symbol systems'.[1] This definition excludes the possibility of communication without conscious intent and so is not universally accepted: habits and emotions are generally regarded as sources of communication that do not involve conscious intention. Sarbaugh preferred to define communication as the process of using signs and symbols that elicit meanings in another person or persons for whatever intent, or even without conscious intent, on the part of the person producing the symbols or signs.[2]

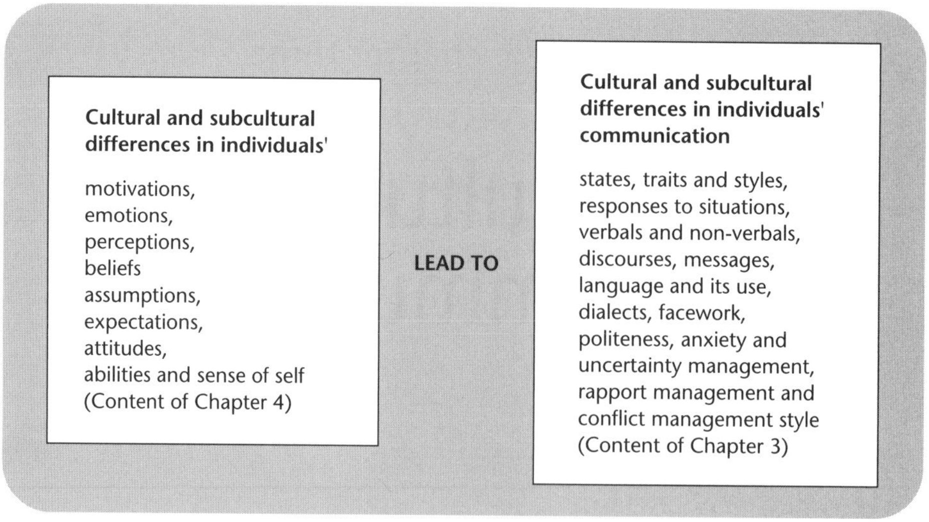

Cultural and subcultural differences in individuals'

motivations,
emotions,
perceptions,
beliefs
assumptions,
expectations,
attitudes,
abilities and sense of self
(Content of Chapter 4)

LEAD TO

Cultural and subcultural differences in individuals' communication

states, traits and styles,
responses to situations,
verbals and non-verbals,
discourses, messages,
language and its use,
dialects, facework,
politeness, anxiety and
uncertainty management,
rapport management and
conflict management style
(Content of Chapter 3)

Figure 3.1   *Relation between the content of Chapters 3 and 4*

Note: Feedback from interlocutors leads to modifications, but these effects are not covered in these chapters

	Traits and styles	Messages	Codes	Verbal communication	Non-verbal communication	Rules	Constraints	Info. seeking	Facework	Etc.
Nationality										
Culture										
Ethnicity										
Age										
(Dis)ability										
Religion										
Social class										

Figure 3.2   *The relationship between Sections 3.2 and 3.3*

N.B. Not all of the cells of this grid are complete in this chapter, or in the available research or possibly in reality.

Universals versus cultural specifics in communication

Do the communication patterns and behaviours of different groups differ significantly? The position taken here is that there are both universals and cultural specifics in communication.[3] Some research suggests that humans may be 'pre-wired' to recognise the communicative importance of language. This 'innate' recognition may, some suggest, account for the speed with which children learn to talk. In addition, as Box 3.1 illustrates, all cultures use both verbal and non-verbal communication systems, including dress and adornment. However, cultural differences in communication have been well documented in non-verbal communication, judgements, intergroup communication and the processes through which a communication episode develops. Some aspects of communication differ among different subcultures, as opposed to cultures. For instance, Scollon and Scollon saw virtually all professional communication as intercultural.[4]

Box 3.1

Ethnographist Donald E. Brown lists the following as universal communication characteristics of peoples: gossip, lying, misleading, verbal humour, humorous insults, poetic and rhetorical speech forms, narrative and storytelling, metaphor, poetry, words for days, months, seasons, years, past, present, future, body parts, inner states (emotions, sensations, thoughts), behavioural propensities, flora, fauna, weather, tools, space, motion, speed, location, spatial dimensions, physical properties, giving, lending, affecting things and people, numbers (at the very least 'one', 'two' and 'more than two'), proper names, possession; distinctions between mother and father. kinship categories, defined in terms of mother, father, son, daughter, and age sequence. Binary distinctions, including male and female, black and white, natural and cultural, good and bad; measures; logical relations including 'not', 'and', 'same', 'equivalent ... opposite', general versus particular, part versus whole; non-linguistic vocal communication such as cries and squeals; recognised facial expressions of happiness, sadness, anger, fear, surprise, disgust, and contempt; use of smiles as a friendly greeting; crying; coy flirtation with the eyes; masking, modifying, and mimicking facial expressions; displays of affection.

Source: Pinker, S. (1994) *The Language Instinct*, London: Allen Lane, The Penguin Press

Although a wide range of categories of communication behaviour are found in all cultures, their precise content may vary from culture to culture.

3.2 CULTURAL DIFFERENCES IN COMMUNICATION

This section introduces aspects of communication that differ cross-culturally or cross-subculturally, with examples to illustrate these differences. The aspects include the following: communication traits and styles, messages, codes, verbal and non-verbal communication, communication rules, conversational constraints, information-seeking, facework, politeness, anxiety and uncertainty management, rapport management, how situations are interpreted and responded to, compliance gaining and conflict management.

Communication traits and styles

Early attempts to analyse behavioural phenomena (leadership is one example) have often included trait or style theories. This is also true for communication. A trait is a tendency to behave in a certain way, in the judgement of the self or others. For some psychologists, a bundle of traits is called a personality; the equivalent for communication theorists is communicator style. Three sets of communication traits are especially important in a cross-(sub)cultural work context – rhetorical sensitivity, assertiveness and argumentativeness.

Rhetorical sensitivity

The tendency to adapt messages to audiences is termed rhetorical sensitivity. People differ in how far they use sensitivity and care in adjusting what they say to allow for

Box 3.2

Concerning the appointment of Supachai Panitchakdi of Thailand as Director-General of the World Trade Organisation, *The Economist* wrote, '… the real test of Mr Supachai lies ahead. How effectively can he persuade trade negotiators to reach a compromise? At the 11th hour of trade talks, this often comes down to personal chemistry. Mr Moore (Supachai's predecessor) played the eternally affable, backslapping politician, who smoothed feathers and brokered deals in a haze of cigarette smoke. Nobody expects that approach from the bookish Mr. Supachai. His style is formal, his manner reserved. All rather Asian, in fact. The doubt is whether the Supachai style will be effective.'

Source: The Economist, 7 September 2002, p. 78

the knowledge, ability level, mood or beliefs of the listener.[5] Some people express themselves without adjusting to others (these speakers are 'rhetorically insensitive'); others (the 'rhetorically reflective') mould themselves completely to what they perceive as likely to please others; rhetorically sensitive people adopt an intermediate way, showing concern for themselves, others and the situation. Research among nurses found age-related and other subcultural differences. Nurses under the age of 35 and those with more education were more rhetorically sensitive, those over 55 more rhetorically reflective. Registered nurses were the most rhetorically insensitive. Most people use all three types of communication but show a tendency to use one more than the others, so displaying a rhetorical trait.

Assertiveness

Putting one's own rights forward without hampering other individuals' rights is called assertiveness. These rights include the rights to make mistakes, set one's own priorities, refuse requests without feeling guilty, express oneself (without infringing the rights of others) and judge one's own behaviour, thoughts and emotions, while taking responsibility for the consequences.[6] Assertiveness is a middle way between submissiveness and aggression. It has been much advocated in the West as a way for women and members of ethnic minorities to communicate, especially with people who are prejudiced against them or who for other reasons are inclined to 'put them down'. It can be effective. However, rights are not separable from the society in which someone communicates. Assertiveness is therefore culture-related – what is assertive in one society is aggressive in another.[7]

Argumentativeness

Willingness to engage in constructive persuasive debate is called argumentativeness.[8] It is a trait that managers have been shown to value in subordinates. However, Kim *et al.* suggested that argumentativeness is a form of verbal aggression. It is acceptable in US culture because the attack is directed against an 'object' – the matter under discussion – rather than a person, but this distinction is probably neither understood nor accepted in other cultures. Research by Kim *et al.* showed that individualism increased argumentativeness.[9] Conversely, other research found no differences in argumentativeness between ethnic groups in the USA or between regional groups of Americans. The groups tested included African Americans, Asian Americans, Hispanics and European Americans.[10]

Communicator style

A signal as to how a message should be received (e.g., as authoritative, friendly or warm) is one meaning of 'communicator style'. Style theorists believe that individuals have dominant styles. Style variables that have been researched include being friendly, relaxed, contentious, attentive, precise, animated, open, dominant, impression leaving and having a positive communicator image. Communicator style is partly individual, partly influenced by social background. The environment plays an important part in the development of an individual's 'communication personality', which thus can be expected to vary among cultures and subcultures.[11]

Situations

Somewhat contrary to the underlying premise of trait and style theories, there is evidence that the meanings attached to both verbal and non-verbal forms of communication are partly determined by the situation in which they are produced. A communication situation is the entire communication event, including the participants, the setting and the activities taking place. According to situation theorists, people normally adjust their communication behaviour for the situation in one or more of the following ways:

- By evaluating the participants differently. For instance, a manager's behaviour will be evaluated differently by subordinates according to whether it takes place in the office or at the office party.
- By adjusting their goals – what they hope to achieve from the encounter. Thus, most people would recognise that they are unlikely to succeed in a request for a salary raise in a large meeting where a major sales dip has been reported.
- By adjusting their behaviour. For example, they may adjust the degree of formality they use in addressing others, whether to make jokes or how much of the 'air time' to take.[12]

There are cultural differences in how people interpret situations. 'Two people socialized to different cultures may react to a situation differently because of differences in internalized conceptions of the content of the situation, of what is normal, what is appropriate and so on.'[13] For example, in some cultures a funeral is seen as a joyful and not a sorrowful occasion. The work context, too, is a situation, or, rather, a large number of different situations with some shared characteristics, such as the norm of focusing on the task. The fact that work communication is different from social or other behaviour applies cross-culturally, although how it differs varies from one (sub)culture to another.

Messages

Only messages can be sent and received; meanings cannot be transmitted. This means that senders of messages must encode their meanings into symbols, choosing those that are likely to be familiar to their audience. Even routines such as greeting people on the street were at some point learned and have to be retrieved from memory.

Receivers, equally, have to decode messages and have to recreate their meaning, often by inference. These facts create scope for miscommunication: for instance, there is no way for Person A to be certain that Person B means the same by 'blue' as they do. Much speech is elliptical: in ordinary work conversation Person A is quite likely to say, 'Bring me the blue folder, please,' even if there are several blue folders, so long as s/he has some reason to think that the person s/he is addressing will be able to infer which blue folder s/he means.

Recently, attention has turned to micro-messages. These are small, often non-verbal and unconscious messages that we constantly send and receive. Micro-messages can be either positive or negative. Some examples in everyday interactions include winking to show understanding, glancing at a watch while someone is speaking, or leaning forward during conversation with a colleague. In a routine ten-minute conversation, two people will send each other, on average, between 40 and 100 micro-messages. Micro-messages sometimes contradict spoken messages, as when a prejudiced person says that they regard everyone present as equal but in practice repeatedly interrupts the speech of minority members. As micro-messages are less under conscious control, they differ more by culture and subculture.

Codes

A distinction can be drawn between restricted and elaborated communication styles or codes. As the names imply, restricted codes explicate less fully than elaborated codes do. For example, if someone approached another person who was waiting at the side of a country road in England, the conversation might run like this: 'What are you waiting for?' 'The 10.15'. Both questioner and responder used a restricted code – neither thought it necessary to elaborate on the fact that it was a bus that was being referred to. The same assumption of shared knowledge could not necessarily be made, even if one of them came from an English town – urban dwellers are used to bus stops being marked by a post and might not be aware that country buses often stop at known but unmarked places. Then the conversation might run differently: The 'What' in 'What are you waiting for?' would have a wider denotation and the answer might correspondingly be, 'The bus'.

Restricted codes express group membership and depend on a context of shared assumptions, social experience and expectations. Vocabulary is smaller and syntax simpler. Non-verbal communication is vital; in fact with their ingroup, people often express themselves solely through body language. For elaborated codes, however, non-verbal communication is much less useful. A study of social class in Britain found that codes differ from one social class to another: the code of the working classes is more restricted than that of the middle classes. This difference indicates that the codes reflect specific views of life and perceptions of reality resulting from the diverse life styles of the social classes.[14] Later critics have contended that identifying restricted and elaborated codes with particular classes is wrong because it implies that there is a deficiency in the language used by some groups. They argue, for instance, that Black English is a fully developed language and that difficulties arise for Black children (in the USA) only because they are not proficient in Standard English, which is the dominant medium in which they must function in formal situations. This criticism may be misplaced. As the author of the study commented, 'Let it be said immediately that a restricted code gives access to a vast potential of meanings, of delicacy, subtlety and diversity of cultural forms.' The difference lies in the speakers' assumption (or otherwise) of knowledge shared with their listener and thus the degree to which they feel required to verbalise. It is likely, however, that closed societies make more use of restricted codes, open societies more use of elaborated ones. People from closed societies might have more difficulty in switching to elaborated codes when they meet outsiders. In any case the criticism does not detract from the idea of different codes used by different groups. 'Some languages and dialects communicate some topics more and others less efficiently than other languages and dialects.'[15]

There is an obvious parallel between the 'elaborated/restricted code' distinction and Hall's high-context/low-context communication distinction (described in Chapter 2), although the code concept is more fluid – the same people might use the restricted code among their familiars and the elaborated code with strangers.

Verbal communication

Verbal behaviour (speech and writing) is particularly good for communicating information and intentions, less useful for communicating relationships and feelings. Communicating verbally requires the use of spoken or written language, in which conventions vary, as Box 3.3 illustrates. Cultural differences in verbal behaviour are highlighted by the concept of a speech community, which is central to the discipline of socio-linguistics. A speech community is based on several core components. Some of these components are considered to be: a common form of socialisation; regular interaction during which norms are established and reinforced; a shared body of words to mean certain things and a certain type of verbal behaviour. All of these combine to create a feeling of belonging (however loosely) and exclusivity (insiders understand the meaning of what is said but outsiders may not).[16]

Box 3.3

'In English, the head of a phrase comes before its role-players. In many languages it is the other way round … . For example, in Japanese, the verb comes *after* its object, not before: they say, "Kenji, sushi ate", not "Kenji ate sushi". The preposition comes after its noun phrase: "Kenji to" not "to Kenji" (so they are actually called "postpositions"). The adjective comes after its complement: "Kenji than taller" not "taller than Kenji". Even the words making questions are flipped: they say, roughly, "Kenji eat did?" not "Did Kenji eat?" Japanese and English are looking-glass version of each other.'[a]

In Sweden, where modes of address became simpler and more intimate during the second half of the 20th century, the 1990s saw a 'reformalisation', marked by such changes as salespeople beginning to address customers in the second person plural (the polite form of address), and it no longer being shameful to put the title 'Professor' before one's name.[b]

Untranslatability: Green Party posters for the German election included one which 'shows Mr. Fischer (German Foreign Minister and a Green Party member) in open-necked shirt and dishevelled hair, and says: "Minister on the outside, green on the inside". (*Aussenminister* translates as 'minister on the outside' but also means Foreign Minister.)'[c]

Sources: (a) Pinker, S. (1994) *The Language Instinct.* London: Allen Lane, The Penguin Press, p. 110

(b) Czarniawska-Joerges, B. (1993) 'Swedish management: modern project, postmodern implementation', *International Studies of Management & Organization*, **23**(1): 13–27

(c) Dejevsky, M. (2002) 'Greens roar back with Schroder's blessing', *The Independent*, 17 September, p. 11

In most languages there are dialects that reflect ethnic, regional and other differences. Dialects employ different pronunciation, vocabulary and grammatical structures. To linguists, the word 'dialect' refers to a way of speaking a language, and not to an incorrect way of speaking a language. While all dialects of a given language are linguistically legitimate, some achieve social prestige. In literate, economically developed societies, the dialect spoken by those with the most formal education, socio-economic status and political power tends to acquire the greatest social prestige. Typically, it becomes the standard dialect for the culture, for writing and education. Standard dialects also provide a medium that persons from different linguistic backgrounds use to communicate with one another. However, there are many kinds of non-standard dialect. These include those tied to social class and educational level. Other aspects of verbal communication that differ cross-(sub)culturally include discourses, speech acts and conversation constraints. These are explained later in this section.

Non-verbal communication

Non-verbal communication has the following characteristics that make it different from verbal communication:[17]

- Much of it, though not all, has universal meaning: threats and emotional displays, for example, may be biologically determined.
- It makes it possible to transmit several messages at once – a person can smile to show friendliness, keep eye contact to show assertiveness and nod to show agreement, all at the same time.
- In many cases it gives rise to an automatic response – laughter, for instance, can be contagious.
- Often it is unintended and hard to control – emotion, particularly, tends to leak out through non-verbal behaviour.
- Like language, non-verbal communication is used to express meaning, but it is particularly important in revealing feelings and attitudes, especially towards the person(s) being communicated with (e.g., 'You bore me', or 'I like you'). It is 'the major contributor to communication of "affect" in messages'.[18] It is also used to simplify and organise the communication of specific messages and to help regulate an interaction (as when a person coughs to indicate that they want to interrupt).
- Meaning can always be assigned to any movement, even when there is no communicative intent; the same individual will generally use the same non-verbal expression for the same emotion or purpose; people are influenced by the visible bodily activity of others; a person's use of bodily activity will have idiosyncratic features but will also be part of a larger social system shared with others.[19] For example, supervisors will often exhibit a more relaxed posture than subordinates.
- Non-verbal behaviour is used to reinforce and communicate identity as a group member. Speech style and accent are the main non-verbal vehicles performing this function, as exemplified in the difference between middle class and working class speech in British English.
- In the world of work, an important function of non-verbal behaviour is its symbolic use to signify occupation or status. For example, doctors wear white coats to symbolise hygiene, police wear uniforms to make them recognisable and to lend them authority and chief executives have large offices with thick pile carpets to show their status. Some symbols are more subtle – in a full-service advertising

agency, although formal suits are worn, there is a greater readiness to leave off jackets than in a bank; in a creative hot-shop, clothing generally will be more 'designer' than in their traditional competitors. People who misread these symbols may behave inappropriately – they may fail, for instance, to give the chief executive his or her due, or they may dress in an inappropriate style that will lead insiders to see them as outsiders.

Many cultural differences in non-verbal behaviour have been recorded. Examples include the following:

- For Americans, forming a circle with thumb and forefinger signals 'O.K.'; it means 'zero' or worthless in France, money in Japan, and calling someone a very bad name in Germany; putting the feet on the table is a (male) American gesture which is offensive to nearly every other country around the globe.
- For some cultures, touching another person is proscribed. These cultures include the people of China, Indonesia, Japan, the Philippines, Thailand, Australia, England, Germany, the Netherlands, Norway, Scotland, America, India and Pakistan. Contact cultures (who use 'touch' with less inhibition) include the people of Iraq, Kuwait, Saudi Arabia, Syria, the United Arab Republic, Bolivia, Cuba, Ecuador, El Salvador, Mexico, Paraguay, Peru, Puerto Rico, Venezuela, France, Italy and Turkey.

Different cultures use the resources of visual communication in ways that are related to their specific underlying value systems. For example, traditional Japanese writing goes vertically; so horizontal writing implies modernity in a way that does not apply in most countries. In Japanese advertisements, the direction suggesting progress and improvement is right to left, whereas the opposite holds in British advertisements. Advertisements showing the image of a woman holding the product are more close-up and have greater direct eye contact with the camera in Britain than Japan, reflecting different attitudes to women. Thus, it can be said, 'Intercultural communication can be deeply conditioned by the degree of understanding of visual semiotics as a cultural code.'[20]

Research has shown that demeanour, which consists primarily of non-verbal and paralinguistic behaviours, is controlled in part by status within a group. It creates and perpetuates status inequalities and beliefs about unequal abilities. It also affects the influence an individual exerts in a group and how credible an impression they make. An autocratic demeanour on the part of a leader reduces group members' satisfaction, while behaving simply 'as the boss' usually increases satisfaction. This research also showed that the demeanour of those involved affects the definitions that people apply to a situation (for instance, whether it is a crisis or a routine event) and so affects their response. The same research also showed that demeanour varies by gender.[21]

Box 3.4

'Shaking hands is important in Madagascar. To omit this little ceremony can be construed as a deliberate insult.'

Source: Murphy, D. (1985) *Muddling Through in Madagascar*, London: Century Press

Rules

Communication is governed by rules, which can vary (sub)culturally. Communication requires people to co-operate, which they do partly by following rules. People generally use rules to interpret what they see and hear (rules of meaning) and then act on the basis of their interpretations. They employ rules of action to decide what kind of action, in this case communication action, is appropriate. In the West, co-operation is achieved by following the rules or maxims of quality (being truthful), quantity (providing enough but not too much information), relevance and manner (not being obscure, disorganised or ambiguous).[22] Communication rules, like other rules, are affected by cultural values. For example, people from collectivist cultures follow a maxim of seeking harmony and may not depend so heavily on the maxim of quality (truthfulness).

Rules also govern speech acts. To speak is to perform an act. Speech is not just used to designate or describe something; it actually *does* something. Speakers do not speak only to give information: they may have a range of intentions.[23] Speech acts, with their associated intentions, may be stating, questioning, commanding, promising or one of a number of other possibilities. If a speech act is successful, the receiver will understand the speaker's intention. If, for example, when Person A asks a question, the receiver, Person B, only understands the words, but not that A intended to ask a question, B is unlikely to give an answer. In this case, A's speech act will not have been a successful one.

Understanding what the speaker's intentions are in saying something is crucial to a receiver. For instance, if a colleague says something like, 'The post has arrived', the literal meaning is easily understood by decoding, but the receiver needs to know why s/he made this announcement. What was the intention behind saying this? It might simply be a desire to impart the information, but usually the speaker intends to communicate more. In the example above, it might be that the speaker wants the receiver to go to the post room to collect the post, or that s/he wants them to know that s/he has been to the post room. Receivers will need to know which of the possible communicative intentions apply or they will miss the full meaning of the message. To decide, they will draw on a set of assumptions that they use to understand their experience. These assumptions are likely to vary cross-culturally.

Speech act theory identifies what it takes to make a successful speech act, that is, to have an intention understood. There are guidelines on how to use speech to accomplish a particular intention – for instance, if A wants something, s/he makes a request, and does it in a form which B will understand to obligate him/her either to grant it or to turn it down. Therefore, when speakers perform a speech act, they must follow rules and those rules must be known to and be understood by receivers, if they are to communicate successfully.

Speech act theory explains how people use intentions to structure communication. It is probable that in all cultures, to speak is to perform an act and to be successful the communicative intention behind the act must be understood by the receiver. However, both intentions and the forms required to communicate them may be culture-specific and hard for outsiders to comprehend. For instance, in some societies, for a guest to praise a host's possession usually obliges the host to offer it as a gift; it is assumed that the guest's intention is to ask for it. Without prior knowledge, Westerners would not understand that implication of praise. There are also rules for discourses. A discourse, as Chapter 2 described, refers to the ways in which language is used in a particular social context. There are (sub)cultural differences in the rules for general discourse.

These rules govern topics of conversation, types of anecdotes, sequences of the elements of a story or account and amounts of speech to use. They also cover how to open and close conversations, take turns during conversations, interrupt, use silence or laughter as communication devices, interject humour at appropriate times and use non-verbal behaviour.[24] Every culture can be shown to consist of a number of internal, intersecting and overlapping discourse systems, such as those of different age groups, ethnic groups, genders, social classes and professions. For instance, many teenagers use media-derived personal idioms, partly in order to identify with other teenagers.

An analysis of interviews with and documents from Indian and Israeli business partners suggested that local discourse systems play a major role in business communication. The findings included the following:

- There was a high level of breakdown of business communication/negotiations between Indians and Israelis.
- Indians' faxes were 2.7 times longer than Israelis'. They included declarations of solidarity, such as, 'On long-term and uninterrupted relationship with concrete and sound foundations, let us build our joint empire', and long paragraphs with no numbers. Negatives, such as a refusal to go to Israel, were expressed indirectly.
- The Israelis commented on the Indian communications, 'Every sentence has two extra degrees of freedom. You can never hold or grasp something. Words have double or triple meaning.' The Indians' comment on the Israeli communication style was that it was aggressive, lacked flexibility, style, patience and human orientation.
- Israelis used 'dugri' discourse, which emphasises faithful projection of one's own feelings, often producing a forceful and confrontational tone; the Indians used Indian English, which is formal, poetic and inefficient, and requires long, indirect sentences to be polite.
- In 15 per cent of cases, each adopted aspects of the other's style: the Israelis used metaphors: 'I must congratulate you for the achievement in receiving the approval for our project and looking forward for the wind to blow in our ship's sail'; the Indians simply stated facts: 'I wish to state that the offer is beyond our scope of investment at this juncture as we have more competitive offers.'[25]

Although there are cultural differences in power distance and uncertainty avoidance between Indians and Israelis, which may be reflected in their discourse systems, it is the difference in those discourse systems themselves that is most noticeable in these findings. This means they conflict with the culture-as-shared-values approach, which portrays culture as having a global influence on people's communication behaviour. That approach has been criticised for failing to explain variations within a culture or variations between cultures that share a broad value. Complexity and variation in communication patterns are often ignored.[26] The culture-in-context approach (also known as the discourse/practice approach), in contrast, builds on the premise that different groups use different discourses. It also treats individuals as active participants (agents) – they make pragmatic choices, decisions and calculations. Thus the discourse/practice approach emphasises individuals' communication choices, particularly as such choices are shaped by the various discourse systems to which the individual belongs. In support of this view, research shows that businesspeople do not fully conform to one cultural code and that they adapt to specific situations; that negotiators from different cultural backgrounds modify their behaviour in intercultural, as opposed to intracultural, interactions; that negotiators tend to match the other's bargaining strategies; and that body movement and language are co-ordinated. Other research in support of the culture-in-context account explored intercultural dialogues between Israeli Jews and Palestinians. The two groups were expected to argue in a manner consistent with their respective cultural communication codes known as dugri and musayra respectively. Thus, the Israeli Jews were expected to be assertive and the Palestinians more accommodating. However, the study found the reverse – the Israeli Jews were more accommodating and the Palestinians more assertive. This finding is claimed to be 'inconsistent with the concept that cultural differences in communication style strongly affect intercultural communication practices'.[27]

Conversational constraints

Conversational constraints (CCs) are criteria for selecting conversational strategies. Three CCs are commonly identified: concern for clarity, for minimising threats to the hearer's face and for minimising imposition. The concerns are linked to interaction goals. Concern for clarity is linked to the goal of getting one's own way. Concern for minimising threats to the hearer's face and minimising imposition are both linked to the goal of avoiding hurting the hearer's feelings. Each interaction goal/CC pair is also linked to a choice of conversational strategy, particularly the choice between direct and indirect forms, as shown in Figure 3.3.[27] Later versions of CC theory add two more concerns: for avoiding negative evaluation by the hearer and for effectiveness.

CC theory is relevant to cultural differences in communication behaviour because it makes links between individuals' self-construals (described in Chapter 4), their needs, psychological make-up and choice of communication strategy. For instance, psychological masculinity leads to concern for clarity; psychological femininity leads to concern for others' face. A study undertaken with 972 undergraduates studying in Korea, Japan, Hawaii and mainland USA found the following. Culture-level individualism correlated positively with concern for clarity and promoting one's own goals in communication but not with the relational constraints of concern for minimising threats to the hearer's face, for minimising imposition or for avoiding negative evaluation by the hearer. In contrast, the results for culture-level collectivism were vice versa. In both cases, the researchers found that a mediating cultural variable – an independent

---

Box 3.5

'When presenting a privatisation proposal to Turkish government officials about a privatisation proposal, one issue is whether to give a balanced view, referring to potential problems, or not. Generally, Turkish history and culture predispose them to believe that any problems referred to are the tip of a very large iceberg and will actually prove fatal to the project. They are not used to working through problems; instead their experience is that problems cause failure. It makes it difficult to follow banking prudence nostrums – you do not know what to say that would make them realise you are being prudent without triggering alarm bells.'

Source: Interview with an investment banker, author's research

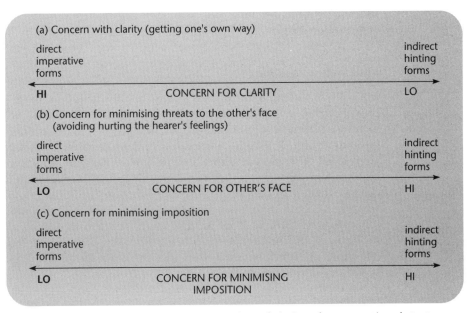

(a) Concern with clarity (getting one's own way)

direct imperative forms → indirect hinting forms

HI   CONCERN FOR CLARITY   LO

(b) Concern for minimising threats to the other's face (avoiding hurting the hearer's feelings)

direct imperative forms → indirect hinting forms

LO   CONCERN FOR OTHER'S FACE   HI

(c) Concern for minimising imposition

direct imperative forms → indirect hinting forms

LO   CONCERN FOR MINIMISING IMPOSITION   HI

Figure 3.3   *Conversational constraints, interaction goals and choice of conversational strategy*

Based on: Kim, M.-S., Hunter, J.E., Miyahara, A., Horvath, A., Bresnahan, M. and Yoon, H. (1996) 'Individual- vs culture-level dimensions of individualism and collectivism: effects on preferred conversational styles', *Communication Monographs*, **63**: 29–49

Box 3.6

'In a Chinese company, if a manager writes a report, he or she must always put, right at the start, that senior managers or other departments shared in the achievement of his or her department.'

Source: Interview with a Chinese expatriate manager in London: author's research

---

or interdependent self-construal – was operating.[28] Again, though Koreans and North Americans both saw the incompatibility of clarity with the three relationally oriented dimensions, Americans saw clearer request strategies as more effective; Koreans saw clarity as counterproductive to effectiveness.[29]

Another study within the same research project showed that participants' gender had no significant direct effect on the perceived importance of any of the CCs; this result was found consistently across all four societies researched. The finding seems to contradict assertions that men use language to assert a 'position of dominance' by coming directly to the point (clarity), whereas women use language to create and maintain relationships of closeness. The apparent contradiction may, however, be related more to the distinction between preferences and behaviour; many researchers have found gender differences in verbal styles (power, politeness, directness) but this still leaves room for men and women to be relatively similar in their *preferred* conversational styles.[30]

Information-seeking

Information-seeking is 'the process by which individuals proactively acquire feedback through the use of ... strategies to understand, predict and control their environments; increase task mastery; and reduce role ambiguity.'[31] Information-seeking facilitates communication by reducing uncertainty and errors based on misinformation. There are cultural differences in information-seeking behaviours, which correspond to the high-context, low-context communication distinction explained in Chapter 2. High-context communicators (HCCs) are more cautious in initial encounters, use more subtle behaviours, make more assumptions about but also ask more questions about a stranger's background. They are also more confident in making attributions about the 'causes' of another person's behaviour. Low-context communicators (LCCs) rely more on verbal expressiveness and are more likely to use interrogation and self-disclosure.

Facework

Face is the 'positive social value people assume for themselves, the image they try to project to the public'.[32] Although face concerns are universal, the meaning and enactment of face are heavily culture-dependent. Face is 'grounded in the webs of interpersonal and sociocultural variability'.[33] Because the relative importance of the self and the group differ in individualist and collectivist cultures, the characteristics of an appropriate face and the nature of facework also differ. In a collectivist culture, facework is used to present the self as an appropriate member of the social network, and people are expected to help others maintain a similarly appropriate face. By contrast, in an individualist society, facework focuses more on maintaining one's own personal identity with less interest in helping others maintain theirs.[34]

The concept of face and its elements has been further analysed in terms of a combination of two theories of culture: individualism–collectivism and low-context/high-context communication.[35] These variables influence the following:

- Whether the person's sense of identity is 'I' or 'we';
- Whether the primary face concern is for the self or the other;
- The relative importance of negative or positive face need;
- Whether the style used is controlling, confrontational and oriented towards solving 'problems' or obliging, conflict-avoiding and oriented towards maintaining positive feelings;
- Whether the person's communicative strategy is competitive or co-operative;
- Whether the person's mode of expression, speech acts and non-verbal behaviour are usually direct or indirect.

Table 3.1 gives a summary of the differences in these constructs in LCCs and HCCs. In addition, members of collectivist cultures have been found to be more likely than members of individualist cultures to use deception, typically as a means of saving face, to avoid confrontation or preserve harmony.

Table 3.1   *A summary of low-context and high-context face negotiation processes*

Key constructs of 'face'	Individualist, low-context communication cultures	Collectivist, high-context communication cultures
Identity	Emphasis on 'I' identity	Emphasis on 'We' identity
Concern	Self-face concern	Other-face concern
Need	Autonomy, dissociation, negative-face need	Inclusion, association, positive-face need
Style	Controlling or confrontation and solution-oriented styles	Obliging or avoidance and affective-oriented styles
Strategy	Distributive or competitive	Integrative or collaborative
Mode	Direct	Indirect
Speech acts	Direct	Indirect
Non-verbal acts	Individualist non-verbal acts, direct emotional expression	Contextualistic non-verbal acts (role-oriented), indirect emotional expression

Based on: Ting-Toomey, S. (1988) 'Intercultural conflict styles: a face-negotiation theory', in Kim, Y. and Gudykunst, W. (eds) *Theories in Intercultural Communication*, Newbury Park, CA: Sage; and Ting-Toomey, S., Gao, G., Trubisky, P., Yang, Z., Kim, H., Lin, S.L. and Nishida, T. (1991) 'Culture, face maintenance, and styles of handling interpersonal conflict: a study in five cultures', *The International Journal of Conflict Management*, **2**: 275–96.

HUMILITY		DIGNITY
Face loss (seen as lacking in dignity)	Face maintenance	Face loss (seen as arrogant)

Figure 3.4   *Face maintenance in Japan*

Based on: Lebra, T. (1971) 'The social mechanism of guilt and shame: the Japanese case', *Anthropological Quarterly*, **44**

Some other facework researchers have included at least one cultural difference variable in their models. In Japan, a collectivist culture, people are exposed to face loss from both excessive humility (seen as lack of dignity) and excessive claims to dignity (seen as arrogance). They strive to remain in an intermediate zone in which face can be maintained (see Figure 3.4).[36] Strategies to protect 'own face' in a collectivist culture include the following:

- Asking someone else to transmit a message (mediated communication).
- Talking to a third person in the intended hearer's presence (refracted communication).
- Acting as if a delegate – 'pretending' to be a messenger from a third person.
- Not expressing wishes explicitly, but expecting the other person to understand (anticipatory communication).
- Corresponding by letter, so avoiding meeting face-to-face.

All these strategies are available to and used by people in a range of cultures, but people from collectivist cultures use them more often. Equally, strategies to protect one's own face and threaten the other's face, such as self-praise or arrogance are commonplace in highly individualist cultures. They also occur in collectivist cultures, but are disapproved of and regarded as anti-social.

Politeness

Politeness theory is an extension of the concept of facework. Some speakers do not seem to aim to construct their messages in the most efficient way, contrary to rule theories. Instead, speakers are often guided by the requirements of politeness. According to politeness theory, there is a relationship between a speaker's face concerns, perceived threats to face and the ways in which a speaker will express a request, explanation, disagreement or any other verbal communication.[37]

Speakers are normally concerned both with their own face and with that of their hearer: they want to maintain their own position without giving offence to the hearer. Speakers who are indifferent to the effect of what they say on the hearer's face are poor communicators: by giving offence they reduce the chances of their message being listened to and understood. However, all communication risks a threat to the faces of either the speaker or the hearer or both. This is because all people have two conflicting desires: for other people's approval (positive face need) and yet to be independent of others and their approval (negative face need). Different kinds of communication, such as requests or apologies, are intrinsically more or less threatening to either the speaker's or the hearer's face. Box 3.7 gives a typology. Threat is also increased by three factors: how much the communication imposes on the hearer (asking for directions is less of an imposition than asking for a loan); the status relations between the speaker and hearer (a schoolmaster is more threatened by a pupil's disagreeing with him than the reverse); and how well the speaker and hearer know one another (knowing one another well

---

Box 3.7

A typology of face-threatening acts (FTAs)

- FTAs which threaten the hearer's positive face include disapproval, criticism, contempt, ridicule, complaints, reprimands, accusations, insults, contradictions, disagreements, challenges, expressions of violent emotions, taboo topics or bad news.
- FTAs which threaten the hearer's negative face include orders, requests, suggestions, advice, reminders, threats, warnings, dares, offers, promises, compliments and expressions of strong emotions.
- FTAs which threaten the speaker's positive face include apologies, accepting compliments, failing to maintain bodily control, making a faux pas, offering a confession of guilt and failing to maintain emotional control.
- FTAs which threaten the speaker's negative face include expressing thanks, accepting thanks, making excuses, accepting offers, responding to the hearer's gaffes and making reluctant promises or offers.

Based on: Brown, P. and Levinson, S.C. (1978) 'Universals in language usage: politeness phenomena', in Goody, E.N. (ed.) *Questions and Politeness: Strategies in Social Interaction*, Cambridge, Cambridge University Press, pp. 56–289

reduces threat). Politeness theory defines politeness in communication as the attempt by the speaker to minimise or reduce the threat to the hearer's face, and postulates that the more intrinsically threatening the situation, the more polite the speaker will be.

There are national, ethnic and gender differences in concepts of politeness, the amount of politeness that people use, the influence of content versus relationship concerns on politeness and the politeness of direct and indirect forms. For instance, Japanese people generally follow different sets of politeness norms from North Americans, including showing a higher level of deference to older people. Politeness is a rule of appropriate behaviour in different ethnic groups across the USA, but the particular behaviours that are defined as polite vary.[38] Again, some women have a pattern of politeness behaviours that is different from men's and can lead to an image of less intelligence. Women have 'learned the language of apology'. Unfortunately, these linguistic politeness patterns can negatively affect credibility and suggest uncertainty in the speaker and triviality in the subject matter.[39] In contrast to North American communication norms, avoiding obscurity or ambiguity (the maxim of manner) is not an expectation in cultures with different value orientations. For example, Koreans do not make negative responses like 'No', or 'I disagree with you'. Instead they are likely to say, 'I agree with you in principle', or 'I sympathise with you'. Koreans' collectivist values and consequent sense of politeness prevent directness of communication.[40]

Anxiety and uncertainty management (AUM)

AUM theory assumes that interacting causes individuals to experience anxiety and uncertainty, especially in a first meeting with strangers. Because these psychological experiences cause discomfort, people attempt to reduce their impact through communication. They do this especially if the strangers will be encountered in future and can provide rewards. Most importantly, uncertainty and anxiety are aroused and people attempt to reduce them when strangers act in a deviant fashion from the perspective of the individual's own culture or subculture. Thus cultural differences in behaviour are central to AUM theory.

Uncertainty is related to a range of communication behaviours: how much communication occurs between people, their non-verbal affiliative expressiveness (the degree to which they show warmth to one another by body language such as smiling, eye contact or touching), information-seeking and how intimately they communicate. Reciprocity, similarity and liking are also related to uncertainty. (In general each of these relations are inverse – thus, the greater the amount of communication and the higher the similarity, the lower the uncertainty. However, information-seeking is higher in the presence of high uncertainty.) People adopt one of three general strategies for reducing uncertainty: a passive strategy (doing nothing in the hope that as time passes things will become clearer); an active strategy (finding out as much as possible from outside sources); and an interactive strategy (seeking out opportunities to interact with people about whom uncertainty exists and using those occasions to obtain as much information as possible).[41] A number of hypotheses based on AUM theory relate anxiety or uncertainty to cultural dimensions. These include:

- An increase in collectivism will produce a decrease in uncertainty in outgroup communication relative to ingroup communication.
- An increase in uncertainty avoidance will produce an increase in anxiety and a decrease in intergroup adaptation and effectiveness.

■ An increase in the strength of ethnolinguistic identities leads to an increase in confidence but also an increase in anxiety, though only when members of the outgroup are perceived as typical and ethnic status is activated.[42]

Rapport management

One important function of language is the effective management of relationships of all kinds, including work relationships. In contrast with some linguists' focus on facework and politeness, scholars concerned with rapport management maintain that linguistic politeness is just one of the resources available for managing relationships. It should be studied within the situated social psychological context in which it occurs. It is therefore important to consider the motivational concerns underlying the management of relations.

Rapport management theorists suggest that face has two interrelated aspects:

1. Quality face: People have a fundamental desire for others to evaluate them positively in terms of their personal qualities, such as competence, abilities or appearance.
2. Social identity face: People have a fundamental desire for others to acknowledge and uphold their social identities or roles, for instance as group leader, valued customer or close friend.

Similarly, rapport management theorists suggest that people have 'fundamental beliefs' that they possess certain 'sociality rights'. These rights have two interrelated aspects:

1. Equity rights: People have a fundamental belief that they are entitled to personal consideration from others, so that they are treated fairly: that they are not unduly imposed upon or unfairly ordered about, that they are not taken advantage of or exploited, and that they receive the benefits to which they are entitled.
2. Association rights: People have a fundamental belief that they are entitled to association with others that is in keeping with the type of relationship that they have with them. People feel, for example, that they are entitled to an appropriate amount of conversational interaction and social chitchat with others (that they are not ignored on the one hand, but not overwhelmed on the other). These association rights also relate to the extent to which people share concerns, feelings and interests. Naturally, what counts as 'an appropriate amount' depends on the nature of the relationship, as well as on socio-cultural norms and personal preferences.

As can be seen, rapport management is conceptualised as having two motivational sources: concerns over face and concerns over sociality rights. Sociality rights are not treated as face issues, because sometimes an infringement of sociality rights may simply lead to annoyance or irritation, rather than to a sense of face threat or loss. Similarly, a request for help, which in politeness theory would be regarded as a face-threatening act, may not in fact be regarded as an infringement or threat at all. On the contrary, it may be regarded either as a boost to quality face, since the request shows trust in the other person's qualities, or simply as an acknowledgement of association rights. The notion of sociality rights relates partly to the concept of negative face but is not synonymous with it: it is broader in scope and is not limited to autonomy-imposition issues.[43]

There is evidence for cross-cultural differences in rapport management. A study compared the preferences of Greeks and Germans for attending to the relationship aspect of communication in telephone conversations. It found that Greeks seem to prefer an exchange of phatic utterances like greetings (which maximise the relational and minimise the informational content of talk), before coming to the reason for calling. Germans opt for a more direct path to the main section of the call. Greeks use more redundancy in closing telephone calls than Germans do, making them more extended. In Greek calls, the decision to end the call is negotiated. In German calls, common ground is invoked.[44]

Compliance gaining

An important purpose for which communication is used at work is to influence. Influencing ranges from the relatively weak effect of getting others to re-evaluate how they think about something to the relatively strong effect of gaining their compliance to doing something. Communication methods for getting other people to comply may correspond to cultural values. One study found that in the USA giving reasons and explanations were favoured over threats or moral pressure. These preferences are probably linked to values of individual autonomy. In contrast in Colombia, which has a collectivist culture, *confianza* (which means the degree of trust and closeness in a relationship, plus responsibility for others) interacts with acceptance of authority. This means that in some relationships it is acceptable for one party to 'command' the other. This can allow the use of threats and moral pressure and remove the need to give explanations. In other words, individualism–collectivism may influence compliance gaining methods.[45]

Compliance gaining with subordinates is using persuasion to influence them to do what they are directed to do and to convince them that the task is worth doing. Such communication is common between superiors and key subordinates. Research suggests that US and European managers use mainly reasoning and friendliness, as opposed to sanctions, bargaining or appeals to higher authority. The probable reasons are that such appeals avoid making superior–subordinate interactions more risky and help both superiors and subordinates to attain their goals. What applies to Japanese managers? Findings based on three samples of 14, 13 and 41 Japanese managers were that reasoning is the most used strategy. However, when Japanese managers see themselves as permanent employees they resort more to the use of assertiveness: they frequently set deadlines for key subordinates, tell these subordinates that they must comply and remind them repeatedly. Permanently employed Japanese managers also make more use of loyalty appeals, even when the subordinates are temporary workers.[46]

Conflict management

Conflict is the 'perceived and/or actual incompatibility of values, expectations, processes, or outcomes between two or more parties over substantive and/or relational issues'.[47] According to Triandis cultures differ on a number of aspects of conflict communication.[48] For instance, in the West, the structure of messages is likely to be: fact 1, fact 2, generalisation, conclusion; in other cultures the conclusion may be stated first, followed by facts that fit the conclusion. This structure permits deviations from a straight line. Another difference is between universalist and particularist cultures: universalists expect all facts to 'fit in' with a position, particularists may feel this is unnecessary. Third, there is a cultural difference between those, like Westerners, who use abstractive communication and those others who use associative communication, for whom the importance of symbols is greater. Conflict intensity, also, may vary as a function of culture because the value attached to a goal is influenced by subjective culture. What one culture may perceive as a major conflict may be quite minor in another. Because on the surface work-related conflict focuses on substantive issues, not relational and image issues, face negotiation has implications for how people manage conflict but is not exactly the same thing. Ting-Toomey and Kurogi argued that culturally competent facework is a critical aspect of conflict management.[49]

A useful distinction can be drawn between simplex relationships, which are confined to a single interest – for instance, that between a doctor and patient – and multiplex relationships, which serve many interests, such as economic, kinship and shared leisure time interests.[50] Because of the significant interdependence involved in a multiplex relationship, continuation of the relationship is very important to the well-being of the participants. In cultures and societies where multiplex relationships predominate, there is likely to be a preference for conflict resolution procedures that allow compromises, so that the relationship can continue smoothly. Examples include negotiation and mediation. Societies where simplex relationships are more common tend to prefer adjudication or arbitration, which lead to win–lose settlements. This might help account for the fact that in 1976, the USA had 18 lawyers per 1,000 people, West Germany four, France two and Japan one. Simplex-relationship oriented societies also tend to prefer adversarial adjudication, where the contending parties compete to make their case, rather than investigative adjudication, where a third party (magistrate or judge) investigates as well as judges. An adversarial system was set up in Japan by the USA after the Second World War, but the Japanese, while retaining its form, subsequently modified it in an investigative direction.

A number of cross-cultural studies of negotiation-related behaviour have provided evidence that members of individualist cultures are more likely to handle conflicts directly through competition and problem solving, whereas members of collectivist cultures are more likely to handle conflict in indirect ways that attempt to preserve the relationship.[51] A study of the conflict style of Vietnamese refugees concluded that they are part of a collectivist (as opposed to individualist), high-context (rather than low-context) culture which often desires to avoid conflict. In a 1994 conflict situation in Louisville, Kentucky, the Vietnamese conflict-avoiding style aided a defusion of tensions.[52] Yugoslavians (collectivists by Hofstede's measures) and Japanese prefer collaboration or compromise in handling a conflict, North Americans prefer competition.[53] Greeks, who by European standards are relatively collectivist, treat their ingroup as a source of protection and social insurance, but are more suspicious of and competitive with outgroup members, such as strangers. This ingroup–outgroup aspect of collectivism affects conflict: for instance, Chinese people are more likely to sue a stranger and less likely to sue a friend than North Americans are.

Cultural collectivism also influences business conflict resolution: a study showed that Japanese managers perceive the level of trust to be higher when an American partner requests a mutual conferral to resolve disputes rather than binding arbitration. However, collectivism, as exemplified in the Chinese preference for 'harmony' does not mean that Chinese people literally avoid conflict at all costs. Fieldwork studies have shown that 'co-operative conflict' occurs in Chinese organisations. Experiments have shown that Chinese people value and use conflict to explore issues, make effective decisions and strengthen relationships. Co-operative conflict in China contributes to effective teamwork, quality service and leadership. Co-operative conflict is achieved through the protagonists communicating that they want to manage the conflict for mutual benefit rather than to win at the other's expense.[54]

Conflict management styles have also been linked to other cultural variables. First, people from feminine cultures, such as the Dutch, have been shown to prefer harmony-enhancing conflict resolution procedures (such as mediation and negotiation) to confrontational procedures (such as threats and accusations). This preference is stronger among the Dutch than among Canadians, who score high on masculinity. Second, members of high power distance cultures (the Philippines, Venezuela, India, France, Belgium) have fewer conflicts with their superiors and are more likely to have superiors intervene in settling their conflicts than do members of low power distance cultures (Denmark, Israel, Austria). Third, members of low-context communication cultures (USA, Germany, Scandinavia, Switzerland) have been found to communicate more directly and to have different communication goals in conflict than members of high-context communication cultures (Japan, China, Korea, Vietnam). Fourth, negotiators who hold monochronic conceptions of time (North Americans, West Europeans) are more likely to process issues sequentially and to negotiate in a highly organised fashion, whereas negotiators with polychronic conceptions of time (Asia, Africa, South America, Middle East) are more likely to process issues simultaneously while ignoring conversational turn-taking (speaking simultaneously) and using frequent interruptions.[55]

Many researchers have conceptualised avoidance styles of conflict management as reflecting low concern for self as well as for the other. This assumption is taken so much for granted in individualist cultures that it has rarely been stated explicitly. The individualist assumption that overt conflict resolution is better than avoidance has led to a focus on limited aspects of conflict resolution and has resulted in ignorance about, or misinterpretation of, alternative conflict management styles.[56] Kim and Leung proposed instead a framework for explaining why people of different cultural identities tend to approach and manage conflict situations differently. The model suggests that collectivists' tendency to avoid conflict can be explained by their desire to preserve relational harmony and their motivation to save others' face. Furthermore, the authors suggested that bicultural individuals are likely to be more flexible and effective than culture-typed individuals (individualist or collectivist) in dealing with conflict situations.[57]

Critique

Though the purpose of this section is to note cultural variations in ways of communicating, the concepts and theories underpinning it derive mainly from a tradition that sees the individual human mind as the independent locus for processing information and for generating and understanding messages. This individualist cognitive approach was dominant in Western social science during the twentieth century; however, it can be challenged both in social science generally and in the study of communication, which is essentially something that happens between people and so cannot be explained solely from the perspective of the individual mind.

(Sub)cultural differences have been found for communication traits, styles and situations. Process-based analyses of communication refer to the exchange of messages and the creation of meaning by assigning signs or interpreting messages. There are (sub)cultural differences in which signs are used and what they refer to. Both verbal and non-verbal signs and their referents can vary. Users of spoken or written languages form different speech communities. Communication rules for achieving the necessary co-operation, for speech acts and for discourses can also differ. Conversational constraints, which link to interaction goals, have been found to vary between masculine/feminine and individualist–collectivist cultures. (Sub)cultural differences have been found in information-seeking, expressing and understanding intentions, facework, politeness, anxiety and uncertainty management, rapport management and in two specific types of interaction, compliance gaining and conflict. These differences partly reflect the cultural values differences described in Chapter 2, but in some cases appear to be independent variables. Apart from 'low-context, high-context', we do not as yet have a taxonomy of (sub)cultural differences in communication per se.

3.3 (SUB)CULTURAL COMMUNICATION

To varying degrees, as the previous section began to show, culture and other psychological variables loosely linked to demography affect how people communicate. This section gives a breakdown of communication similarities and differences by national culture, ethnicity, gender, age and disability, religion and social class. The communication of marginalised groups and professional, business and organisational discourses are also discussed.

National culture and communication

Cultural values play an important part in determining the general tone of communication. For instance, within individualism, it is the individual's responsibility to 'say what's on his or her mind' if s/he expects to be attended to or understood: 'For a person oriented toward the independent construal of self, the general tone of social interaction may concern the expression of his or her own needs and rights.'[58] In individualist cultures, too, highly verbal people are perceived positively because they are more successful at establishing identity. However, the value attached to being talkative varies cross-culturally. The benefit of low verbal output among collectivists comes from being understood without putting one's meaning on record. As a result, understanding is seen, not as the result of putting meaning into words, but rather as the greater understanding of shared perspectives, expectations and intimacy.[59]

The cultural values of individualism–collectivism, power distance, masculinity/femininity and uncertainty avoidance can be used to predict and explain differences between communicator styles in different countries. A study by Gudykunst *et al.*[60] explored this question and found the following:

■ Individualism–collectivism has both a direct effect on communicator styles and an indirect effect that is mediated through self-construals and values. Gudykunst *et al.* found that independent self construals and individualist values mediate the influence of cultural individualism–collectivism on the use of low-context communication, while interdependent self-construals and collectivist values mediate the influence of cultural individualism–collectivism on the use of high-context communication.

■ High power distance in general inhibits direct communication, leading to lower levels of disclosure, openness and informality than in lower power distance cultures. At work, high power distance leads to greater differences according to who is communicating with whom: between managers and subordinates, the above points apply and are reinforced, with subordinates' style conveying deference and managers' condescension or paternalism. On the other hand, between co-workers low down in the hierarchy, it can lead to high levels of informality, with joking, teasing and a private language, as the low level of responsibility required of these workers encourages a playful or childish approach.

- Cultures with strong achievement (masculine) values, like Austria, Venezuela and the Republic of Ireland, tend to use more assertive and competitive forms of communication than cultures with more relational (feminine) values like Sweden, Norway and the Netherlands. Japan, which ranks first on the achievement values index, is an exception, possibly because the strength of collectivism in the culture outweighs even the powerful achievement value.
- High uncertainty avoidance cultures, such as those of Greece, Portugal and the Latin American countries, are cultures where communicator styles are more expressive. 'They are the places where people talk with their hands, where it is socially acceptable to raise one's voice, to show one's emotions, to pound the table.'[61] Conversely, countries known for their low-key style of communication, such as Great Britain, Singapore and the Nordic countries, are also low in uncertainty avoidance.

Gudykunst *et al.* concluded that culture influences communication both directly, guided by cultural norms and rules, and indirectly, through self-construals and values which influence individuals' styles of communication. Table 3.2 summarises the findings. Other cultural influences on communicator style are found in communication rules, the value placed on control, affiliation, content and relationship in communication, and whether communication is usually used for negotiation or ratification.

- Communication rules, like other rules, are affected by cultural values. For example, Americans self-disclose (tell others about themselves) more than Europeans who, in turn, self-disclose more than Asians. In business transactions, Americans generally tolerate open discussion of errors and accept criticism of performance, while Koreans do not. Again, Americans differentiate criticism of a person from criticism of that person's actions, while Koreans view criticism as personal and face-threatening.[62]
- There are differences in the relative value placed by different cultures on control, affiliation, content and relationship in communication. Japanese culture, for instance, places a very high value on communicating subtle aspects of feeling and relationship and a much lower value on communicating information.

Table 3.2 *Relations among different cultural values and communication styles*

Cultural values	Communication styles	Comment
High uncertainty avoidance	Expressive	
Low uncertainty avoidance	Low key	
High masculinity (achievement)	Assertive, competitive	Except among Japanese
High femininity (relational)	Supportive; co-operative	
High power distance	High formality; low disclosure and openness	This applies to manager–subordinate interactions; depends on power balance
Low power distance	Low formality; high disclosure and openness	
High individualism	Competitive	Mediated by self-construals
High collectivism	Co-operative with ingroup	Mediated by self-construals

Most Japanese people also believe that the most important things cannot be communicated in language. Most Western cultures, despite some recent shifts, are the opposite. Not only do they emphasise communicating content at the expense of relationship but they tend to treat what cannot be expressed in language as not worth attending to. (Women from Western cultures, though, are closer to the Japanese in this respect.)

■ In some cultures communication is normally used for negotiation, whereas in other cultures it is normally used for ratification. In some societies relationships are thought of as spontaneously created by individuals and communication is used to negotiate those relationships; in other societies relationships are thought of as pre-determined and set – here communication ratifies pre-existing relationships. In business negotiations, Asians, who follow the ratification model, may state their positions less extremely if they feel that not to do so would disrupt the harmony of the relationship; Westerners may assume that each party has in mind only achieving their own best advantage and may state their positions strongly as a negotiating ploy.

Although the primary focus of this book is on Europe, a comparison of US and Japanese communication is instructive because they perhaps represent polar extremes. Communication in most European countries is located at varying points between.

The USA is a country formed by immigrants and is multicultural, despite past attempts to encourage assimilation. Japan, which was entirely closed to the outside world for centuries, is recognised as ethnically and culturally more homogeneous than any other major country in the world. These differences affect their preferred communication styles. The USA is 'a nation made up of ethnically diverse people who must work and live together. Reliance upon symbolic coding of experience has become a necessary survival skill.' For them, language is *the* mode of communication. For the Japanese, it is *a* mode of communication.

The Japanese prefer a style that employs assumptions about the opinions and feelings of their compatriots. (In Bernstein's terms, they use the restricted code.) The concept of *enryo* translates into a hesitancy about speaking frankly and immediately, which carries the risk of being thought brash. Japanese people are comfortable with silence, which has multiple meanings – for instance, showing respect by waiting for a senior to speak first. In Japan, the form of an event or communication is as important as its content. There are rituals for events, such as leavers' parties, which would be mainly informal in the USA. There are set phrases for apologies, excuses, requests and so on.

For North Americans, interaction formats, especially at work, are persuasive, quantitative and pragmatic; in contrast, for Japanese, they are harmonising, holistic and process-oriented. North Americans expect that each party, whether an individual

---

Box 3.8

An international executive from the UK, interviewed for this book, said that a Russian colleague once said to him that he was a typical Westerner. When he asked why, the Russian said, 'You are always planning for the future or analysing the past, but you never want to talk about what we are doing here and now.'

Source: Author's research

or a small group representative, will state its own point of view and attempt to persuade the other party or parties. Japanese aim to avoid distinguishing individual views or clarifying where differences lie. People are as likely to change their views out of respect or empathy as by responding to logical arguments. The receiver has as much responsibility for understanding what is said, as the speaker has to make him/herself clear. Japanese people tend to give feedback non-verbally rather than by asking questions or in other verbal ways.[63]

National culture and language usage

A culture's preferred communication style is reflected in its use of language. Thus, in cultures where the preferred style is direct (i.e., speakers reveal their intentions through explicit verbal communication), the language used features judgemental adjectives, directives, oppositions, negations, questions and references to quantity; these are less used in cultures whose preferred style is indirect. A preference for succinctness or elaborateness affects how many intensifying adverbs, dependent clauses, sentence initial adverbials ('Well …') and negations are used. Person-centred versus role-centred communication style preferences are reflected in the number of 'I' references, judgemental adjectives, oppositions and negations. Finally, the proportion of references to quantity, place, emotion, oppositions and negations reflect whether the cultural preference is for instrumental communication (which is oriented to the sender's goals) or affective communication (which is oriented to the relationship with the receiver).[64]

Thus, cultural styles are reflected in language features. At the same time, the language used and the communicators' language competency affect both the content and style of communication, which builds culture. Some languages give speakers easier access than others to particular personal and socio-cultural ideas; these in turn relate to or influence message content. For example, English gives ready access to business concepts. Russian supplies fewer of these; Russian speakers often use loan words from English for business concepts. On specialised topics people who are bilingual may use the language that gives them better access to relevant concepts. For example, some speakers of English-as-a-second-language (ESL) speak and write in English professionally because this is the language in which they received training and learned professional concepts.[65] Beyond this, individuals at different language proficiency levels communicate very differently. Low proficiency second-language speakers contribute fewer ideas than do fluent second-language speakers or first-language speakers.[66]

It is sometimes difficult to distinguish between what is cultural and what is linguistic. When Chinese bilingual groups conducted similar decision-making meetings in Cantonese (first language) and English (second language), their communication patterns were interactive and spiral as they interacted in their native Cantonese but linear and sequential as they interacted in English.[67]

The problem of language is most obvious when people speak different languages. Many terms are untranslatable, because the underlying concepts differ; for example, the fact that the Bulgarian word closest to 'ambitious' never carries a negative loading, as it does in the English term 'ambitious schemer'. Loan words can be a particular problem: for instance, in Kazakhstan the loan word 'executive' refers only to the Chief Executive. The terms *sabar, ikhlas* and *setia* identify core personal virtues in traditional Malay culture. They have no exact equivalents in English. For instance, *setia* combines elements of loyal, faithful and true. What counts as a bad event includes words or deeds that could lower someone's *manuah* (roughly dignity) or *nama* (reputation).

Therefore, someone who is *setia* to a politician will be highly reluctant to criticise them or do anything to cause them to have bad feelings.[68]

Differences in meaning can be just as significant, however, when each culture uses the 'same' language. If a British native tells her American friend to put the bags in the boot, the American may not know that she means her to place the luggage in the trunk of the car. While this is an obvious example, objects, events, experiences and feelings have a particular name solely because a community of people have arbitrarily decided so to name them.[69]

Box 3.9

Many colloquial expressions are particular to only one version of a language. For instance the following expressions are mostly used in only one version of English:

Hang in there. (An Americanism meaning, 'Keep trying and don't give up.')

Belt up! (An Anglicanism meaning, 'Shut up!')

Piddling around. (Another Americanism, which is quite rude for the British, meaning not doing anything much.)

She'll be right mate. (An Australianism meaning everything will be OK.)

Bob's your uncle. (An Anglicanism meaning arriving, succeeding or accomplishing.)

It is often not possible to be sure of the meaning without knowing the expressions of that culture. For example, the following differences occur between American and British English:

'Momentarily' in British English means 'for a moment', in American English it means 'in a moment', so that an air stewardess might say, 'We'll be landing momentarily.' This would have a very strange sound in British ears.

'Scheme' and 'collaborate' carry negative implications in US English, but not in British.

The following cultural variations in language use are well established:

Japanese people can speak to another using a selection of many different address forms to indicate explicitly any one of a whole range of relationships – for example, intimate, familiar, neutral, polite, deferential, authoritative. This illustrates the hierarchy and ceremony of interpersonal relationships in the society.

English people, when speaking, continually use the words *please* and *thank you* in their conversations, and often avoid direct statements. English language and behaviour aims to avoid offending or alienating the other person.

The Hindu language, Hindi, has separate words for: my sister's husband (*behnoi*), my husband's elder brother (*jait*), my husband's younger brother (*deva*), and my husband's sister's husband (*nandoya*). Kinship vocabulary is an indication to the nature of the more significant family relations in a culture. The single word *brother-in-law* in English indicates that one behaves similarly towards all the men in those different kinship statuses. The variety of words in Hindi, indicates that each of these categories of people is treated differently.

Greeks, too, have many different words for various family relationships and relatives that are very important in their large and extended families. Many of these words cannot be directly translated into English, as there is no exact word equivalent or in some cases there is not even an approximate word equivalent.

Long breaks in speaking are usual and acceptable between Finns, and are not mistaken for turn-taking signals.

Finns invest themselves personally in what they say, and to openly criticise others' opinions is to criticise them as a person.[a]

Source: (a) Kirra, K.M. (2000) 'Finns in interaction with non-Finns: problematic phenomena perceived as critical incidents', *Intercultural Communication*, 4: 109–23

National culture and non-verbal behaviour

Some non-verbal behaviours differ across culture groups – for example, voice tone. Latinos tend to vary their tone a great deal; Asians tend to favour extreme monotony, while Anglo-Saxons are in between. There are also differences in the way different culture groups sequence their communication. Anglo-Saxons, for example, tend to follow without overlapping (interrupting is rude); Latinos to overlap; and Asians to leave silence gaps.

There are universal features: there is always some norm to regulate non-verbal features of social interaction; bowing where it is used always signifies submission; similarly smiling is a universal sign of wanting to appease another. The meaning of most non-verbal behaviours, however, varies: head nodding and shaking, hissing and spitting, though having the same meaning in many cultures, all have different meanings in at least some – for instance, spitting is a sign of affection among the Masai of East Africa.

Facial expression, which has been shown to be linked to emotion, has both an innate and a cultural basis; culture modifies innate emotional expression in three ways:

- The event that gives rise to the emotion has a different meaning (a funeral could be an occasion of sorrow or joy).
- The reaction to emotions is affected (expressions of anger may not be shown because the person has been culturally induced to suppress anger).
- 'Display rules' such as those which make losers in competitions act as 'good' losers vary across cultures.[70]

Proxemics, the study of the way in which people use space as a part of interpersonal communication, recognises that, 'people of different cultures do have different ways in which they relate to one another spatially.'[71] It is well known that Arabs stand 'very close' when conversing. In fact, Arabs and Europeans differ on distance, facing, touching, loudness and eye contact.

National cultures and assertiveness, facework and rapport management

There are differences in the value that people from different backgrounds place on communication behaviours such as assertiveness. For example, American and Japanese

---

Box 3.10

Working with people in Russia, I'm struck by how they often reflect for several seconds before answering a question. Often they will not answer it and will not even refer to it. This is due to two factors, I was told. First they don't want to say an incorrect or inaccurate thing, so it's culturally better to say nothing, and they are accustomed to people considering their responses before replying. Second, to show yourself as too eager, or to state an incorrect fact in front of your superiors, was (and maybe in some places, still is) dangerous. I had to teach them how to give a quick answer, even if it was to say that they needed more information, but could give a reply later.

Source: E-mail from a financial expert, author's research

people appear to have differing attitudes towards being assertive. One study found that American subjects rated assertive behaviour more highly and as more competent than Japanese subjects did. Japanese subjects discriminated more between ingroup and outgroup members in their attitudes towards being assertive. They rated assertive behaviour more highly when performed by ingroup members than by outgroup members.[72]

A study that investigated face and facework during conflicts across four national cultures, China, Germany, Japan and the USA, found the following:

- Self-construals had the strongest effects on face concerns and facework. Independence was positively associated with self-face and dominating facework; interdependence was positively associated with other- and mutual-face and integrating and avoiding facework.
- Power distance had small, positive effects on all face concerns and on avoiding and dominating facework.
- Individualist, small power distance cultures had less other-face concern and avoiding facework, and more dominating facework than collectivist, large power distance cultures.
- Germans had more self- and mutual-face concerns and used defending more than North Americans.
- Chinese had more self-face concern and involved a third party more than Japanese.
- Relational closeness and status only had small effects on face concerns and facework behaviour.[73]

These findings, and those of earlier research[74] suggest that culture influences facework. However, observation and analysis of rapport management in meetings between the representatives of a British host company and a visiting Chinese business delegation showed that both parties, not just the (collectivist) Chinese, were strongly influenced by group rather than individual face concerns. The British were concerned about the company's reputation: 'They wanted the visitors to learn more about their company, and to go back to China with a deep and positive impression, firstly of the company and secondly of Britain. Similarly, the Chinese delegation presented themselves as a group, and was concerned about the group's face and the reputation of Chinese people in general. "You just tell him. Is it so easy to bully us Chinese, so easy to fool us?" Equally, both parties were more concerned with "own face" than "other face".' The researchers concluded that in different types of interactions and different cultural settings, different kinds of face and sociality rights may arise.[75]

By analysing the tape recording of an initial 'get-to-know-you' meeting between two German and two Chinese students, Günthner[76] identified cultural differences in how the two approach intercultural rapport management situations. After preliminary small talk, the Germans, whose hope was for 'a good argumentative exchange', launched a discussion on the position of women. During this discussion, the Germans used 'highly aggravated forms of dissent', such as distorting quotations of the opposing speaker's utterances and formally continuing the sentence of the previous (opposing) speaker only to show consequences which contradict their argument: 'Housework should be shared by both husband and wife.' 'Yes, and when they neither of them feel like doing it, then the wife has to do it.' The Chinese, on the other hand, showed reluctance to get into an argument and made repeated efforts to return the conversation to 'small talk' – efforts which failed because the Germans responded to concessions by focusing on any contradiction with what they had said before, rejected offers of compromise and only temporarily accepted a change of topic. When the Chinese did participate in the argument, they avoided formal disagreement; instead, they would list further aspects of their position, or formally agree, then give a qualification: 'Do you believe there is a natural limitation?' 'I believe not, but I must say, there is ... a bit.'

In addition to these differing expectations and ways of signalling dissent, there were differing norms for how to behave. The direct way of disagreeing was seen as 'very rude and inconsiderate behaviour' by the Chinese, but the Germans saw it as signs of argumentative involvement. The researcher commented: 'In this [German] culture, getting to know someone means finding out what the others' opinions and positions on different issues are and perhaps debating with them. Chinese responded to this by feeling "the much too strong willingness of the Germans to argue". In China an initial meeting between people who want to get to know one another would involve talking about oneself and the family and asking the others about their families. Only when this kind of rapport is well established may one start to discuss social and political issues.'

National culture and work communication

There is evidence for cultural effects on business communication, despite the common task focus. For instance, according to a study of complaint letters, US and Korean business writers prefer different structures and styles. The majority of the letters written by the US managers in this study followed the 'direct' pattern of identification of the problem, discussion of relevant information, request for action, and a buffer, with the buffer representing an optional move. Only a small proportion of the Korean letters followed the US model, despite the fact that they were written in English to conduct business with US companies. Instead, the standard Korean pattern was indirect: most led with relevant information about the problem before identifying the problem itself. This kind of delay often requires the reader to absorb details, sometimes relevant and sometimes not, before discovering the problem.[77]

In contrast to North American methods, Japanese people use common sense more than 'quantification' in management. For instance, instead of checklists, they use discussions and making resolutions to 'do better'. Information is shared with 'appropriate others', who also participate in making decisions, so that a sense of group involvement results. Making decisions takes longer, but implementation is more certain and often quicker. There is a preference for face-to-face contact, rather than by e-mail, memo or

---

Box 3.11

A Polish engineer called in a British international salesman to help interpret an American manual for a machine. The problem was the term 'stick-up point'. The British salesman had never heard of it and could not make it out from the context. When he got back to England, he telephoned the company and was told the phrase meant 'point of maximum deflection'; it came from the fact that the meter needle would 'stick' in the 'up' position at that point. The US engineer was mystified that its meaning was not obvious.

Source: Author's research

telephone. Japanese offices are usually open plan, allowing day-to-day awareness of others' non-verbal behaviour and its context, which allows them to be interpreted more effectively.

Within Europe, differences have been found in the models of business communication used by national cultures, based on different assumptions about relations and communication between a boss and subordinates. Marked differences in conversation rules were found between Finnish, Swedish and Austrian students of business. Finnish conversation rules encourage observation and reflection before speaking on important, controversial issues. Finns are often more likely to speak openly in one-on-one situations than in a group situation. They try to avoid open conflict and seek consensus via a strategy of listening and observing before speaking. This strategy can also lead to a polite, silent approach that avoids confrontation but leaves core controversial opinions unstated. In contrast, the Swedish and Austrian students in the study communicated according to conversation rules that encourage brainstorming. The goal is to get a variety of views on the table and to use polite verbalisation and phrasing of opinions when talking about problems and seeking consensus. They pursue strategies for talking around the problem with the goal of getting closer to a consensus without directly addressing a controversial issue.

However, the Austrian and Swedish ways of communicating during group discussions also differ from each other. Swedes are talkative and participatory by Finnish standards, but as one Swedish student told Austrians in her group, 'If we talk about it, people will think we consider it important.' The Swedish students used a style of communication that Austrian students occasionally considered blunt, but less blunt than the straightforward Finnish speech that follows the Finnish silence. All three of these approaches to communication differ from an American preference for debating with and/or challenging the 'other'.[78]

According to Aycan[79] in many developing countries, the pattern of communication in organisations is indirect, non-assertive, non-confrontational and usually directed downwards in terms of hierarchy. There is strong preference for face-to-face communication in business dealings. The context determines the way in which information is coded and understood. As such, there is room for subjective interpretation of the content and intent of the message.

Ethnicity and communication

Only a small amount of communication research has so far focused on the communication behaviours of people from different ethnic backgrounds within the same general culture, despite language being the most salient feature of ethnicity in symbolic terms.[80] What evidence there is, suggests that people from different ethnic backgrounds use different communication behaviours. For example, differences have been found in information requesting strategies. Second, differences have been found between the conversational improvement strategies (CIS) used by African and European Americans (AAs and EAs respectively). Conversational Improvement Strategies are used after 'failure' events, such as interactions not running smoothly or expectations being violated. African Americans self-reported as more likely to use active and mutual CISs, especially 'other orientation – involving the other person more, having patience with the other person or focusing on them' and 'avoidance – not bringing up unpleasant topics'. European Americans, in contrast, said they were more likely to use passive strategies that put the onus on the other person, such as 'giving in, apologizing or agreeing'.[81]

Ethnic differences in conveying and interpreting positive and negative messages have been found. A comparison of encoding and decoding of messages by Australian nationals found that positive messages by Australian and Italian men were decoded less accurately than positive messages by British men. On negative and neutral messages, Italian male speakers were decoded less accurately than Australian and British male speakers. There were fewer differences for female speakers. These results suggest that decoding and encoding are influenced by both social skills and attitudes towards the other interactors.[82]

Gender and communication

There is continuing debate about how differently men and women communicate. Most recent scholarship argues that women and men are more similar than different; however, the differences that do exist between men and women are enough to make a difference in how they create and interpret messages as well as in how they are evaluated as communicators. Within marriage, women and men have similar conceptions of friendships, social support, language use, intimacy, responses to anger, sadness and jealousy, encoding and decoding non-verbal deception and how to maintain conversations. In much communication research, being female or male explains less than five per cent of the variance in communication. However, gender differences are found in smiling and non-verbal sensitivity, flirting behaviours, marital conflict communication, especially the demand-withdraw pattern, and everyday conversational topics.[83]

There are gender differences in the basic message transmission and reception processes. Women are slightly better decoders of affect (feelings and attitudes) and considerably better encoders, especially with strangers.[84] A study showed that overall, positive messages were decoded worst and negative messages best; but men were worse on both positive and negative messages. Brain imaging research conducted at the Indiana University School of Medicine found that men listen with only one side of their brains, while women use both. A majority of the men showed activity exclusively in the temporal lobe on the left side of the brain, which is associated with listening and speech. The majority of women showed activity in the temporal lobe on both sides of the brain, although predominantly on the left. The right temporal lobe is associated with non-language listening, such as to voice tone.[85]

Women often soften their messages by adopting linguistic practices such as using tag questions (for instance, 'that's a good idea, don't you think?') and qualifiers (like 'perhaps', or 'might' instead of 'should'). Gender differences in speaking appear easy to recognise: a study found that people are extremely successful at identifying the gender of speakers from short pieces of written-down talk that lack any reference to the gender of the speaker. Socio-economic status and other personal characteristics of the listeners had almost no impact on respondents' ability to identify the gender of the speakers. The authors commented, '(the fact) that respondents should be able to recognize gender from such short excerpts, transcribed and out of context, suggests that distinct male and female voices exist and can be heard'.[86] However, recognition of gender varied dramatically for some of the extracts, suggesting that some talk (called 'voices') may not be gendered. This may be because gender is not always important, but 'waxes and wanes in the organization of group life'.[87]

In 1975, research was published that seemed to show that men interrupt their female conversation partners more than they interrupt other men. Women interrupted speakers of either gender less than men did. (Interruption is 'a device for exercising power and control in conversation' because it involves 'violations of speakers' turns at talk'.) However, a 1998 meta-analysis of 43 published studies indicated that men were more likely than women to initiate interruptions, but only to a slight extent. This effect was higher, though, in the case of intrusive interruptions as opposed to supportive interruptions. Intrusive interruptions occurred more often in unstructured talk, which suggests that work-related conversations may be less prone to male attempts to dominate.[88]

Men perceive women as dominating a discussion even when they contribute as little as 30 per cent of the talk. One explanation is that men think it is the 'natural order of things' for women to contribute significantly less to a group discussion than their male counterparts do. Research has shown that men talk more in formal versus informal tasks and more in public versus private communication. While most members of same-sex task teams produce similar amounts of verbal output, in mixed-sex teams the men produce more than the women. In public, for instance, men speak for a greater length of time and men's speech is more on the task while women's is more reinforcing. Men may tend to hold the floor for long periods, so that they dominate and prevent others from speaking. This dominance also implies higher social status and suggests that men believe themselves more competent to complete the tasks or to discuss the issues at hand than are women. Men use a more adversarial style in discussions, while women are likely to ask more questions.[89] It is, however, possible that women *let* men take more of the air time and that this behaviour reflects their self-perceived lower status – subordinates do the same for managers.

Carter[90] found from extended interview and journal data with nine mid-career women that their professional development is created and sustained largely through talk. This talk achieves transformative learning – learning that significantly revises beliefs, attitudes and values, and not just with instrumental, performance-based learning. Instead of analytical, point-counterpoint discussions, the women professionals' conversations were often highly personal and self-disclosing.

One summary view of gender differences in language use is that women use language on a more co-operative basis – they are concerned with 'connectedness'. Men tend to focus on using language to gain status or establish territory.[91] Politeness theory research shows that women are more likely than men to use a form that minimises the threat to the hearer's face. They may:

- Give their orders as requests, such as 'Please would you mind finishing this letter first?'
- Make their statements sound provisional by using qualifiers.
- Use tag questions as in 'I think we need to call a meeting, don't we?'
- Use disclaimers – 'I may be wrong, but ...'
- Use supportive rather than powerful vocabulary.

One researcher has found that use of politeness of these kinds can lead to some women being rated as less intelligent and less well informed than other people, including other women who do not use them. It is difficult, however, to know whether use of polite forms 'causes' these attributions, because men who use them are not similarly downgraded.[92] There may be a halo effect from the gender of the polite speaker, in the same way as some occupations, such as teaching, have been downgraded in social estimation because they are largely women's occupations.

Some women use body language to express submissiveness. They may take up less physical space in relation to their size than men, hover in the background or lower their eyes when looked at instead of making eye contact. Women managers, in contrast, sometimes show their understanding of the subcultural meaning of non-verbal behaviour by dressing in a masculine way or decorating their offices in a neutral 'sexless' manner.

However, gender differences in communication are not always obvious. For instance, one American study found that in mixed-gender groups of adolescents, young African American women contributed more equally with African American men than White women with White men. This was true overall, in terms of the level of activity and also of one measure of influence. Some of the differences were quite marked – unassertive utterances such as 'yeah, uh-huh' made up 36 per cent of White female adolescents' speech acts, but only 12 per cent to 17 per cent of those of each of the other race-gender categories of participants. This pattern suggests a distinctly less assertive speech style among the White female adolescents than among either African American female adolescents or male adolescents of either ethnic group.[93]

A review of research on interpersonal conflict and anger shows that women and men do not consistently behave in ways indicated by traditional sex stereotypes. Actual behaviour shows that, if anything, women are more competitive than men, that men have a tendency to avoid conflict and that, except for crying, both genders express anger in the same ways. This applies particularly in private life. In public and social domains, such as work, expectations based on sex stereotypes are stronger and more constraining, while power differences between the genders can also lead to differences in the behaviour of men and women.[94]

There are several different kinds of explanation for gender differences in communication. One is based on findings that gender language style preferences parallel those which distinguish national cultures, that is, direct versus indirect, succinct versus elaborate, personal versus contextual, and instrumental versus affective.[95] This might suggest that women and men differ culturally along the lines of individualism–collectivism, etc., though no conclusive studies have been done. Tannen[96] also argues that gender differences can best be observed from a cross-cultural approach, one that does not assume that differences arise from men's efforts to dominate women. Instead, masculine and feminine styles of discourse are viewed as two distinct cultural dialects rather than as inferior or superior ways of speaking. While some scholars do not believe that identifying gendered communication styles is important or even appropriate,[97] others, such as Tannen believe that ignoring those differences is riskier than naming them.

Are women less assertive than men? There is some evidence that compared with male managers, women managers are more inclined to ingratiate; less likely to focus on the importance of their jobs to the organisation and society; less likely to claim success, but more likely to report low performance expectations and make attributions to lack of ability; four times less likely to report that they would move directly to coercive tactics if faced with a non-compliant subordinate. Other findings, though, suggest that both male and female managers display 'masculine' characteristics. The environment in a typical organisation may socialise women into behaving like 'honorary men'.[98]

Whatever the causes, both stereotype-based impressions of and actual differences in ways of communicating tend to be to women's disadvantage at work. For instance, research shows that how credible an individual is judged to be is influenced not only by their status and expertise but also by speech style and vocal and facial qualities linked to gender.[99] Women's linguistic styles affect evaluators' attributions of truthfulness, guilt, deception and dominance. A further effect is to render women 'silent'.

In those discourses that are more highly valued in society (religious, political, legal, scientific and poetic discourses) women's voices are rarely, if ever heard.

One response to the damage done to women by masculine power-based concepts of appropriate talk is feminist critiques which (1) point out the dangers of hierarchies, linear thinking and assuming that logic and science, particularly technology, can solve our problems (2) attempt to root out masculine biases in word choice, metaphor, labels, and the like (3) uncover the power equation in communication settings and more directly engage with and include audience members, and (4) explore the relationship of power and knowledge to demonstrate that by keeping important information from others one participates in a kind of enslavement. Feminist writers also urge black women to use their position as 'outsiders within' to reject imposed hierarchies and take up new positions that they define and determine.[100]

Ethno-cultural and gender effects can be multiplicative. Research found that women in the Mexican region Tenejapa are constrained to be polite, co-operative and meek in their conversation. To express anger and confrontation they are obliged to emphasise only lack of agreement and co-operation with an adversary.[101]

Communication of older people and those with disabilities

How some older people and some people with disabilities communicate is affected by both intrinsic and externally provoked factors. The clearest communication effects of intrinsic disability occur in people with a hearing impairment. Generally, communicators who are born with a hearing impairment speak with low fluency and mispronunciations; they also have difficulty in controlling how loudly they speak. People who are hard of hearing commonly repeat what has already been uttered and interrupt others because they do not hear them talking. Hard of hearing people mainly communicate by relying on their residual hearing, hearing aids, speech reading and bluffing. Some adults who become deaf later in life have difficulty adjusting to their deafness but a few studies show that many late-deafened people can communicate perfectly well.[102] The intrinsic effects of ageing on communication abilities are also variable. Though there is little evidence for changes in communication abilities and practices among people below the age of 60, there is some for progressive changes after that age, although there are wide variations from individual to individual. With age, working-memory capacity and processing speed decline in normal adults. This may lead to them having more difficulty in interpreting complex syntax. In addition, older adults have more problems than younger adults in retrieving proper names. This normal, age-related name-retrieval problem can lead interlocutors wrongly to infer more cognitive disability than simply forgetting a name. Also, some older individuals have been shown to be quite insensitive to the needs and concerns of their younger conversational partners; to introduce embarrassing self-disclosures; and to talk excessively with a lack of focus on the general content of the conversation. However, these findings all relate to private-life situations and we have no evidence on whether the same communication problems arise with older people who are at work.

Whatever the intrinsic communication situation of some older people and those with disabilities, they are likely to be affected by the way they are addressed. It has been shown that messages to negatively stereotyped older adults are shorter, less complex and more demeaning in tone. There is clear evidence that patronising talk from younger individuals to older adults is common. It is likely that being spoken to in these ways affects how older adults communicate.[103] However, except among older people with less education, negative social experiences do not adversely affect older adults' ability to function.[104]

Box 3.12

A study showed that similarity in age influences the likelihood of technical communication between co-workers, but not all that strongly. In a study of a 92–member technical project group, the coefficient of determination between age similarity and communication with other project members was 0.18.

Source: Zengler, T. and Lawrence, B. (1989) 'Organisational demography: the different effects of age and tenure distributions on technical communication', *Academy of Management Journal*, **32**: 331–50

The responses of people with disabilities to how others speak to them include shorter interactions, decreased eye contact and low verbal immediacy.[105] These are ways of avoiding communication. Gaze is influenced by the stereotypes and prejudices about disabled people. People with visible disabilities can be made to feel worthless, unattractive and stressed by how others look at them. This happens especially in the medical context (doctors perform 'public stripping'), but also within everyday social interaction. When one person in an interaction has a visible impairment the other person gains privileged information and therefore power.[106] According to Morris, 'It is not only physical limitations that restrict us to our homes and those whom we know. It is the knowledge that each entry into the public world will be dominated by stares, by condescension, by pity and by hostility.'[107] People whose disability is invisible may fear 'exposure'.

Religion and communication

Are there differences that may be relevant at work in the communication behaviours of religious and non-religious people and between adherents of different religions? It might be expected that religious people will be unlikely to use blasphemy, perhaps less likely than others to use swear words generally, and possibly be more easily offended by others who do.

One study found differences between religious groups in both communication behaviour and the factors underlying it. It found major differences between two denominations – Protestant and Catholic Christians in Northern Ireland – on measures of group identification, self-disclosure, attraction, trust and outgroup contact; on verbal and non-verbal behaviour when speaking with people from the other denominations; and on attitudes and experiences. Such differences imply that there may be a 'religious effect' on communication behaviour generally.[108] Another study found partial support for a relationship between a 'quest' religious orientation and an attentive communicator style, although no more general relationship between religious orientation and communicator style was found.[109]

Communication by religious people about religion has certain characteristics: it cannot be expressed in non-figurative ways, it identifies metaphysical referents that can be grasped but not defined and it is metaphorical. The metaphors that communicators use become fraught with moral and ethical repercussions, as in the use of war metaphors by Christians.[110] Clearly, this is a long way from the usual discourses of business or management. However, we do not know to what extent people can be 'diglossal' between religious and other ways of communicating or to what extent they may 'interpret' from one to the other before speaking or responding.[111] Some religious groups emphasise spontaneity in prayer, which may carry over to other discourses.[112]

Social class and communication

Many working class people, particularly those from mainly oral cultures, tend to prefer a speaking style that presumes knowledge shared with the audience, 'shows' rather than 'tells' and implies linkages among a wide range of topics, which need not be presented chronologically. In working-class environments, 'people simply talk and do not have to prove everything that they say'.[113] Systematic studies show that middle-class speakers tend to talk more, use more varied vocabulary and employ more varied grammatical constructions than working-class speakers. There is evidence that class differences in communication exist also on the non-verbal level – appearing already in pre-school age children; middle-class children are less affected than working-class children by whether an instruction is spoken in a positive, neutral or negative tone of voice. However, the notion that in some (sub)cultures language is more simple or primitive is probably wrong. The basic structuring principles on which language is founded appear to be universal and most linguists now assume that languages do not differ greatly in their underlying structures or in their formal characteristics. In all languages, sentences are hierarchically structured and their interrelationships are equally complex. The same applies to the language of people of different socio-economic status or ethnicity – the rules for constructing sentences are of equal difficulty and complexity in all cases.

Marginalised groups

There is a body of theory and research, termed co-cultural communication, which asserts that in interactions between minority or marginalised group members and those from dominant groups, the communication of those from the subordinate group has particular features. Examples are given in Table 3.3. 'The ongoing research, termed co-cultural theory, explores the common patterns of communication both across and within these different marginalized groups.'[114]

Table 3.3　　*Co-cultural communication practices summary*

Practice	Brief description
Emphasising commonalities	Focusing on human similarities while downplaying or ignoring co-cultural differences
Developing positive face	Assuming a gracious communicator stance where one is more considerate, polite and attentive to dominant group members
Censoring self	Remaining silent when comments from dominant group members are inappropriate, indirectly insulting or highly offensive
Averting controversy	Averting communication away from controversial or potentially dangerous subject areas
Extensive preparation	Engaging in an extensive amount of detailed (mental, concrete) groundwork prior to interactions with dominant group members
Overcompensating	Conscious attempts, consistently enacted in response to a pervasive fear of discrimination, to become a 'superstar'

Table 3.3   *cont'd*

Practice	Brief description
Manipulating stereotypes	Conforming to commonly accepted beliefs about group members as a strategy to exploit them for personal gain
Bargaining	Striking a covert or overt arrangement with dominant group members where both parties agree to ignore co-cultural differences
Dissociating	Making a concerted effort to elude any connection with behaviour typically associated with one's co-cultural group
Mirroring	Adopting dominant group codes in an attempt to make one's co-cultural identity less (or totally not) visible
Strategic distancing	Avoiding any association with other co-cultural group members in attempt to be perceived as a distinct individual
Ridiculing self	Invoking or participating in discourse, either passively or actively, that is demeaning to co-cultural group members
Increasing visibility	Covertly, yet strategically, maintaining a co-cultural presence within dominant structures
Dispelling stereotypes	Countering myths of generalised group characteristics and behaviours through the process of just being one's self
Communicating self	Interacting with dominant group members in an authentic, open way. Used by those with strong self-concepts
Intragroup networking	Identifying and working with other co-cultural group members who share common philosophies, convictions, and goals
Utilising liaisons	Identifying specific dominant group members who can be trusted for support, guidance and assistance
Educating other	Taking the role of teacher in co-cultural interactions; enlightening dominant group members of co-cultural norms, values, etc
Confronting	Using aggressive methods, including ones that seemingly violate the rights of others, to assert one's voice
Gaining advantage	Inserting references to co-cultural oppression as a means to provoke dominant group reactions and gain advantage
Avoiding	Maintaining a distance from dominant group members; refraining from activities or locations where dominance is an advantage
Maintaining barriers	Imposing a psychological distance from dominant group members through the use of verbal and non-verbal cues
Exemplifying strengths	Promoting the recognition of co-cultural group strengths, past accomplishments, and contributions to society
Embracing stereotypes	Applying a negotiated reading to dominant group perceptions and merging them into a positive co-cultural self-concept
Attacking	Inflicting psychological pain through personal attacks on dominant group members' self-concept
Sabotaging others	Undermining the ability of dominant group members to take full advantage of their privilege inherent in dominant structures

Source: Orbe, M.P. (1998) 'From the standpoint(s) of traditionally muted groups: explicating a co-cultural communication theoretical model', *Communication Theory*, **8**(1): 1–26, by permission of Oxford University Press

Six factors have been identified as central to the co-cultural communication process. These are preferred outcome, field of experience, abilities, situation, perceived costs and rewards, and communication approach. These factors are always present but their roles may vary greatly from one co-cultural interaction to another.

Professional, business and organisational discourses and their reception

Professionals, such as doctors and lawyers, business executives in particular industries and company employees often use vocabulary, phrases and ways of speaking that are unknown to outsiders. These discourses may be the most efficient ways of talking about what are specialist areas, but they also have the effect of reinforcing the speaker's group membership and of excluding people who are not members of the group.

A study in two multinational accounting firms found that the work socialisation of trainee accountants led to their professional identities and discourse prioritising 'the client'. As a result, the authors suggested, management control, friends, family and the profit motive are all 'written out' of the accountants' professional discourse.[115] In certain roles, such as that of clergy, 'immediacy' is important in the evaluation of the role holder. From qualitative research, eight categories of immediacy have been identified: personal interest in the 'client' (parishioner) and its opposite, expressing appreciation for commendable work and its opposite, inclusion and exclusion, unexpected role behaviour and support for personal contributions.[116]

The communication expectations of those with whom professionals deal probably reflect their usual discourses. A study found that there were both similarities and differences in US and Hong Kong Chinese patients' expectations of communications from medical staff. The main similarities were expectations of task competence, technical competence and information seeking; important differences were that the US patients looked for friendliness from receptionists and nurses and socio-emotional support from physicians; the Chinese patients did not expect these from their communications with medical staff.[117]

> For most classifications of people, at least some significant differences have been found in their ways of communicating. For the most researched classifications, those of national culture and gender, the significant differences are numerous.

3.4 SUMMARY

This chapter has been concerned with cultural and subcultural differences in how we communicate. Although there are still large gaps in our knowledge, enough has been found through research to suggest that there are important differences between groups. Communication states, traits and styles, responses to situations, verbal and non-verbal communication, discourses, messages, language and how it is used, dialects, facework, politeness, anxiety and uncertainty management, rapport management and conflict management styles all reveal such differences. At least some of the differences in these aspects of communication occur in different cultural and ethnic groups, genders, religious groups, social classes, age groups and those with and without specific disabilities, professions, businesses and organisations. It is too soon to be able to say precisely which differences are to be found in which kinds of group or whether all such will be found eventually in all kinds of group. It is also likely that group membership is not determinate, whatever its influence. Individual and situational variations will sometimes over-ride or compensate for group differences. However, we do know that effective intercultural communication depends on being aware of possible group differences in how others communicate.

QUESTIONS AND EXERCISES

1. In a mixed-culture or subculture group, identify as many differences as possible in ways of communicating verbally and non-verbally.
2. Discuss ways in which cultural and subcultural differences in rhetorical sensitivity, assertiveness and argumentativeness might affect intercultural communication at work.
3. In a mixed-culture group, discuss the meaning of 'argumentativeness' in the different cultures represented, in the light of the material given in the text.
4. Which of the following, if any, apply to people's responses to situations?

   (a) They adjust their goals if the situation requires it.
   (b) They evaluate others differently in different situations.
   (c) They use more energy and time to communicate according to the situation.
   (d) They pursue strategies to achieve their interaction goals.

5. Explain in your own words the key differences between the culture-as-shared-values approach and the culture-in-context (or discourse/practice) approach to communication.
6. How may cultural differences affect how different situations impact on behaviour? Give at least one work-related example.
7. Give two work-related examples of restricted codes that might be used in your culture. Then 'translate' them into elaborated code equivalents.
8. In which of the following circumstances, if any, are restricted codes used?

   (a) in routine situations in which conventional 'goals' and plans are 'given' to actors in closed societies;
   (b) when people want to express group membership rather than individual differences;
   (c) when speakers expect marked differences from those with whom they are interacting;
   (d) when there are marked differences of status among interactors.

9. Add as many examples as possible to the list of cultural or subcultural variations in non-verbal behaviour given in the text. Try to find at least one example of each of the following: posture, gesture, gaze, eye contact, facial expression.
10. Discuss the implications (preferably in a work-related context) of the cultural difference that people from some collectivist cultures depend on seeking harmony to achieve the co-operation needed for communication, whereas people from individualist cultures depend on truthfulness. How can intercultural communicators adjust for these differences?
11. The text gives an example of a culture-specific speech act. The example given relates to some societies' obligations on a host to give away possessions that a guest praises. Find other examples.
12. The following are extracts from business complaint letters: (a) 'You have charged us the wrong amount'; 'Please send us a replacement at your earliest convenience'; (b) 'It appears that there is a discrepancy in the invoice compared with the estimate'; 'We would like to request that you consider replacing this item'. Compare (a) and (b) in terms of clarity, effect on the supplier–customer relationship and overall effectiveness. How far do you think your evaluation is related to your culture?
13. Using the material given in the text on information-seeking by high- and low-context communicators, analyse which of these types of communicator applies to people you meet for the first time in the near future.

14. Complete the questionnaire.

In my culture people at work usually	Strongly agree	Agree	Neither agree nor disagree	Disagree	Strongly disagree
1. Avoid open discussions of of differences					
2. Exert pressure on their peers to make decisions in their favour					
3. Try to find a middle course or compromise to resolve an impasse					
4. Give in to the wishes of their peers					
5. Try to give and take so that a compromise can be made					
6. Try to satisfy the expectations of their peers					
7. Try to avoid unpleasant exchanges with their peers					
8. Keep disagreements with their peers to themselves to prevent disrupting their relationship					

For guidance on how to score and interpret this questionnaire, see Appendix C

15. How would you most naturally express the following in speaking to a subordinate?
    - A criticism of their work
    - Bad news about their hoped-for promotion
    - An order to do a piece of work
    - A compliment on their work
    - An apology
    - Acceptance of a compliment
    - Accepting an offer to work late
    - A promise

    Compare your answers with colleagues from a different culture or subculture.

16. Why do you think that AUM theory predicts that an increase in collectivism will produce a decrease in uncertainty in outgroup communication relative to ingroup communication?

17. In a mixed cultural or subcultural group, discuss the contention of rapport management theory that people are as much concerned with their 'rights' in interactions as with their 'face'.

18. Complete the questionnaire.

When managers ask subordinates to do something they should	Strongly agree	Agree	Neither agree nor disagree	Disagree	Strongly disagree
1. Explain the reason for the request and its objective merits					
2. Aim to create a favourable impression, relying on friendliness					
3. Use loyalty appeals					
4. Employ a forceful manner, making, demands and setting deadlines					

For guidance on scoring and interpreting your answers, see Appendix C

19. Complete the questionnaire.

When conflicts arise at work, people from my culture tend to:	Strongly agree	Agree	Neither agree nor disagree	Disagree	Strongly disagree
1. Seek a compromise					
2. Try to get a third party to adjudicate or arbitrate					
3. Try to bring all their concerns out in the open so that issues can be resolved in the best possible way					
4. Collaborate with their colleagues to come up with decisions acceptable to all					
5. Try to win					
6. Try to work with colleagues for a proper understanding of the problem					
7. Try to get a third party to mediate					
8. Place more emphasis on preserving the relationship than on winning					

For guidance on scoring and interpreting your answers, see Appendix C

20. What explanation would you suggest for Gudykunst *et al.* (1998)'s finding that uncertainty avoidance is correlated with the expressiveness of a culture's communication style?
21. How might Americans' willingness to self-disclose and their tolerance of criticism in business (by comparison to Koreans') be related to the cultural factors described in Chapter 2?
22. Complete the questionnaire.

In my culture, people	Strongly agree	Agree	Neither agree nor disagree	Disagree	Strongly disagree
1. Try to state their points as explicitly as possible					
2. Speak frankly about issues					
3. Feel comfortable with silence					
4. Expect the listener to make as much effort to understand as the speaker to be clear					
5. Respond non-verbally rather than with questions or comments					
6. Rely heavily on hard data at work					
7. Follow conventions closely					

For guidance on scoring and interpreting your answers, see Appendix C

23. Explain why language can be seen as the 'gateway' to culture.
24. Find examples of terms that are untranslatable into English, either from your own language or by interviewing a native speaker of another language.
25. Tannen (1990) argues that gender differences in communication are based in women's lower power-orientation. How good an explanation do you think this is for the differences described in Section 3.2?

NOTES AND REFERENCES

1. Hewstone, M., Stroebe, W., Codol, J.P. and Stephenson, G.M. (eds) (1988) *Introduction to Social Psychology*, Oxford: Basil Blackwell.
2. Sarbaugh, L.E. (1988) 'A taxonomic approach to intercultural communication', in Kim, Y.Y. and Gudykunst, W.B. (eds) *Theories in Intercultural Communication*, Newbury Park, CA: Sage.
3. Haslett, B. (1989) 'Communication and language acquisition within a cultural context', in Ting-Toomey S. and Korzenny, F. (eds) *Language, Communication and Culture: Current Directions*, Newbury Park, CA: Sage.
4. Scollon, R. and Scollon, S. (1981) *Narrative, Literacy and Face in Interethnic Communication*, Norwood, NJ: Ablex Publishing Corporation.
5. Hart, R.P. and Burks, D.M. (1972) 'Rhetorical sensitivity and social interaction', *Speech Monographs*, **39**: 75–91.
6. Langrish, S. (1981) 'Assertive training', in Cooper, C.L. (ed.) *Improving Interpersonal Relations: Some Approaches to Social Skills Training*, London: Gower.
7. Ibid.
8. Waldron, V.R. (1999) 'Communication practices of followers, members, and proteges: the case of upward influence tactics', *Communication Yearbook*, **22**: 251–99.
9. Kim, M.-S., Aune, K.S., Hunter, J.E., Kim, H.-J. and Kim, J.-S. (2001) 'The effect of culture and self-construals on predispositions toward verbal communication', *Human Communication Research*, **27**(3): 382–408.
10. Schullery, N.M. (1998) 'The optimum level of argumentativeness for employed women', *The Journal of Business Communication*, **35**: 346–67.
11. Horvath, C.W. (1995) 'Biological origins of communicator style', *Communication Quarterly*, **43**: 394–407.
12. Cody, M.J. and McLaughlin, M.L. (1985) 'The situation as a construct in interpersonal communication research', in Knapp, M.L. and Miller, G.R. (eds) *Handbook of Interpersonal Communication*, Beverley Hills, CA: Sage.
13. Hall, E.T. (1976) *Beyond Culture*, New York: Doubleday.
14. Bernstein, B. (1971) *Class, Codes and Control: Theoretical Studies Toward a Sociology of Language*, London: Routledge and Kegan Paul.
15. Leigh, J. (2000) 'Implications of universal and parochial behaviour for intercultural communication', *Electronic Journal of Communication*, **4**, November. URL: www.cios.org/www/eju/v4n 23L.htm
16. Trudgill, P. (1983) (Revision of 1974 Edition), *Sociolinguistics: An Introduction to Language and Society*, Harmondsworth, Middlesex: Penguin Books.
17. Harrison, R. (1974) *Beyond Words: An Introduction to Nonverbal Communication*, Englewood Cliffs, NJ: Prentice-Hall.
18. Gallois, C. and Callan, V.J. (1986) 'Decoding emotional messages: influence of ethnicity, sex, message type and channel', *Journal of Personality and Social Psychology*, **51**(4): 755–62.
19. Birdwhistell, R. (1970) *Kinesics and Context*, Philadelphia, PA: University of Pennsylvania Press.
20. Oyama, R. (2003) 'Visual communication across cultures: a study of visual semiotics in Japanese and British advertisements', *Intercultural Communication Journal*, 191–219'. URL: http://www.immi.se/intercultural/nr3/abstract3.htm
21. Rashotte, L.S. (2002) 'What does that smile mean? The meaning of nonverbal behaviors in social interaction', *Social Psychology Quarterly*, **65**(1): 92–102.
22. Grice, H.P. (1975) 'Logic and conversation', in Cole, P. and Morgan, J. (eds) *Syntax and Semantics*, **3**, New York: Academic Press.
23. Searle, J. (1969) *Speech Acts: An Essay in the Philosophy of Language*, Cambridge: Cambridge University Press.

24. Van Dijk, T.A. (ed.) (1997) *Discourse as Structure and Process. Discourse Studies. A Multidisciplinary Introduction. Vol. 1*, London: Sage.
25. Zaidman, N. (2001) 'Cultural codes and language strategies in business communication between Israeli and Indian businesspeople', *Management Communication Quarterly*, **14**(3): 408–41.
26. Ibid.
27. Kim, M.-S., Hunter, J.E., Miyahara, A., Horvath, A., Bresnahan, M. and Yoon, H. (1996) 'Individual- vs. culture-level dimensions of individualism and collectivism: effects on preferred conversational styles', *Communication Monographs*, **63**: 29–49.
28. Ibid.
29. Kim, M.-S., and Wilson, S.R. (1994) 'A cross-cultural comparison of implicit theories of requesting', *Communication Monographs*, **61**: 210–35.
30. Kim, M.-S. and Bresnahan, M. (1996) 'Cognitive basis of gender communication: a cross-cultural investigation of perceived constraints in requesting', *Communication Quarterly*, **44**: 53–69.
31. Baldwin, J.R., and Hunt, S.K. (2002) 'Information-seeking behavior in intercultural and intergroup communication', *Human Communication Research*, **28**(2): 272–86.
32. Goffman, E. (1959) *The Presentation of Self in Everyday Life*, Garden City, NY: Doubleday, p. 3.
33. Ting-Toomey, S. (1988) 'A face negotiation theory', in Kim, Y.Y. and Gudykunst, W. (eds) *Theories in Intercultural Communication*, Newbury Park, CA: Sage.
34. Katriel, T. (1991) *Communal Webs: Communication and Culture in Contemporary Israel*, Albany: SUNY Press.
35. Ting-Toomey, S., Gao, G., Trubisky, P., Yang, Z., Kim, H., Lin, S.L. and Nishida, T. (1991) 'Culture, face maintenance, and styles of handling interpersonal conflict: a study in five cultures', *The International Journal of Conflict Management*, **2**: 275–96.
36. Lebra, T. (1971) 'The social mechanism of guilt and shame: the Japanese case', *Anthropological Quarterly*, **44**(4): 241–55.
37. Brown, P. and Levinson, S.C. (1978) 'Universals in language usage: politeness phenomena', in Goody, E.N. (ed.) *Questions and Politeness: Strategies in Social Interaction*: pp. 56–289. Cambridge, Cambridge University Press.
38. Collier, M.J. (1989) 'Cultural and intercultural communication competence: current approaches and directions', *International Journal of Intercultural Relations*, **13**: 287–302.
39. Stewart, C.M., Shields, S.F. and Sen, N. (1998) 'Diversity in on-line discussions: A Study of cultural and gender differences in Listservs', *Electronic Journal of Communication*, **8**(3/4).
40. Kim, M.S. and Wilson, S.R. (1994) op. cit.
41. Berger, C.R. and Calabrese, R.J. (1975) 'Some explorations in initial interactions and beyond', *Human Communication Research*, **1**: 99–112. See also: Berger, C.R. (1987) 'Communicating under uncertainty', in Roloff, M.E. and Miller, G.R. (eds) *Interpersonal Processes*, Newbury Park, CA: Sage.
42. Gudykunst, W.B. (1988) 'Uncertainty and anxiety', in Kim, Y.Y. and Gudykunst, W.B. (eds), *Theories in Intercultural Communication*: pp. 123–56. Newbury Park, CA: Sage.
43. Spencer-Oatey, H. (2002) 'Managing rapport in talk: using rapport sensitive incidents to explore the motivational concerns underlying the management of relations', *Journal of Pragmatics*, **34**: 529–45.
44. Pavlidou, T.-S. (2000) 'Telephone conversations in Greek and German: attending to the relationship aspect of communication', in Spencer-Oatey, H. (ed.) *Culturally Speaking: Managing Rapport Through Talk Across Cultures*: pp. 121–40. London: Continuum.
45. Fitch, K.L. (1994) 'A cross-cultural study of directive sequences and some implications for compliance-gaining research', *Communication Monographs*, **61**: 185–209.
46. Sullivan, J. and Taylor, S. (1991) 'A Cross-cultural test of compliance-gaining theory', *Management Communication Quarterly*, **5**(2): 220–39.

47. Oetzel, J.G., Ting -Toomey, S., Yokochi, Y., Masumoto, T. and Takai, J. (2000) 'A typology of facework behaviors in conflicts with best friends and relative strangers', *Communication Quarterly*, **48**(4): 397–419.

48. Triandis, H. (2000) 'Culture and conflict', *International Journal of Psychology*, **35**(2): 145–52.

49. Ting-Toomey, S. and Kurogi, A. (1998) 'Facework competence in intercultural conflict: an updated face-negotiation theory', *International Journal of Intercultural Relations*, **22**: 187–225.

50. Gluckman, M. (1954) *The Judicial Process Among the Barotse of Northern Rhodesia*, Manchester: University Press for the Rhodes-Livingston Institute.

51. Bazerman, M.H., Curhan, J.R., Moore, D.A. and Valley, K.L. (2000) 'Negotiation', *Annual Review of Psychology*, **51**: 279–314.

52. D'silva, M.U. and Whyte, L.O. (1998) 'Cultural differences in conflict styles: Vietnamese refugees and established residents', *Howard Journal of Communications*, **9**(1): 57–68.

53. Cushman, D.P. and King, S.S. (1999) *Continuously Improving an Organization's Performance. High-speed Management*, Albany, NY: SUNY Press.

54. Tjosvold, D., Hui, C. and Law, K.S. (2001) 'Constructive conflict in China: cooperative conflict as a bridge between East and West', *Journal of World Business*, **36**(2): 166–83.

55. Bazerman, M. H. *et al.* (2000) op.cit.

56. Cai, D.A. and Fink, E.L. (2002) 'Conflict style differences between individualists and collectivists', *Communication Monographs*, **69**(1): 67–87.

57. Kim, M.-S. and Leung, T. (2000) 'A multicultural view of conflict management styles: review and critical synthesis', *Communication Yearbook*, **23**: 227–69.

58. Thompson, N. (2003) *Communication and Language: A Handbook of Theory and Practice*, Basingstoke: Palgrave Macmillan.

59. Kim, M:-S. (2001) op. cit.

60. Gudykunst, W.B., Matsumoto, Y., Ting-Toomey, S., Nishida, T., Kim, S. and Heyman, S. (1996) 'The influence of cultural individualism–collectivism, self-construals and individual values on communication styles across cultures', *Human Communication Research*, **22**: 507–34.

61. Hofstede, G. (1991) *Cultures and Organizations: Software of the Mind*, London: McGraw Hill.

62. Park, M.Y., Dillon, W.T. and Mitchell, K.L. (1998) 'Korean business letters: strategies for effective complaints in cross-cultural communication', *The Journal of Business Communication*, **35**: 328–45.

63. Ramsey, S.J. (1998) 'Interactions between North Americans and Japanese: considerations of communication style', in Bennett, M.J. (ed.) *Basic Concepts of Intercultural Communication: Selected Readings*, Maine: Intercultural Press.

64. Armstrong, G.B. and Kaplowitz, S.A. (2001) 'Sociolinguistic inference and intercultural coorientation: a Bayesian model of communicative competence in intercultural interaction', *Human Communication Research*, **27** (3): 350–81.

65. Babcock, R.D. and Du-Babcock, B. (2001) 'Language-based communication zones in international business communication', *The Journal of Business Communication*, **38**: 372–412.

66. Park, M.Y. *et al.* (1998) op. cit.

67. Mobo, C. and Gao, F. (2000) 'Influences of native culture and language on intercultural communication: the case of PRC student immigrants in Australia', *Intercultural Communication*, **4**: 33–53.

68. Goddard, C. (2001) '*Sabar, ikhlas, setia – patient, sincere, loyal*? Contrastive semantics of some "virtues" in Malay and English', *Journal of Pragmatics*, **33**: 653–81.

69. Samovar, L.A. and Porter, R.E. (1985) 'Introduction', in Samovar, L.A. and Porter, R.E. (eds) *Intercultural Communication: A Reader, 4th edn*, Belmont, CA: Wadsworth.

70. Ekman, P. and Friesen, W.V. (1968) 'Nonverbal behaviour in psychotherapy research', in Schlein, J.M. (ed.) *Research in Psychotherapy, Vol.3*, Washington, DC: American Psychological Association.

71. Birdwhistell, R. (1970) *Kinesics and Context*, Philadelphia: University of Pennsylvania Press.
72. Singhal, A. and Motoko, N. (1993) 'Assertiveness as communication competence: a comparison of the communication styles of American and Japanese students', *Asian Journal of Communication*, **3**(1): 1–18.
73. Oetzel, J., Ting-Toomey, S., Masumoto, T., Yokochi, Y., Pan, X., Takai, J. and Wilcox, R. (2001) 'Face and facework in conflict: a cross-cultural comparison of China, Germany, Japan, and the United States', *Communication Monographs*, **68**(3): 235–58.
74. Ting-Toomey, S. *et al.* (1991) op. cit.
75. Spencer-Oatey, H. and Xing, J. (2000) 'A problematic Chinese business visit to Britain', in Spencer-Oatey, H. (ed.) *Culturally Speaking*: pp. 272–88. London: Continuum.
76. Günthner, S. (2000) 'Argumentation and resulting problems in the negotiation of rapport in a German–Chinese conversation', in Spencer-Oatey, H. (ed.) Culturally Speaking, pp. 218–39. London: Continuum.
77. Park, M.Y. *et al.* (1998) op. cit.
78. Auer-Rizzi, W. and Berry, M. (2000) 'Business vs. cultural frames of reference in group decision making: interactions among Austrian, Finnish, and Swedish Business students', *The Journal of Business Communication*, **37**(3): 264–92.
79. Aycan, Z. (2002) 'Leadership and teamwork in developing countries: challenges and opportunities', in Lonner, W.J., Dinnel, D.L., Hayes, S.A. and Sattler, D.N. (eds) *Online Readings in Psychology and Culture* (unit 15, chapter 8). URL: http://www.wwu.edu/~culture
80. Thompson, N. (2003) op. cit.
81. Martin, J.N., Hecht, M.L. and Larkey, L.K. (1994) 'Conversational improvement strategies for interethnic communication: African American and European American perspectives', *Communication Monographs*, **61**(3): 236–55.
82. Gallois, C. and Callan, V.J. (1986) op. cit.
83. Canary, D.J. and Dindia, K. (eds) (1998) *Sex Differences and Similarities in Communication: Critical Essays and Empirical Investigations of Sex and Gender in Interaction*, Mahwah, NJ: Lawrence Erlbaum Associates.
84. Hall, E.T. (1976) op. cit.
85. Paper presented Tuesday, 28 November 2002, at the 86th Scientific Assembly and Annual Meeting of the Radiological Society of North America (RSNA).
86. Wolfinger, N.H. and Rabow, A. (1997) 'The different voices of gender: social recognition', *Current Research in Social Psychology*, **2**(6): 50–65.
87. Thorne, B. (1993) *Gender Play: Girls and Boys in School*, New Jersey: Rutgers.
88. Anderson, K.J. (1998) 'Meta-analyses of gender effects on conversational interruption: who, what, when, where, and how', *Sex Roles: A Journal of Research*, **39**(3): 225–52.
89 Stewart, C.M. *et al.* (1998) op. cit.
90. Carter, T.J. (2002) 'The importance of talk to midcareer women's development: a collaborative inquiry', *The Journal of Business Communication*, **39**(1): 55–91.
91. Tannen, D. (1990) *You Just Don't Understand: Women and Men in Communication*: p. 42, New York: William Morrow.
92. Colwill, N. and Sztaba, T.I. (1986) 'Organizational genderlect: the problem of two different languages', *Business Quarterly*, **3**: 64–6.
93. Filard, E.K. (1996) 'Gender patterns in African American and White adolescents: social interactions in same-race, mixed-gender groups,' *Journal of Personality and Social Psychology*, **71**(1): 71–82.
94. Cupach, W.R. and Canary, D.J. (2000) 'Managing anger: investigating the sex stereotype hypothesis', in Braithwaite, D.O. and Thompson, T.L. (eds) *Handbook of Communication and People with Disabilities: Research and Application*, New York: Lawrence Erlbaum.
95. Mulac, A., Bradac, J.J., and Gibbons, P. (2001) 'Empirical support for the gender-as-culture hypothesis: an intercultural analysis of male/female language differences', *Human Communication Research*, **27**(1): 121–52.
96. Tannen, D. (1990) op. cit.

97. Romaine, S. (1999) *Communicating Gender*, Mahwah, NJ: Erlbaum.

98. Gardner, W.L. III, Peluchette, J., V.E. and Clinebell, S.K. (1994) 'Valuing women in management: an impression management perspective of gender diversity', *Management Communication Quarterly*, **8**(2): 115–64.

99. Robinson, K.A. (1998) 'Gender and truthfulness in daily life situations', *Sex Roles: A Journal of Research*, **38**(9): 821–31.

100. Smith, C.R. (2001) 'Multiperspectival feminist critiques and their implications for rhetorical theory', *American Communication Journal*, **4**(3). URL: www.americancomm.org/~aca/acj/acj.html

101. Brown, P. (1990) 'Gender, politeness and confrontation in Tenejapa', *Discourse Processes*, **13**(1): 123–41.

102. McIntosh, A. (2000) 'When the deaf and the hearing interact: communication features, relationships, and disability issues', in Braithwaite, D.O. and Thompson, T.L. (eds) *Handbook of Communication and People with Disabilities: Research and Application*, New York: Lawrence Erlbaum.

103. Nussbaum, J.F. and Baringer, D.K. (2000) 'Message production across the life span: communication and aging', *Communication Theory*, **10**(2): 200–09.

104. Krause, N. and Shaw, B.A. (2002) 'Negative interaction and changes in functional disability during late life', *Journal of Social and Personal Relationships*, **19**(3): 339–60.

105. Fox, S.A., Giles, H., Orbe, M.P. and Bourhis, R.Y. (2000) 'Interability communication: theoretical perspectives', in Braithwaite, D.O. and Thompson, T.L. (eds) *Handbook of Communication and People with Disabilities: Research and Application*, New York: Lawrence Erlbaum.

106. Reeve, D. (2002) 'Negotiating psycho-emotional dimensions of disability and their influence on identity constructions', *Disability and Society*, **17**(5): 493–508.

107. Morris, J. (1991) *Pride Against Prejudice: Transforming Attitudes to Disability*, London: Women's Press.

108. Dickson, D.A., Hargie, O.D.W. and Rainey, S. (2000) 'Communication and relational development between Catholic and Protestant students in Northern Ireland', *Australian Journal of Communication*, **27**(1): 67–82.

109. Baesler, E.J. (1994) 'Religious orientation, persuasion, and communicator style', *The Journal of Communication and Religion*, **17**(2): 61–72.

110. Hostetler, M.J. (1997) 'Rethinking the war metaphor in religious rhetoric: Burke, Black, and Berrigan's "Glimmer of Light" ', *The Journal of Communication and Religion*, **20**(1): 49–60.

111. Lessl, T.M. (1993) 'Toward a definition of religious communication: Scientific and religious uses of evolution', *The Journal of Communication and Religion*, **16**(2): 127–38.

112. Bland, D. (1990) 'Patterns of spontaneous rhetoric: ways of praying among the charismatic bible temple community', *The Journal of Communication and Religion*, **13**(1): 1–11.

113. Hoyt, S.K. (1999) 'Mentoring with class: connections between social class and developmental relationships in the Academy', in Murrell, A.J., Crosby, F.J. and Ely, A.J. (eds) *Mentoring Dilemmas: Developmental Relationships within Multicultural Organizations*, Mahwah, NJ: Lawrence Erlbaum.

114. Orbe, M.P. (1998) 'From the standpoint(s) of traditionally muted groups: explicating a co-cultural communication theoretical model', *Communication Theory*, **8**(1): 1–26.

115. Anderson-Gough, F., Grey, C. and Robson, K. (2000) 'In the name of the client: the service ethic in two professional services firms', *Human Relations*, **53**(9): 1151–74.

116. Pruitt, W., Koermer, C. and Goldstein, M. (1995) 'How the clergy conveys immediacy to parishioners: an exploratory qualitative study', *The Journal of Communication and Religion*, **18**(1): 35–47.

117. Anderson, C.M. (2001) 'Communication in the medical interview team: an analysis of patients' stories in the United States and Hong Kong', *The Howard Journal of Communications*, **12**(1): 61–72.

chapter four

How Culture Affects Behaviour

Communication, from one point of view, is only a particular form of behaviour. This means that we can increase our understanding of how people communicate by learning more about the influences on their behaviour. There are two ways of doing this. One method is to examine the 'internal factors' (actually constructs), which help explain and may even help predict what people do; Section 4.1 describes these internal constructs. The other is to consider the processes that people go through before and while they are communicating; these processes are covered in Section 4.2. In this book there is no space to introduce these vast subjects (but readers are recommended to follow them up: some relevant books are listed in 'Further Reading'). Instead the focus is on how cultural differences are reflected in these constructs and processes that underlie communication. Chapter 3 argued that there are both universals and culture-specifics in communication; the same applies to the constructs and processes described in this chapter, despite the emphasis here on differences.

4.1 INTERNAL FACTORS

The internal factors covered in this section are values, motivations, emotions, perceptions, beliefs, assumptions, expectations, attitudes, abilities and the 'self', which covers personality, identity, self-construals and self-esteem. The relationships among these variables are shown in Figure 4.1. Perceptions, beliefs, assumptions and expectations are all types of cognitions or mental constructs. Perceptions embody an awareness of the environment, both physical and social; beliefs are cognitions to which people attach a degree of credence; assumptions are taken-for-granted beliefs; and expectations are beliefs about the future.

Values

Values have been defined as follows: 'Concepts or beliefs that pertain to desirable end states or behaviors, transcend specific situations, guide selection or evaluation of

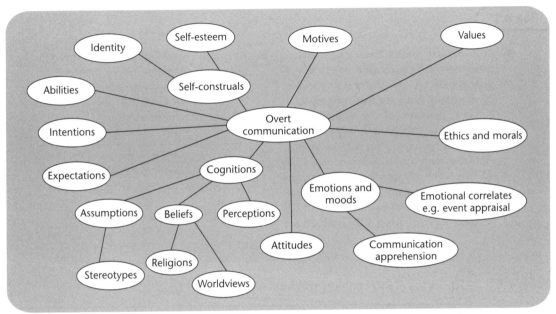

Figure 4.1   *Factors in work communication behaviour which differ cross-culturally*

behavior and events and are ordered by relative importance'.[1] Values are also broad tendencies to prefer certain states of affairs to others. Terms like good or evil and dirty or clean usually express values. Many values have to do with someone's position on and the importance they attach to various moral, religious, political or ecological issues. They have been described as 'the most important indicator in the analyses and prediction of human action and behavior' and 'a means to understanding the underlying motivation (the "why") behind individual behavior'.[2] A literature review found that values are related to such practical work concerns as decision style, strategic action, innovation, creativity, commitment, managerial satisfaction and organisational competitiveness.

Differences in national values are the core concept behind most findings on cultural variation. Unfortunately, such national values found by research cannot legitimately be translated at the individual level, because different individuals have different priorities on values (including the meaning and importance of work). However, the average priorities attached to different values by members of a society 'reflect the central thrust of their shared enculturation. Hence, the average priorities point to the underlying, common cultural values.'[3] Research by Schwartz (1992), has produced a set of 'motivational' values, some of which can be applied at the individual level. Schwartz's study, referred to in Chapter 2, produced a set of 11 'motivational values', which are linked to seven cultural value domains. These are shown in Table 4.1. As Chapter 2 reported, research has linked these cultural values to a range of managerial attitudes and behaviours.[4]

In regard to work values, data from the Meaning of Work Study have consistently shown national cultural differences in three major components: the importance and centrality of work, norms about the rights and duties attached to work, and the work goals sought by individuals in their working lives.[5] For example, in comparison to the

Box 4.1

■ Cross-cultural studies have shown that a preference for equality with one's ingroup peers is most typically found among collectivist nations, such as those in southern Europe. Members of more individualist nations are typically keener on the freedom to receive rewards in proportion to their individual contribution. No more than 30 to 40 per cent of respondents from the Scandinavian nations (except Iceland) choose equality, whereas the pattern from Portugal, Italy and Spain is the reverse.[a]

■ To most western Germans, freedom (49 per cent) matters more than equality (35 per cent). To eastern Germans, it is the other way around (36 per cent and 51 per cent respectively).[b]

Sources: (a) Eyjolfsdottir, H.M. and Smith, P.B. (1996) 'Icelandic business and management culture', *International Studies of Management & Organization*, **26**(3): 61–73

(b) *The Economist*, 18 September 2004, p. 54

Table 4.1 *Schwartz's (1992) primary motivational values and types*

Primary motivational value types	Primary motivational values
Self-direction	Freedom, creativity, independence, choosing own goals, curiosity, self-respect
Stimulation	An exciting life, a varied life, daring
Hedonism	Pleasure, enjoying life
Achievement	Ambition, influence, capability, success, intelligence, self-respect
Power	Social power, wealth, authority, public image, social recognition
Security	National security, reciprocation of favours, family security, sense of belonging, social order, health, cleanliness
Conformity	Obedience, self-discipline, politeness, honouring of parents and elders
Tradition	Respect for tradition, devoutness, acceptance of position in life, humility, moderation
Spirituality	A spiritual life, meaning in life, inner harmony, detachment
Benevolence	Helpfulness, being responsible, forgiving, honest and loyal, mature love, true friendship
Universalism	Equality, unity with nature, wisdom, a world of beauty, social justice, broad-mindedness, protecting the environment, a world at peace

Source: Reprinted from *Advances in Experimental Social Psychology*, **25**, Schwartz, S.H., 'Universals in value content and structure: theoretical advances and empirical tests in 20 countries', pages 1–26, Copyright (1992), with permission from Elsevier

USA, it was found that in Germany work centrality was lower. Meaningful work, good interpersonal relationships, job security and opportunities to learn were all more important but achievement, responsibility and advancement were all less important.[6]

Work values can be subdivided into instrumental work values, such as financial reward and job security, and expressive work values, such as meaningful work. Data from the European and World Values Surveys, shown in Table 4.2, record 1999 levels

Table 4.2   *Instrumental and expressive work values, Europe, 1990–99*

Country	Instrumental work values 1999	Expressive work values 1999	Shift in instrumental work values 1990–99	Shift in expressive work values 1990–99
Latvia	1.5	2.35	+0.05	−0.25
Byelorussia	1.7	2.4	—	—
Czech Republic	2.2	3.2	−1	−0.16
Lithuania	2.6	3.2	−0.4	+0.33
Russia	3.5	2.45	+3.5	—
East Germany	2.4	4	−0.8	−0.175
Ukraine	2.7	4.3	—	—
Bulgaria	3	5	+1.8	+0.4
Poland	3.1	5.2	+1.5	+0.8
Romania	3.1	6	—	—
Montenegro	3.3	6.5	—	—
Hungary	3.7	6.7	+2.6	+0.65
Slovenia	3.4	7.1	+1.5	+0.6
Slovakia	2.4	2.4	−0.6	+0.15
E Europe	2.4	3.5	−0.05	−0.1
Switzerland	3.25	5.5	—	—
Sweden	2.15	4.2	−1.3	−0.8
Norway	n/a	n/a	−0.6	−0.5
Denmark	1.6	3.6	+0.2	−0.07
UK	2.7	3.6	−0.35	+0.61
France	1.75	3.75	+0.4	+0.45
Portugal	2.5	3.75	−1.3	−0.55
Spain	2.9	3.75	+0.45	+0.4
Belgium	2.2	4.2	+0.55	+0.1
Austria	2.25	4.3	+0.35	+0.3
West Germany	2.3	4.4	−0.6	−0.2
Luxembourg	2	4.5	—	—
Netherlands	2	4.5	−0.6	−0.33
Greece	2.8	5	—	—
Eire	3	5	+1	+0.7
Nothern Ireland	3.25	5	+1.5	+1.07
Iceland	2.5	5.1	+0	−0.1
Italy	3.2	6	+1.8	+0.95
Finland	2.25	3.9	+0.5	+0.36

Based on: European Values Study (2002) URL: http://kubnw5.kub.nl/web/fsw/evs/EVSN/online.htm

and shifts between 1990 and 1999 in these values. The data cover a range of European countries. They show considerable cross-country differences in both types of values and in the amount of change over the decade. They also show higher levels overall and wider cross-country differences for expressive than instrumental work values.

In regard to the values of subcultures, the question of whether the values of ethnic minorities within nations align with those of the nation or the ethnic group is complex and not well researched. It probably varies widely by country and ethnic group. Gender appears to have a rather limited effect on the core cultural values, except the masculine/feminine (achievement/relational) dimension, according to Hofstede's (1981) findings. Social class has been shown to affect values. Less educated, low-status employees in various Western countries have more authoritarian values than their higher status co-workers. These authoritarian values are manifested not only at work, but also at home. A study in the USA and Italy showed that working-class parents demanded more obedience from their children than middle-class parents.[7] The difference was larger in the USA than in Italy. However, when Hofstede divided occupations within IBM into six groups according to the level of achievement or relationship (masculine or feminine) values they reported, people in unskilled and semi-skilled occupations recorded the highest level of relationship values apart from office workers. This placed them above managers of all categories, skilled workers/technicians, professional workers and the group with the most masculine values, sales representatives. Hostede's explanation for this finding is in terms of the nature of the work – the sales representatives in the study were paid on commission, creating a highly competitive climate. In contrast, unskilled and semi-skilled workers have 'no strong achievements to boast' and usually work in teams, so that co-operation is important to them. The rankings certainly support such an interpretation. However, another possibility is that members of less skilled occupational classes share the lower valuation of work (working to live rather than living to work) that characterises relationship (sub)cultures.

Ethics and morality

Since moral codes generally reflect values, it is not surprising that researchers have found cultural differences in morality. (However, it is likely that the possession of a moral code of some sort is universal. 'People are motivated to think of themselves as ethical [sic], and rate themselves as more ethical than the average person. When people do engage in ethically questionable behaviour, they often justify it as self-defence.'[8]) It has been argued that business ethical standards are unique to each culture, as a result of the combination of institutional, organisational and personal factors, all of which are based on the 'social foundation' of national culture.[9] The 'trial-and-error process of actual business activity' and personal interaction with other people both play an important role in the way moral reasoning is formed within civil society. Business and its underlying ethical principles of trust and co-operation in the context of civil society are captured in the notion of business as a 'mediating' institution. 'Mediating institutions break down an individual's interaction with the rest of the world into more manageable personal interaction with other human beings.'[10]

There is empirical support for moral beliefs being related to cultural difference. A ten-nation study found that collectivism–individualism, and uncertainty avoidance help explain national differences in judgements of the 'ethicality' of decision items – the particular items were concerned with relations with external stakeholders, with the corporation and with the group.[11] Another study showed that whether individuals in organisations are aware of an issue being a moral one is decided in part by their perceiving a social consensus that an issue is ethically problematic. This finding supports the idea that socio–cultural influences affect individuals' moral beliefs.[12]

Examples of moral standards of individual cultures include Ali's finding that in the Arab world, not only is bribery widespread but political elites encourage it, believing that the more customary the corruption, the more valid their system. 'In July 1992, I visited Jordan and found that, even in a religious court, the clerk openly asked for a bribe (he called it "Ikrameh"). In Syria, it is impossible to get a request processed in any government agency without paying bribes.'[13] A comparison of beliefs about distributive justice found differences between Hong Kong and Indonesia. Hong Kong respondents perceived that the use of merit as a basis for distributing resources was fairer and more

Box 4.2

In Russia since 1990, according to Kazakov *et al.* corruption and crime in business affairs has been widespread. A questionnaire survey of 25 aspiring Russian entrepreneurs revealed 'a definite sensitivity, both moral and utilitarian, to the importance of ethical business practices'. Bribery, breach of word, failure to pay taxes, financial fraud among partners and deceptive advertising were cited as examples of unethical business behaviour prevalent in Russia. Strong resentment was expressed towards these. All respondents agreed that ethical business behaviour is important to society, though some thought that in present-day Russia it might be unprofitable. Most respondents took the position that the development of a market economy and its accompanying wide range of activities contribute to the emergence of ethical business behaviour. There were two notable qualifications, however: 'We need foreign experience'. 'It will take a very long time in Russia.'

Source: Kazakov, A.Y., Taylor, T.C. and Thompson, M. (1997) 'Business ethics and civil society in Russia', *International Studies of Management & Organization*, 27(1): 5–18

principled than the use of need; Indonesian respondents, in contrast, saw the use of need as fairer than the use of merit. (Both groups, however, perceived that the allocator who favoured the needy was nicer and acted more out of concern for others.)[14] Another study found cultural variation in the acceptability of most kinds of lies, although there was cross-cultural agreement that lies perceived as told for malicious or self-benefiting purposes were unacceptable.[15]

A study that compared Indian and American moral choices found cross-cultural differences in the priority given to interpersonal responsibilities relative to justice considerations. More Indians than Americans gave priority to interpersonal responsibilities. This difference was greater in non-life-threatening situations. Americans emphasised the potential harm involved in the choice situation rather than the 'uncaringness' involved in the choice; Indians did the opposite. (Unexpectedly, the various cross-cultural differences were not more marked in older than younger people.) Indians categorised their choice of the interpersonal option in moral terms; the minority of Americans who chose the interpersonal alternative categorised it in personal rather than moral terms.[16]

Perhaps the best resolution of this issue of cultural differences in ethics is that of Argyle.[17] Different societies and religions have arrived at similar moral ideas, such as advocating love, compassion and forgiveness. However, the application of these ideas in society has varied greatly with the circumstances of life at different times.

Motives

At work, motivation and differences in motivational patterns have long been associated with a whole range of outcomes, from productivity to job satisfaction and employee turnover. In a communication context, motivation is a central concept in influencing processes, as well as explaining much about how and why people communicate.

Most current theories of motivation originated in the USA and are now being criticised for being culture-specific. For example, it has been argued that the needs for power, esteem and achievement, which feature strongly in Western motivational theories, are not found in all cultures. Achievement, which means individual achievement, may be a motive limited to individualist cultures; similarly, the need for power may not motivate many people in a high power distance culture, such as India's, where most people accept that they have a 'pre-ordained' position in a social hierarchy. Aycan suggested that, in developing countries, work motivations differ from Western models in the following ways:

- The importance of relationships and networking is 'one of the most salient cultural characteristics' – over-riding rules and procedures in every aspect of social, political and economic life; acting loyally and to preserve harmony, together with ingroup status, determine who gets organisational benefits.
- Work is perceived as a duty done in the service of the family and work achievements are valued as enhancing family status. Work is less important than family, and family reasons are normal excuses for absence. Many organisations are 'families', with paternalistic superior–subordinate relations.
- Job performance is less valued than good interpersonal relations at work. An intention to do well is as important as goal achievement.
- Individuals have a low sense of control, self-reliance may be distrusted as disloyalty and fatalism can lead to low initiative taking.
- Preserving face is very important, resulting in problems in both giving and receiving feedback.
- People respect 'authority' rather than rules – a position that is a prescribed norm in Islam and Confucianism. 'Some paradoxical dualities exist in the superior–subordinate relationship. First, there is high respect but also high affection towards the superior. As such, there is an element of both love and fear in this relationship. Second, being an ingroup member, the superior is considered as "one of us," but being a person with higher status, s/he is "unlike us." Third, superiors have close relationships with their subordinates and are involved in all aspects of their lives, but this does not translate to an informal "friendship" relationship. Instead, the subordinate–superior relationship is formal and distant.'[18]

Recent research has examined the effects on the structure and strength of achievement motivation of individualist and collectivist cultural orientations. The strength of achievement motivation varied markedly across US, Dutch, Israeli, Hungarian, and Japanese samples.[19] Respondents from the USA, a highly individualist culture, demonstrated the strongest tendencies for personal achievement. Respondents from the more collectivist cultures of Japan and Hungary showed the lowest levels of achievement motive. They had a tendency to avoid individual tasks or obligations that involved personal responsibility.

In the literature on culture and work motivation, organisational loyalty or commitment (OC) is a major concern. It has been shown that different cultures conceptualise OC differently. In the USA, for instance, dedication, obligation, integrity and determination emerge as the primary themes, reflecting high individualism. In contrast, four of the five themes from the Japanese sample reflect collectivism: connection, membership, responsibility and co-operation.[20] In Islamic countries, according to a study of 474 employees from 30 organisations in the United Arab Emirates, the Islamic work ethic promotes individuals' commitment to their organisation – an effect that might be less clear for the Protestant work ethic, though no comparison was made.[21]

Differences in communication motives are attracting research attention. One such study investigated the communication motives of different ethnic groups. It first identified issues that African Americans (AAs) find relevant to satisfaction in interethnic encounters. These issues are as follows:

- Acceptance (a feeling of being accepted and respected by the other party).
- Expressiveness (unrestricted communication of thoughts and feelings).
- Negative stereotyping; understanding (interactors feel their meaning is shared).
- Goal attainment (objectives are met through conversation).
- Powerlessness (AAs feel controlled, manipulated and trapped).
- Relaxation (feeling relaxed with one's own self-presentation).
- Relational solidarity (a feeling of closeness or bonding).
- Shared worldview (identity of perspectives or values).

Later research found that powerlessness, relaxation and shared worldview are most salient to AAs. In contrast, identity, goal attainment and relational solidarity are most salient to European Americans (EAs). In low-intimacy relationships, such as those at work, authenticity and relational solidarity are most important for EAs, and understanding (task concern), stereotyping and shared worldview are most salient for AAs. Both groups emphasise acceptance in low-intimacy relationships.[22]

Regarding subcultures, motivational differences between the genders may have been exaggerated. In research into 1001 adolescents, girls were not found to have lower achievement orientations than boys. On the other hand, a review of research into women's and men's professional communication found that women's communication motivations were more affiliative and less power-oriented than men's. In a study of age effects on motivation in the German workforce, measures of personal initiative were examined as a function of age, in combination with other demographic and work characteristics. Overall initiative tended to be greater among older people. Initiative in job behaviour showed no significant age differences among male employees, but a negative age-pattern was found for both men's and women's initiative in educational activities.[23]

Emotions and moods

Emotions have been defined as, 'first and foremost, modes of relating to the environment: states of readiness for engaging, or not engaging, in interaction with that environment'. Aspects of that engagement include, 'modifying inter-individual interactions ... regulating the balance of power ... determining general patterns of social interaction and ... motivating social cohesion'.[24] In the work environment, therefore, communicators must take (sub)cultural variations in emotions into account. Even in complex situations, such as work-related initial intercultural encounters, feelings generally affect behaviour, although thoughts modify the effect. For instance, it has been shown that when the situation is complex, being in a positive mood triggers more confident, direct interpersonal behaviours than being in a negative mood. Again, during complex negotiations, people in a positive mood had more ambitious goals, higher expectations and bargained in a more co-operative and integrative way, leading to greater success, compared with people in a negative mood.[25]

The experience of basic moods and emotions tends to be universal, while their expression and correlates may have both universal and culture-specific elements.[26] Those 'correlates' include antecedent events (which trigger feelings), event categorisation (e.g., as humiliating or flattering), appraisal of the event according to its category (e.g., humiliation as harmful, flattery as pleasant), physiological reaction (like sweating or blushing), action readiness (to run, to leave the room), emotional behaviour (like insulting vengeful speech or crying) and regulation (people can either inhibit or enhance responses). A review article reported that both cultural similarities and differences have been found for nearly all these correlates of emotions. Close attention has been paid to how individuals appraise the events that generate emotions. Appraisal includes evaluating how controllable the outcome of the event seems and what causes it. These elements of appraisal seem to be universal, but the weight placed on some elements varies across cultures. The importance of certain emotions also varies across cultures. Variations in cultural collectivism or individualism seem to explain these differences.[27]

People conceptualise emotion differently – in the West, emotion is usually considered separate from reason, whereas the Eastern ideal is that emotion is a part of reasoning. This difference influences how people deal with their emotional experiences. In one study, directors from 48 separate factories in the People's Republic of China said they experienced intense pleasant and unpleasant emotions as a result of social, moral and material/economic conditions. Some directors expressed these emotions in culturally conforming ways, using reason to understand them; others vented or suppressed them, contrary to their cultural norm. The study concluded that those directors who used culturally conforming methods dealt with their emotions better.[28] Another study showed that African Americans self-report different behaviours as revealing that they feel shy from those reported by White Americans; this implies that behaviours displaying shyness feelings may be culture-specific.[29] Finally, a cross-cultural comparison of the implications of self-disclosure found differences in the Eastern and Western concepts of 'sincerity'.[30]

Subculturally, there are findings of emotional differences between genders and between people with different types of disability. Women managers may be more responsive to emotional issues than men, as shown in Table 4.3. Deaf and hard-of-hearing technical professionals may develop emotional barriers to face-to-face communication. For example, a deaf man who worked as a systems analyst for Procter & Gamble said he was still learning to work on projects as part of a team. 'I grew up with a strong preference for solitary activities. This has been one of my greatest challenges.'[31]

Two aspects of emotion have received particular attention: these are fear of communicating and emotional intelligence.

Table 4.3 *Gender differences in the emotional responsiveness of managers*

Emphasis in interpersonal relationships	Women housing managers	Men housing managers
With own team	Understanding of people; sensitivity; care for individual feelings and development; rich perception of human beings	Support own team; look after their interests; defend them to the hilt
With clients	Empathy; relationships; understanding of different needs	Can use pressure groups

Based on: Sparrow, J. and Rigg, C. (1993) 'Job analysis: selecting for the masculine approach to management', *Selection and Development Review*, **9**(2): 5–8

Communication apprehension

Unsurprisingly, perhaps, the major negative effect of fear of communicating, or communication apprehension (CA) is on communication, though it also affects job satisfaction. Individuals who are high in communication apprehension – whether about speaking or listening – are likely to be less willing to listen than others and to be poor communicators.[32] For instance, CA reduces people's tendency to talk to doctors or seek out health information, though it does not affect health-related behaviours such as taking exercise, going to health fairs or using tobacco.[33]

CA may be culturally induced: Swedish children are more apprehensive than North American children and older children (ages 9–11) are more apprehensive than younger.[34] A comparison of Korean, Hawaiian and US students found that high CA (and low argumentativeness) may be a function of culture-level collectivism.[35] However, there is evidence that who suffers from communication fear and when is not stereotypical. The results of one study indicated that Middle Eastern and European subjects in the USA reported levels of apprehension well *below* statistical norms previously established by US subjects, while Asian and Latin American subjects reported levels just slightly below those norms when communicating in their native languages. All groups indicated that CA was more of a problem when speaking in English, with Asians and Latin Americans reporting the highest levels. Women were slightly more apprehensive overall when communicating in either language, but women in the Latin American sample reported less apprehension than men in every context except public speaking. Neither the subjects' number of years speaking English nor the length of time living in the USA correlated with CA.[36] CA in a first language is a much better predictor of apprehension in a second language than is self-perceived competence in that second language.

Thus, if CA is culturally induced, it nevertheless varies between subgroups. CA is probably personal, though affected by (sub)culture. Among Chinese college students in Taiwan, individuals who held more independent views of the self and who received more encouragement from their teachers to speak up were less likely to be high in CA, though family communication patterns were not shown to have any effect.[37] Women are higher in CA (men are higher in shyness), but it is suggested that this may be linked to cultural norms and stereotypes about gender rather than biological sex. It is not related to self-perceived competence in speaking a language.[38]

Some individuals are apprehensive about communicating with members of other ethnic groups specifically, rather than in general. Such individuals are more likely to be ethnocentric. Interethnic communication apprehension (IECA) affects whether and how people attempt to maintain relations with people from other ethnic groups. High IECAs are less likely than low IECAs to use strategies to maintain interethnic relations. These strategies include performing duties and sharing responsibilities (task), emphasising common affiliations (networking), being optimistic, cheerful and uncritical (positivity), directly discussing the relationship (openness) and stressing the desire to remain in the relationship (assurance). High IECAs may in fact *be* less willing to remain in interethnic relationships, and that may be why they use so few relation maintenance strategies.[39] Scholarship on CA has been criticised as biased by the individualist assumption that communication 'approach' is more desirable than communication 'avoidance'. While it is accepted that extreme forms of communication avoidance and lack of verbal assertiveness can be a handicap in any culture, the view that communication avoidance is solely a deficiency is linked to the Western ethnocentric preoccupation with the self.[40]

Emotional intelligence

Emotional intelligence (EI) is a factor now widely considered to affect work behaviour.[41] It has been defined as the 'accurate appraisal and expression of emotions in oneself and others and the regulation of emotion in a way that enhances living'.[42] Up to now most research into EI has related to the ability to recognise facial expressions. The evidence is that using or judging emotions intelligently does involve this ability. A recent meta-analysis of cross-cultural research on emotion recognition found evidence for both universality and cultural differences.[43] Although emotions are recognised at above chance levels across cultural boundaries, there is also evidence that individuals judge emotions expressed by members of their same national, ethnic or regional group more accurately. In one large-scale study, American and European groups identified from photographs 75–83 per cent of the facial expressions displayed by Americans, while Japanese scored 65 per cent and Africans correctly identified only 50 per cent.[44]

Females are better able than males to perceive facial expressions of emotion. This applies to children as young as three years of age, and across many cultures. 'Psychologists have linked the finding to a wide range of other gender differences, including women's greater empathy, greater expressiveness, greater practice, greater tendency to accommodate others, greater breadth in using emotional information and subordinate role in the larger culture.'[45] Other evidence on subcultures includes that individuals of a higher socioeconomic status (SES) appear to perform better on tests of non-verbal skill in general and on tests of facial expression more specifically than do lower SES individuals.

However, the research so far on EI is extremely partial. EI is 'a multidimensional skill – not an isolated or simple ability – encompassing a range of constructs with complex relationships to each other'. Few of these constructs have been rigorously researched.

Perceptions

Some writers on culture, especially those concerned with culture and management, place perceptions centrally in their analysis of how culture affects individuals' behaviour. For example, Johansson described culture as 'the underlying framework which guides an individual's perceptions of observed events and personal interactions and the selection of appropriate responses in social situations. The framework consists of objective reality, as manifested in terms of societal institutions, and also subjective reality as socialized in terms of predispositions and beliefs.'[46] Culture as framework, according to Johansson, 'serves to highlight certain aspects of a situation and downplay others. It frames reality as observed and interpreted, and provides behavioral rules as a guide for acting on it. Culture involves behavioral constraints imposed by society. This suggests that culture is a strong determinant of observed behavior.' Robinson agreed with the centrality of culture in perception, arguing that culture 'lies at the very roots of perception'.[47] In fact what people perceive is strongly influenced by (Robinson said determined by) their deep culture. Box 4.3 gives some examples of how work-related perceptions can vary with culture.

Cultural influences on social perceptions are of particular interest for this book. People from different cultures exhibit 'dramatic and consequential differences' in constructing social meaning – that is, in their perceptions of the meaning of interpersonal behaviour, according to research by Chi-yue *et al.*[48] The particular study looked at the effect of creating 'need for closure' by increasing the time pressure on people to make

Box 4.3

- An American manager, from a highly individualist culture, expects to gain status at work from the performance produced by his or her department, such as increased market share, higher profitability or product innovation. To a Japanese manager, from a collectivist culture, such achievements belong to the group, and it is mainly from the development of subordinates that his/her own status derives.
- High power distance may tend to make people perceive the top managers in their organisations as infallible, not expect that they themselves will reach positions of power during their career, be motivated to work hard by loyalty to the 'godlike' Chief Executive and think that a steeply hierarchical work organisation is natural and fitting.
- Where some White males perceive a hierarchical structure open to talent and energy, people from ethnic minorities, women and people with disabilities often perceive a glass ceiling.
- There is a direct relationship between the masculinity of clothing worn by female managerial candidates and judgements of masculine managerial traits. But masculinity of dress is unrelated to perceptions of feminine managerial traits because women applicants are rated high on feminine attributes regardless of their attire.
- The language used by speakers affects how they are perceived. For instance, speakers of

all kinds who use 'she' instead of 'he' can come to be seen as less socially attractive, although using 'they' has no such effect. A study found that speakers who addressed the topic of engineering were regarded as more dynamic than speakers who discussed nursing. As public speakers, females were perceived as more credible than males – especially more dynamic and more socially attractive. Male listeners were especially harsh toward same sex speakers with respect to perceived competence. These findings may reflect the 'popular' view that women generally display superior verbal skills.[a]

- A country's relative size, in combination with linguistic similarity, predicts the likelihood of people from one country perceiving another as less sympathetic, more arrogant and less similar to themselves. These findings come from research into Dutch/German, Belgian/French and Dutch-Belgian versus French-Belgian attitudes towards Holland.[b]

Sources: (a) Salter, M.M., Weider-Hatfield, D. and Rubin, D.L. (1983) 'Generic pronoun use and perceived speaker credibility', *Communication Quarterly*, **31**(2): 180–84
(b) Van Oudenhoven, J.P., Askevis-Leherpeux, F., Hannover, B., Jaarsma, R. and Dardenne, B. (2002) 'Asymmetrical international attitudes', *European Journal of Social Psychology*, **32**(2): 275–89

attributions of what caused others to act as they did. Previously, it had been thought that a universal information processing strategy would apply under increased time pressure, leading people to attribute more behaviour to the observed actor's personal dispositions and less to their situation.

However, this research found this predicted pattern among North Americans, but among Chinese people, the need for closure increased attributions, not to personal, but to group dispositions. This finding is consistent with past findings that North American and Chinese attributors have different implicit social theories. North Americans conceive of individuals as autonomous agents; Chinese conceive of groups as autonomous.

It is worth noting that these findings do not mean that individuals' social perceptions are rigidly determined by their culture. Instead they are guided by it only when it is activated – as in the case of heightened need for closure. Additionally, individuals may have other tools for understanding the social world in addition to their 'native' cultural theory. For instance, bicultural people may have developed 'foreign' cultural meaning systems that may be activated to guide their social perceptions.

The group they identify with, the perceived person's communication style, the perceiver's social identity and the situation all affect how people perceive one another. For instance, men are more likely to be evaluated more highly than women in ambiguous situations or in the presence of competent women, women in 'male' contexts or women who behave in ways that are incongruent with their sex-roles. These biases result in women managers often being perceived as less committed to the organisation than their male counterparts are. Because commitment is linked to lower absenteeism, lower turnover rates and increased intention to stay with the firm, negative perceptions of women's commitment may be linked to their lower rates of pay and career progress. These biases apply less in clear-cut situations, for example where quality of performance is obvious, than in more ambiguous cases. Two factors can combine to shape evaluations of commitment. First, single female managers and male and female managers with families evaluate traditional behaviours differently than their single or childless married counterparts, even when controlling for the specific behaviour described and the individual characteristics of the actor. Second, work group gender demographics shape managers' beliefs to the degree that managers conform to the beliefs of the majority. Thus, the more numerically male-dominated the work group, the more likely that traditional indicators of commitment, such as working long hours, will be used.[49]

Which social perceptions are activated also depends on the situation. A survey of 284 American executives affected by foreign or domestic acquisition of their company investigated their perceptions of (organisational) cultural differences, system changes in the acquired company, acquisition negotiations, executives' reasons for staying or leaving after the acquisition and post-acquisition outcomes for the organisation. It was found that the executives' perceptions differed significantly in all five areas according to whether the executive was involved in a foreign or domestic acquisition.[50] Finally, cross-culturally similar perceptions can lead to different reactions. Vigoda found no significant differences between British and Israeli civil servants' perceived levels of organisational politics. Despite this, the British reacted with significantly higher intentions of leaving the organisation, lower levels of loyalty and job satisfaction and a stronger sense that their expectations had not been met.[51]

Beliefs

Belief systems 'help people perceive, interpret, and predict events (e.g., predicting whether people will succeed or fail) and select courses of action (e.g., deciding whether to help a victim of misfortune.'[52]) Belief systems represented by everyday sayings have been related to different levels of prejudice towards a variety of socially stigmatised groups including racial minorities, gay men and lesbians, and overweight persons and women. It has been argued that a taxonomy of beliefs that vary cross-culturally would 'help to move the field beyond its excessive reliance on values'.

Cross-cultural variation has been demonstrated in core beliefs about how the world works, locus of control, belief in a just or unjust world, religion, and beliefs about work.

Core belief systems

Six fundamental belief systems about how the world works have been identified and shown to vary from culture to culture; they have also been linked to prejudice, either positively or negatively. These belief systems are authoritarianism, social dominance orientation, Protestant work ethic, humanitarianism–egalitarianism, beliefs about the malleability of human attributes and beliefs about diversity.[53]

- Authoritarianism has been defined as consisting of three factors: submission to society's established authorities, holding to conventions that they seemingly endorse and support for aggression towards people who break society's rules or conventions. Cross-cultural studies have shown that some people in many cultures score high on authoritarianism (Canada, Ghana, Russia, South Africa, USA included), though in varying numbers. For instance, a greater proportion of people high in authoritarianism was found in the USA than in Russia.

- Social dominance orientation (SDO) refers to the belief in and support for a natural hierarchy among individuals and groups. SDO has been validated in the USA, Canada, Taiwan, Israel and China, but its expression varies across cultures. In the USA, people who strongly agree with SDO blame people in low-status positions (such as poverty) for their misfortunes. However, in Taiwan, people who strongly agree with SDO tend to believe that people's misfortunes are due to forces outside of themselves. Agreeing with SDO predicts a tendency to justify inequality in the culturally endorsed manner. There are also within-culture variations in levels of SDO; in general, people in higher status positions are more likely to strongly agree with SDO. One study found that men support SDO more than women and that this varies little with culture, situation or context. In terms of social status (socio-economic status, ethnicity or 'race') though, support for SDO of high-status groups towards low-status groups depended on the context and situation.[54]

- The Protestant work ethic (PWE) is an individualist belief system that stresses successful outcomes for anyone who works hard, and attributes failure to personal factors such as lack of effort and weakness of character. Tests of PWE beliefs among university students in 13 nations (including India, Germany, USA and Zimbabwe), found that, in general, wealthy countries were less likely to endorse PWE beliefs than countries that were not wealthy. This may be because striving for success is more necessary and useful in poorer societies. The research also found a strong correlation between PWE scores and power distance scores. Of the three European countries in the sample, Great Britain and Germany ranked low on most measures of PWE, whereas Greece ranked much higher.[55]

- Humanitarianism–egalitarianism (H–E) is a belief in and support for equality, social justice and concern for others. It is a belief central to relationship-oriented cultures, such as Norway's, but has also been referred to as an aspect of a US core value, despite that country's high masculinity (achievement) rating.

- Beliefs about the malleability of human attributes refer to beliefs about whether people can change in their human qualities, such as morality, personality and intelligence. Opposing views on malleability have been found in different cultures (USA, Hong Kong and France).

- Beliefs about diversity itself. These are positive or negative attitudes towards ethnic diversity, other specified ethnic groups and women's equality. These beliefs correlate with levels of awareness of racial privilege. Diversity beliefs are also correlated with ethnicity and gender – in sum, with the position of the belief holder's group in society, though the relationship is far from one for one.

Locus of control

The locus of control scale is used to measure beliefs about what controls the outcomes of an individual's actions. Locus of control beliefs are important in predicting individual behaviour. They are closely related to cultural differences in individuals' experiences of control, harmony and submission to their environment. Studies have reported a number of mean differences between country samples in locus of control scores; for instance, Oriental Asians, particularly Japanese, consistently show higher external locus of control scores than North-American Caucasians do. A study in 43 countries found three different dimensions related to locus of control, which varied cross-culturally as follows:

■ Eastern European countries endorsed harmony with the environment; most other countries endorsed mastery of the environment.
■ Cultural collectivism and high power distance predicted low scores on internal locus of control.
■ Four Asian countries endorsed items asserting the role of luck or chance in life, but without an implication of failure. An East German sample produced an extreme negative measure on this dimension.[56]

Belief in a just or unjust world

Belief in a just world and belief in an unjust world are independent variables, not highly negatively correlated. Rank ordered 'just world' and 'unjust world' scores from 12 countries (1700 psychology students) correlated significantly with power distance and individualism. Few sex differences were found across each society, but within societies, richer and more powerful individuals were more likely to believe in a just world. This made it possible for a wealth-polarised country, India, to rank first in both belief in a just world and belief in an unjust world. Of three European countries in the sample, Great Britain and Germany ranked far lower in terms of just world beliefs than Greece.[57]

According to Bond and Smith these dimensions of beliefs, along which countries may be arrayed, overlap only moderately with measures of values for the same countries.[58] This may mean that they have the potential to be used as a different or additional way of analysing culture.

Religion

Religious belief is clearly a strong influence on behaviour, at work as elsewhere, affecting moral judgements and attitudes to wealth and ways of gaining it, such as earning interest on capital, among other factors. Religion has been described as 'a center from which all other forms of human motivation gradually diverged. It is a unifying principle ... with endless varieties of action and passion deriving from it.'[59] Some social scientists contend that too little research concerns the role of religiosity in social interaction. The effects of religious belief on communication have already been introduced in Chapter 3. Research has shown that communal identity and a sense of the importance of community, institution and hierarchy are still strong among religious groups such as Roman Catholics in Australia. These beliefs are reinforced by ritual, story and the variety of social rituals that accompany such events as first communion.[60] Moslems believe that work is a means of worshipping God; thus, in contrast to the PWE Islamic religious belief affects attitudes to the content of work. For example, producing or selling alcohol or working in 'usurious' occupations, such as Western-style banking, are prohibited. In addition, Islam provides a complete set of guidelines for conducting economies in accordance with Islamic teachings, specifying how to deal with such problems as unemployment and inflation.[61,62]

A study of 277 Moslem immigrants to the USA found that acculturation to US organisational practices was related to different factors from those which affected acculturation in private and/or social lives. Willingness to acculturate to the US national culture was promoted by collectivism (presumably because collectivists try to harmonise with the surrounding culture), and affected by religious beliefs and practices (the stronger and more active, the more individuals clung to national culture), gender, education (male and more educated respondents were more willing to integrate) and years lived in the USA. Factors influencing acceptance of US organisational cultures, however, included acculturation to the US national culture but also how much discrepancy in work cultures the person perceived. Despite this, acculturation to US organisational cultures still occurred more readily: most were more inclined to retain their original national culture for their private lives but accepted US organisational cultures. More educated Moslems perceived greater discrepancies between the US and 'own country' organisational cultures; other demographic variables, collectivism and degree of religiosity were unrelated to this variable.[63]

Work-related beliefs

In addition to other beliefs, people also, of course, hold beliefs that are more specifically related to their work. Beliefs about what is important can affect which of the stimuli bombarding managers and others at work are attended to; beliefs about causal relations can affect choice of strategy or action. One cross-cultural analysis found significant differences in beliefs about money, business ethics, social responsibility and guanxi among youths in two Asian economies – Hong Kong and Singapore – and two Western economies – Canada and Hawaii.[64] A study of 292 Russian managers found that organisational beliefs, beliefs about worker participation in decisions, leisure ethic and Marxist-related beliefs showed the same pattern as their worldview beliefs: that is, there were many similarities and some differences associated with managerial level, age and gender. Some of these findings conflict with common stereotypes of the way Russian managers view their work.[65] Against these findings of a link between national culture and work-related beliefs, however, a study in five Hungarian firms with Anglo-Saxon or Western management found that factors such as national culture, functional area, education, age, rank and gender had relatively little influence on beliefs about company strategy compared with the factor of whether or not an individual was located in a unit favourably affected by that strategy.[66]

In fact, there is no conclusive evidence on any relationship between national–cultural background and beliefs about strategic issues. One study, for example, found a positive relationship between national culture and the expressed preferences of US and Japanese managers towards various generic strategies; another, on the other hand, failed to find a relationship between the perceived importance of strategic goals and the national culture of managers.

As far as subcultural variation in beliefs is concerned, the issue is far from clear-cut. Some feminist scholars have described the female worldview as significantly different from the male worldview. Gilligan, arguing from a psychological perspective, stated that female identity revolves around interconnectedness and relationship. Conversely, 'Male identity, stresses separation and independence'.[67] These ways in which concepts of social relationships (and their accompanying communication patterns) differ between genders are parallel to gender differences in worldview. Certainly, there is some evidence that, cross-culturally, males are consistently higher on social dominance orientation than females, reflecting status and power differences between males and females across cultures. Among professional women, having an internal locus of control is negatively linked to perceptions of role ambiguity, role overload and non-participation in the workplace. Both male and female workers with higher externality scores report higher levels of career dissatisfaction and illness.[68] Gender-based worldviews may be reflected in basic work-related beliefs such as those about requesting a higher salary. Women's salary requests and outcomes are lower than men's, and it has been shown that this is linked to their beliefs about requesting a higher salary.[69]

Opposing views on human malleability have been found across age groups (elementary school, middle school and college). The study of 292 Russian managers' beliefs referred to earlier, found, together with many similarities among responding groups, some differences depending upon managerial level, age and gender. These differing beliefs included humanistic belief system and work ethic.[70] In most cases, however, members of different subcultures within a culture share the same core beliefs. Religious beliefs largely transcend subcultural boundaries. When they do vary within cultures, as in many Western societies, there is more variation among individual members of a society than between groups other than religious groups themselves.

Assumptions

Assumptions are taken-for-granted, unquestioned beliefs. This 'knowledge' that people in different cultures and subcultures take for granted is extensive. It affects their behaviour, including their communicative behaviour, in many ways. It influences surface culture, as well as rituals, status differentials and values, including:

- Roles – what is done and not done by people in various categories, such as male/female, supervisor/subordinate, teacher/student.
- Work – how much emphasis is placed on social interaction versus task completion; how supervisors treat subordinates.
- Time – how late a person can be without apologising; whether it is more important to be on time for the next appointment or to complete the business at hand.
- Space – when a person will feel that their 'territory' has been invaded; how acceptable open-plan offices are; how many people can get into a lift before they feel crowded.

Writing specifically in a work context, Schein actually defined culture in terms of assumptions: 'I am defining culture as the set of shared, taken-for-granted implicit assumptions that a group holds and that determines how it perceives, thinks about and reacts to its various environments.'[71] Norms are one manifestation of these assumptions, but it is important to remember that behind the norms lies this deeper taken-for-granted set of assumptions that most members of a culture never question or examine.

Schein identified two subcultures (he called them 'cultures'), based on occupational communities, who are quite stable in the assumptions they hold: 'engineers', the practitioners of the organisation's core technology, who 'prefer solutions without people'; and executives – CEOs especially – for whom their role brings about the perception that 'financial criteria always have to be paramount'. The engineers resist the new organisational learning culture (see Chapter 2) because it does not match their preferred type of solution. The executives resist giving time and resources to building learning capacity, which does not give quick returns; they are over-concerned with the control system and, like the engineers, play down the human factor. As a result, 'New methods of learning or solving problems do not diffuse or even become embedded in the organizations that first used them', and, 'Individual projects learn new methods of operating, but these methods do not diffuse to other groups or organizations'.

Assumptions undoubtedly affect behaviour and are hard to detect, sometimes even by the person holding them. At work, relevant assumptions include those held by managers about their subordinates' work motivations, those negotiators hold about their opponents and those people hold about the members of other social groups. For instance, assumptions about the stereotypical characteristics of women (emotional, sensitive, nurturing and interdependent) and men (independent, dominant, emotionally inhibited and goal directed) are strong unspoken influences on their relative treatment in terms of job segregation and career advancement.

Two sets of assumptions that are especially important for intercultural communication are ethnocentrism and stereotypes.

Ethnocentrism

A biased set of assumptions in favour of one's own ethnic group has been given the label ethnocentrism. To some degree, biases in favour of people's own ingroup and in opposition to outgroups are 'natural'. There are studies that show that people from all cultures:

- Think of what goes on in their own culture as natural and correct and what goes on in other cultures as not natural or not correct.
- Perceive their own customs as universally valid.
- Believe their own norms, roles and values are correct, particularly as concerns their own immediate ingroup or subculture.
- Favour and co-operate with ingroup members while feeling hostile towards outgroups.[72]

These points apply most strongly, however, where the members of a social grouping are concentrated and in day-to-day contact with other members, (as in the case of, say, the Greek–Cypriot community in areas of London) even if the grouping is subordinate and low in attractiveness. It applies less strongly where the members of a subordinate social grouping are spread out among the members of the dominant social grouping. This probably accounts for the fact that, despite feminism, we have not found it necessary to coin the term 'gendercentrism'.

Ethnocentrism is rewarded in interactions within an ethnic group: high ethnocentrics are more likely to conform to its norms, roles and values and therefore to be accepted. A work-based task-group study found that ethnocentrism varied, depending on whether respondents were reporting on task aspects or relationship aspects of their intergroup dynamics. In some conditions groups even seemed to minimise or invert usual ethnocentric tendencies. Over allocation of resources, groups minimised their advantage or emphasised their disadvantage – in 'marked contrast to the usual ingroup–outgroup pattern in which groups see themselves favorably and others unfavorably'.[73] An obvious explanation of this last behaviour, however, is that the groups were motivated to lower the favourability of their self-perceptions in order to try to obtain more resources.

Stereotypes

A stereotype is a stable set of beliefs or preconceived ideas that the members of a group share about the characteristics of a group of people. The concept of stereotype has gradually lost its earlier sense of irrationality and prejudice. Instead stereotyping is now considered an ordinary cognitive process in which people categorise people and entities in order to avoid information 'overload'. There is much evidence that people apply stereotypes to form complex images of others from first impressions. For instance, when 80 students guessed the attitudes of several people whose pictures they were shown, it was found that they expected men to have conservative attitudes on

---

Box 4.4

■ An Indian woman doctor who lived for many years in the Middle East and worked extensively with colleagues from different countries in that area, said, 'Iraqis and Palestinians are very hard working; Syrians are clever and they do work hard but more because there is so much competition there than because it comes naturally; Bengalis and Bangladeshis are not motivated to work hard. They don't seem to want to improve themselves.'[a]

■ 'On the positive side, Germans often see Americans as friendly, open, resourceful, energetic, innovative, and, in general, capable in business ... [with] greater freedom, generally happier, ... more productive and creative than many other people ... ; [and having] opportunities to succeed. ... [Americans find Germans] highly disciplined, well educated, neat and orderly, ... systematic, well organized, meticulous, ... efficient ... Some Americans find them hard to get to know – not unfriendly, but reserved. On the negative side, ... Germans are [seen by Americans as] pushy in service lines ... and often insensitive to the feelings of others.'[b]

■ Research into Black–White communication stereotypes found that Whites saw Black communication as argumentative, emotional,

aggressive, straightforward, critical, sensitive, ostentatious, defiant, hostile, open, responsive and intelligent. Blacks saw White communication as demanding, manipulative, organized, rude, critical, aggressive, arrogant, boastful, hostile, ignorant, deceptive and noisy.[c]

■ In the former Yugoslavia, negative stereotypes of women include regarding them as inefficient, not competent in politics and management, less self-confident than men, less successful in making public speeches, more interested in practical matters (schooling, medical care), and as preferring to spend more time on housekeeping and taking care of others. These stereotypes reflect and support structural inequalities.[d]

Sources: (a) Author's research

(b) Hall, E.T. and Hall, M.R., (1990) *Understanding Cultural Differences: Germans, French, and Americans,* Yarmouth, M.E: Intercultural Press, pp. 75–76

(c) Leonard, R. and Locke, D. (1993) 'Communication stereotypes: is interracial communication possible?', *Journal of Black Studies,* **23**(3): 332–43

(d) Kavcic, B. (1994) 'Women in management: The former Yugoslavia', in Adler, N.J. and Izraeli, D.N., (eds) *Competitive Frontiers,* MA: Blackwell

child discipline, feminism, immigration, and homosexuality, while women were expected to be conservative on religion. Attractiveness was linked to liberalism, age to conservatism. The research also revealed that the participants used sub-stereotypes: the age and attractiveness of the target modified the impression based purely on gender.[74]

People are more likely to create stereotypes of people who are members of different groups from themselves. Stereotypes also tend to favour ingroups. Outgroup members are believed to be less attractive, capable, trustworthy, honest, co-operative and deserving than ingroup members. As a result, people behave differently towards outgroup members. Because stereotypes are constructed socially, group discussion makes members' stereotypes more extreme.[75] A Dutch study showed that stereotypes are 'domain-specific' – for instance, they vary according to whether people are thinking of an ethnic outgroup as neighbours, colleagues, classmates or (marital) partners. The study also showed that how much social distance people impose as a result of stereotypes varies according to the particular attributions in the stereotype – for instance, traditionalism, deviancy or low education/dark skin. (Imposing or maintaining social distance refers to avoiding intimacy or spending time with another person.)[76]

Demonstrations that stereotypes affect behaviour include showing that people whose concept of rudeness was primed interrupted the experimenter more quickly and frequently than did people primed with polite-related stimuli; people for whom an elderly stereotype was primed walked more slowly down the hallway when leaving the experiment than did those from a control group, showing that even their self-concept could be stereotypically primed; and participants for whom a negative African-American stereotype was primed reacted with more hostility to a vexatious request of the African-American experimenter than those for whom a positive stereotype was primed. Stereotypical beliefs significantly affected respondents' attitudes towards the training, promotion and retention of older workers, their willingness to work with older workers, and their support for positive discrimination.[77]

However, other research challenges the idea that implicit biases are automatically and invariantly activated when perceivers come into contact with members of stigmatised groups. For instance, people self-completing race attitude questionnaires showed less race bias when the experimenters were Black than when they were White.[78] Moreover, stereotypes are not continually affecting attitudes and behaviour. For example, when research subjects watched a video of a member of a group about which they had stereotypes, these were first activated (after 15 seconds), then dissipated (after 12 minutes). They were re-activated when the person portrayed expressed disagreement with the research subjects' own view on a court judgement.[79]

Stereotypes of subgroups can be quite specific. For instance, when British listeners gave their social evaluations of audiotaped voices, they upgraded standard accented speakers on competence-related traits but downgraded them on solidarity, regardless of age. However, older speakers were perceived as less hesitant but more benevolent than younger speakers. Older-sounding standard speakers were judged most competent, older-sounding non-standard speakers least competent. Slow-talking younger speakers were most downgraded on competence.[80] However, people tend to overestimate the degree to which they themselves are perceived as different – that is, the extent to which they are stereotyped. This has been demonstrated for stereotypes of and by women, business students, and students from different geographical regions.[81]

Stereotypes of subgroups show both similarity and difference from culture to culture. A widespread stereotype of people with disabilities is that they can be easily offended and highly sensitive about their disability, and can communicate anger and resentment. Similarly, an examination of sex stereotypes in 30 countries concluded

Box 4.5

A woman member of a minority ethnic group was being interviewed about her claim to housing benefit. The officer asked her to describe her circumstances. She replied with a long story about the difficult behaviour of her child, her husband's being out of work, her own poor health and the failures of the (private) landlord to deal with problems in her flat. The officer thought she was being evasive. He interrupted her – 'I didn't mean that, I meant your financial circumstances. How much money do you have coming in each week?' The woman was silent.

Comment

The woman from a collectivist ethnic minority expects the officer to take all her circumstances and problems into account; the officer, mindful of the pertinent rules, wants to know only the relevant facts. If the officer had shown some interest in, or acknowledgement of, the woman's

problems, before *gently* moving on to the matter of money, things might have gone better.

The (high power distance) woman is perhaps silenced by her respect for the officer's authority, though it is unlikely she either understands or accepts the reason for his demands. Her silence may prevent her getting what she is entitled to; it may also lead the officer, if he has the low interpersonal trust attitude typical of individualists, to think that she is trying to get something she is not entitled to.

She might expect sympathy for her 'failed' family and appreciation of her modest silence under what she could experience as an attack (feminine culture).

Had the officer used active listening, the woman claimant might not have fallen silent.

Based on: Author's research

that there is substantial agreement among cultures concerning the psychological characteristics differentially associated with men and women. The stereotypes were scored for activity, strength and favourability of affective meaning. The content of the male stereotype turned out to be more active and stronger in affective meaning, but not any more favourable. However, stronger male stereotypes, that is, a greater attribution of active, strong characteristics to males than to females, were found in cultures with lower levels of literacy and socio-economic development and with a lower proportion of women enrolled in college.[82]

Another study also found cultural differences in stereotypes, in this case of older workers. Compared to a Hong Kong sample, UK respondents saw older workers as more effective but less adaptable. The study also found age-related effects on age stereotypes: older respondents reported positive stereotypes of older people, although not for work effectiveness in the case of older supervisors.[83]

Some stereotypes are positive. Many, though, are negative: for instance, when working-class individuals do not use middle-class speech, they are stereotyped as unintelligent, uneducated and possibly lazy.[84] Other stereotypes may be positive in some contexts but negative in others. For example, stereotypes that are shared by many people about gender differences have men as high in instrumental traits such as aggressiveness and independence, and women as possessing expressive traits such as sensitivity, nurturance and tactfulness. Women's stereotypical traits may well be positively regarded in the context of friendship or the home, but they are generally regarded negatively in the context of work, especially higher-level executive or managerial work.

Because assumptions, including ethnocentrism and stereotypes, are both powerful and inaccessible to self-awareness, they are key variables in encounters. This applies particularly to assumptions about the other party, such as stereotypes. However, such assumptions are not rigidly fixed, but dynamic. There is evidence that one party's assumptions can change the reality for both parties, that 'interpersonal beliefs actively guide social interaction, creating a social world that fits the expectations of the actors. Actors engaged in social interaction behave as if their beliefs about the others are true, and their targets, in turn, tend to act in ways that verify these beliefs. In negotiations, too, the parties, through their belief systems, create the interaction and its outcomes. Negotiators can, and do, "change the game." '[85]

Expectations

Expectations are beliefs about how people do and should behave. In interactions they apply to both verbal and non-verbal behaviour. They influence how people interpret and evaluate what others say and do during interactions; when they are violated, people react, often with negative evaluations of the violator.[86] On the other hand, they may also be changed (co-constructed) during the interaction.[87]

Expectations about both work and communication behaviour are influenced by national cultural differences in values. For instance, individualism influences expectations, commitment and behavioural decision-making patterns. Individualism is reflected in the desire to avoid submission to authority figures as well as a preference for doing things in one's own way. On the other hand, less individualist people have a longer-range view and are more willing to take advice.[88] Cultural values concerning, for instance, the relative importance of self-respect and harmonious work relationships are reflected in both life and personal goals, such as the centrality of work. They are also reinforced by social cues – that is, by information imparted by co-workers and work groups. These cues shape employees' judgments about standards of behaviour and how individuals interpret the actions and communications of others at work, including those perceived as representing the organisation. In high-individualism countries, such as the UK, Italy, Belgium and France, individuals expect others to display self-respect. Collectivist countries, such as Spain, Greece and Portugal expect others to place more emphasis on harmonious relationships and the maintenance of face.

Power distance also plays a role in how individuals interpret organisational actions and standards of behaviour. In high power distance societies such as Spain, Italy, France, Belgium, Greece, Portugal and Turkey, employees expect power within institutions to be distributed unequally and authority to be centralised. It is accepted that power holders will negotiate special privileges for themselves. In contrast, in low power distance countries such as Denmark, Norway, Sweden, the UK, the Netherlands, Germany and Finland, a more democratic contracting style may be expected.

The expectations a person has about the behaviour of people from another culture are related to all of the following:

- How much they know about that culture.
- What they believe and what their attitude is to that culture.
- Stereotypes of individuals from that culture.
- Their own self-concept (e.g., as 'proud to be British' or as 'a citizen of the world').
- Whether they have roles which require interfacing with people from the other culture.
- Previous experience of people from the other culture.
- Perceptions of their own and the others' relative status.[89]

Differences in the definition of honesty may be among the important differences in behavioural expectations of parties in intercultural transactions. Two societies may have the same degree of honesty but may nevertheless define differently the components of honest or of cheating behaviour. Debates about comparative corruption indicate how definitions of honest and dishonest behaviour may vary between societies. Differences in the definition of honesty may mean that people from one society believe that they are being cheated when the other party is behaving honestly by their own code of conduct. This distinction may distort the perception of compliance with contracts or agreements, which of course is fundamental to the relationship between the two parties.[90]

Subcultural variations in expectations are shown by research which found that physician and patient groups had different role expectations of themselves and one another and that age differences affected role expectations in both groups.[91] Other research showed that professional nurses in psychiatric wards were more likely to respond therapeutically to violent patient behaviour directed against staff if they perceived the behaviour as arbitrary rather than intended. In other words, their professional role created expectations about patient behaviour that were different from those most people would have about others' behaviour, and, if the expectations were not fulfilled, their response was affected.[92]

Religion can affect gender role expectations. A study of religious television's depiction of family life suggested that the role of women expected in mainstream American religious groups might be more conservative than in secular life. It might also be becoming increasingly traditional. Women were found to be under-represented, portrayed in minor roles typically associated with the household. Only infrequently did they initiate interaction with other people.[93]

Expectations influence supervisor–subordinate relations. When 'normal' expectations are contravened, as when the supervisor is from an ethnic minority and the subordinate is from the dominant majority, problems arise. When supervisors and subordinates were demographically similar, a study showed, the subordinates' behaviour outside of their roles was favourably affected, probably because similarity creates attraction. Basic task performance was not affected, however. When supervisors and subordinates were dissimilar in ways consistent with social cultural norms (for instance, when the supervisor was a man and the subordinate a woman) both basic task performance and subordinate behaviour outside of the task were positively affected.[94]

Attitudes

Attitudes are a combination of beliefs and affect. 'Affect' means 'enduring positive or negative evaluations about some person, object or issue'. Attitudes received a great deal of attention from psychologists when it was believed that they had a strong influence on behaviour – so strong that a person's behaviour could be predicted from knowing their attitude. It eventually became clear, however, that looking for a direct attitude–behaviour link was not likely to be fruitful. Instead, efforts have been directed at establishing links between the following:

■ Attitudes to performing a behaviour and performing it (e.g., attitudes to working abroad and actually seeking such an assignment).
■ Attitudes to a target person or object and acting accordingly (e.g., attitudes to an overseas job offer and accepting it).

- Attitudes to the context and acting accordingly (e.g., attitudes to a country and seeking to work there).
- Attitudes to time and using it for a particular purpose (e.g., attitudes to one's career and taking a year out to gain international experience).

All four attitudes might need to be favourable before the relevant action is performed, or one might outweigh all the others.[95]

It has been shown, in the context of prejudice, that people may not be fully aware of their attitudes. A study found that although the explicit (self-reported) attitudes of Whites predicted their own assessments of their verbal behaviour towards Blacks relative to Whites observers' assessments of their non-verbal behaviour and bias conflicted with these explicit attitudes. Instead, the Whites' implicit attitudes, assessed by reactions to primary stimuli such as schematic faces, predicted the observers' assessments.[96] Racial attitudes mediate European Americans' display of interaction involvement: Whites with positive racial attitudes display more signs of interaction involvement than African Americans do, but European Americans with negative racial attitudes show less than African Americans. African Americans show awareness of the 'mixed messages conveyed through involvement and stress and the role of these cues as reflections of racial attitudes'.[97]

Trust

Trust is a positive attitude towards another person, assumed voluntarily in order to cope with relational uncertainty. It involves accepting vulnerability, in conjunction with expecting that another's actions will not be harmful. In interactions, trust influences levels of disclosure, openness and formality on the part of speakers and willingness to listen, believe and be persuaded on the part of receivers.

There is a theory that high mutual trust is linked to economic prosperity and so varies from country to country.[98] However, findings from the World Values Survey do not bear this theory out. In Denmark, Sweden, Finland and the Netherlands people do indeed have high mutual trust and, as expected, economic prosperity is generally high. But although France, Belgium and Iceland are also prosperous, their people have much less mutual trust. (The same applies to Luxembourg, the most prosperous country in Europe, which does not have the highest score in terms of mutual trust.) Again, although Eastern European countries are considerably less prosperous than Western European countries, in a few cases the degree of mutual trust is just as high as in many prosperous Western European countries. The figures have changed little over time. Although the trend in most countries is towards a decline in trust, the change is only a few percentage points.[99]

Culture influences the relative importance people attach to different aspects of trust. Findings from a comparative survey of 153 Mexican and 177 US subjects showed that people from individualist cultures valued most the willingness to trust an agent from outside one's group to act on one's behalf, while setting limits to trust. In contrast, people from collectivist cultures most valued setting the level of trust according to the relationship.[100] Power distance is another cultural variable that influences willingness to trust, while gender is a subcultural influence. From hypothesis-testing research on a sample of Hong Kong employees, it was found that, compared with high power distance individuals, those low in power distance were more likely to link trust in their supervisor and belief that their employing organisation was fulfilling its contractual obligations to whether they thought decisions were reached and carried out in a fair way. Similarly, men were more likely than women to believe their employing organisation was fulfilling its contract with them only if they perceived those in authority as acting fairly.[101]

Intentions

Intentions are mental plans of action. They are more closely linked to behaviour than attitudes, though the relationship is still far from one-for-one. Because people are usually aware of their intentions, they are relatively controllable. In addition, as Chapter 3 showed, it is vital to effective communication for receivers to correctly understand speakers' communicative intentions. Intentional actions, it has been suggested, are less strongly influenced by culture than routine, habitual ones or those driven by emotion. However, people usually overestimate how deliberate others' actions are, thus underestimating the influence of culture on others' behaviour.

Abilities

Those individuals who choose to be managers might be more similar in their business skills than they are to non-managers, independent of their national cultural or subcultural backgrounds. This view is supported by a study that found no relationship between managerial skills and national cultural backgrounds of managers in three countries.[102]

Personality

Personality traits are tendencies to show consistent patterns of thoughts, feelings and actions. The Five-Factor Model (FFM) is a taxonomy of personality traits, consisting of neuroticism (N), extraversion (E), openness to experience (O), agreeableness (A) and conscientiousness (C). Studies comparing the mean levels of personality traits across cultures show systematic patterns, but there may be additional personality factors specific to individual cultures, and some factors may be of greater or less importance in different cultures. For example, individual differences in openness to experience may be of little consequence in traditional cultures where life's options are severely limited. In the words of Bond and Smith,

> Studies of implicit personality theory in any language studied to date indicate that a five-factor model can describe the organization of perceived personality. The apparent universality of the broad categories of extraversion, agreeableness, conscientiousness, emotional stability, and openness to experience may arise from their importance in directing universal types of social behaviors such as association, subordination, and formality. Within the general framework of this model, culture exercises its influence by accentuating certain of the Big Five dimensions over others. In free-response trait descriptions of themselves or of others, Chinese, for example, use the category of conscientiousness more often and use the category of agreeableness less often than do Americans. Moreover, the rated importance of each of the five categories varies among cultural groups, and these categories are differentially weighted in guiding social behavior.[103]

There is evidence that personality traits vary across subcultures. They may, for instance, be age-related: studies in the USA found noticeable changes in the mean level of all five factors between adolescence and about age 30. 'N, E, and O decline, whereas

A and C increase. After age 30, the same trends are seen, but at a much slower pace: in terms of personality traits, 30-year-olds resemble 70-year-olds more than 20-year-olds'. Data from Germany, Italy, Portugal, Croatia, South Korea, Estonia, Russia, Japan, Spain, Britain, Turkey and the Czech Republic showed patterns of age differences very similar to those seen in the USA. It appears that increasing age, especially from adolescence to mid-adulthood, tends to make individuals better adjusted, more altruistic and better organised, but also less enthusiastic and less open to new experience.[104]

Personality traits may also be influenced by gender. Using a different taxonomy of personality traits, a study of gender differences across 16 countries found that women scored higher than men in anxiety, vulnerability, straightforwardness and openness to aesthetics; men scored higher in (claimed) competence, assertiveness, excitement seeking and openness to ideas. However, the same study found evidence for cultural differences in the size of gender differences. Contrary to expectations, the greatest gender differences in traits like assertiveness were found in modern European countries and the least in traditional cultures (like South Korea). A possible explanation is that in countries where women are expected to be subservient, they attribute their low assertiveness to their role as a woman rather than their traits. By contrast, European women who are equally low in assertiveness identify it as a part of their own personality.[105]

Argyle records that religion is not much related to the general personality variables known to psychologists, such as extraversion or neuroticism.[106] However, Adorno found that Church members, especially Catholics, in the USA were more authoritarian than those with no religion; fundamentalists – whether Hindu, Muslim, Jew or Christian – were the most authoritarian. In addition, dogmatism – being rigid in thinking, intolerant of ambiguity and unable to deal with new information – was highest among members of strict churches (American Catholics and Southern Baptists), lowest among non-believers.[107]

Identity and self-construals

In some schools of thought, identity, or selfhood, has emerged to replace the concept of personality. Identity is not seen as a fixed, enduring characteristic of the individual, nor as a collection of psychological factors unaffected by wider social concerns. Identity theorists emphasise the social (and cultural) dimensions of identity and the fluid or changing nature of identity over time.[108] Though not synonymous, self-construals and identity are closely related. Self-construals are our mental representations of ourselves, derived, at least in part, reflexively – that is, by interpreting how others seem, from their communication with us, to perceive us. Compared with self-construals, identity is usually considered to include a more affective element and to be associated with group membership; as a result, we all have multiple identities – mother, wife, lawyer, French national and so on. For communication theorists, cultural identification, such as that which causes someone to identify as French, is a process that happens in a constantly changing socio-economic environment and which is also affected by contact with other cultures. Cultural identities are negotiated, co-created, reinforced and challenged through communication. Whereas social psychological perspectives view identity as a characteristic of the person and the self as centred in social roles and social practices, a communication perspective views identity as something that emerges when messages are exchanged between persons. Throughout life, cultural identities are emergent, not created or completed.

According to Thompson culture shapes self-construals through giving meaning to experience. However, he noted, 'we are constrained, not only by the range of possibilities which culture offers – that is, by the variety of symbolic representations – but also by social relations'.[109] The functionalist approach to national cultural differences argues that individualists have independent self-construals: their mental representations of the self are separate from those they have of others. In contrast, for collectivists, self-construals are fundamentally interdependent. Others are in effect considered part of the self. In individualist models, the self 'comprises a unique, bounded configuration of internal attributes, such as preferences, traits, abilities, motives, values and rights, and behaves primarily as a consequence of these internal attributes.'[110] For people with independent self-construals, then, although other people are crucial in maintaining the sense of self and also function as standards of comparison and sources of appraisal, the persistent concern in communicating is to express internal attributes. Against this, people from collectivist cultures are usually more strongly aware of the nature of their relationship to others and of maintaining reciprocity within those relationships. People with interdependent self-construals, such as the Japanese, may have less clarity about their selves than people with independent self-construals, such as Canadians.[111] It is, however, possible to have both interdependent and independent components in the self-construal. (They are orthogonal, not bipolar, constructs.)[112]

Both within and across cultures, individuals with predominantly interdependent self-construals have been found to be more aware of the status of the source of a communication, more influenced by the perceived fairness of a procedure, less inclined to perceive their ingroup as homogeneous, more inclined to use hint strategies, more easily embarrassed and more easily affected by emotional contagion.[113] A study found that people with interdependent self-construals paid closer attention to the characteristics of a high status source than did individuals with independent self-construals. Furthermore, the relative amount of attitude change resulting from persuasive communication by a high status source was significantly larger for those with interdependent self-construals than for those with independent self-construals.[114] Another cross-cultural study built on previous research. This showed that the more fair people thought the procedure by which the outcome of a social exchange was decided, the less they were influenced in assessing it by whether the outcome was in their favour or not. For example, if a performance appraisal was thought to be based on a fair procedure, workers would be less aggrieved by an unfavourable appraisal. The cross-cultural study showed that this applied even more to people with interdependent self-construals than to people with independent self-construals.[115] Finally, a direct link has been found between self-construals and ways of communicating. In making a request, individuals high in interdependence are more likely to use hint strategies on the first and second attempt, while independent individuals are more likely to use direct strategies. However, when non-compliance is high, both interdependent and independent individuals use direct strategies.[116]

Continent-wide or even national cultures may be too broad to define identities or self-construals, which some research shows to vary by subculture and by environmental factors like politics. A study found that Chinese self-construals vary across age, gender and urban-rural residence and are also influenced by the changing political, economic and socio-cultural context in China. As Martin and Nakayama argued, 'Ethnic identity is having a sense of belonging to a particular group and knowing something about the shared experience of the group. For some [US] residents, ethnicity is a specific and relevant construct and for others it is a vague concept.'[117] Ethnic identity is a complex cluster of factors that define the extent and type of involvement with one's ethnic group. It differs both qualitatively and quantitatively among ethnic group members; two individuals who belong to the same group may differ widely on

Box 4.6

- Europe-wide only three in 100 Europeans put 'Europe' first as the place they identify with. Many people, it seems, do not identify with 'Europe' because of the lack of continuity down the generations, shared memories, symbols etc. People identify with their immediate surroundings, the town or city (49 per cent), province (13 per cent) or country (28 per cent) where they live. This general low figure does not, however, mean that people reject Europe. Only around 8 per cent of Europeans overall feel they belong least of all to Europe, but in Great Britain the figure rises to one in three, and a relatively large proportion of respondents in Ireland, Denmark and France also reject Europe.

Even Russians and other Central and Eastern Europeans are less likely to reject Europe.[a]
- Typically, Muslims, and Arabians in particular, hold two sets of identity: one, immediate, social and spatially particular; the other, historical, cultural and global.[b]

Sources: (a) Halman, L. and Kerkhofs, J. (2001) The European Values Study: Selected results. URL: www.romir.ru/eng/research/01_2001/european-values.htm
(b) Ali, A. J. (1993) 'Decision-making style, individualism and attitudes toward risk of Arab executives', *International Studies of Management & Organization,* **23**(3): 53–74

their identification with the group and their commitment to it. They may differ in how salient the group is for them and in what it means subjectively. Furthermore, ethnic identity can vary within one individual over time. The psychological correlates of ethnicity are likely to differ depending on the quality of this identity. However, although the implications of ethnicity vary widely across individuals, ethnicity is 'a highly salient and meaningful construct'.[118]

Ethnic identities ascribed to an individual by others can create 'treacherous cross-currents' that have to be negotiated. University students in Hong Kong, for example, perceived themselves as similar to but distinct from typical Hong Kong Chinese. They ascribed to themselves elements of a valued Western identity in equal measure to their Hong Kong identity.[119] This creative synthesising of local identities provides an escape from the intergroup conflict that must arise when there is no alternative to ascribed ethnic identity. The identifications achieved by individuals rather than ascribed to them by others then become the basis for various forms of intergroup behaviour, such as linguistic differentiation and styles of conflict management.[120]

Gender is fundamental to most people's identity. In all cultures, men and women differ in their self-reports of masculine and feminine characteristics, although the gender difference is typically less than that reflected in gender stereotypes.[121] Gender difference in the total affective meaning of self-reports was reportedly greater in countries where power distance was high and where the socio-economic level, percentage of Christians and proportion of female college graduates were low. In the West, women may be more like people from collectivist cultures than Western men are, in having more interdependent self-construals: Cross and Madison argued, 'Many gender differences in cognition, motivation, emotion and social behavior may be explained in terms of men's and women's different self-construals'.[122] For US women, but not for men, a positive relationship has been found between self-esteem and motives that favour acting in friendly or helpful ways. Self-enhancement strategies used by US men often involve boasting and exaggeration of their abilities, operating with a 'false uniqueness' bias – the false belief that one's own abilities are exceptional – and overestimating their performances against objective standards. In contrast, US women are more likely to adjust their self-enhancement strategies for the feelings of others. For instance, women students with high grade-point averages are more likely to take into account the assessments received by their interlocutors before talking about their own grades.

US women also respond more to feedback than US men do. This finding has also been interpreted in terms of their having more interdependent self-construals. On the other hand, women's greater responsiveness to feedback may be because they have lower self-esteem, rather than being directly linked to their self-construals. The fact that women have lower status than men may lower their self-confidence, leading them, among other things, to place a low valuation on their own opinion of themselves and to be more responsive than men to others' evaluations.[123]

Significant differences have been found in how accurately men and women perform the following:

- Estimate their own intelligence.
- Evaluate their productivity.
- Evaluate their performance at finding a route and on tests of sports trivia and knowledge of politics.
- Report prior grades.
- Judge their own attractiveness.

In almost all cases, women underestimate themselves. Replicating an earlier study, Beyer found that women expected to perform worse, judged themselves as having performed worse and wrongly remembered that they had performed worse (showed a greater negative recall bias) on tests of masculine knowledge (such as American football). However, there were no significant differences in men's and women's expectations, judgements and recall of performance on tests of 'feminine' knowledge (of film and TV stars and fashion) or neutral tests of common knowledge, character detection, practical questions and anagrams. 'This emphasizes that females' inaccurate self-perceptions are highly task specific rather than generalized'.[124]

Social class often enters into identity. Hoyt found that high-flying working-class individuals entering middle-class environments can feel stress and feelings of incompetence, because of a lack of 'cultural necessities', that is the speech, manners, clothing and experiences of the middle class. Such individuals may be 'conflicted'. One said, 'Part of our identity was middle class while another part remained back in the working class world of our roots.'[125] According to Huntington, religions give people identity by positing a basic distinction between believers and non-believers, between a superior ingroup and a different and inferior outgroup.[126]

People with disabilities have been shown to have self-construals not significantly different from those of others, contrary to stereotypes. A study of 177 students registered with a university's disabled service and 160 other students found that students with and without disability tended to rate each other in a stereotypical manner. Students with disabilities were seen as more conscientious and cultured than were students without disabilities, whereas students without disabilities were seen as more extraverted and emotionally stable than students with disabilities. When the students rated themselves, however, no such differences emerged between the groups with and without disabilities.[127]

Personal characteristics may affect the level of cultural identity exhibited. People with high levels of national identification have been shown to be more likely to display the individualist or collectivist characteristics associated with their national culture than people with low levels of national identification.[128] Kim and Leung criticised the conceptualisation of individualism and collectivism as polar opposites, arguing that a person can simultaneously maintain high independent and interdependent construals, that self-construals are dynamic, not fixed – they vary with context and over time – and that there is an increasing incidence of biculturals. Asian students are higher than Americans on interdependent scales but not lower on independence. These authors saw 'biculturals' as having the most fully developed self-construals, 'independents' as having underdeveloped interdependence construals and 'interdependents' as having underdeveloped' independence construals. They also suggested there is a fourth category, 'marginals', who have underdevelopment of both construals.[129]

Huntington argued that everyone has multiple identities that may compete with or reinforce each other: identities of kinship, occupation, culture, institution, territory, education, party, ideology and others. In the contemporary world, cultural identification is dramatically increasing in importance compared to other dimensions of identity. This is the result of social/economic modernisation. At the individual level, dislocation and alienation create the need for more meaningful identities; at the societal level, the enhanced capabilities and power of non-Western societies stimulate the revitalisation of indigenous identities and culture. Identity at any level – personal, tribal, racial, civilisational – can only be defined in relation to an 'other', a different person, tribe, race or civilisation. The intra-civilisational 'us' and the extra-civilisational 'them' is a constant in human history. These differences in intra- and extra-civilisational behaviour stem from feelings of superiority (and occasionally inferiority) towards people who are perceived as being very different. Other sources are fear of and lack of trust in such people, difficulty of communication with them as a result of differences in language and what is considered civil behaviour and lack of familiarity with the assumptions, motivations, social relationships and social practices of other people.[130]

Critique

There is an ongoing debate about how relevant cultural identities (and so self-construals) are at work. One study suggests that they are relevant, but to differing degrees. Homogeneous work groups which differed in terms of ethnicity and gender were found to vary significantly in how far cultural identity was articulated, whether ethnicity, gender or religion was the most salient identity, whether the focus was on the ingroup or the outgroup and whether the references were positive or negative. However, discourses of separateness, narrowly defined identity and inequality were common.[131] Another study suggests that identities at work are affective (emotion-based) and can be measured on dimensions of 'niceness', powerfulness and liveliness. The study found that German managers and subordinates, constrained to behave according to the prescriptions of their American employing company (prescriptions which corresponded to American cultural norms), had both to adjust substantially and lost status. When the managers' affective identities were measured, they reflected substantially lower levels of niceness and powerfulness. 'This redefinition shows that he [sic] had lost any basis for corporate leadership', according to the author. Managers experience identity problems when following culture-centric behaviour prescriptions instead of using the affective meaning of their professional identities as guidance for their behaviour.[132]

The concepts of self-construal and identity and cultural differences in them have attracted criticism. Varela *et al.* criticised the whole concept of a 'self' as a Western myth, arguing that when people look inside themselves for a fixed, unitary self, no such animal can be found. Instead, they find that who they are is completely bound up with and relative to their environment. The inability to catch one's self without a perception, to separate the self from the world, can lead to anxiety, restlessness and self-grasping.[133]

Self-esteem

It has been asserted that culture influences the perceived gap between our actual self and our ideal self, and so decides how we evaluate our self-esteem. This implies that self-esteem is a cultural creation. The evidence, however, is somewhat conflicting. On the one hand, Farh *et al.* found cultural differences in self-esteem strongly reflected when they investigated modesty bias among Taiwanese and Western workers. Modesty bias means that subjects give self-ratings of work performance that are lower than supervisors' ratings; Western workers' self-ratings of performance are usually higher than ratings obtained from supervisors – they do not exhibit modesty bias. Farh, *et al.* found that Taiwanese workers do exhibit modesty bias.[134] Their findings were explained in terms of broad cultural differences between Taiwanese and Western workers. On the other hand, a replication study using data from several organisations in mainland China showed leniency in self-ratings – that is self-ratings higher than supervisor or peer ratings – which suggest that broad cultural factors may not fully explain the reported modesty bias.[135] However, measures of self-esteem used in cross-cultural comparisons are often based on individual attributes rather than group attributes. Cross-cultural comparisons may therefore miss differences in self-evaluation derived from a person's 'collective identity'. Thus findings on whether people from certain cultural groups are more socially modest or internally depressed may be premature.[136]

Box 4.7

North Africans in France use a range of rhetorical tools for rebutting French racism to prevent it damaging their self-esteem:

- They claim that people of all races, nations and religions are equal. Moral rules are emphasised: 'Whether black or white, if they don't do evil, they are OK.'
- They demonstrate cultural similarities between the French and Moroccans, Tunisians, Algerians or Kabyles, using historical and socio-cultural evidence.
- They argue that they personally conform to what they perceive to be universal moral criteria highly valued by the host (French) society. This distances the individual from the race/nation/religion in order to show that the group to which s/he belongs does not necessarily define a person.

- They demonstrate the superiority of Moslems (or their own national group) to the French – embracing an Islamic moral universalism: 'In France, old people are badly treated and their children don't come to see them. In contrast, in our country. ...
- They explain racism by the characteristics of the racist (e.g. lack of experience of members of ethnic minorities). Only a small number of North Africans in France use this rhetoric.

Source: Lamont, M., Morning, A. and Mooney, M. (2002) 'Particular universalisms: North African immigrants respond to French racism', *Ethnic and Racial Studies*, **25**(3): 390–414

Values, motivations, emotions, perceptions, beliefs, assumptions, expectations, attitudes intentions, abilities and the 'self' – are affected by many individual factors. These range from genetic make-up to school environment during upbringing, from the innate element in intelligence to experiences at work. In particular, though, they are affected by the way people have been taught by their culture to look at the world. Other influences are people's societal positions, which are affected by such factors as their gender, age, (dis)ability, social class and so on. In turn, these psychological factors affect individuals' communicative styles, emphases (content versus relationship, control, affiliation), strategies and ways of using language.

4.2 SOCIAL COGNITION PROCESSES

This section concerns the processes that produce the kinds of cognitive constructs described in Section 4.1. Cognitive processes receive, select, transform and organise information, construct representations of reality and build knowledge. Many activities are involved, including perceiving, learning, memorising, thinking and verbalising. These processes continuously influence one another. They are subject to a number of distorting influences. They do not directly predict particular communication behaviours such as reciprocity or defensiveness, but do so indirectly by their influence on thoughts. The emphasis in this section is on how these processes themselves may vary cross-culturally and how they may lead to differences in the resulting constructs.

Social perceiving

People are exposed to more complex and varied information than they can process. They therefore use a number of devices to reduce the mental work involved. These devices include selective attention, limited arousal, categorisation and simplification. Culture influences these processes. For example, there are cultural differences in how likely it is that someone 'samples' – that is be aware of and seek information on – the verbal content of communication more than its non-verbal accompaniments, such as voice tone or gesture. Again, people in some cultures tend to sample processes internal to individuals, such as attitudes or beliefs, more than externals, such as social influences or roles. Others do the reverse.[137] These devices are also, necessarily, some of the sources of bias in social perception. This was demonstrated when holders of the belief that traits are unalterable consistently displayed greater attention to and recognition of consistent information about another person, whereas holders of a belief that people's traits change incrementally paid more attention to inconsistent information about that person. Thus beliefs can lead to processing that supports or limits stereotype maintenance.[138]

The process that introduces most cultural difference into social perceiving, however, is attribution. This term refers to deciding, often subconsciously, whether another person's disposition or situation causes their observed behaviour. People make attributions in order to predict future events, exercise control and gain understanding. For example, in order to decide whom to make redundant, a sales manager may need to decide whether a salesperson's poor sales record is the result of his or her incompetence and laziness or of market conditions. There are different kinds of personal attributions and these differ cross-culturally. Some cultures give greater weight to ascribed attributes of persons, such as ethnicity or religion and others to achieved attributes, such as attitudes or past performance. Several types of attribution bias have been well documented. Of these, one has been most clearly demonstrated to vary cross-culturally. This is the self-serving bias, or tendency for someone to attribute successful outcomes of their own actions to themselves and unsuccessful outcomes to the situation. According to the theory of self-esteem in attribution, self-serving bias helps to protect self-esteem; the extent of the need for such protection depends partly on cultural factors. The self-serving bias occurs in most cultures, but more frequently in North American and some European individuals than in Japanese, Indians, Asians or southern Europeans.[139] A study showed that Finns use self-serving bias less than Americans. In comparison to the Americans, the Finns were less likely to attribute good outcomes to internal, stable and global factors, pointing to a difference between the two Western cultures. Another study found that Dutch subjects made attributions similar to the Finns'. These findings suggest that some Western societies may exhibit more collectivist patterns of self-serving bias than originally presumed from studies of mainly Americans.[140]

Attribution processes in non-Western cultures may be 'context-dependent and occasion-bound'.[141] Their attributional logic may be less personal. Accordingly, members of non-Western cultures are more likely to make external/situational attributions than to believe that others' behaviours are consistent with internal factors such as attitudes.[142] Attribution research has found a strong bias towards attributing male, rather than female, gender to a gender-unspecified individual, even when no descriptive pronouns (such as he or she) are used.[143] Girls tend to attribute their own failure in mathematics/science more to a learned-helpless orientation than boys do.[144]

At work, there is bias in attributions of managers' success – women's being more often attributed to the situation, men's more to personal qualities.[145] Attributions of blame for sexual harassment at work are also biased. Men allocate more blame overall than women and specifically more to the target of the harassment.[146] Gender also influences attributions and emotions in helping contexts – men perceive themselves as having more responsibility and become angrier.[147] In laboratory research, people tend to offer different explanations for the same level of performance, depending on the gender of the performer. Women's success tends to be attributed more strongly to high effort, luck or the ease of the task, but their failure to lack of ability. However, a field test of gender effects on managers' attributions for the performance of their direct subordinates found that employees of both genders were in the main attributed personal responsibility for both their successes and their failures. They were seen to succeed mainly because of their ability and because they worked hard; they were seen to fail chiefly because of limitations in the same two areas. The managers' own gender was unrelated to how they attributed the performance of their staff. In this study, unlike in laboratory studies, there was no support for the hypothesis that the performance of female employees would be explained differently and less favourably than that of men.[148]

Religious orientation has some effect on attributions. A Swedish study found that religious participants preferred secular attributions, especially when assessing the causes of failure. People with high extrinsic religious orientation (who view religion instrumentally and as one of many influences on life) were most likely to make different attributions depending on the topic.[149]

Thinking

Several aspects of mental processes may differ between cultures. These include categorising, logic style, learning style and problem-solving processes.

Categorising

How people classify or differentiate other people, things or issues is not 'natural', but rather learned, mainly through communication. The complexity of the categories in a child's cognitive system increases as the child gains experience. In mature individuals it varies – some people differentiate more finely than others and most people differentiate more finely on subjects they are interested in or knowledgeable about. Because the categories that people use are learned, not 'natural', they are culturally influenced. For example, English uses the word 'aunt' to mean both 'mother's sister' and 'father's sister'. Other cultures distinguish between the two. Chinese has different words for 'older brother' and 'younger brother', as age is an important indicator of status.

'Categorising is a fundamental and natural human activity. It is the way we come to know the world.' As a result, 'any attempt to eliminate bias by attempting to eliminate the perception of differences is doomed to failure'.[150] More subtle categorical distinctions bring stereotypes closer to reality. People should make more, not fewer distinctions. For instance, Europeans and Americans should divide Japanese people into male and female, rather than see both genders in terms of the same national stereotype.

Logic style

Western logic emphasises atomistic analysis, dichotomisation, deduction and induction from empirical data by an accepted set of procedures and abstractions. There are variations within Western cultures on which of these is more emphasised – French and German cultures are more concerned with ideas and abstractions than the British culture. Overall, however, Western logic systems can be contrasted with those of Eastern cultures. In these, again with internal variations, holism and intuition predominate, together with an emphasis on seeing the relationships between the external and internal world.

Learning style

While the capacity to learn from experience is clearly universal, there are (sub)cultural differences in what is learnt, how it is learnt and the degree to which mature adults remain open to such learning. For instance, if people believe that it is proper to accept the world as it is rather than to try to change it, learning based on problem-solving and future forecasting may be difficult. The relative emphasis placed on memorising versus understanding, knowledge versus skill acquisition and passive versus active learning similarly varies across cultures, as it has, historically, within single cultures, such as Britain's.

In regard to formal learning, if, as in many Central and Eastern European countries, teachers are highly honoured and hierarchies are important, then people may be used to learning from a lecture rather than from the give and take of a discussion. One of the greatest difficulties experienced by Western academics and others attempting to inculcate Western business education methods in the transition economies has been to make workshops, case studies and other participative learning techniques effective.

Problem-solving processes

How people work and their preferences for certain actions or solutions to work-related issues are affected by how they approach obtaining and manipulating information and their approach to problem-solving. There is evidence that these processes, which are known together as cognitive style, are affected in turn by cultural influences. There is also evidence that people with different cognitive styles experience difficulties in communicating with one another. These interaction problems can lead to conflict. A study of Canadian and Japanese cognitive styles found differences: Canadians were found to have a tendency to seek fast decisions and to rush to closure on data collection. The Japanese were found to resist fast decision-making because of a preference to obtain large amounts of information.[151]

> There are (sub)cultural differences in how people perceive, including what they notice about other people and to what causes they attribute others' behaviour. They also affect how they categorise people, things and issues as well as their preferred styles of logic, learning and problem-solving. These differences affect how they interact at work with culturally different others.

4.3　SUMMARY

The purpose of this chapter has been to deepen and widen the analysis of (sub) cultural differences in communication discussed in Chapter 3. To achieve this, it has explored psychological constructs and processes underlying overt communication behaviour. The chapter has shown that individuals' values, motivations, emotions, perceptions, beliefs, assumptions, expectations, attitudes, abilities and even their sense of 'self' differ from group to group. How individuals perceive other people and how they think also differ according to their (sub)culture. However, other factors than group memberships, including heredity, interact with these group effects to influence behaviour.

The three chapters of Part I of this book provide a foundation for awareness of cultural and subcultural similarities and differences in diverse workforces and populations. They also help analyse how and why people from different groups communicate differently at work.

QUESTIONS AND EXERCISES

1. What would make a psychological construct 'universal'? How can universal psychological constructs differ from culture to culture?
2. Devise a questionnaire to test for at least two of the primary motivational values of Schwartz given in the right hand column of Table 4.1. Test it out on three people from different backgrounds.
3. Interview at least two people from different backgrounds about (a) the importance and centrality of work, (b) norms about the rights and duties attached to work or (c) their work goals. Then devise a questionnaire to test for these values.
4. What might account for the finding of the European Values Survey that the data 'show higher levels overall and wider cross-country differences for expressive than instrumental work values'?
5. Research has shown that social class affects individuals' work values. Would you expect demographic differences, whether based on ethnicity, gender, age, disability, religion or sexual orientation, to affect work values? If so, explain how. If not, give your reasons.
6. Discuss the contention that 'the "trial-and-error process of actual business activity" and personal interaction with other people play an important role' in honing moral reasoning.
7. Table 4.3 shows differences between male and female housing managers' approaches to interpersonal relations with their staff and clients. How would you expect these differences to affect their work?

8. Complete the questionnaire. Note that 'stranger' here just means a person whom one has not met before.

	Strongly agree	Agree	Neither agree nor disagree	Disagree	Strongly disagree
1. I often find that encounters with strangers turn awkward					
2. I rarely ask questions early on in encounters with strangers					
3. I think most people would regard me as a competent communicator					
4. I try to avoid too many meetings with new people					
5. I usually tell new people I meet, a good deal about myself					
6. Meeting strangers of the opposite sex is more awkward than other meetings with strangers					
7. Meeting strangers with disabilities is more awkward than other meetings with strangers					
8. Meeting strangers from foreign countries is more awkward than other meetings with strangers					
9. Meeting strangers who are ethnically different from myself is more awkward than meeting other kinds of strangers					

Guidance on how to score and interpret this questionnaire is given in Appendix C

9. In the study of how Chinese managers deal with emotional issues at work (Ref. 28), they identified the best processes as: (a) to pay attention to or recognise the seriousness of the disruption (b) to divert attention and thinking away from the disruption (c) to calm unpleasant inner feelings, either privately or in connection with others (d) either to maintain or to calm pleasant emotions (e) to keep up their employees' pleasant emotions (f) to come to a better understanding of problems and possible solutions by thinking and feeling through them (g) to learn from emotional experiences so that pleasant ones can be sustained and unpleasant ones can be avoided in future. How would these processes differ from those most likely to be used by managers in your own culture? Where there are differences, which would you expect to be more effective in your own culture and why?

10. The text describes six 'fundamental belief systems about how the world works'. These are authoritarianism, social dominance orientation, Protestant work ethic, humanitarianism–egalitarianism, beliefs about the malleability of human attributes and beliefs about diversity. Other 'core' beliefs include locus of control and belief in a just or unjust world. Discuss possible reasons why such belief systems vary cross-culturally. Would you expect such belief systems to show less variability within than between cultures? Give your reasons.

11. Research more consistently shows a relationship of national culture to beliefs about aspects of organisation, such as worker participation, than to strategy. Why might this be?

12. What is ethnocentrism? How does it differ from stereotyping? How can it affect work behaviour?

13. An ethnic minority householder went into the local authority offices to complain that a large item of furniture left for collection was not picked up with the rest of their rubbish. He spoke to the receptionist. The item (a double bed) had to be picked up that day or it would affect arrangements for a cultural celebration. The receptionist tried to explain to him that special arrangements had to be made with the Council for the removal of large items and that a standard charge was levied. (Co-incidentally neighbours had phoned to complain that this large item had been left in the street outside the house in question.)

   During the discussion it emerged that the householder had offered the refuse men money to remove the item. He was angry because they declined. Now he wanted to negotiate a price for the item to be picked up. He asked if it would be cheaper if he put it in the street. The receptionist was young and female, the householder male and older. He wondered if she had enough authority to make decisions – was he being palmed off? He demanded to speak with manager (whom he assumed to be male). In turn, the receptionist wondered if he was sexist – she could not understand why it was so important that the item was moved that day. She also wondered if the offer of money to the refuse men was an attempt at a bribe.

   Analyse the factors influencing the behaviour of the participants in this scene. The case may also be used as the basis for a role play.

14. What factors influence the expectations that a person has about the communication behaviour of someone from another culture?

15. Complete the table from the material in the text or other sources:

(Sub)cultural differences which influence expectations	Expectations that may be influenced
Individualism	Desire to avoid submission to authority figures

16. What is trust? What aspects of communication does it influence? How does trust vary (a) in different economies and (b) between individualist and collectivist cultures?

17. What is the core difference between a communication perspective on identity and a social psychological perspective?

18. Draw an identity map equivalent to the one in Figure 2.1 for yourself. Compare yours with a colleague and discuss the reasons for the differences.
19. Complete the questionnaire.

	Strongly agree	Agree	Neither agree nor disagree	Disagree	Strongly disagree
1. When I communicate with others, I am always aware of my relationship with them.					
2. In communication with others, I am mainly concerned to have them understand where I am 'coming from'.					
3. I like the people I meet to know my tastes and preferences at an early stage in our acquaintance.					
4. When I communicate with others, I try to maintain an even balance between meeting my own needs and meeting theirs.					
5. I place a high value on self-expression.					
6. I like the people I meet to understand my important beliefs and values.					
7. It is important to get across one's personality in social conversations.					
8. I am generally concerned with how other people see me – what they think of me.					
9. I am very concerned that my interactions with others should be at all times harmonious.					
10. I use other people's attitudes and behaviours as ways of setting standards for my own.					

For guidance on how to score and interpret your responses to this questionnaire, see Appendix C

20. Find examples additional to those given in the text of cultural or subcultural differences in the following aspects of the thinking processes: categorising, logic style, learning style and problem-solving.

NOTES AND REFERENCES

1. Schwartz, S.H. (1992) 'Universals in value content and structure: theoretical advances and empirical tests in 20 countries', *Advances in Experimental Social Psychology*, **25**: 1–66.
2. Ali, A.J. and Wahabi, R. (1995) 'Managerial value systems in Morocco', *International Studies of Management & Organization*, **25**(3): 87–96.
3. Hofstede, G. (1981) *Cultures and Organizations: Software of the Mind*, London: Harper Collins, p. 31.
4. Sagiv, L. and Schwartz, S.H. (2000) 'A new look at national cultures: Illustrative applications to role stress and managerial behavior', in Ashkanasy, N.N., Wilderom, C. and Peterson, M.F. (eds) *The Handbook of Organizational Culture and Climate*, Newbury Park, CA: Sage, pp. 417–36.
5. England, G.W. (1995) 'National work meanings and patterns: Constraints on managerial action', in Jackson, T. (ed.) *Cross-Cultural Management*, Oxford: Butterworth-Heinemann.
6. Lingnan, O.S. (2003) 'Job stress and job performance among employees in Hong Kong: the Role of Chinese work values and organizational commitment', *International Journal of Psychology*, **38**(6): 337–47.
7. Kohn, M.L. (1969) *Class and Conformity: A Study in Values*, Homewood, Illinois: Dorsey Press.
8. Bazerman, M.H., Curhan, J.R., Moore, D.A. and Valley, K.L. (2000) 'Negotiation', *Annual Review of Psychology*, **51**: 279–314.
9. Stajkovic, A.J. and Luthans, F. (1997) 'Business ethics across cultures: a social cognitive model', *Journal of World Business*, **32**(1): 17–34.
10. Kazakov, A.Y., Taylor, T.C. and Thompson, M. (1997) 'Business ethics and civil society in Russia', *International Studies of Management & Organization*, **27**(1): 5–18.
11. Jackson, T. (2001) 'Cultural values and management ethics: a 10-nation study', *Human Relations*, **54**(10): 1267–302.
12. Butterfield, K.D., Treviño, L.K. and Weaver, G.R. (2000) 'Moral awareness in business organizations: influences of issue-related and social context factors', *Human Relations*, **53**(7): 981–1018.
13. Ali, A.J. (1995) 'Cultural discontinuity and Arab management thought', *International Studies of Management & Organization*, **25**(3): 7–30.
14. Murphy-Berman, V. and Berman, J.J. (2002) 'Cross-cultural differences in perceptions of distributive justice', *Journal of Cross-Cultural Psychology*, **33**(2): 157–70.
15. Seiter, J.S., Bruschke, J. and Bai, C. (2002) 'The acceptability of deception as a function of perceivers' culture, deceiver's intention, and deceiver-deceived relationship', *Western Journal of Communication*, **66**(2): 158–80.
16. Miller, J.G. and Bersoff, D.M. (1992) 'Culture and moral judgment: how are conflicts between justice and interpersonal responsibilities resolved?', *Journal of Personality and Social Psychology*, **62**(4): 541–54.
17. Argyle, M. (2000) *Psychology and Religion: An Introduction*, London: Routledge, p. 170.
18. Aycan, Z. (2002) 'Leadership and teamwork in developing countries: Challenges and opportunities', in Lonner, W.J., Dinnel, D.L., Hayes, S.A. and Sattler, D.N. (eds) *Online Readings in Psychology and Culture* (Unit 15, Chapter 4), URL: http://www.wwu.edu/~culture
19. Sagie, A., Elizur, D. and Yamauchi, H. (1996) 'The Structure and Strength of Achievement Motivation: a Cross-Cultural Comparison', *Journal of Organizational Behavior*, **17**(5): 431–44.
20. Guzley, R.M., Araki, F. and Chalmers, L.E. (1998) 'Cross-cultural perspectives of commitment: individualism and collectivism as a framework for conceptualization', *Southern Communication Journal*, **64**(1): 1–19.

21. Yousef, D.A. (2000) 'Organizational commitment as a mediator of the relationship between Islamic work ethic and attitudes toward organizational change', *Human Relations*, **53**(4): 513–39.

22. Martin, J.N., Hecht, M.L., Moore, S. and Larkey, L.K. (2001) 'African American conversational improvement strategies for interethnic communication', *Howard Journal of Communication*, **12**: 1–27.

23. Warr, P. and Fay, D. (2001) 'Age and personal initiative at work', *European Journal of Work and Organizational Psychology*, **10**(3): 343–53.

24. Frijda, N.H. and Mesquita, B. (1994) 'The social roles and functions of emotions', in Kitayama, S. and Markus, H.R. (eds) *Emotion and Culture: Empirical Studies of Mutual Influence*, Washington, DC: American Psychological Association, pp. 51–87.

25. Forgas, J.P. and Vargas, P. (1998) 'Affect and behavior inhibition: The Mediating role of cognitive processing strategies', *Psychological Inquiry*, **9**(3): 205–10.

26. George, J.M., Gonzalez, J.A. and Jones, G.R. (1998) 'The role of affect in cross-cultural negotiations', *Journal of International Business Studies*, **29**(4): 749–72.

27. Mesquita, B. and Frijda, N. H. (1992) 'Cultural variations in emotions: a review', *Psychological Bulletin*, **112**(2): 179–204.

28. Krone, K.J., Chen, L., Sloan, D.K. and Gallant, L.M. (1997) 'Managerial emotionality in Chinese factories', *Management Communication Quarterly* **11**(1): 6–50.

29. Cutspec, P. and Goering, E.M. (1988) 'Acknowledging cultural diversity: perceptions of shyness within the black culture', *Howard Journal of Communications*, **1**(1): 75–87.

30. Wolfson, K. and Pearce, W.B. (1983) 'A cross-cultural comparison of the implications of self disclosure on conversational logics', *Communication Quarterly*, **31**(3): 249–56.

31. McKee Ranger, L. (2002) 'Communication is key for deaf and hard of hearing technical pros', *Diversity/Careers Professional*, Oct/Nov. URL: http://www.diversitycarrers.com/articles/pro/octnov02/fod_com_deaf.htm

32. Roberts, C.V. and Vinson, L. (1998) 'Relationship among willingness to listen, receiver apprehension, communication apprehension, communication competence, and dogmatism', *International Journal of Listening*, **12**: 40–56.

33. Booth-Butterfield, S., Chory, R. and Beynon, W. (1997) 'Communication apprehension and health communication and behaviors', *Communication Quarterly*, **45**(3): 235–50.

34. Watson, A.K., Monroe, E.E. and Atterstrom, H. (1989) 'Comparison of communication apprehension across cultures: American and Swedish children', *Communication Quarterly*, **37**(1): 67–76.

35. Kim, M.-S., Aune, K.S., Hunter, J.E., Kim, H.-J. and Kim, J.-S. (2001) 'The effect of culture and self-construals on predispositions toward verbal communication', *Human Communication Research*, **27**(3): 382–408.

36. Allen, J.L. (1985) 'The relationship of communication anxiety, avoidance and competence of non-native English Speakers in the U.S.', Paper presented at the 35th Annual Meeting of the International Communication Association, Honolulu, HI. URL: http://www.flstw.edu/pderic.html.

37. Hsu, C.-F. (2002) 'The influence of self-construals, family and teacher communication patterns on communication apprehension among college students in Taiwan', *Communication Reports*, **15**(2): 123–32.

38. McCroskey, J.C., Fayer, J.M. and Richmond, V.P. (1985) 'Don't speak to me in English: Communication in Puerto Rico', *Communication Quarterly*, **33**(3): 185–92.

39. Toale, M.C. and McCroskey, J.C. (2001) 'Ethnocentrism and trait communication apprehension as predictors of interethnic communication apprehension and use of relational maintenance strategies in interethnic communication', *Communication Quarterly*, **49**(1): 70–83.

40. Kim, M.-S. (1999) 'Cross-cultural perspectives on motivations of verbal communication: Review, critique, and a theoretical framework', *Communication Yearbook*, **22**: 51–89.

41. Goleman, D. (1998) *Working with Emotional Intelligence*. New York: Bantam Books.

42. Mayer, J.D., DiPaolo, M. and Salovey, P. (1990) 'Perceiving affective content in ambiguous visual stimuli: A component of emotional intelligence', *Journal of Personality Assessment*, **54**: 772–81.

43. Elfenbein, H.A., Mandal, M.K., Ambady, N., Harizuka, S. and Kumar, S. (2002) 'Cross-cultural patterns in emotion recognition: Highlighting design and analytical techniques', *Emotion*, **2**: 75–84.

44. Izard, C.E. (1971) *The Face of Emotion*. New York: Appleton-Century-Crofts.

45. Elfenbein, H.A., Marsh, A.A. and Ambady, N. (2003) 'Emotional intelligence and the recognition of emotion from facial expressions', in Barrett, L.F. and Salovey, P. (eds) *The Wisdom of Feelings: Processes Underlying Emotional Intelligence*, NY: Guilford Press.

46. Johansson, J.K. (1994) 'Cultural understanding as managerial skill: Japan, North America and Europe', Presentation made at the David See-Chai Lam Centre for International Communication – Pacific Region Forum on Business and Management Communication, Simon Fraser University at Harbour Centre. URL: http://www.cic.sfu.ca/forum/

47. Robinson, S. (1997) 'Intercultural management: the art of resolving and avoiding conflicts between cultures' AIESEC Global Theme Conference: Learning and Acting for a Shared Future.' URL: http//www.eye.ch/~gtc97/intercul.html.

48. Menon, T., Chi-yue C., Morris, M.W. and Hong, Y.Y. (2000) 'Motivated cultural cognition: the impact of implicit cultural theories on dispositional attribution varies as a function of the need for closure', *Journal of Personality and Social Psychology*, **78**(2): 247–59.

49. Porter, D.M., Jr. (2001) 'Gender differences in managers' conceptions and perceptions of commitment to the organization', *Sex Roles: A Journal of Research*, **45**(5/6): 375–98.

50. Krug, J.A. and Nigh, D. (2001) 'Executive perceptions in foreign and domestic acquisitions: an analysis of foreign ownership and its effect on executive fate', *Journal of World Business*, **36**(1): 85–105.

51. Vigoda, E. (2001) 'Reactions to organizational politics: a cross-cultural examination in Israel and Britain', *Human Relations*, **54**(11): 1483–518.

52. Bond, M.H. and Smith, P.B. (1996) 'Cross-cultural social and organizational psychology', *Annual Review of Psychology*, **47**: 205–35.

53. West, T. and Levy, S.R. (2002) 'Background belief systems and prejudice', in Lonner, W.J., Dinnel, D.L., Hayes, S.A. and Sattler, D.N. (eds) *Online Readings in Psychology and Culture* (unit 15, chapter 4). URL: http://www.wwu.edu/~culture

54. Sidanius, J., Levin, S., Liu, J. and Pratto, F. (2000) 'Social dominanceorientation, anti-egalitarianism and the political psychology of gender; an extension and cross-cultural replication', *European Journal of Social Psychology*, **30**: 41–67.

55. Furnham, A., Bond, M.H., Heaven, P., Hilton, D., Lobel T. *et al.* (1993) 'A comparison of Protestant work ethic beliefs in thirteen nations', *Journal of Social Psychology*, **133**: 185–97.

56. Smith, P.B., Trompenaars, F. and Dugan, S. (1995) 'The Rotter locus of control scale in 43 countries: a test of cultural relativity', *International Journal of Psychology*, **30**: 377–400.

57. Furnham, A. *et al.* (1993) op. cit.

58. Bond, M.H. and Smith, P.B. (1996) op. cit.

59. Burke, K. (1966) *Language as Symbolic Action*, Berkeley, CA: University of California Press.

60. Greeley, A. (1990) *The Catholic Myth*, New York: Macmillan.

61. Alkhazraji, K.M., Gardner III, W.L., Martin, J.S. and Paolillo, J.G.P. (1997) 'The acculturation of immigrants to US organizations: the case of Muslim employees', *Management Communication Quarterly*, **11**(2): 217–65.

62. Stewart, R.A. and Roach, K.D. (1993) 'Argumentativeness, religious orientation, and reactions to argument situations involving religious versus nonreligious issues', *Communication Quarterly*, **41**(1): 26–39.

63. Alkhazraji, K.M. (1997) op. cit.

64. Swee, H.A. (2000) 'The power of money: a cross-cultural analysis of business-related beliefs', *Journal of World Business*, **35**(1): 43–60.

65. Puffer, S.M., McCarthy, D.J. and Naumov, A.I. (1997) 'Russian managers' beliefs about work: Beyond the stereotypes', *Journal of World Business*, **32**(3): 258–76.

66. Markoczy, L. (2000) 'National culture and strategic change in belief formation', *Journal of International Business Studies*, **31**(3): 417–42.

67. Gilligan, C. (1982) *In a Different Voice: Psychological Theory and Women's Development*, Cambridge, MA: Harvard University Press.

68. Gianakos, I. (2002) 'Predictors of coping with work stress: the influences of sex, gender role, social desirability, and locus of control', *Sex Roles: A Journal of Research*, **42**: 1059–79.

69. Barron, L. (2003) 'Ask and you shall receive? Gender differences in negotiators' beliefs about requests for a higher salary', *Human Relations*, **56**(6): 635–62.

70. Puffer, S.M. *et al.* (1997) op. cit.

71. Schein, E.H. (1992) *Organizational Culture and Leadership* (2nd edn), San Francisco, CA: Jossey-Bass.

72. Triandis, H.C. (1990) 'Theoretical concepts that are applicable to the analysis of ethnocentrism', in Brislin, R.W. (ed.) *Applied Cross-Cultural Psychology*, Newbury Park, CA: Sage.

73. Alderfer, C.P. and Smith, K.K. (1982) 'Studying intergroup relations embedded in organizations', *Administrative Science Quarterly*, **27**: 5–65.

74. Grant, M.J., Button, C.J., Hannah, T.E. and Ross, A.S. (2002) 'Uncovering the multidimensional nature of stereotype inferences: a within-participants' study of gender, age and physical attractiveness', *Current Research in Social Psychology*, **8**: 2. URL: http://www.uiowa.edu/~grpproc/crisp/crisp.html

75. Brauer, M., Judd, C.M. and Jacquelin, V. (2001) 'The communication of social stereotypes: the Effects of group discussion and information distribution on stereotypic appraisals', *Journal of Personality and Social Psychology*, **81**(3): 463–75.

76. Hagendoorn, L. and Kleinpenning, G. (1991) 'The contribution of domain-specific stereotypes to ethnic social distance', *British Journal of Social Psychology*, **30**: 63–78.

77. Chiu, W.C.K., Chan, A.W., Snape, E. and Redman, T. (2001) 'Age stereotypes and discriminatory attitudes towards older workers: an East-West comparison', *Human Relations*, **54**(5): 629–62.

78. Devine, P.G. (2001) 'Implicit prejudice and stereotyping: how automatic are they?', *Journal of Personality and Social Psychology*, **81**(5): 757–9.

79. Kunda, Z., Davies, P.G., Adams, B.D. and Spencer, S.J. (2002) 'The dynamic time course of stereotype activation: activation, dissipation, and resurrection', *Journal of Personality and Social Psychology*, **82**(3): 283–99.

80. Giles, H., Henwood, K., Coupland, D., Harriman, J. and Coupland, J. (1992) 'Language attitudes and cognitive mediation', *Human Communication Research*, **18**(4): 500–27.

81. Rettew, D.C., Billman, D. and Davis, R.A. (1993) 'Inaccurate perceptions of the amount others stereotype: estimates about stereotypes of one's own group and other groups', *Basic and Applied Social Psychology*, **14**: 121–42.

82. Best, D.L. and Williams, J.E. (1994) 'Masculinity/femininity in the self and ideal self-descriptions of university students in fourteen countries', in Bouvy, A.M., van de Vijver, F.J.R., Boski, P., and Schmitz, P. (eds) *Journeys into Cross-Cultural Psychology*, Amsterdam: Swets & Zeitlinger, pp. 297–306.

83. Chiu, W.C.K. *et al.* (2001) op. cit.

84. Hoyt, S.K. (1999) 'Mentoring with class: connections between social class and developmental relationships in the Academy', in Murrell, A.J., Crosby, F.J. and Ely, R.J. (eds) *Mentoring Dilemmas: Developmental Relationships within Multicultural Organizations*, Hillsdale, NJ: Lawrence Erlbaum.

85. Williams, J.E. and Best, D. (1990) *Sex and Psyche: Gender and Self Viewed Cross-Culturally*, Newbury Park, CA: Sage.

86. Burgoon, J.K. and Le Poire, B.A. (1993) 'Effects of communication expectancies, actual communication and expectancy disconfirmation evaluations of communicators and their communication behavior', *Human Communication Research*, **20**(1): 67–96.

87. Ducharme, D. and Bernard, R. (2001) 'Communication breakdowns: an exploration of contextualisation in native and non-native speakers of French', *Journal of Pragmatics*, **33**: 825–47.

88. Ali, A.J. (1993) 'Decision-making style, individualism and attitudes toward risk of Arab executives', *International Studies of Management & Organization*, **23**(3): 53–74.

89. Berger, C.R. and Zelditch, M. (1985) *Status, Rewards and Influence*, San Francisco: Jossey-Bass.

90. Thompson, A.G. (1996) 'Compliance with agreements in cross-cultural transactions: some analytical issues', *Journal of International Business Studies*, **27**(2): 375–90.

91. Cichon, E.J. and Masterson, J.T. (1993) 'Physician-patient communication: Mutual role expectations', *Communication Quarterly*, **41**(4): 477–89.

92. Apel, D. and Yoram, B.-T. (1996) 'Nursing staff responses to violent events in closed psychiatric wards: a comparison between attributional and cognitive neo-associanistic analyses', *British Journal of Social Psychology*, **35**: 509–21.

93. Abelman, R. (1991) 'The depiction of women in religious television', *The Journal of Communication and Religion*, **14**(2): 1–14.

94. Tsui, A.S., Porter, L.W. and Egan, T.D. (2002) 'When both similarities and dissimilarities matter: extending the concept of relational demography', *Human Relations*, **55**(8): 899–930.

95. Ajzen, L. (1991) 'The theory of planned behaviour: some unresolved issues', *Organizational Behavior and Human Decision Processes*, **50**: 179–211.

96. Dovidio, J.F., Kawakkami, K. and Gaertner, S.L. (2002) 'Implicit and explicit prejudice and interracial interaction', *Journal of Personality and Social Psychology*, **82**(1): 62–8.

97. Ickes, W. (1984) 'Compositions in black and whites: determinants of interaction in interracial dyads', *Journal of Personality and Social Psychology*, **47**: 330–41.

98. Fukuyama, F. (1995) *Trust: The Social Virtues and the Creation of Prosperity*, New York: Free Press.

99. Halman, L. and Kerkhofs, J. (2001) The European Values Study: selected results. URL: www.romir.ru/eng/research/01_2001/european-values.htm

100. Nicol, D. (1994) 'Trust: critical and cultural'. URL: http://blue.temple.edu/~eastern/nicol.html

101. Lee, C., Madan, P. and Law, K. (2000) 'Power distance, gender and organizational justice', *Journal of Management*, **26**(4): 685–704.

102. Lubatkin, M.H., Ndiaye, M. and Vengroff, R. (1997) 'The nature of managerial work in three developing countries: a test of the universalist hypothesis', *Journal of International Business Studies*, **284**: 711–33.

103. Bond, M.H. and Smith, P.B. (1996) op. cit.

104. McCrae, R.R. (2002) 'Cross-cultural research on the five-factor model of personality', in Lonner, W.J., Dinnel, D.L., Hayes, S.A. and Sattler, D.N. (eds), *Online Readings in Psychology and Culture* (unit 6, chapter 1). URL: http://www.wwu.edu/~culture

105. Ibid.

106. Argyle, M. (2000) *Psychology and Religion: An Introduction*, London: Routledge.

107. Adorno, T.W. (1991), *The Culture Industry: Selected Essays on Mass Culture*, London: Routledge.

108. Thompson, N. (2003) *Communication and Language: A Handbook of Theory and Practice*, Basingstoke: Palgrave Macmillan.

109. Ibid.

110. Markus R.H. and Kitayama, S. (1994) 'A collective fear of the collective: implications for selves and theories of selves', *Personality and Social Psychology Bulletin*, **20**(5): 568–79.

111. Abramson, N.R., Lane, H.W., Nagai, H. and Takagi, H. (1993) 'A comparison of Canadian and Japanese cognitive styles: implications for management interaction', *Journal of International Business Studies*, **24**(3): 515–87.

112. Singelis, T.M. (1994) 'The measurement of independent and interdependent self-construals', *Personality and Social Psychology Bulletin*, **20**: 580–91.

113. Singelis, T.M. and Sharkey, W.F. (1995) 'Culture, self-construal and embarassability', *Journal of Cross-Cultural Psychology*, **26**: 622–44.

114. Tasaki, K., Kim, M.-S. and Miller, M.D. (1999) 'The effects of social status on cognitive elaboration and post-message attitude: focusing on self-construals', *Communication Quarterly*, **47**(2): 196–214.

115. Brockner, J. (2000) 'Culture and procedural fairness: when the effects of what you do depend on how you do it', *Administrative Science Quarterly*, **45**: 138–59.

116. Kim, M.-S., Shin, H.-C. and Cai, D. (1998) 'Cultural influences on the preferred forms of requesting and re-requesting', *Communication Monographs*, **65**(1): 47–66.

117. Martin, J.N. and Nakayama, T. (1997) *Intercultural Communication in Contexts*, Mountainview, CA: Mayfield Publishing Company.

118. Phinney, J.S. (1996) 'When we talk about American ethnic groups, what do we mean?', *American Psychologist*, **51**: 918–27.

119. Weinreich, P., Luk, C. and Bond, M.H. (1994) 'Ethnic identity: identification with other cultures, self-esteem and identity confusion', *International Conference on Immigration, Language Acquisition and Patterns of Social Integration*, Jerusalem.

120. Ting-Toomey, S. (1988) 'Intercultural conflict styles: a face-negotiation theory', in Kim, Y.Y. and Gudykunst, W.B. (eds) *Theories in Intercultural Communication*, Newbury Park, CA: Sage.

121. Best, D.L. and Williams, J.E. (1994) op. cit.

122. Cross, S.E. and Madison, L. (1997) 'Models of the self: self-construals and gender', *Psychological Bulletin*, **122**(1): 5–37.

123. Roberts, T.-A. (1991) 'Gender and the influence of evaluations on self-assessments in achievement settings', *Psychological Bulletin*, **109**(2): 297–308.

124. Beyer, S. (1998) 'Gender differences in self-perception and negative recall biases', *Sex Roles: A Research Journal*, **38**: 103–33.

125. Hoyt, S.K. (1999) op. cit.

126. Huntington, S.P. (1997) *The Clash of Civilizations and The Remaking of World Order*, London: Simon & Schuster, p. 97.

127. Kelly, A.E., Sedlacek, W.E. and Scales, W.R. (1994) 'How college students with and without disabilities perceive themselves and each other', *Journal of Counseling and Development*, **73**: 178–82.

128. Jetten, J., Postmes, T. and McAuliffe, B.J. (2002) ' We're all individuals: group norms of individualism and collectivism, levels of identification and identity threat', *European Journal of Social Psychology*, **32**(2): 189–207.

129. Kim, M.-S. and Leung, T. (2000) 'A multicultural view of conflict management styles: review and critical synthesis', *Communication Yearbook*, **23**: 227–69.

130. Huntington, S.P. (1997) op. cit.

131. Lind, R.A. (2001) 'The relevance of cultural identity: relying upon foundations of race and gender as laypeople plan a newscast', *Journalism and Communication Monographs*, **3**(3): 113–45.

132. Schneider, A. (2002) 'Behaviour prescriptions versus professional identities in multicultural corporations: a cross-cultural computer simulation', *Organization Studies*, **23**(1): 105–32.

133. Varela, F., Thompson, E. and Rosch, E. (1991) *The Embodied Mind*, Cambridge, MA: MIT Press.

134. Farh, J.L., Dobbins, G.H. and Cheng, B. (1991) 'Cultural relativity in action: a comparison of self-ratings made by Chinese and US workers', *Personnel Psychology*, **44**: 129–47.

135. Yu, J. and Murphy, K.R. (1993) 'Modesty bias in self-ratings of performance: a test of the cultural relativity hypothesis', *Personnel Psychology*, **46**: 357–73.

136. Bond, M.H. and Smith, P.B. (1996) op. cit.

137. Triandis, H. (2000) 'Culture and conflict', *International Journal of Psychology*, **35**(2): 145–52.

138. Plaks, J.E., Stroessner, S.J., Dweck, C.S. and Sherman, J.W. (2001) 'Person theories and attention allocation: preferences for stereotypic versus counterstereotypic information', *Journal of Personality and Social Psychology*, **80**(6): 876–93.

139. Chandler, T.A., Shama, D.D., Wolf, F.M. and Planchard, S.K. (1981) 'Multiattributional causality for social affiliation across five cross-national samples', *Journal of Psychology*, **107**: 219–29.

140. Nurmi, J. (1992) 'Cross-cultural differences in self-serving bias: responses to the attributional style questionnaire by American and Finnish students', *Journal of Social Psychology*, **132**(1): 69–76.

141. Shweder, R. A. and Bourne, E.J. (1982) 'Does the concept of the person vary cross-culturally?' in Marsella, M.J. and White, G.M. (eds) *Cultural Conceptions of Mental Health and Therapy*, Dordrecht: Reidel, pp. 97–137.

142. Morris, M.W. and Peng, K.P. (1994) 'Culture and cause: American and Chinese attributions for social and physical events', *Journal of Personality and Social Psychology*, **67**: 949–71.

143. Merritt, R.D. and Kok, C.J. (1995) 'Attribution of gender to a gender-unspecified individual: an evaluation of the "people = male" hypothesis', *Sex Roles: A Journal of Research*, **33**: 145–57.

144. Peckham, P. and Ryckman, D.B. (1987) 'Gender differences in attributions for success and failure situations across subject areas', *Journal of Educational Research*, **81**(2): 120–5.

145. Martin, L.R. and Morgan, S. (1995) 'Middle managers in banking: an investigation of gender differences in behavior, demographics, and productivity', *Quarterly Journal of Business and Economics*, **34**(1): 55–68.
146. De Judicibus, M. and McCabe, M.P. (2001) 'Blaming the target of sexual harassment: impact of gender role, sexist attitudes, and work role', *Sex Roles: A Journal of Research*, **41**: 401–17.
147. Macgeorge, E.L. (2003) 'Gender differences in attributions and emotions in helping contexts', *Sex Roles: A Journal of Research*, **48**(3): 175–82.
148. Rosenthal, P. (1996) 'Gender and managers' causal attributions for subordinate performance: a field story', *Sex Roles: A Journal of Research,* **34**: 121–36.
149. Hovemyr, M. (1998) 'The attribution of success and failure as related to different patterns of religious orientation', *International Journal for the Psychology of Religion*, **8**(2): 107–24.
150. Kashima, Y. and Triandis, H.C. (1986) 'The self-serving bias in attributions as a coping strategy: a cross-cultural study', *Journal of Cross-Cultural Psychology*, **17**(1): 83–97.
151. Abramson, N.R. *et al.* (1993) op. cit.

part two

Intercultural Communication at Work

chapter five

Barriers to Intercultural Communication

Common experience teaches that face-to-face communication is imperfect and can lead to misunderstanding and even conflict. Communication theorists generally take it as given that communication can never be perfect.[1] There are many sources of miscommunication. They include 'noise', in the technical sense of interference, whether physical or psychological, which prevents messages being received; poor encoding by the sender; distortion by the medium; and selection, inaccurate decoding, distorted interpretation and indiscriminate categorisation by the receiver. The two-way nature of face-to-face communication creates possibilities for reducing miscommunication by feedback (the sender can find out how well the receiver is understanding and responding). However, it also imposes demanding time pressure on each receiver in turn to respond, so reducing opportunities for thinking through what they say.

In the case of people from different backgrounds, there are two additional sources of miscommunication. Section 5.1 describes those sources of miscommunication which are 'universal' barriers, but which apply with particular force in intercultural situations. Section 5.2 describes those obstacles arising from the fact that, as the previous two chapters showed, differences of background, whether cultural or subcultural, ethnic, gender-based or based on some other distinction, do affect how people communicate. These two kinds of barrier are illustrated by the following comments of African Americans (A-As) about their communication with European Americans (E-As):

- 'When E-As introduce a stereotypical subject (basketball), A-As feel offended or patronized.'
- 'When most A-As see disliked behavior or don't understand what an E-A is saying, they label the other person as racist.'
- 'A-As who speak a non-standard dialect are more often faced with stereotyping.'
- 'A-As "overtalk" in an attempt to control the conversation "in compensation" and to prevent E-As displaying stereotyping.'
- 'A-As stress "being cool" – not letting the other know what you are thinking or feeling – there is a lot of underlying anger.'

- 'A-As query the authenticity of many inter-ethnic conversations: they are phony. Even a sincere effort [by a White liberal] may come across in this way.'
- 'Blacks and Whites may come away with different meanings from a conversation because concepts aren't defined in the same way.'
- 'White Americans would find Black intracultural conversation aggressive.'[2]

Larkey put forward a view that cultural differences affect intercultural encounters, usually by leading to misunderstanding or conflict, at both the individual and the group level. Interpersonal misunderstanding and conflict can arise at the individual level as different values, beliefs or worldviews are manifested in communication behaviours and as culture creates differing expectations (especially about communication rules) and differing styles or patterns of speech.[3] At the group level, intergroup processes can be triggered by, for instance, an individual's non-verbal behaviour or ways of speaking which stereotypically represent a group.

There is, however, still some debate about whether such differences actually do create barriers to communication and if so how. This chapter will attempt an answer to this question; it will argue that they do and try to show how. In this book, the term 'miscommunication' is used broadly, even to cover cases where communication is intended but none occurs – as when A speaks to B but B is not listening and does not hear. This broad definition means that miscommunication includes at least all the following cases:

- Communication is intended but none occurs.
- The receiver makes no sense of the message.
- The receiver misunderstands the message – the speaker's meaning and the receiver's understanding of the meaning are different.
- The speaker's communicative intention (to ask a question, make a request, make a promise, etc.) is not understood.
- Information imparted by the speaker, which s/he intended to have believed, is not believed.
- An attempt to persuade fails.
- An attempt to exert power fails.
- A communication is understood but provokes unintended conflict.

So broad a use of 'miscommunication' extends its usual definition, but allows it to refer to all cases where barriers to communication are effective. However, this does not mean that all cases of disagreement, for example, constitute miscommunication: a process of working through disagreement can increase understanding.

Section 5.3 builds on the analysis of cultural differences in behaviour given in Chapter 4 to consider how those differences can create barriers to intercultural communication. Section 5.4 introduces two specifically work-related types of barrier – heterogeneity of work groups and task-related conflict.

5.1 'UNIVERSAL' BARRIERS

As the introduction to this chapter stated, some barriers apply to all or most communication, but create particular problems in intercultural communication. This section discusses three such barriers: the general problem of intergroup communication, stereotyping and prejudice.

The general problem of intergroup communication

Modern work generally involves meeting or working with individuals from different ethnic backgrounds, socio-economic classes, age groups, occupational categories and so forth. In these encounters, people may communicate with each other not just or even mainly as individuals with unique temperaments and personalities but to a considerable extent as undifferentiated representatives of social groups. For example, Person A might deal with Person B as a 'Polish Catholic lawyer' or 'White male doctor' and Person B might deal with Person A as a 'Welsh Protestant client' or an 'Afro-Caribbean woman nurse'. (When people respond to one another primarily in terms of their group membership, the terms 'intergroup encounter' and 'intergroup communication' apply even if only two people are present.) This tendency to emphasise group membership is especially strong at initial meetings with 'strangers', which here means anyone who is believed to lack understanding of the social world inhabited by members of the other person's or people's ingroup.

Whether people do or do not treat an encounter as intergroup usually depends on the four factors shown in Figure 5.1. Recognising that someone's ethnicity, religion or gender is different can lead to an interaction being treated as intergroup. It may not, however, if the individual's personal attitudes or the subject of the interaction make group memberships seem irrelevant. For example, perceived religious difference might have no bearing on a discussion of software capability. A second factor is whether the other person's language is perceived as a major one; if not, as in the case of English people interacting with Welsh people, the English might not treat the encounter as intergroup (but the Welsh might). Third, where people draw their ingroup boundaries varies from person to person and occasion to occasion. A French person might, on some occasions, perceive his or her ingroup as 'European' and so not regard an encounter with a German as intergroup. Finally, an individual may disregard social group differences if s/he perceives the status of the other person's ingroup as high and identifies with it or perceives an overlap in social categories ('You may be an English

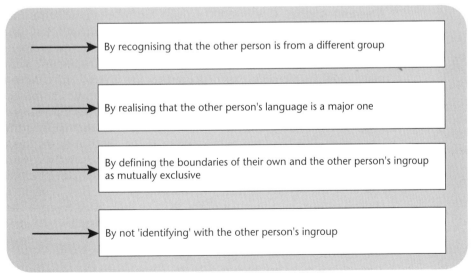

Figure 5.1   *How people define an encounter as intergroup*

Based on: Rogers, E. and Kincaid, D. (1981) *Communication Networks: Toward a New Paradigm for Research*, NY: Free Press

businesswoman, but, like me, you are a woman.') Where none of these exceptions applies, awareness that the other person is from a different major group usually leads to the encounter being treated as intergroup.

Outgroup co-variation effect

Part of the explanation for treating strangers as group members rather than individuals is the 'outgroup co-variation effect'. People generally see their outgroups as less variable (more similar) along single characteristics, such as intelligence or cleanliness, than their ingroup. They may also be affected by intergroup bias – a tendency to see members of their ingroup more favourably than members of outgroups. Intergroup bias is a complex phenomenon. For example, people without disabilities tend to display more bias towards people with disabilities than the latter do toward the former. The former also tend to be derogatory about people with disabilities. In contrast, following a rewarding interaction experience with a member of a 'no-disability' outgroup, people with disabilities display an evaluative bias in favour of, and identify with, the 'no-disability' outgroup. An explanation can be found in social identity theory, which states that people identify more strongly with groups that they find socially rewarding.[4] Intergroup bias occurs so easily that it is common even between 'minimalist' groups – where individuals are randomly allocated to groups and know that that is how the groups have been formed.[5]

Ingroup favouritism

It has been shown that people from a wide range of categories favour their ingroup. It may be caused by individuals' needs to simplify their complex environment (need for cognitive economy) and for self-enhancement.[6] However, so far as the second of these is concerned, recent research tends to contradict this prediction. No support was found for the hypothesis that, following a group's showing ingroup favouritism in a particular domain, such as artistic ability, individual group members' self-esteem in that domain would increase. A similar finding applied to members of a religious group – American Baptists. One possible explanation for these negative findings is that the group members felt guilty about having shown favouritism.[7] How legitimate members of a group consider their status in relation to other groups profoundly affects their intergroup attitudes, emotions and behaviour. If their ingroup's status seems illegitimately low, its members experience higher perceived relative deprivation, prejudice and a desire for social change; they may engage in realistic and/or social competition, collective protest or action and intergroup conflict. Perceiving an ingroup's status to be illegitimately high leads to pro-social instead of discriminatory attitudes and action tendencies. This has been found among White South Africans towards Black South Africans and West Germans towards East Germans. The perceived legitimacy of an outgroup's status seems to be related to how far the outgroup members conform to prototypical norms. When Germans were asked whether they thought that Turkey was entitled to become a member of the EU, the more they thought Germany was relatively more prototypical for Europe than Turkey, the less they thought Turkey was entitled to membership in the EU.[8]

It has been shown that how people evaluate an ingroup's standing on an ability dimension is based partly on performance outcomes of an ingroup in comparison with an outgroup and partly on circumstances related to their performance. Thus, when people know their ingroup is disadvantaged, there is an increase (1) in their beliefs that together they can improve their performance, (2) in their individual effort on behalf of the ingroup and (3) in their tendency to hinder the future performance of an outgroup.[9]

Effects of intergroup problems

Communicating with others as representatives of their groups can create barriers and complications in at least the following ways:

- People's group membership is not always obvious: identifying it is often a creative process in which linguistic 'work' must be done and group membership must be inferred.
- Interpersonal factors cannot be ignored in intergroup encounters, so both group and personal factors must be handled, creating complexity.
- Intergroup communication involves at least one of the individuals present being regarded as a 'stranger'. Interactions with strangers can create anxiety and often are experienced by both parties as a series of crises.[10]
- As Chapter 4 showed, people attribute other people's behaviour to their disposition or their situation. When they treat an encounter as 'intergroup', they commonly use their knowledge of the group to 'decide' their attributions. This increases the likelihood that they will attribute different others' behaviour to their disposition as opposed to their situation, and possibly to judge it more harshly.[11] In addition, they may not know much about the culture of the different other's group, leading them to make false attributions or, if they are aware of the problem, to make limited and provisional attributions that inhibit openness.[12]
- Ethnocentrism is readily activated in intergroup encounters, leading to hostility towards the different others.
- Criticism from outsiders provokes high levels of defensiveness and intergroup suspicion, leading to rejecting the truth of the comments. In contrast, criticism from ingroup members is tolerated 'surprisingly well', and is seen to be more legitimate and constructive than outgroup criticisms. Positive comments from outsiders are received as well as from insiders, suggesting that the effect of outsiders' criticism is not due to general outgroup negative bias.[13]
- Intergroup relations are more competitive and discordant than relations between interacting individuals; this is particularly so when the people involved depend on one another. Highly interdependent research subjects endorse threat more and acceptance of others' demands less to a relatively greater degree in an intergroup as opposed to an inter-individual conflict.

These sources of potential miscommunication are summarised in Figure 5.2.

Stereotyping

Stereotypes were explained in Chapter 4. Stereotyping, though a natural and necessary process, can distort intergroup communication. It may lead people to base their messages, their ways of transmitting them and their reception of them on false assumptions.

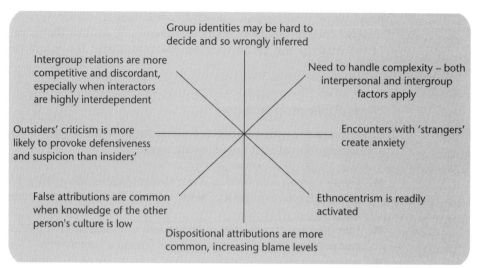

Group identities may be hard to decide and so wrongly inferred

Intergroup relations are more competitive and discordant, especially when interactors are highly interdependent

Need to handle complexity – both interpersonal and intergroup factors apply

Outsiders' criticism is more likely to provoke defensiveness and suspicion than insiders'

Encounters with 'strangers' create anxiety

False attributions are common when knowledge of the other person's culture is low

Ethnocentrism is readily activated

Dispositional attributions are more common, increasing blame levels

Figure 5.2   *Factors increasing the amount of poor communication in intergroup encounters*

These distortions arise in at least the following five ways:

1. Stereotypes can influence how information is processed. More favourable information is remembered about ingroups, less favourable about outgroups; for instance, someone who has a stereotype of Scottish people as 'mean' is likely not to notice or quickly to forget if a Scottish person shows generosity.
2. Objectively, there is often more variation within groups than between them. This applies even to fundamental cultural values and still more to more superficial characteristics such as 'meanness'. Stereotyping, though, leads to individuality being overlooked.
3. Stereotypes create expectations about 'others' and individual others often feel a pressure to confirm these expectations. It may seem unlikely that Scottish people will try to confirm expectations that they are mean, though it can happen; but research has shown that schoolchildren under-perform if teachers expect less of them because of their background.
4. Stereotypes constrain others' patterns of communication. Conventions and politeness may prevent people who perceive they are being treated in accordance with a stereotype from disputing it. Even if they do react, this is likely to disrupt the conversation or discussion.
5. Stereotypes create self-fulfilling prophecies, leading to stereotype-confirming communication. A clear example is the way that, as Chapter 3 showed, women use 'powerless' ways of speaking to conform to stereotypes of femininity.[14]

In addition, negative stereotypes can contribute to prejudice. For instance, 76 per cent of African Americans said they felt that Whites are insensitive to people, 76 per cent that Whites do not want to share with non-Whites and 79 per cent that Whites see themselves as superior and able to boss others around. These communication stereotypes may be 'a key piece of the interracial relations puzzle'.[15]

Prejudice

Prejudice is a thoughtless, derogatory attitude or set of attitudes towards all or most of the members of a group. It includes racism, sexism, homophobia and ageism. Religious

Box 5.1

X is a manager in local government. He is interviewing an applicant for a post in the Authority's Committee Section. The job description calls for a person with strong organisational and communication skills, who is excellent at meeting deadlines, has or is able to develop a detailed knowledge of procedures and constitutions and is prepared to work in the evenings. The interviewee is from an ethnic minority and is older than the interviewee.

During the interview, an observer records noticing differences in body language and eye contact – the manager sits well forward in his seat with his body slanted towards the interviewee and makes considerable use of gesture; he maintains a steady gaze directed at the interviewee; throughout he speaks loudly, clearly and fast. The interviewee, in contrast, sits still, with hands folded, and appears to back gradually away from the interviewer. She looks down at the space between them, and speaks quietly and slowly, though clearly.

The interviewee appears uncomfortable with detailed questions. More than once she proffers CV and qualifications certificates, but the manager will not take them or look at them.

Questions include asking whether she would be able to fulfill the long hours and evening working sometimes required and asking what her written English is like. The observer reads into the manager's conduct that he is making assumptions like 'Aren't your lot a bit laid back?' and that foreign qualifications are of less value than those of his own country.

Source: Author's research

prejudice, too, can be as potent and thoughtless as any of these. Prejudice gives rise to myths, such as that some dialects or accents indicate lower intelligence. From a linguistic point of view, all languages and dialects are complex, sophisticated sets of systems and it makes little or no sense to argue that one is 'superior' to another.

One major strand in approaches to the origins of prejudice is to view it as a personality trait linked to authoritarianism (measured by an 'F' – for Fascist – scale) resulting from early socialisation. However, a cross-cultural study of prejudice in South Africa and the United States showed that racists in those countries did not necessarily have high levels of authoritarianism.[16] Furthermore, individual-level explanations of extreme prejudice fail to account for its widespread incidence in some societies. For these reasons, socio-cultural factors are now considered better at explaining prejudice.

Research into how prejudice operates is beginning to reveal some unexpected aspects. For example, people seem to be more, not less, willing to act in a prejudiced way after they have, for instance, disagreed with blatantly sexist statements or selected a member of a stereotyped group, such as an African American, for a job. They might then reject a woman for a stereotypically male job or reject a member of a minority group for a job stereotypically suited to majority members. This may be because they feel they have previously established their moral credentials and so act according to their prejudices.[17]

Ethnic prejudice

Although most people in Western countries will no longer explicitly deny ethnic equality, they may instead exhibit 'aversive racism'. This is defined in terms of feelings of discomfort and uneasiness that motivate people to avoid ethnic outgroups and maintain social distance from them.[18] A Swedish study found that classical (overt or direct) racial prejudice and modern (covert or subtle) racial prejudice are distinct.

Box 5.2

'Few bits of London are a better advertisement for prosperous and tolerant multi-racial Britain than Finsbury Park. Crowded Greek, Kurdish, Turkish, Arab and African shops and restaurants rub shoulders with a mighty indigenous business, Arsenal football club. Cultural barriers count for little in the search for profit: the Algerian-owned Café Paradise offers birthday cakes with iced greetings in both Amharic (for Ethiopians) and Tigrigna (for Eritreans).'[a]

'In some of the most ethnically mixed parts of the country [Britain], assimilation has done a lot to dissolve prejudice. London, which has both ethnic minorities and refugees in abundance, used to be a place where the far right enjoyed a toe-hold. Now the capital consistently displays the lowest levels of intolerance of any region in the country.

Feelings are strongest in regions where an ethnic divide is accentuated by poverty and the resulting competition for access to public services.'[b]

A trainer of social workers at a UK airport reported that White South Africans arriving in Britain would treat Black social workers with respect: 'They knew that they were entering a different situation – that in Britain Black people have both power and status.' On the other hand, Black people arriving from African countries would often be disrespectful toward Black social workers: 'They thought that Black people here were powerless.'[c]

Sources: (a) *The Economist*, 25 January 2000, p. 27
(b) *The Economist*, 11 October 2003, p. 33
(c) Interview, author's research

It showed that a scale to measure modern prejudice distinguished both between native Swedes and immigrants and between men and women, the former in each case being more prejudiced in the modern sense. In contrast, a scale to measure classical prejudice found few differences.[19] Another piece of research found that white French subjects showed significantly different psycho-physiological responses, such as change of heartbeat rate, to pictures of outgroup members (Arabs) as against ingroup members (other white French). This applied even though, when self-report measures were used, the subjects did not exhibit anti-Arab prejudice.[20] Between 1990 and 2000 most countries of Eastern Europe saw a significant decrease in ethnic prejudice as measured by the percentages stating that they would not want members of another race as neighbours.[21] Exceptions were Poland, where there was a very small increase, and Hungary, where the figure more than doubled, from 22 per cent to 51 per cent. In Western Europe, the picture was more mixed. Leaving aside the three countries (Greece, Montenegro and Luxembourg) for which these data are only available for 1999, nine countries saw a decrease, which was largest in Finland and Portugal, bringing the latter down to below the Western European average. Denmark, Northern Ireland, Eire, Spain and Italy saw an increase, which was largest in Eire, where the figure doubled from 6 per cent to 12 per cent.[21]

Prejudice against other subgroups

There is evidence of gender prejudice. A meta-analysis of research in which actual performance indicators were equalised between men and women found an overall tendency to favour male leaders. Although the bias was slight, it was real. It was larger in the following conditions:

■ Where the woman leader's style corresponded to male stereotypes (that is, was not interpersonal and participative).

- For roles usually occupied by men as against those occupied equally by both sexes or where the sex distribution was unknown.
- In some organisational contexts, such as sports and athletics coaching or business and manufacturing. The evaluation of male business managers was generally slightly more favourable than that of female business managers.
- Men were more likely to devalue women than women were. Women were largely neutral.[22]

Religious belief has been linked to prejudice. Members of Christian churches are usually more racially prejudiced towards Jews and Blacks than non-members, although in Holland church members are less prejudiced than others against immigrants. Intrinsics – the 'uncritically orthodox' as opposed to those with multiple motivations for religiosity – are less racially prejudiced but are prejudiced against homosexuals. High correlations have been found between prejudice and measures of fundamentalism, not only for populations of Christians but also for Jews, Moslems and Hindus.[23]

Perceptions of prejudice are themselves often biased. There is a tendency to believe that certain groups (such as older White male managers) are prejudiced or that its victims are members of certain groups (such as Bangladeshi women). That is, perceptions of prejudice are influenced by expectations about who is typically prejudiced about whom.[24] In an interview with the author, the Personnel Director of a major UK car manufacturer said,

> We find that the stereotypes of who will be prejudiced are often wrong. We tend to think that it will be the older males, especially from the engineering or factory side, that will be most biased. Often, though, it's the 'young Turks' – mostly graduates – in Sales and Marketing. I think perhaps they see them – the women – as rivals, in a way the older ones don't.

False suspicions of prejudice can create communication problems in a wide range of organisational, work, social and educational settings.

Effects of prejudice at work

Direct effects are mainly discrimination and harassment, which have been discussed in Chapter 1. Both these, in addition to their negative effects on individuals and the organisation, are intrinsically barriers to communication, but so is prejudice itself, even when it is not overt. Prejudiced people distort and misread communication from those about whom they hold prejudiced views. On the other side, people who become aware of others' prejudices about themselves or others are likely to develop negative attitudes to the prejudiced individual's opinions in general, regardless of how soundly based those other opinions may be.

Prejudice is often displayed in negative micro-messages. These are subtle, semi-conscious, devaluing messages, which discourage and impair performance, possibly leading to damaged self-esteem and withdrawal. For example, negative micro-messages (micro-inequities) can occur within a team when a manager or a colleague communicates different messages to people, usually linked to a difference between them such as race, gender, age, sexual orientation or level. Micro-messages can affect such things as employee productivity, morale, absenteeism and turnover – all critical to the success of a company. Negative micro-messages can cause employees to withdraw, complain, question their own abilities, be absent from work frequently and possibly quit; conversely, positive micro-messages can encourage employees to excel in their work, commit to the company, and feel motivated. Individuals who belong to groups that have been historically excluded and devalued because of their difference may have stronger reactions to micro-inequities.[25,26]

Past experience of prejudice naturally affects the response of members of minority groups to communications they receive at work. Excuses, apologies and explanations, which are collectively called 'social accounts', may be counter-productive when used by members of dominant groups with members of minority groups. In areas such as negative pay decisions and layoffs, researchers have found that a well-constructed account that explains what happened and why can reduce perceptions of injustice and anger. However, social accounts may be ineffective when used by White managers to Black subordinates. The pattern of responses across four studies demonstrated a 'persistent injustice effect'. Black employees had more experience than White with unjust acts; they reported higher levels of both past and expected future injustices, and greater mistrust. This experience of 'persistent injustice' may account for the findings that a social account reduced perceived injustice less for Black respondents observing Black than White victims or than for White respondents observing either Black or White victims. Black respondents observing Black victims when there was higher racial identification or higher levels of personal experience with injustice were similarly less influenced by social accounts. The same applied when Black respondents observed Black victims hurt by White harm-doers. Black respondents also perceived higher initial levels of injustice, disapproval and intentionality when observing Black victims hurt by White harm-doers. These findings are consistent with earlier studies that found that social accounts were less effective at diminishing perceptions of injustice for union officials and female managers when the hypothetical victim was a member of their ingroup. When there is a persistent injustice effect, it is likely to be invisible to a manager who has given what on the surface may be received as a successful excuse, apology or explanation. As a result, ' "solutions" end up being partial and temporary, and the conflicts get driven underground, to incubate and surface again at some other time, in some other form'.[27]

The effects of discrimination depend partly on how negative behaviours of one group towards another are interpreted. It has been found that the more members of low-status groups endorse the ideology of individual mobility, the less likely they are to attribute negative outcomes from higher status group members to discrimination. Conversely, the more members of high-status groups endorse this same ideology, the more likely they are to attribute negative outcomes from low-status group members to discrimination.[28]

> Contributory causes and effects of three 'universal' sources of miscommunication were discussed. Dealing with other people as representatives of their group leads to ingroup favouritism and intergroup negative bias. Stereotypes distort intergroup communication when they lead people to base their messages, their ways of transmitting them and their reception of them on false assumptions. Some kinds of prejudice may be diminishing in Europe but still are widely prevalent and lead to transmitting negative micro-messages. Past experience of prejudice naturally affects the responses of members of minority groups.

5.2 COMMUNICATION DIFFERENCES AS BARRIERS

National, ethnic, gender and social class differences in how people speak and interact can lead to them being perceived as disorganised, poor thinkers or as being insulting.

Finnish respondents to a survey perceived the following dimensions of communication as problematic in their interactions with non-Finns: lack of language proficiency, transfer of mother tongue patterns into a foreign language, mistaking a concept to mean the same in the other culture as in their own, use of a concept unfamiliar in the other person's culture, words taken too literally or personally, use of directness or indirectness, Finnish use of indirectness in criticism, self-presentation, acceptance of an offer or invitation, choice of topic, register or form of address perceived as unexpected or inappropriate, turn-taking perceived as difficult, back-channelling perceived as unexpected or negative, use of silence perceived as excessive or insufficient, eye contact, smiles, gestures misinterpreted (e.g., wrongly seen as inviting intimacy), use of space perceived as unexpected, territoriality behaviour and attitudes to time perceived as negative or unexpected, treating the other person on the basis of stereotyped views, gender attitudes and behaviour perceived as negative or unexpected and Finns' low power distance orientation perceived as negative or unexpected. Example comments from the respondents included the following: 'I expected everybody to listen to what I had to say. This was not the case but the Italians interrupted me in what I considered to be a harsh way and started all to give their own opinion in chorus.' 'We were sitting in a bus on an excursion with our group when she asked me if I shaved my legs. I was surprised at the question as I considered it all too personal to be asked in a public place.' 'An American fellow passenger kept asking too personal matters such as whether I was married and why I was not married.'[29]

Subcultural as well as national differences create problems. For instance, in the UK, schoolchildren of Afro-Caribbean ethnic origin, and elsewhere in Europe children of Algerian, Turkish or Indonesian ethnicity display differences from the majority in dialect, frequency of interruption, story telling and conversational rules. These differences have resulted in lower performance expectations from teachers, excessive speech or language therapy placements, and communication differences being treated as discipline problems. For the children themselves, their treatment often results in lowered self-expectations and a tendency to see the school climate as negative. Gender differences in ways of talking and non-verbal behaviour can also cause problems: the male sex may be seen as powerful and decisive and the female as submissive and indecisive. Tannen argued, 'Communication between men and women can be like cross cultural communication, prey to a clash of conversational styles.'[30]

Disability is another source of communication barriers. For instance, this applies to communicators who do not have normal hearing thresholds. Even in ideal conditions, skilled lip-readers accurately interpret less than 50 per cent of what is being said. The late-deafened communicator, especially, has a difficult time adapting to new communication strategies. People talking to interlocutors who are hard of hearing may not have the skills to repair communication breakdowns, leaving both parties dissatisfied with the communication encounter.[31] Within the first few interactions with people without disabilities, people with disabilities must manage or fend off requests for information and invasions of privacy in an attempt to retain individuality and control. At the same time they have to try to build relationships. If uncertainty about the disability is not reduced, it has a negative impact on interability relationships, including premature termination of the relationship.[32]

A three-tier model of intercultural communication consists of the intrapersonal, interpersonal and systemic. At the intrapersonal level, social demands, such as the one to treat people with disabilities with kindness, might be in conflict with others, such as to treat them as equals. This paradox constrains interability interactions, especially those between strangers. At the interpersonal level, people without disabilities, operating with stereotypes, may be unclear as to what constitutes appropriate behaviour (e.g., to help or not to help). This leads them to constrain their behaviour. At the systemic level, which concerns power relations, people without disabilities, who have the upper hand in conversations, may misconstrue statements made by people with disabilities and guide behaviour in a way that supports negative stereotypes. A study had female confederates (trained to use a wheelchair) either feign a disability or remain visibly non-disabled when interacting with a non-disabled respondent. The study found that the non-disabled respondents sought more information and were more aware of behaviour from the non-disabled confederate than from the apparently disabled confederate. The results showed that less positive predicted outcomes led to less information-seeking behaviour.[33]

Problems persist even when efforts are made to overcome them. A deaf man who developed software for a big company could speak and lip-read, but said, 'I lose a lot of information, which leads to misunderstandings. I prefer written means to be sure I'm getting the full message.' He relied mostly on e-mail, instant messaging, a text pager and a whiteboard, and said, 'I work closely with my supervisor to get assignments that let me be most productive. That usually means they require minimal face-to-face communication.' He said he found that his company's strong diversity awareness programmes reduced common workplace problems and misconceptions about the deaf and hard of hearing. 'But I still need to encourage co-workers to include me in their conversations and meetings. Over time, the communication barrier does break down as the comfort level increases. But in our fast-paced work environment, it takes longer for this to happen.' One deaf man whose firm gave him a text pager device discovered that not everyone was ready to use it. 'Most hearing people who have not used a text pager shy away from it because they don't feel comfortable with it,' he said.[34] Finally, differences brought about by education and professional training can also cause frequent misunderstandings and misinterpretations.

The rest of this section aims to show how many of the communication practices introduced in Chapter 3 can lead to misunderstanding and even conflict in intercultural encounters. The practices covered include encoding and decoding of messages, language ambiguity, inferences, elaborated codes, the topic–comment structure of a communication, social knowledge, relevance, face issues, politeness, non-verbal behaviour, low-context communication and high-context communication, detecting deceptions, communication strategies, conflict management and the functions talk is used for.

Encoding and decoding of messages

Intercultural communicators often have problems both in encoding their own messages so they can be understood by the other party and in accurately decoding what the other party says. Bias increases this difficulty. Gallois and Callan considered that the results of their study of message decoding in Australia, described in Chapter 3, revealed that the negative attitudes of Anglo-Australians to Italian men are reflected in the difficulty they have in decoding these speakers when the Italian voice and accent are present. They concluded that the listener's own goals and perception of the context as threatening may lead to an overall distortion of the speaker's messages.[35]

Language ambiguity

Language is fundamentally ambiguous,[36] giving rise to much confusion, especially for non-native speakers. For instance, in English, there is nothing in the words themselves

Box 5.3

The following are examples of ambiguity in English:

My son has grown another foot; visiting relatives can be boring; vegetarians don't know how good meat tastes; I saw the man with the binoculars.

The following examples are from newspaper headlines:

The judge sentenced the killer to die in the electric chair for the second time.

Dr. Tackett Gives Talk on Moon.

No one was injured in the blast, which was attributed to the buildup of gas by one town official.

The summary of information contains totals of the number of students broken down by sex, marital status and age.[a]

Other examples include:

On a packet of soya milk: There are many more delicious products from Alpro; why don't you try them?

Overheard in a lift: 'I want the porter to turn off the TV thing; I don't want to see people.' (Actually he meant he only wanted an audio entry phone, not a video one).

On a poster advertisement: The less you pay to travel, the more you have to spend when you get there.[b]

Sources: (a) Pinker, S. (1994) *The Language Instinct*, London: Allen Lane, The Penguin Press
(b) Author's research

to say, 'This is the important point.' That emphasis is supplied by the expectations each speaker has that the other speaker will use language in the same way that s/he does. In the case of English this means they have to grasp the subtle English use of voice modulation. For example, questions can be expressed as statements spoken in a rising voice pitch, as in, 'So you went to the bank this morning.' This is a statement if spoken in a level pitch and a question if spoken in a rising pitch. Because we have no choice but to draw inferences about meaning, when language is ambiguous we rely on two main sources: (1) the language a speaker has used and (2) our knowledge about the world. A statement like, 'There is a man at the door,' *could* mean, 'There is a man sitting on the doorstep playing the guitar.' However, we are likely to discount this in favour of assuming it to mean, 'There is a man at the door waiting to be let in,' or a similar one. In other words, we are likely to assume, unless a speaker states otherwise, that the obvious common-sense assumption is correct. However, what constitutes 'common sense' varies across cultures. In fact, even within interactions by native speakers of the 'same' language from different cultures, such as speakers of British and American English, there are at least four categories of language differences that have the potential to confuse. The four categories are (1) the same expression with differences in style, connotation, and/or frequency (2) the same expression with one or more shared and different meanings (3) the same expression with completely different meanings (4) and different expressions with the same shared meaning.[37]

Inferences

There are subtleties of language use that enable receivers of messages spoken in their native language to draw accurate inferences about the speakers' meanings. These subtleties will tend to escape non-native speakers. Equally, the other source of inference, knowledge of the 'world', may be defective when the speaker is from another culture, as the two participants' 'worlds' will be influenced by their culture. For example, Kotani noted that English speakers assume that, 'I'm sorry,' means 'I admit responsibility,' and that the words closely represent the speaker's feeling; conversely, Japanese speakers mean, 'I acknowledge that you have suffered,' and there can be low correspondence between the words and the feeling. This may lead to English speakers judging Japanese people insincere.[38] Misunderstanding also arises interculturally because of misinterpreting the 'cues' used to decide what kind of language event is occurring. Expectations about how conversational exchanges should develop, appropriate ways of speaking and the interpersonal relations and speaking rights of those involved are based on these cues, which may be missed or misread by people from outside the culture.[39] Differences in what aspects of a communication receivers 'sample' (e.g., attitudes or roles) also 'have profound implications for the probability of conflict and the type of conflict that will develop between individuals and groups'.[40]

Elaborated codes

When people realise that they are interacting with someone from a different background, they usually adapt their discourse by using elaborated rather than restricted codes.[41] This adaptation is necessary, but can mean that intercultural encounters are marked by formality. This formality slows the pace at which relationships develop while people from some (sub)cultures, such as the North Americans, find it unfriendly. In addition, the requirements for adapting to the elaborated code place heavy demands on people's communication resources. On the other hand, what a person from one culture overhears in a discussion between two people from a different culture using a restricted code can be mystifying or misleading.

The topic–comment structure of a communication

Speakers may either give the context of what they want to say first and then their main point or vice-versa. Topic–comment order varies between cultures and this can cause confusion, especially in languages like English that (unlike Japanese, for instance) have no semantic way of marking the main subject. Research in a major East Asian city studied situations that could be considered to require professional communication. It found that amongst people from North American / European cultures, it was usual to put the comment, main point or suggested action first and then give the topic, background or reason. People from Asian cultural backgrounds did the reverse: they put the topic, background or reason first and then their main point, comment or the action they were suggesting.[42] For example, a North American might say, 'We could announce price cuts on 100 items for the next three months – we'd run a big press campaign and an in-store sales promotion, try to get lots of publicity [suggested action]. That way we'd really cut the ground out from under our competitors with their selective weekly price cuts [reason].' An Asian listener, expecting to hear the reason for any action first, might find this abrupt, or might interpret the opening sentence as the reason and become confused. By contrast, an Asian speaker would be more likely to say, 'Our competitors are launching a campaign of weekly price cuts. This could have very serious consequences for our sales and market share [reason]. We could look at announcing price cuts on 100 items for the next three months ... [suggested action].' A North American listener might grow impatient, especially if the reasons were elaborated, as they might well be. The North American might then be inattentive when the speaker reached the point of proposing action.

Social knowledge

Intercultural communicators, even those with high technical understanding of the other culture's language, will often be hampered by lack of social knowledge. For instance, they might not know the definitions and boundaries of situations that are well understood in the other culture, the precise nature of role relationships occurring in those situations or the linguistic and non-verbal codes to use.[43] Errors result when people impose the social rules of their own (sub)culture in a situation where the social rules of another (sub)culture would be more appropriate. One type occurs when a speech strategy is employed which is inappropriate for the language being spoken: for instance, speaking loudly and forcefully in Japanese. Another type involves getting the balance between talk and silence wrong for the culture. On the other hand, attempting to adapt to the perceived needs of the person being spoken to can itself produce problems – for instance, using a simplified 'foreigner talk' register, as the Japanese often do, even when the person they are addressing is highly competent in the language, limits discussion as well as possibly giving offence.

Relevance

Interlocutors have to decide which is the relevant intention of various possibilities that might underlie a communication. In intercultural situations, however, using relevance to decide another person's intention can create problems. The speaker may have a limited ability to make their intention correspond to the beliefs most likely to be relevant to the receiver. For instance, in the example given in Box 3.5, a Western banker explained that in dealing with Turkish officials he had difficulty in conveying an intention to be 'properly and prudentially' cautious because of not knowing what beliefs would be relevant to them in the situation at issue.

Face issues

In uncertain situations, which may threaten their sense of their identity, people experience problems with facework. In uncertain situations, active facework is needed. The parties engage in two kinds of facework: those concerned with their own face and those with the other party's face.[44] Important work meetings, negotiations or interviews, which involve meeting people from another culture for the first time, are examples of uncertain situations. Culture influences people's use of facework and which kind of facework they will more often select. For instance, people from one culture may choose strategies that avoid face issues while people from another culture select strategies that defend their face. Non-alignment or misalignment of facework strategies can lead to miscommunication – the people who are interacting misread each other's signals and so respond inappropriately. This can lead to spiralling conflict.

Politeness

Another source of intercultural communication problems arises from the miscommunication of politeness. As Ambady *et al.* speculated in conclusion to research about cultural differences in politeness strategies, 'Perhaps many misunderstandings that occur between cultures are due to the miscommunication of politeness.'[45] What constitutes a face-threatening act varies cross-culturally. For instance, making a request is generally a less face-threatening act for North Americans (as shown by their dictum 'always ask') than to many British people. Some intercultural miscommunication is produced by directness and indirectness in certain situations involving greetings, farewells, compliments and negative observations. Directness perceived positively is called 'honesty'. However, if it is negatively perceived it quickly becomes 'rudeness'. Indirectness perceived positively is regarded as 'politeness' or 'friendliness', but if perceived negatively is seen as 'superficiality' or 'insincerity'. This issue has been found to affect communication between North Americans and Germans. North Americans often show politeness through behaviours and language perceived as 'friendliness', while Germans show it through what they might label 'respect'. Many Germans stress 'honesty' in encounters, while many North Americans wish to maintain an agreeable attitude and do not want to disappoint their interlocutors. Thus, when they meet, if they are expecting behaviour from the others that they find in their own cultures, North Americans and Germans often do not have their expectations met and they become disappointed in the members of the other culture.[46]

Non-verbal behaviour

In intercultural encounters, non-verbal behaviour is easily misinterpreted. Some examples are given in Box 5.4. Trait and style differences can also create communication

Box 5.4

Kinesics: Asians in general tend to smile or laugh more readily than Westerners when they feel difficulty or embarrassment. Westerners then misinterpret this as normal pleasure or agreement and the source of difficulty is missed.

Proxemics: Hall put forward the notion of a 'space bubble' in which each individual moves and feels comfortable. The size of this space bubble varies by culture: Arabs and Latin-Americans feel comfortable with a smaller space bubble than Anglos. This leads them to stand closer, creating discomfort for an interacting Anglo, who may move backwards, thus giving an impression of unfriendliness to the Arab. Responses to perceived invasion of space have been shown to differ between men and women. While men may respond aggressively, women tend to yield space rather than challenge the intruder.[a]

Speed of delivery: Faster speakers almost always evaluate slower speakers negatively. Thus Europeans and people from the Northern USA often wrongly regard people from the Southern states of the USA as slow thinking.

Speech styles: Language and communication norms among young African American males, particularly those of lower socio-economic status, are related, at least in part, to their higher

rate of disciplinary problems and special education placements. Speaking ethnically based English vernaculars and the use of urban argots can be seen by such youths as markers of masculinity and defiance of White standards, but it 'virtually guarantees' academic problems and, sometimes, social problems by conflicting with the school's communication norms.[b]

Communicator style: A study examined the role that culture plays in communication distortion by using observation and interviewing techniques to gather data while applicants from West Africa and Westerners applied for a visa. The results suggested that speech patterns, body posture, eye contact, information disclosure and verbal aggression are interpreted differently depending on culture, which leads to communication distortion.[c]

Sources: (a) Hall, E.T. (1959) *The Silent Language*, New York: Doubleday

(b) CNORSE 'Cross-cultural communication: an essential dimension of effective education', http://www.nwrel.org/cnorse

(c) Olaniran, B.A and Williams, D.E. (1995) 'Communication distortion: an intercultural lesson from the visa application process', *Communication Quarterly*, **43**(2): 225–40

barriers. For instance, the point has already been made that there are cultural differences in what counts as assertiveness and the value attached to it. Using a level of assertiveness which is appropriate in one culture with interactors from another will probably be seen as aggression or, on the other hand, lack of assertion.

Low-context communication (LCC) and high-context communication (HCC)

Misunderstanding arises easily between users of LCC and HCC. When a speaker uses HCC, the problem for LCC receivers is literally to grasp their meaning: so much is left unsaid and they are not attuned to the implicatures and inferences being used, nor to the extensive use of non-verbal communication. Indirectness and an emphasis on relationship data compound the problem. When the speaker uses LCC, the problem for HCC receivers is less to grasp their overt meaning than to avoid over-interpreting and seeing inferences that may not be present. They may also be affronted by directness or the 'brutality' of the concentration on hard content; or simply suffer from information overload.

Detecting deceptions

Three types of assessment are generally used to decide whether a speaker is telling the truth: whether the speaker's non-verbal behaviour breaches common expectations, whether the message being communicated is plausible and how nervous the speaker is. People from a different background can misread all these indicators. For example, most able-bodied people would not know enough about cerebral palsy to assess the plausibility of a statement about its symptoms and treatment which they were told by a person with this disability.

Communication strategies

Differences of communication strategy can produce conflict, especially between members of different subcultures. For example, in discussions with men, women's communication strategies often express the subordinate, non-aggressive role allocated to women, but this can be misleading. Soft-spoken women who use multiple hesitations and tag questions may nevertheless be highly determined and power-oriented; they may be deliberately, and even successfully, adopting a 'feminine' style or they may lack awareness of their own style and so miscommunicate their attitudes or intentions. Communication strategies that impede real communication may, however, reflect the interactors' real intentions or attitudes, and these may be culturally induced. For instance, a study of group encounters between Israeli Jews and Palestinians highlighted how the participants pursue their rhetorical goals in ways that frustrate dialogue. These ways include using symbols of ethnic identity to support a case in argument, unquestioned assumptions by each side that forestall progress, and various argumentative strategies (e.g., question asking, collaboration argument, limited topical space).[47] Similarly, cultural differences between 'professional' and lay members of religions can emerge in communication breakdown. Research among practising Roman Catholics found that the prevailing Catholic culture has led to 'a breakdown in communication between people at different positions in the political structure'. Individuals who said they were trying to find a way to be heard gave many examples of encounters with priests, nuns, other ministers of religion and lay religious practitioners who responded with incomprehension and contempt. None of those interviewed used mediation or consensus procedures successfully to work through their issues. In some cases they compromised themselves. This meant they withdrew physically, emotionally and/or spiritually from stress-causing situations.[48]

Conflict management

Cultural differences in how conflict is usually conducted may increase the difficulty of resolving intercultural conflicts. Triandis pointed out that conflict is greater when two cultures are very different than when they are similar. The degree of difference is called cultural distance, which is a function of language, social structure (e.g., family structure) and religion, among other factors.[49]

Functions of talk

The functions to which talk is put can differ between groups, at least in emphasis, and so create misunderstanding. One function is to distribute control of the interaction; another is to determine the level of affiliation. Some women see talk as the essence of a relationship while some men use talk to exert control, preserve independence and enhance status.

> This section has shown that differences of background, whether cultural or subcultural, ethnic, gender-based or based on some other distinction, not only affect how people communicate but can also be a serious cause of miscommunication.

5.3 BEHAVIOURAL BARRIERS

All of the underlying psychological factors, which, as Chapter 4 showed, vary cross-culturally, are capable of leading to behaviours that disturb effective intercultural communication. These include values, emotions, beliefs, assumptions, expectations, intentions and self-construals. The processes of social perception and thinking are similarly vulnerable.

Values

Between people from different sides of cultural divides, communication can be inhibited by non-acceptance of the others' values. For example, the attempt of someone with high power in a high power distance society to receive the attentions 'due' to their status will grate on people from more egalitarian communities. On the other hand, many university lecturers in Central Europe regard the egalitarianism between students and staff, which is now usual in British universities, as damaging the learning process by undermining their authority. This has led to cases where lecturers from Britain, working for a semester in a Central European country to help introduce Western business studies or management courses, have found themselves isolated as their local colleagues distance themselves.

Both deep and surface cultural values can be problematic in intercultural communication: deep culture because communication which conflicts with others'

Box 5.5

Many Indians look down when acknowledging authority, an attitude that many North American and European managers interpret as untrustworthiness.

The British find the French analytical approach arid; the French find British pragmatism confused.

Giving public reprimands is acceptable in US culture, even effective, but probably in few others.

Argentinians and South Americans need time to elapse for trust building before doing deals; this is in conflict with Americans' need not to waste time because 'time is money'.[a]

Western European companies negotiating joint ventures with Russians 'face difficulties in assessing their counterparts' trustworthiness. In particular, there are misunderstandings regarding commitment to the given word. While Westerners may consider a verbal agreement binding, this does not seem to be the case for Russians.' Verbal agreements may be reached one day and ignored the next.[b]

The Germans value experience, seniority and age and so to send a young manager to deal with seniors is considered a mistake. Germans also feel that jokes are inappropriate in a business setting.

It is easy for people visiting Africa to give offence by taking photographs of local people. First, for Moslems, there is a Koranic prohibition on representations of the person; second, 'local colour' to them is the backward aspect of their society; third, some people may associate being photographed with becoming a victim of witchcraft.

Sources: (a) Adler, N. (1991) *International Dimensions of Organizational Behavior* (2nd edn), Belmont, CA: Wadsworth
(b) Abramov, M., Arino, A., Rykounina, I., Skorobogatykh, I. and Vila, J. (1997) 'Partner selection and trust building in West European–Russian joint ventures: a Western perspective', *International Studies of Management & Organization*, **27**(1): 19–37

values is very likely to be misunderstood, rejected and found offensive; surface culture because it determines matters such as what is polite and what is not (for instance, in the West to proffer the wrong hand for a hand shake is a mere error; to do so in Arab countries is a grave offence against manners). Sometimes the problem is one of false interpretation: Example 1 in Box 5.5 illustrates such a case: a difference in the conventions governing eye contact can lead to Westerners finding Indians untrustworthy. At other times, there are genuine differences in values or attitudes that, when accurately communicated, create negative responses: the second example in the same Box may reflect such a situation. It is probable that differences in education and upbringing between the French and British (both of which may be rooted in differences in their cultural levels of uncertainty avoidance) do lead at least some of the people of these two nations to approach issues differently. It is also quite possible that both have low tolerance for the other's approach.

Universalism and particularism, as Chapter 2 explained, contrast a preference for drawing general principles with a preference for anecdotes or lists of specific items. People who think and speak in universal modes can under-rate the quality of thinking of those who think and speak particularistically. Conversely, particularistic thinkers can regard universalistic thinkers as 'academic' and out of touch with the real world. In both cases, these attitudes lead to poor listening – a lack of serious attention and consideration of the views being expressed or the information being imparted. When these attitudes to others are transmitted, often unintentionally, to the person to whom they apply, a natural reaction for them is to withdraw, reducing the amount of communication they offer, or to get angry. Either reaction can lead to a breach in communication. Again, people from specific cultures, with their small areas of privacy clearly separated from public life, have considerable freedom for direct speech. This may result in 'insulting' people from diffuse cultures, for whom the principle of losing face is 'what happens when something is made public which people perceive as being private'. The importance of avoiding loss of face is the reason why in diffuse cultures so much more time is taken to get to the point: it is necessary to avoid confrontation because it is impossible for participants not to take things personally. Many similar examples could be cited to show how differences in core values lead to miscommunication broadly defined.

Several of the core cultural values have the property of constituting barriers to communication in themselves, regardless of whether intercultural communication is at issue. For example, if everyone were an individualist, one might predict a world of poor communication – individualists show low concern for 'other face'; if all were collectivists, one could predict poor communication and conflict between groups. Collectivists erect barriers to communication with outgroup members, regardless of whether those outgroup members are themselves collectivists or not. People in high power distance cultures erect barriers against those in a different power position from themselves, though their communication with those in a similar power position to their own may be enhanced, because similarity fosters liking, acceptance and persuasibility. High uncertainty avoidance leads to reluctance to engage in uncertain communication situations regardless of whether they are with culturally different people. High masculinity as a trait (as opposed to a value) has been shown to correlate with low ability to 'read' others' emotional states or to express emotion; it seems probable that the equivalent value tends to lead to similar communication deficiencies.

Inter-ethnic differences in values have been revealed by American research as a reason why inter-ethnic conversation is often unsatisfying and does not go smoothly. African Americans' core values are: sharing (which endorses the ingroup, reflects collectivism and implies bonding), uniqueness (individuality), positivity (emotional vitality), realism ('tellin' it like it is) and assertiveness. European Americans prioritise the individual, the right to choose, the self, traditional social roles, being honest, sharing and communication. Even where the labels are the same, they are understood differently: for European Americans 'sharing' means sharing opinions, not bonding; honesty means expressing one's true understanding but that may not be realistic (it might be optimistic); their 'self' implies less interpersonal connectedness than African Americans' 'uniqueness' implies.[50] Similarly, the differences, reported in Chapter 4, in the communication motives of the members of different ethnic groups may reduce the chances that either side will find their communication satisfying.[51]

Emotions

As Chapter 2 revealed, Trompenaars contended that the amount of visible display of emotion is a major difference between cultures. A further aspect of this difference is the degree of separation from objective and impersonal matters. Americans, for example, are high in emotional expression but also high in separation; Italians are high in emotional expression but low in separation; Dutch and Swedish people are low in emoting visibly and high in separating.[52] These differences in culturally inculcated rules for emotional display can create severe difficulties for participants in intercultural encounters. The English, with their famous 'stiff upper lip' have traditionally been embarrassed, to the point where their ability to empathise or sympathise was subverted, by the more demonstrative displays of affection and grief shown by Mediterranean people.

The same applies to subcultures – men in Western cultures often fear the 'emotionalism' of women (and so take the route of avoidance) although the gender differences here may be more closely related to culturally induced differences in what it is legitimate to display than in the real level of emotion.

In addition to the obstacles created by these cultural differences, the intercultural encounter itself often gives rise to emotions that can create further barriers. For example, in encounters between people with and people without disabilities, anxiety, as well as negative stereotypes and expectations, affects both parties and leads to miscommunication.[53] In international negotiations, 'increasingly negative' emotional reactions can cause ill will, harm the negotiation process and even bring it to an end. 'In negotiations between Japanese and US negotiators, the latter may be prone to experiencing frustration and the former may be prone to experiencing anxiety. The anxiety of the Japanese negotiators results in increasing frustration on the part of the US negotiators, leading to a vicious circle of increasingly negative feelings.'[54]

Communication fear or apprehension (CA), which was described in Chapter 4, impedes communication. Individuals who experience CA ask few questions during the first minute of an interaction, engage in high levels of self-disclosure and are considered less competent by their communication partners. Individuals who experience high levels of CA are high in global uncertainty and lack expertise when playing out acquaintance scenarios.[55] Intercultural communication apprehension (ICA) is often objectively unjustified. On structured communication tasks, inter-ethnic dyads (e.g., a French Canadian with an English Canadian) were just as efficient at communicating with each other as intra-ethnic dyads (e.g., a French Canadian with a French Canadian). Likewise, in the unstructured situation of a free interaction, mixed-ethnicity pairs showed the same pattern of conversational topics, did not take longer to begin communicating and did not talk less than same-ethnicity pairs. Yet, despite this evidence that inter-ethnic communication can be as successful as intra-ethnic communication, it has been found that not only do subjects enter these intergroup encounters with negative expectations but they also leave them with an unfavourable impression of what has been achieved. Such negative expectations no doubt serve as an important deterrent to intergroup interaction.

Five other 'problem' emotions are common in intercultural encounters:

1. Disconfirmed expectations – being upset not because a situation is bad, in and of itself, but rather because it is not what was expected.
2. Frustrated desire to belong – not being part of the 'ingroup' of a culture; always feeling like an outsider. This feeling can be provoked by physical difference – being tall and fair among people who are short and dark – or the perceived attitudes of the culture's members.
3. Ambiguity – not being sure what is 'going on' or how to interpret events.
4. Confrontation with one's own prejudices – In being socialised into their own culture, people learn to categorise people as 'like me' and 'not like me', and develop ways of treating people in those two groups differently. In another culture, where the majority of people are 'not like me', they have to rethink how they treat other people. Sometimes they may be dismayed to find themselves prejudiced.
5. Anxiety – feeling anxious because of not knowing if a given behaviour is appropriate, what is safe, how to negotiate a situation and so on.[56]

(Some of these points relate particularly to sojourning.)

Other common negative emotions in intercultural situations include a need to be dependent or a feeling of being overwhelmed and a need to withdraw. It is not, of course, the emotion itself that constitutes a communication barrier: it is how the individual responds to that emotion. If their response is withdrawal or aggressiveness, communication is impeded. Having strong emotional reactions to intercultural situations is normal, and one of the skills of becoming interculturally competent is learning how to deal with such emotions in productive ways.

Beliefs

Probably more disagreement arises over differences in conscious beliefs than anything else. Disagreement should not be confused with miscommunication, even on a broad view. However, to the degree that conflict can be taken as a measure of miscommunication, the amount of conflict prevailing throughout history and still raging today around issues of religion is an indication of how this aspect of beliefs produces barriers. Huntington argued that intercultural conflicts centring on beliefs are perhaps the most intractable of all. While ideological differences can at least be debated, and differences in material interests negotiated, core beliefs are not negotiable or even discussable. 'Hindus and Muslims are unlikely to resolve the issue of whether a temple or a mosque should be built at Ayodhya by building both, or neither, or a syncretic building that is both a mosque and a temple. Similarly, neither French authorities nor Muslim parents are likely to accept a compromise which would allow schoolgirls to wear Muslim dress every other day during the school year. Cultural questions like these involve a yes or no, zero-sum choice.'[57]

Chapter 4 described a set of beliefs, consisting of authoritarianism, social dominance orientation, Protestant work ethic, humanitarianism–egalitarianism, beliefs about the malleability of human attributes and beliefs about diversity. These belief systems are linked to prejudice. Social distance orientation is associated with negative attitudes towards policies that promote equality across gender, social class, ethnic or racial groups, and sexual orientation, and towards the groups that would benefit from such policies. In North America, people who agree with SDO are more likely to agree with sexism, racism, and ethnocentrism (seeing one's own culture as superior) than people who agree with authoritarianism. Following directly from beliefs that people who are stigmatised are responsible for their lesser outcomes, people who agree with the Protestant work ethic in the USA tend to dislike overweight persons and to be prejudiced toward racial minorities. A belief in the Protestant work ethic has been positively associated with behavioural measures of prejudice, including, in Australia, opposition to public assistance programmes and, instead, support for 'tough-minded' solutions to the problem of unemployment, such as restricting immigration and reducing unemployment benefits. The other three beliefs systems, humanitarianism–egalitarianism, positive beliefs about the malleability of human attributes and positive beliefs about diversity, are linked to low levels of prejudice. For instance, holders of these beliefs tend to attribute Blacks' negative outcomes such as experiencing discrimination, to causes located outside of the individual, believe that society, rather than the individual, should change to improve those outcomes, agree less strongly with stereotypes of ethnic and occupational groups and less readily form extreme trait judgements of novel (unfamiliar) groups.[58]

Box 5.6

Women from Western countries can often misunderstand signals if they are not completely briefed on the country's customs. 'In an accounting center, I got talking to the Deputy Minister for Taxation who said he was interested in financial reporting in the UK. I started discussing moves to international standardisation, etc. He then invited me out to dinner at his house. Innocently, I accepted. We then moved to a communal lunch. There was uproar as I got about five different offers from people I knew to either meet them at their offices, or their houses etc. It turned out that as an apparently single woman accepting an invitation to a man's house, I had agreed to more than I might be anticipating.'

Women can also be misunderstood. 'In the early evening in my hotel in a Central Asian country a young man was visiting me to give me his brother's CV to see if I could help get him work in the West. I was feeling ill and wanted to access the only decent telephone in the major hotel, about 1 kilometre down the road, so that I could get medical help. I didn't feel it was safe for me to walk alone at night. I asked him, "Will you please accompany me to the Hotel XXXX?" He said, "Certainly not!" in a shocked voice. I had to explain my motives, as my request had been misunderstood.'

Source: An accounting expert on her experiences while working in Central Asia: e-mail, author's research

Assumptions

Making false assumptions based on the situation in someone's own culture can lead to impeding communication through giving or taking offence by, for example, not giving deference where it is expected or expecting it where it will not be granted. Who is important, whom it would be useful to get to know and who is to be respected may be different in one culture than it is in another. A religious leader may be more important in one culture, someone with wealth in another. In one culture Black people may be the 'insiders' in another it may be South Asians. People who are insiders in their own culture, due to their economic, professional or educational status, may be outsiders in another culture, because their skills are not important there, or because of ethnicity or gender, or simply because they are from another culture and can never be fully accepted in the host culture.

Expectations

Violations of expectations, including role and norm expectations, often lead to people evaluating the violator negatively. People have expectations about both the verbal and the non-verbal behaviour of others, based on social (cultural) norms, previous experience with the situation and, where applicable, previous experience of the other person. These expectations refer both to how they think others do behave and to how they think others should behave. However, as norms for behaviour vary from social group to social group, these expectations are often violated in intercultural encounters. For instance, in the European American middle-class subculture of the USA, 'one expects normal speakers to be reasonably [sic] fluent and coherent in their discourse, to refrain from erratic movements or emotional outbursts and to adhere to politeness norms'.[59] What counts as reasonable fluency and coherence, erratic movement, emotional outburst or politeness varies considerably from one culture (and subculture) to another, so European American middle-class people interacting with many other groups in the world are likely to have their expectations violated. Insofar as fear of violations of expectations means that people expect interactions with people from outside their own social circle to be more costly in terms of effort than rewarding in terms of social gain, people may be more inclined to avoid such interactions.[60]

Intentions

Inferring the intentions of a speaker, which, as Chapter 3 showed, is crucial to communication, is highly problematic for receivers from another culture. Some of the problems have already been pointed out in the discussion of language ambiguity.

Self-construals

A final factor is the different self-construals held by people from different cultures. This applies particularly to people from individualist and collectivist cultures. It means that each group is likely to make false assumptions about members of the other group. For instance, 'Asians will possibly overestimate a Westerner's concern about his [sic] group's response to an issue, while a Westerner is likely to assume a greater degree of independence on the part of an Asian with whom he is negotiating.'[61]

Social perception and thinking

These processes are subject to difficulties and errors particular to intergroup and intercultural encounters. The increased tendency to make errors when making intergroup attributions was noted in Chapter 4. Categorisation is another error-prone process; there is evidence that some people categorise narrowly and both some of them and some others categorise rigidly. Narrow categorisers group together only cases which are closely similar on a particular criterion: for instance, a narrow categoriser might apply the label 'manager' only to people who are responsible for the work of others. Broad categorisers, in contrast, allow more cases to fit into the same category by using an increased number of criteria. Thus, broad categorisers might count as managers people who manage budgets or brands as well as those who manage people. Both narrow and broad categorisers might be flexible or rigid categorisers, willing or unwilling to shift their category 'definitions' on receiving new information. There is, though, a tendency for rigidity and narrowness to go together. Rigidity and narrowness, especially when combined, create obstacles to intercultural communication by leading people to over-emphasise differences and ignore similarities and by reducing their willingness to search for appropriate interpretations of different others' behaviour. Finally, (sub)cultural differences in logic style, learning style and problem-solving, such as those described in Chapter 4, obviously impede mutual understanding.

This section has been concerned with how the behavioural factors and processes underlying communication behaviour can contribute to miscommunication between people from different groups. To date, most attention has been paid to the barriers created by different values, by emotions, especially fear, and by the violation of expectations.

Box 5.7

X was attending a meeting of the French subsidiary of the global organisation he worked for. He was acting as the representative of another subsidiary in a discussion of the basis on which his company would supply the French company with components.

The meeting was formally convened by the Chairman [sic], then the French company's Purchasing Director began describing X's company's offer in negative terms. (1) X interrupted, addressing the last speaker directly, not through the Chair. X explained the rationale for his company's offer. (2) The next speaker said, 'Chairman, I'm afraid I must disagree with X. Just because we have received a concessionary price, it does not follow that we should accept delivery delays. These matters are not directly connected.' (3) X thought they would never get to the point of stating their demands. 'Analysis-paralysis', he thought. (4) However, when they finally did say what they wanted, he felt trapped – they had constructed so powerful a rationale to support their demands that it was difficult to find any weakness where their position could be attacked. (5) X found the outcome of the meeting unsatisfactory – nothing had been decided. (6) Though probing continuously for his company's aims and objectives, the French negotiators had side-stepped every effort on his part to get them to reveal theirs. (7) At times, the discussion had seemed more like an intellectual exercise than a business meeting.

The following help explain the barriers which led to X finding the meeting unsatisfactory:

(1) X's interruption, and especially his lack of formality in not going through the Chair, would be regarded as a serious breach of etiquette in many French organisations.

(2) French negotiators often concentrate on weaknesses in the other party's logic, rather than on 'getting to yes' by building areas of agreement.

(3) French use of logic can lead to extensive analysis of all matters under discussion.

(4) Instead of a process of making initial offers and concession-making, demands follow a careful build-up of supporting rationale, which is often very powerful.

(5) Important decisions are rarely taken in meetings.

(6) The French do not regard disclosure of business information as a mutual win-win matter, but as a competitive win-lose 'game'.

(7) Prolonged discussion allows French negotiators to grasp their opponents' weaknesses.

Based on: The author's research

5.4 WORK-SPECIFIC BARRIERS

In the work context, a number of additional issues arise to limit intercultural communication effectiveness. For example, organisational cultures of blame and defensiveness reduce communication effectiveness, while different cultures within organisations can lead to a breakdown of inter-organisational communication.[62] Two areas have attracted particular attention: (1) the effects of the heterogeneity of problem-solving and task groups and (2) task-related conflict.

Heterogeneity of work groups

Because organisations are increasingly moving to team-based job design, communication within both task groups and decision-making groups is increasingly important. This has led to research being undertaken into the effects of heterogeneity in work groups on how well people working in them communicate and on related matters such as their creativity.

A study of 20 actual work units with 79 respondents suggested that heterogeneity is associated with lower levels of groups' social integration. This, in turn, is associated with higher staff turnover. The study focused on age heterogeneity. It found that group members more distant in age are the ones likely to leave. 'Individuals in an age-heterogeneous [work] group have higher turnover rates as do individuals distant in age from an otherwise homogeneous group.' One possible explanation comes from an earlier finding that after controlling for an individual's demographic characteristics, the greater the difference in superior–subordinate dyads, in terms of age, education, race and sex, the lower the supervisor's rating of the subordinate's effectiveness and the higher the subordinate's role ambiguity. If subordinates experience 'prejudiced' assessments when they are in a mixed work group or when they are different in background from their supervisor, they may decide that the easiest solution is to leave.[63]

Work-related conflict

There is clear evidence for poor work relations in intercultural situations. For instance, studies of Chinese–American joint ventures reported the following:

- '[Chinese] workers ... evaluated Chinese managers by a simple standard: whoever quarrelled with Americans the most aggressively would be considered comrade in arms, and whoever co-operated with the Americans would be nicknamed 'Er Gui Zi' (fake foreigners).'[64]
- 'American managers complained that the Chinese do not recognize the importance of deadlines and schedules; that the Chinese are not proactive and will not take risks; that the Communist party representative at the firm often has more power than the Chinese managers; and that the hardship of working in China is a chronic stressor, which exacerbates inter-cultural conflict. The Chinese managers complained that Americans do not try to understand and learn from the Chinese; that the American management style is too abrupt; that Americans fail to recognize the importance of relationships; and they overemphasize the importance of formal rules and regulations. "The atmosphere [at Beijing Jeep] became so tense that even the most trivial business dealings between the American and Chinese became bogged down in charges and countercharges." '[65]

Larkey proposed that there are five dimensions of interaction in culturally diverse groups at work.[66] Being dimensions, they have positive as well as negative poles, but it is the negative poles that are most often associated with workforce diversity. The dimensions are inclusion/exclusion, convergence/divergence, conforming/varied ideation, understanding/misunderstanding and positive/negative evaluation.

- Exclusion in the workplace is the practice of marginalising members of certain groups by limiting contact and restricting entry into certain job arenas. The related communication behaviours include simple exclusion from conversations. This is done by avoidance or starting conversations only when selected individuals are absent or by non-verbally or linguistically excluding outsiders who are present. Other exclusions are changes in the content of information, especially to exclude individuals from job-related information, either deliberately or by the assumption that they are not appropriate recipients, the use of privileged forms of discourse and exclusion from the normative expectations.

■ Convergence/divergence is a concept already introduced in Chapter 4 (and to be further explained in Chapter 6). Convergent communication means adjusting ways of speaking (such as style, dialect, rules and primary language choice) to match those of a partner perceived as different or to show a wish for affiliation; divergence is adherence to one's own way in spite of perceived differences. It is open to individuals in diverse work groups to diverge deliberately in order to increase social distance.

■ Conforming ideation means suppressing divergent points of view and converging towards normative views in decision-making; varied ideation is the reverse. A climate of conforming ideation is likely to lead to suppressing the views of minorities.

■ Misunderstanding here means the mismatching of expectations and meanings for people in interaction. Both employees and managers are predisposed to interpret the communication of others according to specific culture-based expectations. For instance, views of what makes a good leader or a good employee may vary substantially, leading to misinterpretations of the behaviour of individuals in those roles. Among the resulting communication practices are complaints of inappropriate responses or expectations.

■ Negative evaluations can be explained by perceptions of ingroup/outgroup membership and associated responses to social identity, reinforced by stereotyping (the communication of even positive stereotype beliefs may elicit negative responses from those being categorised). The resulting behaviours include harassment, overt statements of negative stereotyping and stories with negative implications.

Figure 5.3 shows the relations between cultural diversity in groups and the above five communication practices.

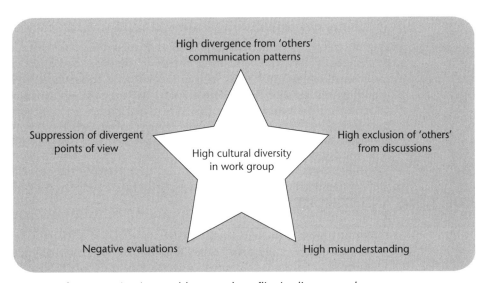

Figure 5.3   *Sources of communication problems and conflict in diverse work groups*

Based on: Larkey, L.K. (1996) 'The development and validation of the workforce diversity questionnaire', *Management Communication Quarterly*, **9**(3): 296–337

Box 5.8

Some scholars dispute the idea that intercultural communication is a special kind of communication in which misunderstandings arise because the participants do not share meanings and communication practices. Instead, they argue, all communication requires interactors to go through a process to establish common ground. Misunderstandings are part of that process. 'Existing research on intercultural misunderstandings usually explain them as caused by culturally different conventions ... here misunderstanding is understood as part of the process of constructing a discursive inter-culture.'

Source: Koole, T. and ten Thije, J.D. (2001) 'The reconstruction of intercultural discourse: methodological considerations', Journal of Pragmatics, **33**: 571–87

Heterogeneity of work groups has been shown to increase staff turnover rates, probably because some people experience discrimination from colleagues and supervisors. Diversity in workforces can lead to communication practices that generate conflict and poor working relationships.

5.5 SUMMARY

This chapter was concerned with sources of intercultural miscommunication. These barriers are real in their consequences and seem often to have their greatest effect for not being perceived. When they are recognised, people often try to overcome them, and often succeed.

Cultural and sub-cultural differences in the ways in which people from different backgrounds communicate were shown to create these barriers to communication, while associated behaviours such as stereotyping, prejudice and harassment, ingroup/outgroup differentiation and discrimination increase them. At work, these barriers create misunderstandings between individuals, whether in the roles of colleagues, professionals and their clients or suppliers and their customers. These misunderstandings often result in emotional distress and reduced performance. Other consequences are that heterogeneous work groups, while potentially more creative, take longer to perform and are more likely to break down and that transnational negotiations and business operations can be fraught with conflict.

The next chapter shows how these barriers can be overcome and how effective intercultural communication can be achieved.

QUESTIONS AND EXERCISES

1. The text gives examples of how differences in communication practices can lead to misunderstanding and even conflict in intercultural encounters. Collect a list of other examples.
2. List four ways in which stereotypes can distort intergroup communication.
3. Use the pro forma below to record your beliefs about a minority group* to which you do not belong. Then use another blank pro forma to record your beliefs about how a minority

group to which you do belong* is perceived. Compare the two and discuss the results in your multi-cultural group.

* the group could be national, regional, ethnic, gender, lesbians and/or gays, people with a specific disability, people of a given age group, social class, educational level, or occupation.

Members of this group	Strongly disagree/ disagree	Neutral	Strongly agree/ agree
Have fewer accidents			
Are unfairly treated by many companies			
Are harder to train			
Are absent more often			
Produce higher quality work			
Are more dependable			
Can't keep pace with technology			
Are most loyal			
Are less interested in challenging jobs			
Do not want responsibility			
Are less co-operative			
Resist change			
Are a poor investment for training			

4. What are the sources of miscommunication in the example given in Box 5.1?
5. Discuss the findings on direct (overt) and subtle (covert) racism given in the text. What consequences for work behaviour would you predict from the substitution of covert for overt prejudice?
6. Referring to a story about a ban on gays in the Armed Forces, a columnist for The *Times* of London, himself openly gay, wrote, 'If prejudice among soldiers runs so deep and wide, it should be respected.' Do you agree? Why or why not?
7. What conclusions do you draw from the meta-analysis of research into prejudice directed against women managers and leaders described in Section 5.1?
8. Give three examples of positive and three of negative micro-messages.
9. Explain the persistent injustice effect. How might it be overcome in a work context?
10. The text gives a list of 23 dimensions of communication that Finns perceive as problematic in their communication with non-Finns. How many of those dimensions do you perceive as problematic in your communication with people of nationalities other than your own? Which are most important? Are there any others not in the Finns' list?
11. Devise a questionnaire to test whether respondents are more concerned about 'control' or 'affiliation' in communication and administer it to a sample of equal numbers of men and women.
12. Reword the following to put the topic, background or reason first and the main point, suggested action or comment second: 'You take the ring road to go to the factory.'

Reword the following to put the main point, suggested action or comment first and the topic, background or reason second: 'Because of difficulties in transit which have led to delivery delays and increases in packaging costs which are beyond our control, we have been forced to reconsider our pricing policy, leading to a new price structure from 1st November.'

13. Give an example of misalignment of facework strategies.

14. From the face-threatening acts listed in Table 3.2, select the ten that you think are most threatening in your culture. Put them in order of decreasing threat. Compare your list with those of colleagues from a different culture.

15. Give examples showing how the behaviour of non-disabled people can reinforce stereotypes of disabled people.

16. Discuss the challenges people with disabilities face in asserting a positive identity in interability situations.

17. How does viewing a person with a disability as atypical because he or she does not act in a stereotypical way help to keep stereotypes intact?

18. Give examples of how communication between people from different cultures can be inhibited or distorted by non-acceptance of the others' core values.

19. Give examples of how cultural differences in the following antecedents of communication can create barriers:

■ the self
■ conscious beliefs
■ assumptions
■ display of feeling

20. Complete the following questionnaire.

	Strongly agree	Agree	Neither agree nor disagree	Disagree	Strongly disagree
1. I think other people, no matter how different their background to my own, are easy to understand					
2. During the first few minutes of an encounter with people from a different background, I usually tell people a good deal about myself					
3. I generally have a clear idea of what is going on in any meeting, even with strangers in a new situation					
4. My expectations about the behaviour of others from different backgrounds are usually confirmed					
5. I think the world is hard to understand and make sense of					
6. My expectations about the outcomes of encounters with people from different backgrounds are usually confirmed					

	Strongly agree	Agree	Neither agree nor disagree	Disagree	Strongly disagree
7. I generally have a clear idea of how to behave in any circumstances, however new to me.					
8. I experience high levels of anxiety whenever I meet people who are very different from me.					
9. I find it hard to get to know new acquaintances.					
10. There are many kinds of situations at work, from interviews to speaking up in meetings, which make me nervous.					

For guidance on how to score and interpret this questionnaire, see Appendix C

21. List and explain the five emotions that Brislin describes as giving rise to difficulty in intercultural encounters.
22. In discussing the effects of beliefs on intercultural communication, Kincaid (1987)[67] wrote, 'Absolute certainty renders communication inoperable.' Discuss this contention in relation to the material on core beliefs and prejudice in the text.
23. What are the implications of the following finding for Black/White relations at work?

    In a study with a full intergroup design, Black and White participants rated Black and White racial groups. Members of both groups underestimated how favourably their own group was rated by members of their respective outgroup. (Krueger, J. (1996). 'Personal beliefs and cultural stereotypes about racial characteristics', *Journal of Personality and Social Psychology*, **71**: 536–548).

24. '[Intergroup] conflict, despite appearances, still leads to intergroup influence.' Discuss this statement.

NOTES AND REFERENCES

1. Burke, K. (1966) *Language as Symbolic Action*, Berkeley, CA: University of California Press.
2. Hecht, M.L., Ribeau, S. and Alberts, J.K. (1989) 'An Afro-American perspective on interethnic communication', *Communication Monographs*, **56**(4): 385–410.
3. Larkey, L.K. (1996) 'The development and validation of the workforce diversity questionnaire', *Management Communication Quarterly*, **9**(3): 296–337.
4. Guimond, S., Dif, S. and Aupy, A. (2002) 'Social identity, relative group status and intergroup attitudes: when favourable outcomes change intergroup relations for the worse', *European Journal of Social Psychology*, **32**(6): 739–60.
5. Ashburn-Nardo, L., Voils, C.I. and Monteith, M.J. (2001) 'Implicit associations as the seeds of intergroup bias: how easily do they take root?', *Journal of Personality and Social Psychology*, **81**(5): 789–99.
6. Stangor, C. and Thompson, E.P. (2002) 'Needs for cognitive economy and self-enhancement as unique predictors of intergroup attitudes', *European Journal of Social Psychology*, **32**: 563–75.

7. Hunter, J.A. (2003) 'Ingroup favoring allocations and domain-specific self-esteem in the minimal group setting', *Current Research in Social Psychology*, **8**(13): 177–87.

8. Weber, U., Mummendey, A. and Waldzus, S. (2002) 'Perceived legitimacy of intergroup status differences: its prediction by relative ingroup prototypicality', *European Journal of Social Psychology*, **32**: 449–70.

9. Ouwerkerk, J.W. and Ellemers, N. (2002) 'The benefits of being disadvantaged: performance-related circumstances and consequences of intergroup comparisons', *European Journal of Social Psychology*, **32**: 73–91.

10. Wiemann, J.M. and Giles, H. (1988) 'Interpersonal communication', in Hewstone, M., Stroebe, W., Codol, J.-P. and Stephenson, G.M. (eds) *Introduction to Psychology*, Oxford: Blackwell.

11. Hewstone, M. and Jaspars, J. (1984) 'Social dimensions of attributions', in Tajfel, H. (ed.) *The Social Dimension vol. 2.*, Cambridge: Cambridge University Press.

12. Detweiler R. (1975) 'On inferring the intentions of a person from another culture', *Journal of Personality*, **43**: 591–611.

13. Hornsey, M.J., Oppes, T. and Svennsson, A. (2002) ' "It's ok if we say it, but you can't": responses to intergroup and intragroup criticism', *European Journal of Social Psychology*, **32**: 293–307.

14. Hewstone, M. and Giles, H. (1986) 'Social groups and social stereotypes in intergroup communication: review and model of intergroup communication breakdown', in Gudykunst, W.B. (ed.) *Intergroup Communication*, London: Edward Arnold.

15. Leonard, R., and Locke, D. (1993) 'Communication stereotypes: is interracial communication possible?' *Journal of Black Studies*, **23**(3): 332–43.

16. Pettigrew, T.F. (1958) 'Personality and sociocultural factors in intergroup attitudes: a cross-national comparison', *Journal of Conflict Resolution*, **2**: 29–42.

17. Monin, B. and Miller, D.T. (2001) 'Moral credentials and the expression of prejudice', *Journal of Personality and Social Psychology*, **81**(1): 33–43.

18. Hagendoorn, L. and Kleinpenning, G. (1991) 'The contribution of domain-specific stereotypes to ethnic social distance', *British Journal of Social Psychology*, **30**: 63–78.

19. Akrami, N., Ekehammar, E. and Araya, T. (2000) 'Classical and modern racial prejudice: a study of attitudes toward immigrants in Sweden', *European Journal of Social Psychology*, **30**: 521–32.

20. Dambrun, M., Desprès, G. and Guimond, S. (2003) 'On the multifaceted nature of prejudice: psychophysiological responses to ingroup and outgroup ethnic stimuli', *Current Research in Social Psychology*, **8**: 187–206.

21 Halman, L. and Kerkhofs, J. (2001) The European Values Study: Selected Results. URL: www.romir.ru/eng/research/01_2001/european-values.htm

22. Eagly, A.H., Makhujani, M.G. and Klonsky, B.G. (1992) 'Gender and the evaluation of leaders: a meta-analysis', *Psychological Bulletin*, **111**: 3–22.

23. Argyle, M. (2000) *Psychology and Religion: An Introduction*, London: Routledge.

24. Inman, M.L., and Baron, R.S. (1996) 'Influence of prototypes on perceptions of prejudice', *Journal of Personality and Social Psychology*, **70**: 727–39.

25. Stangor, C., Swim, J.K., Van Allen, K.L. and Sechrist, G.B. (2002) 'Reporting discrimination in public and private contexts', *Journal of Personality and Social Psychology*, **82**(1): 69–74.

26. Wanguri, D.M. (1996) 'Diversity, perceptions of equity and communicative openness in the workplace', *The Journal of Business Communication*, **33**: 443–57.

27. Davidson, M. and Friedman, R.A. (1998) 'When excuses don't work: the persistent injustice effect among Black managers', *Administrative Science Quarterly*, **43**: 154–83.

28. Major, B., Gramzow, R.H., McCoy, S.K., Levin, S., Schmader, T. and Sidanius, J. (2002) 'Perceiving personal discrimination: the role of group status and legitimizing ideology', *Journal of Personality and Social Psychology*, **82**(3): 269–82.

29. Kirra, K.M. (2000) 'Finns in interaction with non-Finns: problematic phenomena perceived as critical incidents', *Intercultural Communication*, **4**: 109–23.

30. Tannen, D. (2001) *You Just Don't Understand Men and Women in Conversation*, New York: Quill.

31. McIntosh, A. (2000) 'When the deaf and the hearing interact: communication features, relationships, and disability issues', in Braithwaite, D.O. and Thompson, T.L. (eds) *Handbook of Communication and People with Disabilities: Research and Application*, New York: Lawrence Erlbaum.

32. Fox, S.A., Giles, H., Orbe, M.P. and Bourhis, R.Y. (2000) 'Interability communication: theoretical perspectives', in Braithwaite, D.O. and Thompson, T.L. (eds) *Handbook of Communication and People with Disabilities: Research and Application*, New York: Lawrence Erlbaum.

33. Ibid.

34. Ranger, L.M. (2002) 'Communication is key for deaf and hard of hearing technical pros', *Diversity/Careers Professional*, Oct/Nov. URL: http://www.diversitycareers.com/articles/pro/octnov02/fod_com_deaf.htm

35. Gallois, C. and Callan, V.J. (1986) 'Decoding emotional messages: influence of ethnicity, sex, message type and channel', *Journal of Personality and Social Psychology*, **51**(4): 755–62.

36. Sperber, D. and Wilson, D. (1986) *Relevance: Communication and Cognition*, Cambridge, MA: Harvard University Press.

37. Scott, J.C. (2000) 'Differences in American and British vocabulary: implications for international business communication', *Business Communication Quarterly*, **63**(4): 27–39.

38. Kotani, M. (2002) 'Expressing gratitude and indebtedness: Japanese speakers' use of "I'm sorry" in English conversation', *Research on Language and Social Interaction*, **35**(1): 39–72.

39. Thompson, N. (2003) *Communication and Language: A Handbook of Theory and Practice*, Basingstoke: Palgrave Macmillan.

40. Triandis, H.C. (2000) 'Culture and conflict', *International Journal of Psychology*, **35**(2): 145–52.

41. Bernstein, B. (1971) *Class, Codes and Control*, St Albans: Paladin.

42. Yum, J.O. (1987) 'Asian perspectives on communication', in Kincaid, D. (ed.) *Communication Theory: Eastern and Western Perspectives*, New York: Academic Press.

43. Armstrong, G.B. and Kaplowitz, S.A. (2001) 'Sociolinguistic inference and intercultural coorientation: a Bayesian model of communicative competence in intercultural interaction', *Human Communication Research*, **27**(3): 350–81.

44. Ting-Toomey, S. (1988) 'Intercultural conflict styles: A face-negotiation theory', in Kim Y.Y. and Gudykunst, W.B. (eds) *Theories in Intercultural Communication*, Newbury Park, CA: Sage.

45. Ambady, N., Koo, J., Lee, F. and Rosenthal, R. (1996) 'More than words: linguistic and nonlinguistic politeness in two cultures', *Journal of Personality and Social Psychology*, **70**: 996–1011.

46. Wierzbicka, A. (1991) *Cross-Cultural Pragmatics: The Semantics of Human Interaction*, Berlin: Mouton de Gruyter.

47. Maoz, I., and Ellis, D.G. (2001) 'Going to ground: argument in Israeli–Jewish and Palestinian encounter groups', *Research on Language and Social Interaction*, **34**(4): 399–419.

48. Coco, A. (1999) 'Can't hear you: barriers to communication in the Roman Catholic culture', *Electronic Journal of Communication*, **9**(2,3,4). URL: http://www.ios.org/www/ejc/v(n23499.htm

49. Triandis, H. (2000) op. cit.

50. Martin, J.N., Hecht, M.L. and Larkey, L.K. (1994) 'Conversation improvement strategies for interethnic communication: African-American and European-American perspectives', *Communication Monographs*, **61**(3): 236–55.

51. Hecht, M.L., Larkey, L. and Johnson, J. (1992) 'African American and European American perceptions of problematic issues in interethnic communication effectiveness', *Human Communication Research*, **19**: 209–36.

52. Trompenaars, F. (1993) *Riding the Waves of Culture*, London: Nicholas Brealey.

53. Coleman, L. and De Paulo, B. (1991) 'Uncovering the human spirit: moving beyond disability and "missed" communication', in Coupland, N., Giles, H. and Wiemann, J. (eds) *"Miscommunication" and Problematic Talk*, Newbury Park, CA: Sage.

54. George, J.M., Gonzalez, J.A. and Jones, G.R. (1998) 'The role of affect in cross-cultural negotiations', *Journal of International Business Studies*, **29**(4): 749–72.

55. Douglas, W. (1991) 'Expectations about initial interaction: an examination of the effects of global uncertainty', *Human Communication Research*, **17**: 355–84.
56. Brislin, R., Cushner, K., Cherrie, C. and Yong, M. (1986) *Intercultural Interactions*, Beverly Hills, CA: Sage.
57. Huntington, S. (1997) *The Clash Of Civilizations And The Remaking of World Order*, London: Simon & Schuster.
58. West, T. and Levy, S. R. (2002) 'Background belief systems and prejudice', in Lonner, W.J., Dinnel, D.L., Hayes, S.A. and Sattler, D.N. (eds), *Online Readings in Psychology and Culture*, (unit 15, chapter 4). URL: http://www.wwu.edu/~culture.
59. Burgoon, J. and Hale, J. (1988) 'Nonverbal expectancy violations', *Communication Monographs*, **55**: 58–79.
60. Hoyle, R., Pinkley, R. and Insko, C. (1989) 'Perceptions of social behavior', *Personality and Social Pscyhology Bulletin*, **15**: 365–76.
61. Yum, J.O., (1987) op. cit.
62. Thompson, N. (2003) op. cit.
63. O'Reilly III, C.A., Caldwell, D.R. and Barnett, W.P. (1989) 'Work group demography, social integration and turnover', *Administrative Science Quarterly*, **34**: 21–37.
64. Grub, P.D. and Lin, J.H. (1991) *Foreign Direct Investment in China*,: p. 194, New York: Quorum Books.
65. Mann, J. (1989) *Beijing Jeep: The Short, Unhappy Romance of American Business in China*,: p. 180, New York: Simon and Schuster.
66. Larkey, L.K. (1996) op.cit.
67. Kincaid, D.L. (1987) 'The convergence theory of communication, self-organization and cultural evolution', in Kincaid, D.H. (ed.) *Communication Theory: Eastern and Western Perspectives*, New York: Academic Press.

chapter six

Communicating Interculturally

Chapter 5 discussed barriers to intercultural communication. Awareness of these barriers is shown by a recent study, which found that native speakers of American English who interacted with non-native speakers perceived interaction as more difficult than did their counterparts who interacted with other native speakers. They also had more thoughts showing confusion, but also more thoughts focused on the partner and fewer on the content of the conversation, more focus on understanding the other's message, less on clarifying their own message and less on displaying their own involvement.[1] Many of these responses to being aware of barriers may improve intercultural communication, though others impede it.

This chapter focuses on how intercultural encounters can be made more effective. Section 6.1 covers inclusive language, Section 6.2 discusses ethical issues in intercultural communication, Section 6.3 describes effective intercultural communication behaviours and Section 6.4 analyses effective intercultural communication processes, many of which are interactive and mutual. It also offers a critique of theoretical approaches to intercultural communication. The final Section, 6.5, is an examination of what effectiveness means in an intercultural communication context.

Box 6.1

Digh reports that to get messages across, American companies are now providing 'Ads in Spanish, TV commercials featuring people with disabilities, marketing messages using cross-generational icons such as Britney Spears and Bob Dole. ..."There's no longer one solution or message that will work for everyone," says Myrna Marofsky, President of ProGroup Inc., a diversity consulting firm. "For example," she says, "if a company wants to tell employees something about health benefits, human resources should consider: not what's easiest, but what would make the value of health benefits clear to all the cultures represented in your workplace." '

Source: Digh, P. (2002) 'One style doesn't fit all: to get your message across to diverse groups within your workforce, send it in various ways – each version tailored to their distinct needs', *HR Magazine*, November 2001

6.1 INCLUSIVE LANGUAGE

None of the ways of overcoming intercultural communication barriers described later in this chapter is likely to work if, whether unintentionally or out of a perverse or misguided intention not to be 'politically correct', biased language is used. Biased language has been shown to affect adversely the self-image of members of the group excluded or negatively portrayed. There is therefore a strong argument from social justice (equal opportunity) in avoiding it. In addition, it naturally provokes resentment among members of such groups, which contributes to social disharmony and disrupts intercultural communication. For instance, as research among French women managers showed, they disliked, 'remarks and compliments concerning their physical appearance and comments emphasizing how their behavior differed from men's model of professional behavior. In the workplace, women managers wanted to be recognized for their abilities. The French language allows a job title to indicate the gender of the person holding the job, but most women managers chose to use the masculine form rather than the feminine form of their professional title, especially on their visiting cards.' The women managers disliked men stressing their views on women's maternal responsibilities; the women felt that making reference to their 'feminine' characteristics was a method men used to remind women of the traditional gender hierarchy.[2]

Non-inclusive language reinforces barriers which prevent all members of an organisation or society from participating fully in its work; it also undermines policies aimed at diversity. Non-inclusive language is of three main kinds:

1. Using generic masculine words or titles to refer to all persons.
2. Using terms or expressions that reinforce inappropriate, outdated or demeaning attitudes or assumptions about persons or groups. These may be based on age, disability, ethnicity, gender, national origin, race, religion or sexual orientation.
3. Misusing stereotypes, which too often represent an oversimplified opinion, subjective attitude or uncritical judgment. They become particularly offensive and demeaning when used to make assumptions about the intellectual, moral, social or physical capabilities of an individual or a group. Neither individuals' demographic and other characteristics, nor their group membership should be mentioned, unless it is specifically relevant to the topic being discussed. Inclusive language aims to respect the wishes of the group to or about whom the communication is taking place.[3]

In addition to these general points, care should be taken over terms for people's ethnicity, gender, age group, type of disability and sexual orientation.

Ethnicity is a social and political phenomenon, and, as such, its categories are not fixed. As society changes, so do the labelling conventions that define groups. Within broadly drawn groups, individual members may not agree about which term they feel best defines them. In the UK, 'White' and 'Black' (sometimes distinguishing 'Black Caribbean' and 'Black African') are current; Indian, Pakistani and Bangladeshi are generally used specifically, though 'Asian' also occurs. Interestingly, the equivalents of terms such as 'Black American' or 'Asian American' – for example, 'Black Briton' or 'Asian Briton' – are not current, which perhaps points to a lack of inclusiveness in British social attitudes. On the other hand, the term 'people of colour', which is widely used in the USA, ceased to be acceptable in the UK in the mid-1990s.

Referring to members of both genders by traditional terms such as 'man' and 'mankind' and the masculine pronouns 'he', 'him' and 'his' has two costs: ambiguity and exclusion. Using these terms requires the listener or reader to decide whether the reference really does include women as well as men. More seriously, studies have shown that girls and women do feel excluded by this usage. Feeling excluded from history books, policy statements, professional titles and the like can have a powerful impact on the self-image and aspirations of women. Stereotyping by gender often takes the form of assigning complementary and opposing characteristics to men and women, such as active/passive, strong/weak and rational/emotional. In these formulations, it is usually the characteristic associated with masculinity that is viewed as more positive and desirable, at least in a work context. Men and women should be treated primarily as people, and not as members of different genders. Their shared humanity and common attributes should be stressed. Neither gender should be stereotyped. Both men and women should be represented as whole human beings with human strengths and weaknesses, not masculine and feminine ones.

Using ageist language shows ignorance of the fact that in many countries, people are living longer in good health. Just as some people in their twenties and thirties are not as vigorous as others of their age, people in their sixties and seventies differ greatly in their physical health and abilities. Expressions such as, 'Even at 75, x can do y', or 'Octogenarian w still does y' are ageist; even describing someone as 'old' depends on a judgement which may be prejudiced. At the other end of the scale, young men and women should not be referred to as 'boys' and 'girls'. Giving the age of individuals in reports, as newspapers do (especially for women), reinforces ageism (and sexism). Unless age is the topic being written or spoken about, it is generally preferable not to refer to it. People with disabilities prefer that others focus on their individuality, not their disability, unless, of course, it is the topic that is being written or spoken about. The terms 'handicapped', 'not able-bodied', 'physically challenged', and 'differently abled' are also discouraged and so is the article 'the' with an adjective (e.g., 'the deaf') to describe people with disabilities. The preferred usage, 'people with disabilities', ('people who are deaf') stresses the essential humanity of individuals and avoids objectification. Alternatively, the term 'disabled people' ('deaf people') may be acceptable, but still defines people as disabled first and people second. It is important to be careful not to imply that people with disabilities are to be pitied, feared or ignored, or that they are always somehow more heroic, courageous, patient or 'special' than others. The term 'abnormal' (or 'normal' in contrast) should never be used.

Sexuality is now generally regarded as determined early in life. As a rule, it cannot be changed. Thus, 'sexual orientation' is a more accurate term to describe a person's sexuality than 'sexual preference' or 'choice'. The clinical term 'homosexual' may be appropriate in certain contexts, but generally the terms 'gay men', 'lesbians' and 'gay people' are preferable. The euphemisms 'lifestyle' or 'alternative lifestyle' should be avoided, because gay people, like heterosexuals, have a variety of lifestyles. The term 'domestic partner' is being used increasingly to refer to the person with whom one shares a household on a permanent basis, whether married or not.

> Although during conversation finding the acceptable term for members of a group may be tricky, it becomes easier with practice. Where possible, use the term preferred by members of the group themselves. When speaking about any group or individual, emphasise accomplishments and deeds, and concentrate on the person's essential humanity, not on characteristics such as ethnicity, gender or age.

6.2 ETHICAL ISSUES

Intercultural business ethics addresses moral issues that emerge when the norms and values of stakeholders, including employees, reflect cultural differences in the way described in Chapter 4. For example, while Western cultures tend to turn moral issues into issues of conscience or law, this might not be the case in other cultures.

Ethical relativism claims that there is no culture-free, universal morality and therefore no way of ranking moral views and practices as more or less right, at least across cultures. Ethical relativism runs counter to assumed cultural superiority (or ethnocentrism) and to top-down morality. However, ethical relativism has been criticised on grounds such as the following:

■ Obvious empirical differences of moral beliefs and practices do not prove that they are all right.
■ Even though some practices that vary from place to place are justifiable, surrender of principles in the face of disagreement hurts integrity.
■ Disagreement about judgements does not necessarily prove disagreement about the principles upon which such judgements are based.
■ Relativism can confuse behaviour and analysis rather than enlighten them.
■ There is no moral-free space, although there are many moral grey zones.

These arguments suggest that ethical dilemmas arising in intercultural work communication cannot be evaded by a resort to ethical relativism.

What is needed (and sufficient), according to Brinkmann, is an intercultural consensus about an ethical minimum. Ethics integrates people by seeking a consensus around good principles and procedures.[4] The communication ethics approach of Habermas suggests, as a principle, fair and open communication among all the stakeholders affected in order to build a consensus.[5] However, individual conscience, moral customs and positive law vary more cross-culturally than minimum ethics.

Brinkman proposed the following model, described as a 'virtuous (but vulnerable) circle of delaying judgement and transcending ethical relativism'. If a moral conflict or dilemma is faced in an intercultural setting, intercultural communication, ideally, could contribute with (1) unprejudiced, non-ethnocentric description and interpretation and with (2) tools for communication and barrier reduction, while ethics would focus (3) on moral and value conflicts and (4) on possibilities for solutions, preferably consensus-building. Such an interdisciplinary mix of competencies could then (5) reach a preliminary minimum consensus, a first step towards transcending ethical relativism and (6) produce positive examples and experiences for future situations. Such idealism, that is, a virtuous circle, is self-reinforcing once it works, but is also vulnerable, that is, can fail or even turn into a vicious circle.[6]

Deetz *et al.* considered that the international business situation poses unique and complex issues of ethics and responsibility. Only a stakeholder approach to organisation, combined with 'adequate' conceptions of communication and micro-practices of negotiation can lead to ethical daily practices in modern organisations. Because the organisation is part of the community, the values and ethical standards of the community should be both represented and considered. The problem is to give the minority or marginalised stakeholders a sufficient 'voice' or representation so that their views are reflected. Deetz *et al.* argued that to increase the 'voice' of multiple stakeholders in organisations that are intrinsically biased against weaker stakeholders, such as the surrounding community, requires four changes. These are:

1. An end to the fixing of roles (e.g., by the division of labour) and to the suppression or ignoring of the complexity of people's identities and aspirations. These identities include those such as being a parent, citizen or softball player as well as an employee or customer.
2. Ending the limits imposed on discussion by rules and authority relations; such limits make stakeholders unequal in power.
3. Opening information production activities to stakeholder discussion: in most cases the information available to stakeholders is manufactured by management groups and is both limited and skewed.
4. Ensuring that discussion focuses on ends rather than means.[7]

Many of the intercultural communication skills given later in this chapter, including empathy and tolerance for ambiguity, may be seen as indicators of individual cultural relativism, which means trying to understand different others according to their own frame of reference. It should be distinguished from ethical relativism but may be considered an interculturally ethical stance. Hall added the point that 'ethical efforts to assist others must include a deep concern for the value systems of others involved in the process. ... It means that we should be concerned about others' dignity, rights, values and concerns as much as we are about our own. Of course, such an attitude can also result in applauding the learning and growth processes of individuals and nations as their intercultural and international communication efforts become more effective, more caring, and their judgments of situations and people more adequate.'[8]

> Ethical issues are among the most problematic in intercultural work. Ethical relativism, which evades ethical issues by the contention that no moral system is better than any other, appears to be logically flawed. Consensus building by fair and open communication based on cultural relativism, finding a way to increase the power and voice of weaker stakeholders and having a deep concern for others' value systems are among the suggested ways to achieve ethical intercultural work communication.

6.3 INTERCULTURAL COMMUNICATION BEHAVIOURS

Many factors may affect the success or failure of intercultural communication. Some of these are not within a person's immediate control – for instance, their status in the eyes of the person with whom they are interacting or the prejudices of other participants. However, the person's own behaviour during the interaction impacts very directly and is within their control. This section looks at behaviours that help intercultural communication. It begins with skills that improve intercultural understanding of others' communication. Skills for effective intercultural self-presentation follow. Next the section deals with general traits for intercultural effectiveness. The last set of behaviours covered is the application of skills to particular situations.

Enhanced intercultural understanding of others

A first stage in skilled communication behaviour is to understand the values, motives, beliefs, attitudes and intentions of an interlocutor. As Figure 6.1 suggests, some factors

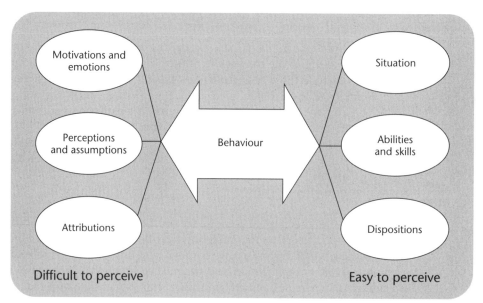

Figure 6.1   *Ease and difficulty of perceiving factors influencing others' behaviour at work*

that influence behaviour are relatively easy to perceive; others are more difficult. In an intercultural context, both interpersonal and intercultural understandings are needed. The skills involved include increasing intercultural social perceptiveness, unlearning and learning, accurately predicting others' behaviour and responses, tolerating ambiguity, being non-judgemental, being mindful and developing positive expectations about intercultural encounters.

Intercultural social perceptiveness

To perceive accurately in intercultural contexts, communicators need self-awareness and awareness of others' culture sensitivities, of the context and of perceptual barriers.

■ Some trainers in intercultural communication now consider that working to enhance self-awareness is the most essential preparation for working in another culture as a sojourner or on international assignments. Most people remain unaware that their own behaviours, attitudes and beliefs are culture-specific, unless they are exposed to at least one other culture. Therefore, a first step towards better intercultural understanding is to seek out such exposure at work or at leisure. Learning from such experiences then needs to be enhanced and speeded up by reflective observation, either alone or in discussion. The purpose is to understand one's own stereotypes, prejudices, ethnocentrism, values and attitudes as much or more than those of others.

■ It is easy, when ignorant of the sensitivities of another culture, not only to set up barriers to good communication but also to cause serious offence. The problem is how to avoid such situations and develop cultural awareness. Studying the culture of the people with whom we interact in order to know what sensitivities they are likely to have is one possible solution. However, many people face the problem that they interact with people from a wide range of cultures and subcultures. For instance, if the computer teacher quoted in Box 6.2 worked in a central London

Box 6.2

'I had a student from an African nation. He was having problems with understanding the English and computer terms. I paired him with another man who was a jolly soul who loved computers. One day this man discovered the connection between the commands and the purpose for giving them in DOS (before Windows). He was so excited, I reached over and gave him a hug. The poor man got hysterical, screamed and ran out of the class. I was shocked and his partner went to check on him. He was crying so hard in the hall, and I couldn't figure what I had done so wrong. *Moral of the story*: A young white women hugged him. That was a death sentence in his home town. A young woman touched him, he had to marry her (me) or I would be shamed. Yicks, his partner calmed him down, told him no one would kill him, I didn't have to marry him and everything was o.k.

It wasn't a fun lesson to learn, the young man dropped my course. I now have learned the art of praise without a touch, or just a touch of hands. A hard lesson, but fair when you work in an university environment that has many cultures.'

Source: Frazier, J. (1996) 'Stories from a computer teacher'. URL: frazier@ccit.arizona.eduää

university, she might find in her classes people from several different European, African and Asian nations, from several different British ethnic and religious minority religious groups (e.g., Bangladeshi, Indian, Pakistani, Afro-Caribbean, Jewish, Muslim, Sikh, Catholic, Church of England), plus, of course of different genders, sexual orientations and levels of physical ability. In addition, often the answer to the question 'How can I learn about culture X?' is the discouraging information that there is no comprehensive book (or list) available about culture X.

There is, anyway, no substitute for experience in gaining knowledge of other cultures. However, realistically, few service providers are likely to be able to visit all the countries represented among their students, patients or clients or even to get well acquainted with all the ethnic or religious groups so represented. There is no easy solution, but there are some principles that can be applied:

1. The best, and most neglected, source of information on a culture is people from that culture. Often they can be met in the course of work. Setting aside time to talk with as many of them as possible about the sensitivities inculcated through their culture is an excellent use of time. Most will be willing to help someone who explains that they want to understand more out of respect and to avoid giving offence. If the people concerned are clients, patients, advisers, customers or suppliers it may be necessary to arrange a special time for the discussion; with colleagues, opportunities may arise naturally in the course of the work.

2. The following points should be kept in mind:
   - ☐ First hand experience is necessary to understand many subtleties of any culture.
   - ☐ What is logical and important in a particular culture may seem irrational and unimportant to an outsider.
   - ☐ In describing another culture, people tend to stress the differences and overlook the similarities; in contrast, in interacting with people from another culture, they tend to assume more similarity than actually exists.

Box 6.3

X was a visiting official from the international parent organisation of the Hungarian Business Association, which was holding a presentation and reception for members to meet a VIP. The Hungarian President of the Association spoke first. X had agreed with him beforehand that he would convey a 'message' about the Association's mission. (1) The President began by telling several funny anecdotes. It was clear that the audience obviously enjoyed these. Then he began to get quite emotional, even melancholy, and philosophical. (2) After a while, X began to feel that the agreed 'message' was not going to be conveyed. (3) During the networking at the reception after the presentations, X found, as she had before, that while the Hungarian men were very courteous to her (one even attempted to kiss her hand!), (4) they dominated the conversation in a series of unstoppable monologues and she had difficulty getting any chance to speak. (5) When she did manage to make herself heard, though, she was careful to open with a couple of sentences in praise of Hungary and its cultural heritage. After that, things became easier. (6) Nevertheless, as soon as the topic turned to Association business, she found that her interlocutors quickly confronted her with a series of problems. It would be wrong, she thought, to describe them as complaints – they were presented just as problems – but there was no attempt to identify solutions. (7) Instead, there seemed to be an expectation that finding ways round the problems was up to someone else.

The following cultural knowledge would help the visiting official to understand better:

(1) Hungarians are great raconteurs and equate fluency with intelligence.

(2) As they develop their arguments, Hungarians may become emotional and philosophical more than logical, and so it is easy for non-Hungarians to lose the thread. This does not seem to be a problem for Hungarian members of audiences themselves, though.

(3) 'Old-fashioned' courtesy towards women is still common in Hungary.

(4) Hungarian conversational rules do not require equality in turn-taking (often several people will speak at once). This increases the tendency for men to dominate conversations.

(5) Small talk usually precedes business; displaying a knowledge and appreciation of things Hungarian is an accepted, even expected, form of compliment.

(6) and (7) Possibly as a residue of communism (or of subjection under the Austro-Hungarian Empire), some Hungarians display a kind of fatalistic pessimism, which recognises problems but has no expectation that they will be put right and certainly no sense that they themselves can put them right.

Based on: Author's research

☐ Stereotyping may be inevitable among those who lack frequent contact with another culture but an understanding of the limited truth of stereotypes is essential.

☐ Personal observations of others about another culture should not be taken as objective evidence.

☐ Many subcultures often exist within a single ethnic or language group, religion or nationality. These subcultures are differentiated by education, age, gender, socio-economic status, education, and exposure to other cultures. Highly educated people of a given cultural group are less likely to reveal indigenous language and communication patterns than less educated persons.

☐ All cultures have internal variations.

Box 6.4

'I think if they are talking to people from their own cultures, it's much more – it's very tiring for people to work in a second language or third language all the time. What's quite interesting 'cause you get used to it. It doesn't worry you. I mean in some situations out in sort of the real world, people talk in another language, people might get kind of upset about this. What are they talking about? Well, after a while, you realize they're just talking about what everyone else is talking about anyway. So, it's not worth getting worried about' (laughter).

Source: Quoted in Harris, H. (2001) 'The Perceived influence of culture and ethnicity on the communicative dynamics of the United Nations secretariat', *Business Communication Quarterly*, **64**: 205–10

☐ Cultures are continually evolving. Understanding another culture is a continuous process.

☐ To best understand a culture, one should understand the language of that culture.[9]

■ Communication takes place within a context that fundamentally affects the knowledge needed by participants.[10] Therefore, they need awareness of contexts. A context has at least four dimensions, each of which can magnify, reduce or have neutral impact on how aware the participants are of their cultural differences.

1. Power and status. These exert an influence over whose cultural preferences are accepted and in some cases who controls the discussion. A British study showed that in contact between White and Black people, the White person typically controls access to valued resources that the Black person needs or wants.[11]

2. Cultural assumptions defining the 'rules of the game'. For example, in a high power distance culture, a subordinate from a low power distance culture would probably be frustrated by the restraints on free speech in talking to a manager. This would probably not bother a subordinate from the high power distance culture.

3. Attitudes, based on personal experiences.

4. The role the participants assign to the immediate encounter. For instance, if two colleagues of different sexes, ethnicity and professional status were discussing their annoyance at the inconvenience of a photocopier breakdown, their awareness of their cultural differences would probably be low. It would be higher, though, if they were negotiating with one another over the pay of one of them.

An appreciation of the context of an encounter is a useful tool in increasing intercultural effectiveness. Intercultural encounters have distinctive characteristics and texture, according to their context: for instance, tourism encounters, unlike some others, essentially celebrate, rather than try to overcome or pacify, the experience of cultural difference. When Western tourists tell stories of bargaining in 'native' stores, they are relating their enjoyment of the, to them, unusual experience. International trade, diplomacy and scholarly exchanges are other examples of encounters with their own distinctive characteristics and texture. All these contexts 'create differences in the expectations of the parties to encounters and the requirements for effective communication'.[12] In work encounters the nature of the task also has a strong contextual influence.

Box 6.5

A research study found the following. 'Blacks reported more discussion about racial issues, both within their own group and outside it, than Whites did. ... Members of the minority group are forced to deal with intergroup issues and to come to grips with their relationships in intergroup terms. Members of the majority group can overlook group forces and can attempt to explain their relationships mainly in terms of the individuals involved.'

Source: Alderfer, C.P. and Smith, K.K. (1982) 'Studying intergroup relations embedded in organizations', *Administrative Science Quarterly,* **27**: 5–65

Another contextual factor influencing intercultural encounters is how well the participants know one another – how often they have met. Initial encounters are generally the most difficult. Not surprisingly, the influence of cultural norms and stereotypes diminishes as people get to know one another. Therefore, being able to communicate successfully when the level of cultural dissimilarity is high is most important on first acquaintance or in formal settings. (These contexts, of course, occur often at work.) Work contexts can sometimes reduce intercultural communication difficulties, because where both parties concentrate on the task, the near-universalism of 'technology' (in its broadest sense) creates a bridge. Unfortunately, though, there has often been an over-reliance on this factor, with resulting poor work relations between people from different cultures.

■ Being aware of stumbling blocks can help in avoiding them, so interactors need awareness of perceptual barriers to intercultural communication. Intercultural communication is improved by learning not to assume that others have the same values and attitudes, by becoming more sensitive to differences in others' verbal and nonverbal language, more aware of societal preconceptions and stereotypes which portray other groups from our own as 'different', or in the case of the other gender as 'opposite', and by reducing the tendency to evaluate another's culture as inferior.

Unlearning and learning

Increasing all the forms of awareness described earlier is really a matter of unlearning and learning. Unlearning may often be a necessary preliminary to improving social perception: it means being freed from past attitudes, preconceptions, prejudices and expectations in order to absorb new ideas and information. Unlearning is, of course, learning by another name; but it is a difficult type of learning because it involves a change in self-organisation – in the self-construal. Such changes are threatening and tend to be resisted.

Learning (and hence unlearning) is easier when the subject matter is perceived as having relevance for someone's own goals. Therefore learning about cultural difference and intercultural communication comes more easily just before an important meeting with someone from a different background or before an overseas journey. In addition, when external threats are at a minimum, learning which is threatening to the self is more easily perceived and assimilated, because there is a limit to the level of threat to the self that most people can tolerate.[13]

The following behaviours also facilitate learning:

■ Activity – much significant learning is acquired by doing (to understand why and how, see the Kolb learning cycle in Figure 7.5).

- Responsible participation by the learner in the learning process. This means abjuring passive learning models in favour of active learning, in which the learner drives and steers the process.
- Self-initiated learning which involves the whole person – feelings as well as intellect – is the most lasting and pervasive.
- Formative evaluation by the learner is more helpful than summative evaluation by others. If learners can assess, somewhat objectively, their own progress, strengths and weaknesses as they go along, they will gain independence, creativity and self-reliance as well as knowledge.
- Learning how to learn. This requires a continuous openness to experience and incorporation into oneself of the process of change.

Predicting others' behaviour and responses accurately

Predictive skill is needed to guide choices of communication strategy, to avoid giving offence inadvertently and to keep the flow of discussion smooth. Without necessarily being aware of doing so, all communicators predict others' responses repeatedly during interactions. Often, however, their predictions are inaccurate. This is especially likely if they are members of a dominant subculture interacting with members of a 'minority' subculture, as they may receive little feedback about their communication performances, especially if they as individuals are in positions of power. Fear or a wish to ingratiate may lead minority group members to conceal negative responses. Everyone, though, relies on stereotypes and rules based on past experience to predict others' responses and these necessary simplifications often produce inaccuracy.

Predicting others' responses more accurately depends on the following:

- Obtaining as much information as possible both before and during interactions,
- Becoming more aware of sensitive issues, language and non-verbal behaviour,
- Examining and modifying stereotypes, implicit theories and rules, and
- Encouraging others to give us feedback.

Tolerating ambiguity

People who tolerate ambiguity can control their feelings in situations where it is unclear what is happening, why, or what the outcome is likely to be. Tolerating ambiguity involves managing the feelings associated with unpredictability: it is not suggested that discomfort or other negative feelings should not be experienced when confronted with uncertain situations, but that both those feelings and their display can be controlled. Individuals with a high tolerance for ambiguity are more inclined to seek out 'objective' information, which means that their intercultural behaviour is more likely to be based on a realistic appreciation. People with lower tolerance for ambiguity tend to seek supportive rather than objective information – that is, in order to feel less psychological discomfort they select and distort incoming information.

Behaviours that support being or becoming tolerant of ambiguity include:

- Delaying the decision on how to approach a new person or situation until as much information as possible has been gained by observation,
- Having flexible short-term aspirations or goals (for instance, not being fixated on achieving a particular goal in the present encounter – being willing to try again at a later date if necessary),
- Using trial and error rather than the same formula until what works becomes clear,

- Consciously relaxing muscles, especially those in the back and neck,
- Avoiding tense behaviours such as frowning, growling, pacing, sounding exasperated, clenching teeth, fidgeting, talking fast or pounding anything (remembering that how someone behaves affects how they feel as much as the reverse), and
- Projecting confidence to oneself through positive messages: 'I feel confident, I can handle this, and I feel relaxed.'

Other traits related to being tolerant of ambiguity are uncertainty-orientation and field-independence. Uncertainty-oriented individuals seek information more than certainty-oriented individuals. People whose sense of self is not too much affected by their environment experience less stress on entering a new culture than field-dependents, who are strongly affected by their environment.[14]

Being non-judgemental

Judging others' behaviour or them as people, especially early in initial meetings, risks making errors of judgement, especially because it increases reliance on stereotypes. As a result, it can lead to basing one's own behaviour on false premises. It also leads to communicating to interlocutors the fact that they are being judged, which can lead them to have negative attitudes to the speaker. Behaviours that support and communicate a non-judgemental perspective include:

- Withholding preconceived opinions – asking, not telling,
- Framing questions openly: 'What do you think?', 'What do you mean by …?', 'Can you give me an example of …?',
- Soliciting feelings specifically: 'How do you feel about … –?',
- Asking questions to find out explanations of others' behaviour that may be deep-seated in their values or culture,
- When expressing views, making it clear that it is understood that they are only opinions with which other people may disagree,
- Acknowledging different values, beliefs and perceptions as valid,
- Listening openly,
- Listening to another's view without interrupting or criticising,
- Acknowledging the other's point of view as valid: 'I see what you mean',
- Providing reassurance: 'Don't worry – this won't be taken as agreement',
- Avoiding calling a view which is disagreed with bad or wrong,
- Sorting 'objective' facts from more subjective feelings, perceptions and stereotypes,
- Avoiding over-generalisations, and
- Making statements in a form which acknowledges one's own subjectivity, such as, 'I feel uneasy when Mr Ling does not appear to react to what I am saying', rather than generalising or laying claims to objectivity, as in, 'Chinese people are hard to read'.

Being mindful

To correct the tendency to misinterpret others' behaviour, people need to become more aware of their own mental processes – more 'mindful'. Mindfulness means tuning in consciously to habituated mental scripts; mindlessness is the rigid reliance on old categories, whereas mindfulness means the continual creation of new ones. Mindfulness carries a certain degree of existential vulnerability (openness). As shown in Figure 6.2, it occupies an intermediate zone between uncaringness and monitored constraint – between not caring about learning or improving and an inhibited caution

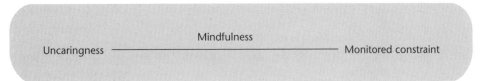

Uncaringness — Mindfulness — Monitored constraint

Figure 6.2   *The mindfulness continuum*

which is defensive and closed to new ideas. Mindfulness includes creating new categories, being open to new information and being aware of more than one perspective.[15]

Having positive expectations about intercultural encounters

People's expectations influence their ability to understand different others. The attitudes someone has about a particular other (sub)culture or other (sub)cultures in general create expectations about experiences in interactions with different others. The stereotypes someone has about people also affect expectations. Someone who is open to other (sub)cultures, with a positive attitude towards the specific (sub)culture, and positive stereotypes about the people of the (sub)culture will probably have positive expectations about their experiences, and vice-versa.

Negative attitudes and stereotypes create negative expectations. Negative expectations, in turn, tend to create self-fulfilling prophecies; that is, lead to interpreting the behaviour of members of the other (sub)cultures negatively and therefore to having negative experiences. On the other hand, expectations transferred without mindfulness from the 'own' culture are particularly likely to be violated. These are further reasons for avoiding, or at least postponing, evaluating the behaviour of 'different other' people.

These pointers are based on Expectations States Theory whose core idea is the influence of expectations, which were introduced in Chapter 4, on behaviour in interactions. People 'choose among various communication strategies on the basis of predictions about how the person receiving the message will respond'.[16] Three types of information are used in making predictions: cultural, social (roles and group memberships) and personal. (North Americans use more personal than social information; Japanese vice-versa.) We saw in Chapter 4 that the expectations people have about how others will respond to what they say strongly influence their communication behaviour. Chapter 5 showed how communication barriers can arise when expectations are violated. Expectations themselves are a function of knowledge, beliefs/attitudes, stereotypes, self-conceptions, roles, prior interaction and status characteristics.[17] Figure 6.3 shows the relationships among these variables.

The knowledge referred to in the model is mainly knowledge of the group to which people who are being met for the first time are thought to belong. When a person meets 'strangers' without any previous knowledge of the strangers' group, s/he predicts how they will behave by watching and listening to what they do and say. These observations are, of course, selective, and the impressions gained are influenced by the individual's own cultural framework. Those observed and interpreted behaviours are then treated as 'typical' and inferences are drawn from the impressions.

The need to make inferences is greater when dealing with people who are unfamiliar; this can lead to extreme predictions and expectations. The more previous knowledge people have about the other group, the less they are inclined to over-interpret small samples of behaviour, such as are observed on first meeting. Thus, prior knowledge affects expectations and so behaviour. If this knowledge is accurate, the effect is likely to be beneficial. If, however, they have false beliefs or the 'knowledge' consists of

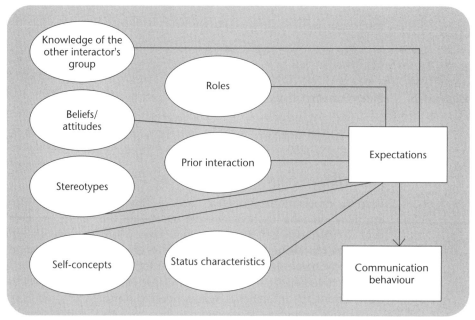

Figure 6.3 *Expectations states theory: factors influencing expectations and behaviour in intercultural encounters*

simplified and inaccurate stereotypes, the resulting expectations can distort behaviour with adverse effects on communication. Videotaped conversations between 46 US students and confederates from India showed significant differences in the Americans' communication behaviour depending on their previous knowledge or beliefs about India.[18]

People employ one or more of three strategies for gaining information about another group. One is a passive strategy such as watching TV (which is the strategy most likely to lead to over-reliance on stereotypes), or observing directly but without interacting. The second is an active strategy of asking others from their own group about the other (sub)culture, and the third is an interactive strategy of meeting members of the other (sub)culture, asking them questions, self-disclosing and trying to detect deceptions. This last sounds on the surface like the best information-gathering strategy, and it can be. However, to gain accurate information, contacts with other (sub)culture members must be made under conditions that do not increase prejudice.

Status is widely used in all cultures as input to the expectations individuals form about others with whom they will interact. In general, a wider range of behaviour is expected and tolerated from a high-status person than others. Status is assessed from external factors (e.g., race, ethnicity, sex, attractiveness, education, occupation) and expressive cues (e.g., dialect, eye contact, speech styles, skin colour) or indicative cues (such as someone's statement that they grew up in Mexico). Although these factors are used in all cultures to assess status, they are not used in identical ways. In Japan, professional position is so important that people need to know it in order to know how to address one another correctly, and an introductory exchange of business cards is de rigueur. In the USA, in contrast, questions directing at ascertaining someone's professional status can be rude, and physical attractiveness is often a key status factor for both sexes, even at work.

Expectations States Theory makes predictions about others' responses the main intervening variable between behaviour in intercultural encounters and a range of independent variables. In doing so, it inevitably leaves out the possibly equally powerful variables put forward in other theories – goals, for instance, or episode representations.

Skills for effective intercultural self-presentation

The skills required to achieve an effective intercultural impression include language choice, following appropriate conversational rules, achieving clarity, adjusting for non-routine interactions, showing empathy, communicating a relationship as well as a task orientation, communicating appropriate assertiveness, being a resourceful communicator and sharing information.

Language choice

People usually appreciate it when an interlocutor speaks their language. However, when one person speaks the other's language well but the reverse is not true, using the language best understood by both parties increases understanding. Sometimes, though, partial bilingual communicators may in fact be more effective, as their encoded blunt or 'rude' messages are more likely to be tolerated and attributed to their language deficiencies than would be the case for full bilinguals or native speakers. Silence and pauses in conversation are normal and accepted parts of communication between partial bilinguals, so they can strategically use breaks in the conversation flow, even in situations where they could process information faster and send messages sooner. For instance, they may use pauses to avoid introducing unproductive and destructive comments into conversations and to provide breaks for reflection. However, while the norms of some languages, such as Chinese and Japanese, mean that such silences do not cause anxiety, the same might not be true for some Westerners. Language choice has implications for the nature of the relationships that bilingual speakers develop and for whether they are included in informal communication channels. Bilingual expatriates who choose to use their own language remain outsiders and so are less likely to be sanctioned for not following the country's customs and social norms. By choosing the host country language, however, they become insiders, develop closer interpersonal relationships with colleagues and have more access to 'soft' information.[19]

Following communication rules

As Chapter 3 explained, communication requires people to co-operate, which they do, in part, by following conversational rules. Schwarz suggested the following lists of requirements for speakers and receivers. Speakers should:

- Take the receiver's characteristics into account,
- Be coherent and comprehensible,
- Give neither too much nor too little information,
- Be relevant,
- Produce a message that is appropriate to the context, the circumstances and the communicative purpose,
- Convey the truth as they see it, and
- Assume that the receiver is trying, as much as possible, to follow the rules of communication.

Receivers should:

- Take the speaker's characteristics into account,
- Determine the speaker's communication intent or purpose,
- Take the context and circumstances into account,
- Pay attention to the message and be prepared to receive it, and
- Try to understand the message and provide feedback, when possible, to the speaker concerning their understanding of the message.[20]

In intercultural communication both speakers and receivers need also to allow for cultural differences in communication rules. Learning what those cultural differences are is another aspect of developing cultural awareness.

Achieving clarity

Communicating clearly is often, though not always, an important communication objective, especially in work-based situations where the requirements of the task demand it. For instance, for a doctor, important though it is to communicate empathy and concern for relationship, clarity is even more important because of the importance of accuracy in diagnosis and in patients' following of instructions.

The distinction between restricted and elaborated codes, referred to in Chapter 3, is relevant to how clarity is achieved in intercultural communication. In communication with people who are familiar, language use goes on largely at a level below consciousness, with varying degrees of effectiveness; with new acquaintances or people from different backgrounds, effectiveness depends on heightened consciousness of how language is being used. This need for high awareness applies widely in work situations. When speakers expect marked differences from other people with whom they are interacting, they both do and should use more formal language, that is the elaborated code, instead of the restricted code that they use when they can assume that the receiver will understand their assumptions.[21] An expectation of marked difference leads the speaker to express fully those meanings that are expected to be misunderstood. In other words, these meanings have to be put into words rather precisely to make them available to the receiver. Therefore elaborated codes require a large vocabulary and complex syntax, though not too large and complex for the receiver to understand.

Clear communication requires the following actions:

- Stating points concisely and precisely,
- Adjusting to the other person's level of understanding without being demeaning,
- Simplifying language,
- Explaining or avoiding jargon,
- Where possible and acceptable, using the idiom of the other (sub)culture,
- Avoiding slang,
- Slowing down (but not speaking louder),
- Starting from where the other person is 'at',
- Using progressive approximations,
- Dividing explanations into smaller, more specific units,
- Repeating in alternative ways,
- Getting the other person to ask questions,
- Giving short answers – stopping after a partial reply and waiting for their response, and

■ Checking understanding to ensure messages are communicated clearly and completely: for example by asking 'Am I being clear?', 'Will you say it back to me in your own words?', 'Let me show you what I mean', 'Why don't you give it a try now?'

Adjusting for non-routine interactions

In non-routine contexts, people cannot achieve their communication goals by just applying cultural rules, conventions and codes. Instead they need to use person-centred messages.[22] Person-centred messages recognise other people's perspectives and explain the reasons for requests or orders in terms of the other's perspective. To construct person-centred messages, speakers first use open questioning to obtain information about the other's attitudes, beliefs and values. They then take others' attitudes and beliefs into consideration and acknowledge them when appropriate. Person-centred messages demand more thought from the communicator. They have, though, been shown to be more effective in gaining others' compliance. Since intercultural encounters are usually non-routine, communicators should expect to use more inquiry, less advocacy and more attempts to see and acknowledge the other's point of view and emotions than they do in routine situations.

These suggestions are based on the constructivist approach. Much current social science research uses a metaphor of 'person-as-a-naive-scientist' attempting to make sense of his/her world; the constructivist approach, on the other hand, argues that when people are interacting, their inferences and behaviour are aimed at accomplishing goals. When they respond to each other, they typically are less concerned with understanding why others behave as they do than with understanding the immediate implications of what others do and say for their ability to achieve their own goal(s). These goals differ and may include personal goals or goals brought into being by the situation. Often the goal is simply to respond appropriately and keep the conversation on track.

In routine situations, communication is dominated by conventional goals and plans 'given' to the interactors. For instance, at the end of routine work meetings, people discuss and decide the date of the next meeting without thinking about why or how. It is in such situations that the influence of culture and cultural differences on communication is most obvious. Thus, in a high power distance culture, the forward engagements of the most senior person present will be the deciding factor on the date of the next meeting; in a more egalitarian culture, a gap will be sought in everyone's diary. However, because these conventions are so well known, people entering into intercultural communication often are unaware that the conventions of the other culture may be different. Therefore, the influence of culture on communication may be strongest, as well as least recognised, not in initial interactions but in later stages of work relationships. This conflicts with most other views of the influence of the stage of relationship.

Constructivism offers a partial explanation for individuals' motivations within intercultural interactions, although, being goal-based, it is a highly cognitive one, which leaves 'needs theories' out of account. It also provides little explanation for why people enter such encounters in the first place or how their motives in entering interaction relate to their goals within them.

Showing empathy

Being empathic means accurately understanding the thoughts and motivations of another person in an interaction and putting oneself in their place when making a judgement about them. It does not necessarily mean agreeing with them or sympathising with them – only really trying to understand them. Total empathy with another person is probably impossible, even when both are from the same culture and subculture. However, most people's communication with others would be more successful if they could increase their ability to empathise and, equally importantly, if they could convey to their interlocutor an intention to empathise.

To communicate empathy involves the following actions:

- Asking open-ended questions, such as, 'What was the experience like for you when …?',
- Listening actively,
- Paraphrasing the other person's words (e.g., 'What I think I hear you saying is …', 'Is this what you mean?') to check for understanding and to show a sincere attempt to understand,
- Checking out verbal and non-verbal cues to find out what another is feeling: 'I sense you are feeling … angry … sad … glad … afraid. Am I reading you correctly?', and
- Paying attention to any of one's own non-verbal messages that may make another person uncomfortable; and mirroring elements of the other person's body language, tone and pace, when appropriate.

Communicating a relationship as well as a task orientation

People from individualist cultures, especially men, are at risk of provoking a culture clash if they act with people from collectivist cultures according to what may be their usual priority of getting on with the task 'regardless'. It is well known that Arabs and other Middle-Easterners prefer to do business by building a relationship and then, when trust has been established, proceeding to the negotiation or discussion. The same applies to people of many other nationalities and ethnicities. Equally, men who wish to move away from the position in which their dominance imposes a style which may be inimical to their women colleagues, clients or patients and/or counterproductive for the organisation, should try to increase the amount of 'relationship' orientation they communicate at work.

Methods include:

- Remembering people's names and small details about them learnt unobtrusively or by asking,
- Using their names according to their culture (e.g., patronymic first),
- Initiating conversations on non-work topics,
- Being sensitive to nuances,
- Reciprocating acts of consideration,
- Using humour appropriately and with care,
- Finding common ground with counterparts,
- Supporting others' communication,
- Bringing others in to discussions,
- Thanking others for their work or contribution,
- Praising above standard work (in public or private according to the other person's culture), and
- Where appropriate giving candid feedback (in private).

Communicating appropriate assertiveness

Chapter 3 made the point that assertiveness, while fundamentally desirable as a communication attribute, is a variable; the level appropriate in one culture appears as aggression or submission in others. There is a matter of judgement here. Some people may be unwilling to compromise their own assertiveness level even if they are aware that the other person is likely to regard their behaviour as aggressive or submissive. However, the optimal intercultural communication approach is to seek the appropriate level of assertiveness for the culture of the person being interacted with.

Being a resourceful communicator

Communication resourcefulness is the knowledge and ability to apply cognitive, affective (emotional) and behavioural resources appropriately, effectively and creatively in diverse interactive situations.[23] Like other forms of resourcefulness, it is related to approaching new situations as learning opportunities.

■ Whether someone thinks of an intercultural encounter as an opportunity or as an anxiety-ridden event has a profound influence on how they approach interaction with strangers. Being secure in one's own cultural identity and not feeling threatened by another person's different cultural identity allows a person to approach an encounter as an opportunity to learn. If one person conveys a sense of identity security it tends to evoke the sense of security in the other, and vice-versa.

■ The emotions of an intercultural encounter are either ego-focused or other-focused, or more often some combination of the two. Culture plays a major role concerning the emotional meanings and reactions attached to encounters. For individualists, ego-focused emotions are most common: they are concerned with 'justice' and revolve around conflicting claims which are seen as able to be resolved by invoking impartial rules, principles or standards. Conversely, other-focused emotions, most commonly experienced by collectivists, revolve around issues of relationships. In both cases, demands are made on the individual's affective resourcefulness (which is similar to emotional intelligence) to resolve emotional issues.

■ To deal with the diverse identity needs of different persons in different situations, intercultural interactors need the behavioural resourcefulness to develop a wide range of verbal and non-verbal repertoires. Being responsive to strangers and open to learning from them are other aspects of behavioural resourcefulness.

Thus, to become a more resourceful intercultural communicator, there are three aspects to work on:

■ Regarding intercultural encounters as opportunities to affirm their own and endorse other people's identities rather than as sources of anxiety.

■ Achieving an acceptable and appropriate balance between 'ego' concerns and 'other' concerns in interactions. This also means achieving a good balance between relying on principles, rules and procedures for guidance and regulation of the encounter, and on the other relying on trust and caring – a relationship approach. Highly individualist, achievement-oriented people are often deficient in the 'other' dimension of affective resourcefulness and should attempt to shift in

Box 6.6

'In a major city in Siberia I was training about 40 local administration employees to give presentations to potential providers of finance. I asked them what laws the region had to support new enterprises. No one said a word. I suggested to them that they all knew this information and told them I was now going to act like an international financier. I packed up my papers and stomped out of the room, muttering that I had wasted my time. I then returned and listed five major benefits that their recent law gave to local and foreign investors. I also stated that any international financier would find out such information in advance (I had found it from a website) and would expect the people working to promote business to both know the law and explain how it actually worked. "Silence is not an option." One person in the audience called out, "You didn't tell us silence wasn't an option."

Soviet ways led to people finding that keeping silent was the safest option. Such a response is likely in any currently or formerly authoritarian society and needs to be anticipated.'

Source: Email from a financial expert: author's research

that direction; other groups, including many women, may gain in affective resourcefulness by more emphasis on their own needs and on principles rather than feelings.

■ Developing a wide range of verbal and non-verbal repertoires to deal with the diverse identity needs of different persons in different situations. Another key theme is behavioural adaptation and flexibility.[24]

Sharing information

A study has shown that, by sharing information, individuals can create more favourable impressions among colleagues from whom they are demographically different and who negatively stereotype them as outgroup members. Such information sharing comes more naturally to extraverts and to high self-monitors, described next, but is available to all. When others' impressions of them are more positive, the study showed, demographically different people performed better, were more satisfied and reported higher levels of social integration, no matter how different they were from their work colleagues.[25]

General traits for intercultural effectiveness

Self-monitoring, dealing with intercultural communication emotions and cultural relativism and biculturalism are the traits that support intercultural effectiveness.

Self-monitoring

The habit of self-observation and analysis is known as self-monitoring. There is substantial research evidence that it has positive effects on intercultural communication. High self-monitors are better able to do all the following:

■ Discover appropriate behaviour in new situations,
■ Have control over their emotional reactions,

- Create the impressions they wish,
- Modify their behaviour to changes in social situations,
- Make more confident and extreme attributions,
- Seek out information about others with whom they anticipate interacting, and
- Initiate and regulate conversations more.[26]

They also have a greater need to talk, and are more likely to be leaders. This applies to both genders.

Dealing with intercultural communication emotions

Because people's behaviour is affected by their moods and emotions as well as by their thoughts, attitudes and values, intercultural interactors need to take moods and emotions into account. Chapter 5 described some sources of negative emotions that can arise during intercultural encounters. These emotions include anxiety and communication fear. Moreover, individuals' previous experience in interactions with a particular other party or with people from a related group is likely to evoke thoughts about the past experiences, to which positive or negative emotions may be attached. These evoked emotions have the potential to influence the emotions that are experienced during the current interaction.

Although there are situations where it is desirable to increase the level of anxiety felt during an interaction, in intercultural interactions, particularly with strangers, it will more often be appropriate to lower harmfully high anxiety levels.[27] There are three main reasons: fear will make interaction unpleasant or painful, it will make it difficult to concentrate enough to behave in a skilled way and it will communicate itself to interlocutors. Ability to manage anxiety and communication fear should mainly be developed away from interaction itself, through introspection, observation and the following practices:

- Identifying, as precisely as possible, situations that give rise to communication fear,
- Observing, carefully, from memory if possible and from future interactions just how, if at all, past expectations were proved wrong (the fear usually originates in past experiences of disconfirmation of expectations),
- Taking equally careful note of when expectations were confirmed (there is a tendency to notice our failures but not our successes, which undermines confidence unnecessarily), and
- Checking that when a situation requiring communication gives rise to apprehensiveness in future, the problem is not caused by over-generalising. Communication situations have multiple aspects: two people may be from different continents, but both may be mothers; the discussion may be about accounts, which make a person nervous, but with fellow-students to whom they can talk without fear on other subjects. Instead of concentrating on the difficulties, it is more effective to concentrate on the emotionally easy aspects.[28]

Cultural relativism and biculturalism

Achieving real and ethical intercultural communication requires cultural relativism. This involves a shift away from a position in which the norms, roles, values and behaviours into which a person was socialised are seen as uniquely valid. Instead, the person sees others' norms, roles, values and behaviours as equally valid in themselves, possibly beneficial, and eligible for adoption. Unfortunately, this shift is difficult to achieve: following norms into which one was socialised is reflexive and requires little effort; not following them, or following others, is non-reflexive and requires substantial effort. The key skill required is mindfulness, which, with practice, can become habitual.

Biculturalism goes beyond this and involves accepting role-taking as part of the human condition, avoiding stylised verbal behaviour, being willing to accept the strain of adaptation, being well aware of conversational constraints and showing flexibility in conversational adaptation.[29] There are, however, individual differences in whether biculturals see their two cultures as oppositional or compatible. It is easier for people who see their two cultures as compatible to switch between culturally different interpretive lenses or frames. For example, they may make external attributions in the Chinese cultural manner after Chinese primes and internal attributions after American primes.

Applications of skills to particular situations

Situations calling for both general and specific intercultural skills to be applied include interability communication, avoiding and proscribing harassing or discriminatory behaviour, coping with others' harassment, bullying, prejudice or discrimination, subverting the suppression of motherhood in the workplace and helping change others' stereotypes about outgroup members.

Interability communication

Relying on broad 'disability knowledge' is not enough in interactions with a particular person with a disability. Implying that another person cannot enact any role outside his or her 'disabled' identity threatens both their fellowship and their competence face. Instead, the following can help develop interability relationships:

- Notice cues that help to reveal others' preferred identities instead of relying on one's own impression.
- Emphasise personal, not (sub)cultural identities.
- Treat people and relationships as unique, not as representatives of any category.
- Anticipate face needs and learn to overcome face threats by including the other person and respecting his or her abilities. When face threats do occur, apologise.
- Be aware that it may take several interactions to achieve effective interability communication.[30]

Disclosing a disability, its type and cause, can reduce tension and uncertainty so that the initial focus on the disability will recede and the individual, not the disability, will become the focus. However this strategy disregards the needs and feelings of the person with a disability and makes them responsible for disclosure. Both parties prefer the other to take the initiative, but since the privacy issue most concerns the person with a disability, it is important that the decision to disclose information remains theirs.[31] As the examples in Box 6.7 show, people with disabilities are often the ones to undertake the roles of enabling communication and of educating or training people without disabilities to achieve interability communication.

Box 6.7

A man who is deaf works on satellite technology at Walgreens (a US pharmacy chain). He explained: 'If words fail I try body language, writing or typing … . It's a matter of perseverance to prove to the hearing that my deafness will not interfere with my work. But in this age of advancing communication technology the barriers are diminishing quickly.'

A woman who is deaf and works in consumer documentation at Microsoft uses a hearing aid to help her use her residual hearing. 'I read lips and speak fairly well', she says, 'I've learned how to put people at ease. And of course many discussions are conducted through e-mail or IM [instant messaging].'

A development engineer in the design automation group of Eastman Kodak's R&D engineering technology centre (Rochester, NY) said, 'I try to educate my co-workers on how

they can help me understand them. Keep your hands away from your mouth, face me when you talk, and e-mail me or stop by my office rather than call or leave voice mail'. He added, 'I have reaped the benefits of … interacting with people who have an understanding of deafness.'

The availability manager for global Web applications in IT for IBM wears two hearing aids and hears quite well with their help, but finds that unusual speech patterns and phone conversations can be a challenge. She copes by not being shy about asking people to repeat things she may have missed.

Source: Ranger, L.M. (2002) 'Communication is key for deaf and hard of hearing technical pros', *Diversity/Careers Professional*, Oct/Nov. URL: http://www.diversitycareers.com/articles/pro/octnov02/fod_com_deaf.htm

Avoiding and proscribing harassing and discriminatory behaviour

Any kind of harassing or discriminatory behaviour is not only wrong and unacceptable in itself, it also creates barriers to communication, not only with its victims but also with all who perceive and condemn it. Although these subjects have been covered in Chapters 3 and 5 they are so important that a reminder at this point is worthwhile. Some perpetrators of harassment, especially sexual harassment, do not always understand that what they do is harassment.

The European Commission identifies five categories of sexual harassment:

1. Non-verbal (e.g., pin-ups, leering, whistling and suggestive gestures),
2. Physical (unnecessary touching),
3. Verbal (unwelcome sexual advances, propositions or innuendo),
4. Intimidation (offensive or superfluous comments about dress, appearance or performance), and
5. Sexual blackmail.

Not all harassment at work is done by men to women; however, the majority is. While awareness of some of these behaviours as harassment has increased and most men avoid them, others continue to be a problem.

People accused of harassment are generally rated more credible, more likeable, more dedicated and more competent when they accept responsibility, compared to when they rely on excuses or denials. Excuses lead to more warnings, punishments and advice for the accused; denials prompt respondents to study the matter further or refer the entire incident higher up.[32]

Coping with others' harassment, bullying, prejudice or discrimination

Sexist, racist and other prejudiced behaviours are not the fault of the victims. Responsibility for preventing them and putting them right is primarily the perpetrators' and secondarily any relevant managers, organisations or institutions. Despite this, victims do often need to handle them in order not to be damaged emotionally or in their ability to communicate and maintain relationships at work.

There are both positive and negative coping strategies for dealing with work stress, however caused. Positive (control-related) coping styles include help-seeking (which reflect actively pursuing consultations with others in the work situation, publicly announcing decisions about what should be done, and undertaking policy changes to prevent future problems), positive thinking and direct action (devoting more time and energy to do what is expected, using more effective planning methods, and working harder and longer hours). A study found that high scores on gender identity roles, whether masculine or feminine were linked to positive coping styles. Low scores on gender identity were associated with the escape-related coping styles of alcohol use and avoidance/resignation. High masculinity, but not high femininity, was linked to help-seeking scores. 'Such activities seem to require certain levels of assertiveness and analytical decision-making skills, traits more descriptive of a masculine rather than feminine gender role.' (These findings relate to gender role, which was more closely linked than biological sex to ways of coping with work stress.) Having an internal locus of control increased people's tendency to use help-seeking and positive, direct action coping strategies; an external orientation, that either powerful other people or chance control what happens, increased the tendency to use escape-related strategies. Older workers are less likely to avoid or resign themselves to workplace stressors. This finding is consistent with other research that finds older workers exhibit a greater sense of being in control and more accurate self-appraisals; these may result from their longer experience with effective coping behaviours.[33] Suggestions for how women and other 'minority' groups can learn to cope with others' damaging behaviours include the following:

- Having one's own clear parameters and consistent commitment to fair treatment,
- Judging when to 'let it go' and when to react strongly,
- Recognising allies in the oppressing categories,
- Getting a mentor,
- Getting better qualifications and experience than the 'competition', and
- Accepting the need to prove oneself over and over.

A German study found that most victims started with constructive conflict-solving strategies, changed their strategies several times but, regrettably, ended with trying to leave the organisation. The unsuccessful victims, in their fight for justice, often contributed to the escalation of the bullying conflict. On the other hand, successful copers (those victims who believed that their situation at work had improved as a result of their coping efforts) less often fought back with similar means, less often used avoidance behaviour such as absenteeism, and were better at recognising and avoiding escalating behaviour.[34]

Subverting the suppression of motherhood in the workplace

Gendered and discriminatory organisational practices can coerce women into disguising their commitments as mothers. These practices include pervasive assumptions that working mothers are less reliable, less committed or less professional than their child-less colleagues. A qualitative study found that women interpret supervisory patterns and interactions and often decide to edit ties to motherhood, express their 'public' and 'private' identities differently and operate self-surveillance and control. However, most also engage in family talk and 'bring children to work' through conversation.[35]

Helping change others' stereotypes about outgroup members

In order to promote a good atmosphere for intercultural communication in an organisation, there can be a need to influence co-members of an ingroup to change their stereotypes of other (sub)cultural groups. Research has shown that members of an attractive ingroup can help shift stereotypes held by other members. A study reported in the British Journal of Social Psychology discussed referent information influence. This is the motivation individuals have to agree with (i.e., share the beliefs of) other members of a group, where their social identity as a group member is salient. In these circumstances, people expect to agree with the other group member. When disagreement occurs, they may be motivated to reduce the subjective uncertainty that arises from disagreement with people with whom they expect to agree. Then they may change their views in one of three ways. They may alter them to become consistent with other ingroup members (e.g., by shifting their own stereotypes – as in, 'My sister Mary works with Asian women and she says they are not nearly as submissive as people think – she could be right'); attribute the disagreement to perceived relevant difference in the stimulus situation (e.g., as in, 'My sister Mary works with Asian women and she says they are not nearly as submissive as people think – but she's talking about the ones who've been brought up in the West – they're different'); or recategorise the disagreeing ingroup members as an outgroup (e.g., as in, '... but Mary's always had some peculiar ideas – she's not like the rest of our family').[36]

Another approach is based on attribution theory. Counter-stereotypic behaviour by one member of an outgroup often fails to change outgroup stereotypes because it can be dismissed as an exception to the rule. Thus, for instance, Mrs Thatcher's behaviour as UK Prime Minister failed to change many men's stereotypes of women because they chose to regard her as an 'honorary man', that is, not a typical woman. However, a study has shown that the impact of an individual outgroup member's behaviour on stereotypes can be increased. This happens if two conditions apply: the behaviour is attributed to a stable internal cause such as personality, rather than to an external cause, such as 'luck' or an unstable internal cause such as mood; and the outgroup member is seen as typical, because in other ways their behaviour is similar to the behaviour of many members of the outgroup. Thus, by dressing in a feminine way to confirm male stereotypes of women but consistently making the 'hard' decisions, women managers increase their chances of shifting their male colleagues' stereotypes of women. Unfortunately, though, negative beliefs are often more resistant to change than positive ones.[37]

A wide range of behaviours and traits can contribute positively towards achieving effective intercultural communication. They include skills that enhance intercultural understanding of others, skills for effective intercultural self-presentation, general traits for intercultural effectiveness and applications of skills to particular situations such as interability communication. Some of these fall into the category of 'self-management'; others are directed at reassuring interlocutors of having good intentions and a desire to establish good relations.

6.4 INTERCULTURAL COMMUNICATION PROCESSES

This section discusses processes that increase intercultural communication effectiveness but that require both parties to co-operate. These processes are grounding, communication accommodation, adapting in initial intercultural encounters, developing shared representations of intercultural episodes, managing uncertainty and anxiety in intercultural encounters, conflict resolution, mutual conversational improvement strategies and marginalised groups' strategies.

Grounding

In attempting to speak so as to be understood, speakers make assumptions about the common ground they share with their interlocutors. Each time they are understood and each time they understand what the other person says, the common ground is extended, so that 'in orderly discourse, common ground is cumulative'.[38]

This process by which people establish and continuously update their shared understanding in conversations is called grounding. It occurs naturally, but can be enhanced by asking and answering questions or by one party anticipating the other's information needs and supplying them without being asked. In either case, unsuccessful grounding can occur if the information supplier does not correctly understand the other person's needs; however, a process of 'successive approximations' can be successful. The more intercultural pairs ground, the better they communicate. It has been suggested, however, that they are less inclined to ground than monocultural pairs, although one study found the contrary.

A study that analysed authentic spoken data revealed that common ground more often comes to be established between two persons through shared belief than through mutual knowledge. Shared beliefs are held to be true by virtue of indirect information/ experience as a result of a prior discussion and interaction with another individual concerning the same belief. In contrast, mutual knowledge is held to be true by direct experience of both parties.[39]

Box 6.8

The following example of grounding occurred during an interview in English between an immigration lawyer and her Chinese client:

Lawyer: 'Another option would be to switch into another category, like the "Highly Skilled Migrant Programme". Do you understand?'

Client: 'Do you mean, instead of getting my employer to support my application for permanent residence?'

Lawyer: 'Yes. It's a points system – so many for a degree, so many for relevant experience. You have to have enough points.'

Client: 'Do you get points for professional qualifications?'

Lawyer: 'Yes.'

Client: 'So that might be better for me?'

Lawyer: 'It's another option.'

Client: 'Yes, I'll have to decide which is best.'

Lawyer: 'Yes.'

Source: Observed by author, author's research

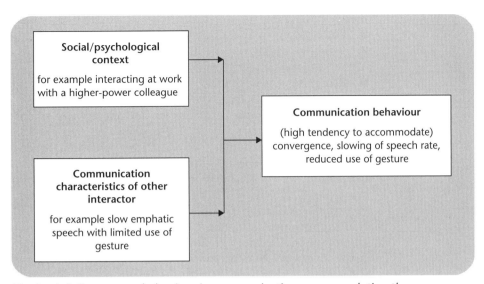

Figure 6.4 *The basic influences on behaviour in communication accommodation theory*

Based on: Gallois, C., Franklyn-Stokes, A., Giles, H. and Coupland, N. (1988) 'Communication accommodation in intercultural encounters', in Kim, Y.Y. and Gudykunst, W.B. (eds) *Theories in Intercultural Communication*, Newbury Park, CA: Sage.

Communication accommodation

When two or more people are communicating face-to-face, they often adjust features of their speech or behaviour, including accent, speed, loudness, vocabulary, grammar, voice tone or gestures. Sometimes they adjust in a way that makes their communication more like the other person's (converging), sometimes to make it more unlike (diverging). Diverging usually accentuates a person's own group membership. Converging and diverging are probably strategies to signal communicators' attitudes towards one other. They may converge to gain approval or identify; they may diverge to distinguish themselves.[40] Communication accommodation theory (CAT) identifies factors that influence whether people try to converge or diverge; it is illustrated in Figure 6.4.

According to CAT, people from different cultures (or groups) can increase their ability to communicate with one another by converging through a process of attuning.[41] Attuning consists of

■ Using increasingly similar phrasing and vocabulary, formality levels and non-verbal behaviour.
■ Sharing the choice of topic, taking turns to speak and listen, responding to what others say and supporting others' 'face'.
■ Minimising interruptions, corrections and evaluations.
■ Adjusting speech-rate, loudness, framing and focusing moves to maximise ease of understanding for the partner.

Other important CAT processes include the following:

1. Learning when to expect people to behave more in intergroup terms and more in accordance with their norms; being more careful about breaches of norms. This

means learning to:

- Realise when an interaction is likely to involve status issues.
- Recognise people who are highly dependent on their group and those whose sense of solidarity with their group is high.
- Recognise people who feel that they or their group are disadvantaged and be aware of its implications (see Section 5.1).
- Distinguish members of dominant and subordinate groups and know how that status is likely to affect their behaviour (see Sections 5.1 and 6.3).
- Treat initial encounters as particularly occasions when people will be conscious of and behaving in accordance with their group memberships.

2. Being aware that the long-term motivations of interactors to build relationships or otherwise will affect how much they are likely to accommodate.
3. Paying attention to others' needs and behaviours.
4. Noticing how much attention interlocutors pay to others' needs and behaviours.
5. Monitoring interlocutors' communication strategies to identify them as convergence, divergence or maintenance; becoming aware of the possibility of using a wider range of strategies than are normally used; trying to gain the level of personal control which will allow using an appropriate strategy rather than simply adopting a strategy unthinkingly.
6. Being sensitive to the other party's evaluations of one's own interactive behaviour as accommodative or not and attributable to oneself, one's situation or one's group; monitoring one's own equivalent evaluations and ensuring they are soundly based.
7. If interlocutors are converging, being aware that that probably implies one of the following on their part:
   - They desire social approval.
   - They perceive the 'costs' of attuning as lower than the perceived rewards.
   - They desire to meet the perceived communication needs of their interlocutor(s).
   - They desire a mutual self-presentation and equal-status role relations.
8. Similarly, the presence of these factors suggests that attuning can be expected.
9. If interlocutors are diverging, being aware that that probably implies that they desire:
   - To communicate a contrastive self- or group-image.
   - To dissociate personally from their interlocutors or their definition of the situation.
   - To signal differences in experience/knowledge/intellectual capability/ communicator style.
   - To achieve or maintain a high-status role.
10. Knowing the counter-intuitive findings on people's use of interaction strategies – for instance, that people from collectivist cultures use politeness to create distance.[42]

Adapting in initial intercultural encounters

Adaptation theory complements communication accommodation concepts. It is concerned with the conditions under which individuals who are interacting interculturally make more or less effort to adapt; in particular it concerns how responsibility for adapting is allocated between two participants. Adaptation is regarded as a burden that the participants will assume equally or differentially according

Box 6.9

In a British joint venture in Taiwan, the secretary appointed to a British executive had lower English language proficiency than the executive was used to. The appointment was a success, however, because her 'guanxi' gave the CEO access to and provided understanding of the communication and decision-making process in Taiwan. The executive accommodated by not pointing out grammatical errors and awkward English paragraph and sentence construction, speaking as precisely and simply as possible, avoiding slang and colloquial expressions, and providing illustrations and examples. The result was that the Chinese secretary could make accurate translations of the executive's English messages into written Chinese and oral Mandarin, despite her low English language proficiency.

In another case in the same joint venture, an expatriate's secretary had obtained an advanced degree in the US, so she possessed excellent oral and written English communication skills. She was also comfortable working in an English-speaking environment and interacting with Westerners. In this case, it was she who accommodated to the direct style of her boss.

Where neither party has adequate language proficiency in the other's language (or a third language), to adjust successfully both need to converge towards a common vocabulary and communication style. They may also seek to increase the proportion of messages exchanged directly and thereby expand the outer boundaries of the communication zone. For example, a Taiwanese product manager had negotiated previous sub-contracting agreements for small appliances with the same French engineers and designers, and the parties had developed an effective communication channel. One time, however, the language proficiency required for specifying the appliance prototype exceeded their capacity, so they were unable to finalise the prototype arrangements, but they were able to communicate well enough to pinpoint the source of their communication difficulties and agree on the initial steps towards developing a workable prototype: namely, to purchase a competitor's product, take the product to Taiwan for disassembly and analysis, and thereby learn the required circuitry for French appliances.

Source: Babcock, R.D. and Du-Babcock, B. (2001) 'Language-based communication zones in international business communication', *The Journal of Business Communication*, **38**: 372–412

---

to their relative power in the interaction or their relative dependence on it for desired outcomes. Adaptations are the changes that individuals make in their emotions, thoughts, sense of identity and communication behaviour as they interact in a new cultural environment. The extent and nature of the adaptation depends on their motivation.

People are more likely to adapt when they have a goal in an interaction, as opposed to merely engaging in a casual conversation. If the goal is shared, if, for instance, both are trying to 'get to yes' in a negotiation, both participants will adapt; if only one participant has a goal which will be served by adaptation, then only that person will adapt. Goals arise from needs for co-operation, participation or agreement in such areas as commerce, manufacturing, defence, education, science, technology, politics, agriculture, medicine, the arts and scholarly research.

When one person adapts ineffectually, the other participant will respond by invoking culture-based beliefs about difference. So, if a European in negotiation with someone from China suddenly starts 'stone-walling', in a clumsy attempt to adopt what s/he regards as Chinese negotiating style, the Chinese person might ascribe the behaviour to Western deviousness, if that is part of his or her culture-based belief about Europeans. Adaptation is disrupted when culture-based beliefs are invoked. If they are not, other impediments, such as status differences, are more likely to be overcome.

Adaptation theory concerns first-time encounters. These are less predictable than later meetings and their outcomes often determine whether there will be further contact. In first-time encounters, the theory states, people will probe one another's beliefs, especially those related to the task or purpose of the meeting, in order to identify areas of agreement or disagreement. An important outcome of this process is reinforcement or modification of prior cultural stereotypes. This learning will become a cognitive resource for future encounters. Whether such learning proves to be positive or negative for such future encounters depends on how closely 'strangers' met in future conform to the stereotype. Experience does not necessarily increase competence in intercultural communication, although it has the potential for doing so. Also important is self-examination. Adaptation involves confronting not only the 'other', but also the self. In this process, the personal cultural stereotype is reinforced or modified, and this learning also becomes part of the background of the individual's future intercultural encounters.[43]

The implications of this theory for improving intercultural communication are that it is beneficial to:

- Realise that both participants may be wrongly diagnosing the intercultural situation. (This could happen if they both wrongly identify the culture of the different other person. It could also occur if they have incomplete or inaccurate knowledge of the cultural stereotype with which the other has been correctly identified or how closely the individual actually conforms to the stereotype.)
- Expect beliefs to be probed for areas of agreement and disagreement; understand the importance of agreement for building relationships.
- Anticipate that how either party sees the interaction will affect whether they will take on, reject or intend to share the 'burden' of adaptation. They are likely to adapt their own communication behaviour more than they expect of the other party in the following circumstances: if they see the encounter as purposeful, its goals as shared, the benefit as mutual or theirs, the 'territory' as the other's and their power and status as lower than the other's. If any of the above conditions do not apply, they are likely to adapt less than they expect of the other.
- Understand that adaptation itself is likely to change the attitudes and perceptions of adapters, both about the other party and their culture and about themselves and their own culture.
- Avoid invoking culturally based beliefs which may conflict with the other person's.

To speed progress with the task it is beneficial for each party to:

- Offer more functional adaptive behaviour; if there is inequality in adaptive behaviour to shift towards parity (i.e., assume more of the 'burden' than would be 'natural').
- Expect the major beneficiary of task completion to take responsibility for accelerating adaptive behaviour.
- Disregard differences of status or territory which are to their advantage; or invoke them to increase the amount of adaptation the other party will supply.[44]

Developing shared representations of intercultural episodes

Intercultural communication is effective to the extent that the participants think of interactions in similar ways. 'For interaction to succeed, participants must essentially agree in their social situation definition.'[45] It has been argued that members of a given culture or subculture have a 'shared, implicit cognitive representation of interaction episodes'. These representations cover assessments of the episode's intimacy, involvement and friendliness; the importance of task- versus relationship-orientation; participants' own self-confidence and anxiety levels; their positive or negative evaluation of each encounter. These representations usually differ from those held by members of different cultures, influenced by cultural values such as individualism–collectivism and achievement/relationship.[46] For instance, research among Chinese and Australian subjects found that Chinese subjects perceived episodes mainly in terms of communal values, power distance and usefulness, rather than pleasantness. Australians were more aware of competitiveness and individualism. Age, sex and personality also predicted how social episodes were seen in both cultures, but the pattern of such links was culture-specific. Other research includes a comparative study of students and housewives. This study showed that for housewives, episodes were mainly thought of in terms of intimacy and friendliness, self-confidence and positive or negative evaluation. Results are not given for students, but it is implied that they were different.[47] A comparative study of Faculty, research students and other staff showed that decreasing status was associated with an increasing role for anxiety in episode perceptions; involvement was a criterion used mainly by Faculty; and students were least evaluative but placed the greatest importance on task-orientation.

The greater the differences between how communicators think about interaction episodes, the harder it is for them to understand one another. Thus these cultural and subcultural differences can create barriers, though at work factors such as common technical expertise favour intercultural understanding. These barriers can be overcome by understanding how people from a different culture think about interactions and so coming to have 'shared representations' of interaction episodes. Two other factors can assist: thinking about interactions in more complex ways and being generally socially skilled. A study compared more successful and cohesive with less successful and cohesive student teams. The more cohesive teams had more complex episode representations, based on three dimensions: friendliness, intimacy and activity than the more fragmented teams. These had two-dimensional representations, based on evaluation and friendliness. It has been shown that how someone thinks about encounters is related to social skill. Highly socially skilled individuals see episodes more in terms of evaluation and intensity, while less socially skilled persons are primarily affected by anxiety in their mental representations of social episodes.

Managing anxiety and uncertainty in intercultural encounters

To adapt successfully to working with different others, individuals need to manage the levels of uncertainty they experience about others' behaviour and the anxiety they feel about interacting with different others. This means that they must be able to understand the different others (manage uncertainty) and to manage their emotional reaction to the differences (control anxiety).[48] They may also be able to help the other party manage uncertainty and anxiety and so to interact more effectively. Several factors contribute towards people's ability to manage uncertainty and anxiety.

These factors include:

- Knowledge of the other's culture or subculture – for instance, its communication rules and behavioural norms,
- Open, flexible and accurate stereotypes,
- Positive attitudes towards the other (sub)culture and its members,
- Intimate and rewarding contact with members of the other (sub)culture,
- Perceiving similarities between their own (sub)culture and the (sub)culture of the different others,
- Sharing communication networks with members of the (sub)culture,
- A positive cultural identity. (With a negative cultural identity, the insecurity and anxiety stimulated by intercultural contact will seem greater, perhaps too great, leading to avoidance), and
- A demeanour that may help shift other participants' definition of a situation from 'difficult interaction with strangers', which would tend to be an anxiety-provoking definition that would lead to heavy reliance on stereotypes, to a more relaxed one where individual characteristics can be taken into account. Research has shown that the demeanour of those involved in a situation affects the definitions that people create for situations (for instance, whether it is a crisis or a routine event) and so how people respond to the situation.[49]

By decreasing uncertainty and anxiety, these factors may allow people to adapt more and be more effective in intercultural communication. Managing uncertainty and anxiety in intercultural encounters requires the skills to make accurate predictions, tolerate ambiguity, be mindful, empathise, self-monitor and adapt behaviour through cultural relativism and biculturalism. Competence in a second language, which need not necessarily be used in the interaction, also reduces anxiety. These skills, with some suggestions on how to develop them, were described in Section 6.3.

This guidance on factors and skills for reducing uncertainty and anxiety in intercultural encounters comes from Anxiety/Uncertainty Management (AUM) theory. Core elements of AUM theory are the concepts of the stranger, initial encounters, uncertainty and anxiety.

- Strangers are people who are different because they are members of other groups. When strangers act in a way that is deviant in terms of an individual's own culture, the individual experiences uncertainty and anxiety, especially when those strangers will be encountered in future or can provide rewards.
- Initial encounters, by definition, are between strangers. It was noted earlier that culture forms an implicit theory (about the rules being followed and the 'game' being played) that individuals use to guide their behaviour and interpret others' behaviour. Much culturally influenced behaviour is habitual and therefore not 'conscious'.[50] The matter is different, though, in the initial stages of intercultural communication. When interacting with a stranger, individuals become aware that the stranger does not share their own implicit theory about the rules or the game. Therefore they become more conscious of that implicit theory. The result is that interactions between strangers take place at high levels of behavioural awareness.
- Uncertainty is of two distinct types: not being able to predict what strangers' attitudes, feelings, beliefs, values and behaviour will be and not being able to explain why they behave in the way they do. When uncertainty is too high for comfort, people will either try to reduce it by gaining information or end the

interaction. When uncertainty is too low for comfort, people may be too bored to act effectively.

■ Anxiety refers to the feeling of being uneasy, tense, worried or apprehensive about what might happen. This is an affective (emotional) response, whereas uncertainty is a cognitive (thought process) one. Anxiety is usually based on people's negative expectations, such as that their self-concepts will be damaged or that they will be negatively evaluated. When anxiety is too high for comfort, people either avoid encounters or their attention is distracted from the communication. Then they rely on information like stereotypes to predict other people's behaviour, and therefore may misinterpret it. When anxiety is too low, people may not care what happens in the interaction, not pay attention and miss important cues.

Thus, effective communication occurs when levels of uncertainty and anxiety are optimal – intermediate between too high and too low. However, in interactions with strangers, both are normally too high for effective communication. In these cases, effective intercultural communication depends on controlling anxiety through tension-reducing behaviour and reducing uncertainty by information-seeking. In intercultural as against intracultural interactions, information seeking involves more interrogation, self-disclosure and non-verbal affiliative expressiveness, but no more direct questions are asked. Self-monitoring, attributional confidence and attraction are related to how much information seeking takes place in an interaction.[51]

Support for the existence of uncertainty reduction as part of the dynamic of interaction with strangers has come from research which showed it applies to both low-context communication and high-context communication cultures,[52] friendship relations across cultures,[53] interactions between Blacks and Whites in the USA,[54] and interethnic communication generally in the USA.[55] A study of Japanese and Caucasian subjects found, as AUM would predict, that ethnicity, stage of relationship, shared networks and ethnolinguistic identity strength influenced how much interlocutors self-disclosed, how many questions they asked, whether their body language expressed affiliation, whether they saw one another as similar and how confident they were in making attributions about the causes of different others' behaviour, using both high- and low-context measures.[56]

AUM theory has been criticised for being static and for taking the individual interactor, rather than the dyad or group, as the unit of analysis. However, because behavioural contagion is known to be particularly common when one party is anxious, the theory has the potential to be interactive and dynamic. AUM theory has also been criticised for assuming that uncertainty will always produce anxiety.[57] These critics further suggest that it would be more appropriate to focus on communication and uncertainty management. To better explain these processes, they argue, answers are needed to questions about the experience and meaning of uncertainty, the role of appraisal and emotion in uncertainty management and the range of behavioural and psychological responses to uncertainty. Despite these criticisms, AUM's focus on initial interactions and the early stages of acquaintanceship makes it valuable for understanding those aspects of intercultural work communication which involve meeting strangers, such as opening interviews between professionals and clients or international negotiations.

Conflict resolution

'Dispute settlement is already no easy task. ... With the addition of cultural barriers, cross-cultural negotiation may seem next to impossible.'[58] The cultural barriers consist not only of differences in beliefs and values, such as were described in Chapter 4, or in ways of communicating, as recounted in Chapter 3, but also in models of conflict resolution itself. Low-context cultures, with their 'enlightenment-based rationalism', attempt to resolve disputes by a 'means-end rationality', an emphasis on technical ways to break problems down into their component parts and a guiding ethic which is 'instrumental and manipulative'. In contrast, high-context cultures attempt dispute resolution through adaptation and eschewing dichotomous either/or possibilities. For ethical conflict management, it is widely agreed following Habermas, that there is no alternative to 'fair and open intercultural communication'.[59] Unfortunately, however, it is precisely in an intercultural setting that, according to some researchers, open communication is least likely. Whereas similarity encourages people to adopt a co-operative, integrative approach, lack of cultural similarity is a significant factor in explaining reliance on a legalistic strategy. The feeling of a lack of common ground may lead to a higher level of perceived behavioural uncertainty and so to reliance on legal mechanisms for resolving conflicts.

Conflict resolution, with open problem-solving and compromising, are widely advocated to enable participants to escape from deadlock situations. In international joint ventures, for instance, both partners need to adopt a give-and-take attitude in resolving disagreements.[60] Critics suggest, though, that conflict and instability are not anomalous or uncharacteristic, but inevitable; therefore the aim should be for resolutions that 'privilege instability and difference within a more stable whole'. Any positions, standpoints or solutions should always be understood as subject to being revised, changed, deleted or replaced. Most methods rely too much on linear logic, quasi-legalistic approaches and formalism that 'undermine other discourses (e.g., based on needs, differences, multicultural diverse voices, etc.) and possibly more liberating narrative constructions.'[61]

Two approaches that attempt to answer these criticisms respectively emphasise sources of conflict that stem from frustrated needs and the mental processes of the disputants. Needs, as opposed to interests, are universal.[62] Needs also differ from interests in other important ways. First, they are non-negotiable. People will not trade away their identity or their security. Identity and security are so necessary to all human satisfaction, that people will do almost anything, even things that violate fundamental norms, or diminish their ability to attain their interests, in an effort to obtain their basic needs. Second, needs are usually not mutually exclusive. While interests may be structured in such a way that only one side can get what it wants, needs are usually mutually supporting. Insecurity tends to breed aggression against others; security allows one to leave others alone. Similarly, if one's own identity is secure, there is no need to threaten another's sense of identity. If a group's identity is denied, however, it is likely to respond by asserting its identity against that of the opposing group(s).

A second approach emphasises the mental processes of the disputants. One important aspect is how the parties perceive their situation, as opposed to how it might appear to an independent observer. Second, especially where some participants are 'subaltern voices', such as those of women or ethnic minorities, the complexities of people's group identities must be allowed for. 'It is fundamentally important for all participants in a conflict to be heard and understood.' These understandings underpin an approach that aims for conflict transformation rather than dispute settlement. It sees conflict as both caused by and causing changes in relationships. 'Destructive interaction patterns need to be transformed into positive or constructive relationships and interactions … development of empowerment and mutual recognition, along

Box 6.10

A Building Control Officer (BCO) for a local authority visited a householder to explain that the extension the householder built on to his house did not comply with the Building Regulations and that he needed to make alterations. (1) The householder came from an ethnic minority community. (2) and (3) About an hour into the discussion, it emerged that the householder had used a family member as architect. (4) The householder was inclined to use expansive gestures and 'shout'.

In this example, differences in culture and communication styles are likely to lead to violations of expectations. The following guidance might help resolve the conflict:

(1) The householder is probably a collectivist and so answerable to a 'constituency' of extended family.

(2) The BCO should aim for tolerance for ambiguity in the early stages of the discussion and not fall into the trap of judging indirectness as devious.

(3) The involvement of a family member as architect may make the householder more sensitive about what he sees as an accusation of incompetence on the architect's part: to him, family pride is at stake.

(4) The BCO should bear in mind that vivid emotional display is common in some cultures and is not necessarily aggressive.

The BCO needs to stick to the point that the rules apply to everybody. A possible resolution of the conflict is for the BCO to speak to the architect (as intermediary); this would fit well with some cultures that often use third parties in such cases.

Based on: Author's research

with interdependence, justice, forgiveness, and reconciliation.' One technique is 'dialogue' in which small groups of people who hold opposing views on highly divisive and emotional issues are brought together to have a 'new kind of conversation'. Dialogue does not always lead to settlement, but may produce a transformation in the way the conflict is pursued.[63]

Conversational improvement strategies

To repair communication failures, as Chapter 3 explained, people say they use one or more conversational improvement strategies.

- Asserting a point of view: being more persuasive, expressing disagreement, arguing one's point of view.
- Open mindedness: being less judgemental, not dismissing ideas or opinions, letting the other person express their own opinion.
- Avoidance: not bringing up unpleasant topics.
- Giving in: apologising, agreeing.
- Interaction management: more talking, listening, turn taking, questioning, exploring topics on the part of both.
- Other orientation: involving the other person more, having patience with other person, focusing on them.

Respondents also mention a seventh 'strategy', acceptance that nothing can be done; it seems unlikely, however, that this strategy will actually repair failures.[64]

Marginalised groups' strategies

Co-cultural communication theory, introduced in Chapter 3, creates a framework for understanding the processes by which marginalised group members negotiate attempts by others to mute their voices within dominant societal structures.[65] Table 6.1 sets out communication behaviours corresponding to three strategies – separation, accommodation and assimilation.

Critique

It would be wrong to create the impression that intercultural communication theories are non-problematic. Jehn and Weldon, for example, criticised the ethnocentric assumption that Western theories can be applied in any culture. Although their criticism focused on conflict management theories in particular, there is every reason to believe that it applies equally to the intercultural communication theories discussed earlier. They wrote:

> The problem centers on the way that conflict management behavior is conceptualized, and the way it is measured in studies of cross-cultural differences. In each case, a theory of conflict management behavior developed in the West is adopted. These theories focus on dimensions that differentiate strategies of conflict management. ... These (Western-originated) dimensions of conflict management behavior are then linked to dimensions of cultural variability.[65]

These shortcomings, they argued, suggest that research based on these theories provides little useful information. To produce useful information, Western-based measures must be discarded. Instead, an inductive search must be conducted for etic dimensions (outsiders' descriptions of what people do and why they do it, developed using the tool kits of linguistics and anthropology) and emic constructs (what people themselves tell

Table 6.1   *Co-cultural communication orientations*

	Separation	Accommodation	Assimilation
Non-assertive	Avoiding Maintaining inter-personal barriers	Increasing visibility Dispelling stereotypes	Emphasizing commonalities Developing positive face Censoring self Averting controversy
Assertive	Communicating self Intragroup networking Exemplifying Strengths Embracing stereotypes	Communicating self Intragroup networking Utilizing liaisons Educating others	Extensive preparation Overcompensating Manipulating stereotypes Bargaining
Aggressive	Attacking Sabotaging others	Confronting Gaining advantage	Dissociating Mirroring strategic distancing Ridiculing self

Source: Reprinted from Orbe, M.P. (1998) 'From the standpoint(s) of traditionally muted groups: explicating a co-cultural communication theoretical model', *Communication Theory*, **8**(1): 1–26, by permission of Oxford University Press

you about what they do and why they do it). Discovering true etics allows meaningful comparisons across cultures on a set of common dimensions, and the discovery of emics contributes to a full understanding of each culture.

Other difficulties with these theories are the fact that they are partial and yet each theory stands alone as if its proponents believe it to be a complete account. Little effort has so far been made to integrate them and, with limited exceptions, insights from other theorists' and researchers' work are not incorporated. However, this defect is probably characteristic of a young and vigorous subject area in the social sciences and while it reduces the immediate value of the work, it may well be productive for the further development of the field.

In addition, there are some obvious gaps in the variables covered. With the possible exception of CAT, accounts of motivation – why some people and not others are motivated to achieve effective intercultural communication – are weak or lacking; in one case, motivational analysis is reduced to the proposition that 'length of sojourn' is the key underlying variable (see Chapter 7). Little attempt has been made so far to draw on motivational theories from psychology and social psychology.

More surprisingly, perhaps, there is a lack of recognition of cultural difference in some of the theories. With the partial exception of AUM Theory, they are silent on such questions as whether collectivists are more or less likely than individualists, those high in power distance than those low in power distance, universalists than particularists to perceive interactions in terms of cultural identity, to have their expectations violated, to adapt and so on. (It is true that one of the reported pieces of research on CAT relates part of the theory to cultural variability, but the theory per se does not do this.) Equally, only Cultural Identity Theory presents cultural difference as in any way a dependent variable, affected by the process of intercultural interaction. There is clearly potential for including cultural differences in the various models by a fairly simple logic, but the work has not yet been done, or not yet published.

> Reducing intercultural misunderstandings and increasing the ease and effectiveness of intercultural communication can be attained by grounding (mutual interactive checking for understanding), accommodating to the interlocutor's communication style, being willing to assume a more than equal share of the adaptation 'burden', developing shared representations of intercultural episodes, managing anxiety and uncertainty, conflict resolution techniques, conversational improvement strategies and learning from the positive ways in which marginalised groups cope. Intercultural communication theories can be criticised for being Western-centric, partial and static.

6.5 INTERCULTURAL COMMUNICATION EFFECTIVENESS

Clearly any work on communication needs a framework that allows an examination of whether or not any particular piece of communication or episode has been effective. 'Communication studies should aim to explain what works and what does not work in various situations; behavior that is typical may not be effective.' The framework offered by the communications literature is mainly in terms of communication competence. Competence implies being adequate to preserve a relationship within a desired definition, such as a 'good' working relationship, but not necessarily to do more than that. Perfect communication is probably unattainable.

Communication theorists' understandings of communication competence, not surprisingly, vary according to their understanding of communication itself.

■ For linguistic pragmatists, communication competence includes a capacity for using language. However, situations do not all make identical demands on language, so competence must be evaluated in terms of some particular social circumstance. Communication requires both linguistic knowledge (for instance, participants must attach similar meanings to the messages transmitted) and non-linguistic knowledge. A minimal requirement for competence is that the individual is being co-operative – that is, makes his or her contributions as and when needed, according to the purposes of the interaction.[66]

■ Communication competence can be measured either situationally or disposition-ally. That is, it can be seen as particular to a given encounter or as a property of an individual. Cupach and Spitzberg showed that these are separate variables.[67] They also found that situational measures of competence predicted 'feel-good' reactions after an encounter better than dispositional measures.

■ Cognitive communication theorists define competence in terms of the mental processes required to achieve effective and efficient communication. Duran and Spitzberg found the following mental processes linked to communication competence:
  1. Planning (thinking before a conversation what people might be going to talk about, mentally practising what to say, during a conversation thinking about what topic to discuss next).
  2. Modelling (watching who is talking to whom when first entering a new situa-tion, trying to 'size up' the event; generally, studying people and being aware of people's interests).
  3. Presence (during a conversation being aware of when a topic is 'going nowhere', of when it is time to change the topic, paying attention to how others are reacting to what is said).
  4. Reflecting (after a conversation thinking about your performance and how to improve it and about what the other person thought of you).
  5. Consequence (thinking generally about how others might interpret what you say and how what you say may affect others).[68]
  Mindfulness is another view on how communication competence is achieved, which also focuses on individual mental processes.

■ Writers on communication strategy argue that competence is grounded in rational efficiency, rather than just effectiveness, that 'Given a desired end, one is to choose that action which most effectively, and at least cost, attains the end.'[69] In other words, both inputs and outputs must be considered in assessing communication strategies. Effectiveness is an 'output' consideration; it focuses on the results of strategy used and not on what effort or other resources it takes to employ a strat-egy. Conversely, efficiency focuses on both inputs and outputs; it considers the effort and resources that are used to achieve a given result.

■ There is an alternative view of communication competence that it consists, not in the attributes or performance of an individual, but in a given relationship.[70] According to this view, an individual may be socially skilled, but only particular communication relationships will be competent. This is because even the most skilled individual will certainly experience some failures of communication, and even the most unskilled will certainly experience some successes when they find people with whom they are congruent. This assertion receives some support from the research cited earlier which found that situational factors prevailed over individuals' dispositions. However, the term 'effectiveness' can still be used for analysis of communication relationships, 'competence' and 'skill' for the performance of each of the participating individuals.

Understandings of *intercultural* communication competence and effectiveness also vary according to different theoretical perspectives.[71]

■ In AUM theory effective communication means that participants attach similar meanings to the messages transmitted. (The importance of this factor is shown by research that found that when Black and White people interact in public meetings, they often assign different meanings to the matters under discussion. However, they tend to believe that the meanings they assign are the same, and on this basis ascribe negative motives to the other group.[72]) Effective intercultural communication also requires that individuals from one culture can attribute others' behaviour to causes, whether situation or personal or group disposition, that are the same as those of a native of the other's culture under the same conditions.

■ The facework approach to intercultural communication competence is a developmental model with four stages:
Stage 1 – unconscious incompetence: the individual is fundamentally ignorant both cognitively and behaviourally;
Stage 2 – conscious incompetence: the individual understands the behaviour issues but cannot deal with them; so, for example, an interlocutor may be aware that there are too many awkward pauses and silences but not be able to correct this;
Stage 3 – conscious competence: the individual cognitively understands communication differences between cultures and is conscious of facework;
Stage 4 – unconscious competence: this is the final, fully effective stage. As with driving a car or swimming, at a certain point it becomes spontaneous and natural. Adjustment and adaptation occur without conscious effort.[73]

Satisfaction with an intercultural encounter can be one measure of its effectiveness. A study found that the level of satisfaction expressed by participants in initial intercultural encounters was linked to three factors: perceptions of how well synchronised the conversation was, how difficult it was and how much common ground there was.[74] Chen provided a set of intercultural communication competence measures, which are shown in Figure 6.5.[75]

In a work context, international business managers identified the following seven dimensions of communication competence as predictors of the success of international and intercultural business management.[76] These predictors were confirmed by other empirical studies.[77]

1. How appropriately individuals adapt to new or ambiguous situations, acquire new learning and perform according to the standards and practices of the host society. Those who are unwilling or slow to adapt to new situations may have many problems in intercultural interaction.

2. The ability to show respect and positive regard for another person in interpersonal and intercultural relations. Respect is conveyed in a variety of ways – through eye contact, body posture, voice tone, voice pitch and general displays of interest.

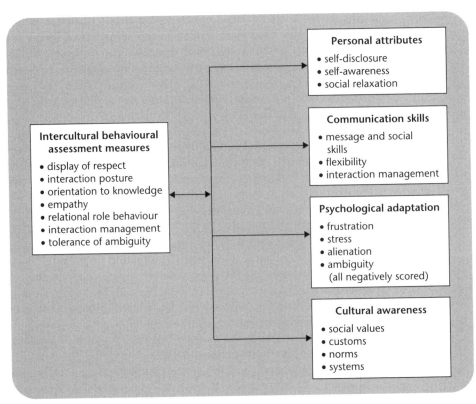

Personal attributes
- self-disclosure
- self-awareness
- social relaxation

Communication skills
- message and social skills
- flexibility
- interaction management

Intercultural behavioural assessment measures
- display of respect
- interaction posture
- orientation to knowledge
- empathy
- relational role behaviour
- interaction management
- tolerance of ambiguity

Psychological adaptation
- frustration
- stress
- alienation
- ambiguity (all negatively scored)

Cultural awareness
- social values
- customs
- norms
- systems

Figure 6.5   *Intercultural communication competence measures*

Based on: Chen, G.M. (1988) 'Relationships of the dimensions of intercultural communication competence'. Paper presented at the 79th Annual Meeting of the Eastern Communication Association, Baltimore MD.

Showing respect is a very important managerial skill for international business success.

3. The ability to understand others' situations and feelings through giving and receiving feedback, or empathy.

4. Interaction management, including negotiation of topics discussed, turn taking, entering and exiting episodes and handling topical development smoothly. Holding negotiations, conducting meetings, communicating decisions and making presentations are important for international business management.

5. The ability to respond to others in a descriptive and non-judgemental way. Judgement, evaluation and appraisal are major barriers to interpersonal communication. Withholding judgement is important in international business management.

6. Having the flexibility to explain things to different people in different situations in order to reach the same results. Research findings showed that maintaining flexibility in explanations predicted culture awareness and effectiveness in intercultural communication.[78] A survey indicated that the Vice Presidents of international business corporations perceived maintaining flexibility as an important skill for international business success.[79]

7. The ability to perform both relationship and task roles and to avoid self-centred roles. In intercultural interaction, developing a working relationship is the basis on which two parties can facilitate task roles. Without a good working relationship, business cannot be conducted between two parties.

There are cultural variations in what counts as communication competence and effectiveness, whether intercultural or not. Using low-context communication in a high-context culture counts as incompetent – too many words, too little use of silence; the reverse is also true – in a low-context culture, high-context communication may be seen as inarticulate and hesitant. Indirectness is ineffective where directness is the rule and vice-versa. An emphasis on relationship data is seen as 'soft' where content data is usually predominant (and, as the case of women illustrates, it also conveys a lack of authority and assertiveness); an emphasis on content data in a (sub)cultural milieu that prefers an emphasis on relationship data may be seen as an incompetent lack of subtlety and refinement. Cultural variations mean that the skills, such as tolerance of ambiguity, and the processes, such as uncertainty reduction, which have been tested and argued to be generalisable, may not be universally effective. Flexibility, respect, openness, confidence or self-control may reflect a Western cultural bias on individualism or low social distance.[80]

Some results have suggested a challenge to traditional intercultural competence criteria. The type of situation and the other participants within the situation may be more powerful determining factors than the particular intercultural communication competence traits possessed by individuals. Trait criteria are considered of 'limited value in differentiating between the actual behaviour *in situ* of culturally different persons'. For instance, the situation of firing an employee elicited communication behaviour judged less competent than that for promotion or selection, regardless of the culture or gender of the stimulus person.[81]

> Approaches to communication effectiveness and intercultural communication effectiveness include both stage models and lists of dimensions. Definitions vary with the theoretical perspective of the definer.

6.6 SUMMARY

The main psychological constructs, individual-level processes and interactive processes described in this chapter are set out in Figure 6.6. Despite the criticisms given in Section 6.4, the intercultural communication theories and research presented in this chapter collectively have carried our understanding a considerable way forward. Many of them also have the benefit of being readily applied in practice.

The techniques and approaches suggested in this chapter present individuals with a more complex interactional task than they may have understood to be necessary. However, it may be that such individuals have been living in a 'fool's paradise' in which lack of understanding, offence and even hostility went unrecognised; or that they have been imposing their 'definition of the situation' as members of a dominant group in an undemocratic and damaging way. There is an investment of energy and commitment needed to move through the stages of unconscious and conscious incompetence to first conscious and ultimately unconscious competence but there are both ethical and instrumental reasons for making that investment. Ethically, attempts to create a level playing field for members of minorities can be pointless if they are excluded or undermined by unskilled communication. Instrumentally, appropriate intercultural communication can help organisations win goodwill, attract the best talent, gain government business, do business with people from 'other' (sub)cultures, and have good industrial relations. For individuals, intercultural communication skills

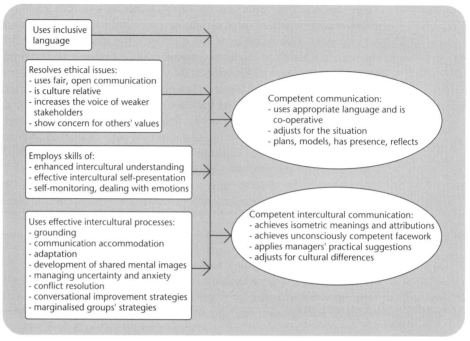

Figure 6.6 *Effective intercultural communication*

are an essential tool for providing services to, working as colleagues with or doing business with, people from backgrounds different from the individual's own.

QUESTIONS AND EXERCISES

1. Give inclusive alternatives to the following non-inclusive terms: businessman, chairman, clergyman, fellow worker, fireman, forefathers, foreman, freshman, layman, mankind, manpower, man-made, postman, poetess, spokesman, stewardess, suffragette, workman, gentleman's agreement, man on the street, straw man, right-hand man.

2. How realistic do you consider the various proposals for ethical intercultural work communication? Give your reasons.

3. Give an example of a cultural norm that you have which might be reviewed in the interest of cultural relativism. Explain your reasons.

4. Explain how intercultural social perceptiveness can be improved by the four kinds of awareness described in the book.

5. Suppose that in two days' time you will meet an important potential client from a country that you know little about. What steps could you take to enable yourself to predict more accurately his or her expectations, attitudes, behaviours and responses?

6. The text states, 'An appreciation of the context of an encounter is a useful tool in increasing intercultural effectiveness.' What assumptions underlie this statement? Discuss how far such assumptions are justified.

7. Can being aware of perceptual barriers to intercultural communication really help to increase effectiveness?

8. How might you set about trying to unlearn a prejudice that you have about people from a different culture?

9. Explain in your own words the behaviours that support becoming tolerant of ambiguity.
10. Complete the questionnaire.

	Strongly agree	Agree	Neither agree nor disagree	Disagree	Strongly disagree
1. An expert who doesn't come up with a definite answer probably doesn't know too much.					
2. I would like to live in a foreign country for at least a year.					
3. There is really no such thing as a problem that can't be solved.					
4. People who fit their lives to a schedule probably miss most of the joy of living.					
5. A good job is one where what is to be done and how it is to be done are always clear.					
6. It is more fun to tackle a complicated problem than to solve a simple one.					
7. In the long run it is possible to get more done by tackling small, simple problems rather than large and complicated ones.					
8. Often the most interesting and stimulating people are those who don't mind being different and original.					
9. What we are used to is always preferable to what is unfamiliar.					
10. People who insist upon a yes or no answer just don't know how complicated things really are.					
11. A person who leads an even, regular life in which few surprises or unexpected happenings arise really has a lot to be grateful for.					
12. Many of our most important decisions are based upon insufficient information.					
13. I like parties where I know most of the people more than ones where all or most of the people are complete strangers.					

cont'd

	Strongly agree	Agree	Neither agree nor disagree	Disagree	Strongly disagree
14. Teachers or supervisors who hand out vague assignments give one a chance to show initiative and originality.					
15. The sooner we all acquire similar values and ideals the better.					
16. A good teacher is one who makes you wonder about your way of looking at things.					

For guidance on how to score and interpret this questionnaire, see Appendix C

11. Give an example to illustrate three processes that comprise mindfulness.
12. What factors, according to Expectation States Theory, influence expectations and behaviour in intercultural encounters?
13. How can expectations of people from another (sub)culture be made both more supportive of intercultural communication effectiveness and less subject to violations?
14. Discuss Schwarz's list of communication rules for speakers to follow. Would they be appropriate for someone communicating with a person from your culture? Give reasons.
15. How can a relationship orientation be communicated? Does it conflict with getting the job done? Give your reasons.
16. An ethnic minority member of staff approached a manager with a request for extended leave to visit family abroad. S/he asked for a month off work to visit family and participate in a wedding/cultural celebration. S/he had two weeks of paid holiday unused and would expect to take the remainder of the time as unpaid leave. The manager found the request inconvenient, because its timing coincided with a peak workload period. The manager also feared that if this staff member were allowed this extra time off, all the other staff would want the same.

    (a) How should the manager respond?
    (b) Role play the meeting between the manager and the staff member.

17. How might individualist, achievement-oriented interlocutors need to adjust their behaviour in order to increase their affective resourcefulness?
18. A male asylum seeker entered an office and went straight up to a female receptionist. It was her task to understand what the issues were and to contact the appropriate officer for an interview. The asylum seeker arrived without an appointment, wanted to see someone straight away and seemed to behave aggressively. He jumped the queue, and demanded to see 'a professional'. The receptionist had experience of people from this asylum seeker's country and knew that they are normally polite in the old fashioned sense. It was possible that his perceived lack of courtesy had some underlying cause. Nevertheless, she gradually became annoyed.

    (a) How could the receptionist resolve the tension in this situation?
    (b) Role play the encounter between the receptionist and the asylum seeker.

19. Discuss ways of improving your communication with people with disabilities. Should your strategy vary according to the type of disability? Give reasons.
20. Discuss ways for members of minority groups to cope with others' prejudice, discrimination or harassment.

21. With a colleague from another culture, practise grounding in order to understand how a given business activity, such as advertising, or work activity, such as manager–labour negotiations, differ in their culture from yours.

22. List five implications of Adaptation theory that point to behaviours, expectations and understandings that are beneficial to intercultural communication and speeding progress with the task.

23. How can an interactor develop greater social skill by following the precepts of Episode Representation theory?

24. Complete the questionnaire.

	Strongly agree	Agree	Neither agree nor disagree	Disagree	Strongly disagree
1. I am guarded about the impression I make on others.					
2. I adapt my behaviour to the response I get from others.					
3. I have little difficulty in managing my feelings in new or unpredictable situations.					
4. In new or unpredictable situations I use trial and error until I see what works.					
5. I do not mind taking decisions in uncertain situations.					
6. In new and unpredictable situations I set my own feelings aside and act according to objective facts.					
7. I consider that other cultures are equal to my own, though different.					
8. Even with unfamiliar people or strangers I usually feel confident that I know why they say the things they do.					
9. I think it is very important to my sense of who I am that my mother tongue is the language that it is.					
10. My mother tongue is a major world language.					
11. I have an independent self-construal.					
12. I am a competent speaker of a second language.					

For guidance on how to score and interpret this questionnaire, see Appendix C

NOTES AND REFERENCES

1. Chen, I. (2003) 'Conversation orientation and cognitive processes: a comparison of U.S. students in initial interaction with native- versus non-native-speaking partners', *Human Communication Research*, **29**: 182–209.
2. Serdjénian, E. (1994) 'Women managers in France', in Adler, N.J. and Izraeli, D.N. (eds) *Competitive Frontiers*, Cambridge, MA: Blackwell.
3. This section is developed from The Human Relations Code of the University of Maryland at College Park. URL: http://www.inform.umd.edu/Student/Diversity_Resources.
4. Brinkmann, J. (2002) 'Business ethics and intercultural communication: exploring the overlap between two academic fields', *Intercultural Communication*, **5**. URL: http://www.immi.se/intercultural/nr5/abstract5.htm#brinkmann
5. Habermas, J. (1998) *On the Pragmatics of Communication*, Cambridge, MA: MIT Press.
6. Brinkmann, J. (2002) op. cit.
7. Deetz, S., Cohen, D. and Edley, P.P. (1997) 'Toward a dialogic ethic in the context of international business organization', in Casmir, F.L. (ed.) *Ethics in Intercultural and International Communication*, Mahwah, NJ: Lawrence Erlbaum Associates.
8. Hall, B.J. (1997) 'Culture, ethics, and communication', in Casmir, F.L. (ed.) *Ethics in Intercultural and International Communication*, Mahwah, NJ: Lawrence Erlbaum Associates.
9. Gudykunst, W. and Kim, Y.Y. (1997) *Communicating With Strangers: An Approach to Intercultural Communication,* 3rd edn, Boston, MA: McGraw-Hill.
10. Katriel, T. (1989) 'From "context" to "contexts" in intercultural communication research', in Ting-Toomey, S. and Korzenny, F. (eds) *Language, Communication and Culture: Current Directions*, Newbury Park, CA: Sage.
11. Mason, D. (1995) *Race and Ethnicity in Modern Britain*, Oxford: Oxford University Press.
12. Katriel, T. (1989) op. cit.
13. Rogers, K. (1951) *Client-centred Therapy*, London: Constable.
14. Gudykunst, W.B. (1988) 'Uncertainty and anxiety' in Kim, Y.Y. and Gudykunst, W.B. (eds) *Theories in Intercultural Communication*: pp. 123–56. Newbury Park, CA: Sage.
15. Langer, E. (1989) *Mindfulness*, Reading, MA: Addison-Wesley.
16. Burgoon, J.K. and Le Poire, B.A. (1993) 'Effects of communication expectancies, actual communication and expectancy disconfirmation evaluations of communicators and their communication behavior', *Human Communication Research*, **20**(1): 67–96.
17. Manusov, V. and Hegde, R. (1993) 'Communicative outcomes of stereotype-based expectancies: An observational study of cross-cultural dyads', *Communication Quarterly*, **41**(3): 338–54.
18. Ibid.
19. Babcock, R.D. and Du-Babcock, B. (2001) 'Language-based communication zones in international business communication', *The Journal of Business Communication*, **38**: 372–412.
20. Schwarz, N. (1994) 'Judgment in a social context: biases, shortcomings and the logic of conversation', In Zanna, M.P. (ed.) *Advances in Experimental Social Psychology*, **26**: 123–62, NY: Academic Press.
21. Berger, C.R. and Calabrese, R.J. (1975) 'Some explorations in initial interactions and beyond', *Human Communication Research*, **1**: 99–112. See also: Berger, C.R. (1987) 'Communicating under uncertainty', in Roloff, M.E. and Miller, G.R. (eds) *Interpersonal Processes*, Newbury Park, CA: Sage.
22. Applegate, J.L. and Sypher, H.E. (1988) 'A Constructivist theory of communication and culture', in Kim, Y.Y. and Gudykunst, W.B. (eds) *Theories in Intercultural Communication*, Newbury Park, CA: Sage.
23. Ting-Toomey, S. (1989) 'Communicative resourcefulness: an identity negotiation perspective', in Asante, M.K., Gudykunst, W.B. and Newmark, E. (eds) *Handbook of International and Intercultural Communication*, Newbury Park, CA: Sage.
24. Flynn, F.J., Chatman, J. and Spataro, S.E. (2001) 'Getting to know you: The influence of personality on impressions and performance of demographically different people in organizations', *Administrative Science Quarterly*, **46**(3): 414–42.

25. Snyder, M. (1974) 'Self-monitoring of expressive behavior', *Journal of Personality and Social Psychology*, **30**: 526–37.
26. Gudykunst, W.B. (1988) op. cit.
27. McCroskey, J.C. (1984) 'The Communication apprehension perspective', in Daly, J.A. and McCroskey, J.C. (eds) *Avoiding Communication: Shyness, Reticence and Communication Apprehension*: pp. 13–38. Beverley Hills, CA: Sage.
28. Kim M.-S., Hunter, J.E., Miyahara, A., Horvath, A., Bresnahan, M. and Yoon, H. (1996) 'Individual vs. culture-level dimensions of individualism and collectivism: effects on preferred conversational styles', *Communication Monographs*, **63**: 29–49.
29. Merrigan, G. (2000) 'Negotiating personal identities among people with and without identified disabilities: the role of identity management', in Braithwaite, D.O. and Thompson, T.L. (eds) *Handbook of Communication and People with Disabilities: Research and Application*, New York: Lawrence Erlbaum.
30. Fox, S.A., Giles, H., Orbe, M.P. and Bourhis, R.Y. (2000) 'Interability communication: theoretical perspectives', in Braithwaite, D.O. and Thompson, T.L. (eds) *Handbook of Communication and People with Disabilities: Research and Application*, New York: Lawrence Erlbaum.
31. Ibid.
32. Dunn, D. and Cody, M.J. (2000) 'Account credibility and public image: excuses, justifications, denials, and sexual harassment', *Communication Monographs*, **67**(4): 372–91.
33. Gianakos, I. (2002) 'Predictors of coping with work stress: the influences of sex, gender role, social desirability, and locus of control', *Sex Roles: A Journal of Research*, **42**: 1059–79.
34. Zapf, D. and Gross, C. (2001) 'Conflict escalation and coping with workplace bullying: a replication and extension', *European Journal of Work and Organizational Psychology*, **10**(4): 497–522.
35. Farley-Lucas, B.S. (2000) 'Communicating the (in)visibility of motherhood: family talk and the ties to motherhood within the workplace'. URL: http://www.nwrel.org/cnorse
36. Haslam, S.A., Oakes, P.J., McGarty, C., Turner, J.C., Reynolds, K.J. and Eggins, R.A. (1996) 'Stereotyping and social influence: the mediation of stereotype applicability and sharedness by the views of ingroup and outgroup members', *British Journal of Social Psychology*, **35**: 369–97.
37. Northwest Regional Educational Laboratory: CNORSE. 'Cross cultural communication: an essential dimension of effective education'. URL: http://www.nwrel.org/cnorse
38. Schwarz, N. (1994) op. cit.
39. Lee, B.P.H. (2001) 'Mutual knowledge, background knowledge and shared beliefs: their roles in establishing common ground', *Journal of Pragmatics*, **33**: 21–44.
40. Giles, H. (1977) *Language, Ethnicity and Intergroup Relations*, London: Academic Press.
41. Beebe, L.M. and Giles, H. (1984) 'Speech accommodation theories: a discussion in terms of second-language acquisition', *International Journal of the Sociology of Language*, **46**: 5–32.
42. Gallois, C., Giles, H., Jones, E., Cargile, C. and Ota, H. (1995) 'Accommodating intercultural encounters: elaborations and extensions', *Intercultural Communication Theory (International and Intercultural Communication Annual)* **XIX**: 115–46, Thousand Oaks, CA: Sage.
43. Ellingsworth, H.W. (1988) 'A theory of adaptation in intercultural dyads' in Kim, Y.Y. and Gudykunst, W.B. (eds) *Theories in Intercultural Communication*, Newbury Park, CA: Sage.
44. Leodolter, R. and Leodolter, M. (1976) 'Sociolinguistic considerations on psychosocial socialisation', in McCormack, W. and Wurm, S. (eds) *Language and Man*: p. 327. The Hague: Mouton.
45. Forgas, J.P. (1983) 'Social skills and episode perception', *British Journal of Clinical Psychology*, **22**: 26–41.
46. Forgas, J.P. (1976) 'The perception of social episodes: categorical and dimensional representations in two different social milieus', *Journal of Personality and Social Psychology*, **33**: 199–209.
47. Gudykunst, W.B. (1988) op. cit.
48. Rashotte, L.S. (2002) 'What does that smile mean? The meaning of nonverbal behaviors in social interaction', *Social Psychology Quarterly*, **65**(1): 92–102.

49. Triandis, H.C. (1980) 'Values, attitudes and interpersonal behavior', in Page, M. (ed.) *Nebraska Symposium on Motivation 1979*, **27**, Lincoln: University of Nebraska Press.

50. Baldwin, R. and Hunt, S.K. (2002) 'Information-seeking behavior in intercultural and intergroup communication', *Human Communication Research*, **28**(2): 272–86.

51. Gudykunst, W.B., Nishida, T., Koike, H. and Shiino, N. (1986) 'The influence of language on uncertainty reduction: an exploratory study of Japanese–Japanese and Japanese–North American interactions', in McLaughlin, M. (ed.) *Communication Yearbook Vol. 9*, Beverley Hills, CA: Sage.

52. Ibid.

53. Gudykunst, W.B., Yang, S.M. and Nishida, T. (1985) 'A cross-cultural test of uncertainty reduction theory: comparisons of acquaintance, friend and dating relationships in Japan, Korea and the US', *Human Communication Research*, **11**: 407–55.

54. Gudykunst, W.B. and Hammer, M.R. (1988) 'Strangers and hosts: an uncertainty reduction based theory of intercultural adaptation', in Kim, Y.Y. and Gudykunst, W.B. (eds) *Intercultural Adaptation*, Newbury Park, CA: Sage.

55. Gudykunst, W.B., Nishida, T. and Chua, E. (1986) 'Uncertainty reduction in Japanese–North American dyads', *Communication Research Reports*, **3**: 39–46.

56. Gudykunst, W.B., Sodetani, L.L. and Sonoda, K.T. (1987) 'Uncertainty reduction in Japanese–American/Caucasian relationships in Hawaii', *Western Journal of Speech Communication*, **51**(3): 256–78.

57. Brashers, D.A. (2001) 'Communication and uncertainty management', *Journal of Communication*, **51**: 477–97.

58. Leung, K. (1997), 'Negotiation and reward associations across cultures', in Earley, P.C. (ed.) *New Perspectives on International Industrial/Organizational Psychology*: pp. 640–75. Jossey-Bass, San Francisco, CA.

59. Brinkmann, J. (2002) op. cit.

60. Lin, X. and Germain, R. (1998), 'Sustaining satisfactory joint venture relationships: the role of conflict resolution strategy', *Journal of International Business Studies*, **29**(1): 197–214.

61. Lederach, J.P. (1995) *Preparing for Peace: Conflict Transformation Across Cultures*, Syracuse: Syracuse University Press.

62. Burton, J.W. (1996) *Conflict Resolution: Its Language and Processes*, Maryland: Scarecrow Press.

63. Lederach, J.P. (1995) op. cit.

64. Martin, J.N., Hecht, M.L. and Larkey, L.K. (1994) 'Conversational improvement strategies for interethnic communication: African American and European American perspectives', *Communication Monographs*, **61**(3): 236–55.

65. Jehn, K. and Weldon, E. (1992) 'A comparative study of managerial attitudes toward conflict in the United States and the People's Republic of China: issues of theory and measurement', *Annual Meeting of the Academy of Management 1992*, Las Vegas, NV.

66. Banks, S. (1989) 'Power pronouns and the language of intercultural understanding', in Ting-Toomey, S.F.K. (ed.) *Language, Communication and Culture*: pp.180–98, Newbury Park, CA: Sage.

67. Cupach, W.R. and Spitzberg, B.H. (1983) 'Trait versus state: a comparison of dispositional and situational measures of interpersonal communication competence', *Western Journal of Speech Communication*, **47**(4): 364–77.

68. Duran, R.L. and Spitzberg, B.H. (1995) 'Toward the development and validation of a measure of cognitive communication competence', *Communication Quarterly*, **4**: 259–75.

69. Kim, Y.Y. (1991) 'Intercultural communication competence: a systems-theoretic view', in Ting-Toomey, S. and Korzenny, F. (eds) *International and Intercultural Communication Annual*: pp. 259–75, Newbury Park, CA: Sage.

70. Wiemann, J.M. and Giles, H. (1988) 'Interpersonal communication', in Hewstone, M., Stroebe, W., Codol, J.P. and Stephenson, G.M. (eds) *Introduction to Social Psychology*, Oxford: Basil Blackwell.

71. Collier, M.J. and Thomas, M. (1988) 'Cultural identity: an interpretive perspective', in Kim, Y.Y. and Gudykunst, W.B. (eds) *Theories in Intercultural Communication*, Newbury Park, CA: Sage.

72. Kochman, T. (1983) *Black and White: Styles in Conflict*, Urbana, IL: University of Illinois Press.
73. Chen, G.M. (1988) 'Relationships of the dimensions of intercultural communication competence', Paper presented at the 79th Annual Meeting of the Eastern Communication Association, Baltimore, MD. http://www.flstw.edu/pderic.html
74. Chen, L. (2002) Perceptions of intercultural interaction and communication satisfaction: a study on initial encounters', *Communication Reports*, **15**(2): 133–47.
75. Chen, G.M. (1988) op. cit.
76. Kealey, D.J. (1989) 'A study of cross-cultural effectiveness: theoretical issues, practical applications', *International Journal of Intercultural Relations*, **13**: 387–428.
77. Zhao, J.J. and Ober, S. (1991) 'Communication skills needed by US international business persons', *Delta Pi Epsilon Journal*, **33**: 52–60.
78. Ruben, B.D. and Kealey, D.J. (1979) 'Behavioral assessment of communication competency and the prediction of cross-cultural adaptation', *International Journal of Intercultural Relations*, **3**: 15–47.
79. Zhao, J.J. (1991) op. cit.
80. Collier, M.J. (1989) 'Cultural and intercultural communication competence: current approaches and directions', *International Journal of Intercultural Relations*, **13**: 287–302.
81. Dinges, N.G. and Lieberman, D.A. (1989) 'Intercultural communication competence: coping with stressful work situations', *International Journal of Intercultural Relations*, **13**: 371–85.

part three

Extensions and Applications

chapter seven

Skills for Working Abroad

Increasing numbers of people have opportunities to take on international assignments or become expatriates working and living in a foreign country. For business managers and other staff these opportunities arise from factors such as increasing international competition and the resulting need to market products worldwide, international merger and acquisition activity and new market access opportunities (for instance in Eastern Europe). Globalisation of telecommunications, the rapidly increasing prevalence of the English language and specific developments such as the Erasmus programme of the European Union have created similar international opportunities for a wide range of non-business personnel, from students to doctors, footballers to musicians. Young people, particularly, have shown themselves eager to seize these opportunities for international experience. However, any international assignment poses challenges in terms of adaptive capabilities and cultural sensitivity; longer-term assignments require the person to cope with culture shock and the processes of sojourner adaptation as well as dealing with new roles and responsibilities in an unfamiliar context.

This chapter is concerned with how people who are working abroad can learn to cope with and in their new cultural environment. Clearly, all encounters taking place in an overseas host culture occur in a different context from those with different others in the 'home' country. Equally clearly, overseas visitors staying for a few days before returning home or moving on to another country are in a different situation from sojourners – people who are staying for at least a month in another country, either for work or study. (Immigrants are in a different situation again; this book does not cover issues confronting immigrants.) Therefore the chapter considers first the needs of all visitors who go to another country to work: Section 7.1 addresses cultural orientation skills. These include knowledge of the host country and culture, what problems to expect, and learning how to learn from in-country experience. Section 7.2 covers cultural adaptation – how to deal with culture shock, sojourner adjustment, acculturation, training and preparation. The material given in Chapter 6 is, of course, just as relevant and important to the subject of this chapter.

7.1 CULTURAL ORIENTATION SKILLS

Working internationally gives rise to problems of mutual understanding and appropriate self-presentation. Experiencing these difficulties can be stressful for the individuals

Box 7.1

(1) The consultant knocked, then immediately entered the manager's office, without waiting for a 'Come in.' (2) He was wearing a smart new sweater. (3) He held out his hand and said, 'Hi, Werner, how are you doing?' The manager looked somewhat cold, but shook hands and said, 'Good morning, Dr. X.' (4) X moved forward to a comfortable conversational distance. Werner backed away.

They sat down. (5) X said, 'You got my message, telling you I'd be late? Werner replied, still coldly, 'I'm afraid not.' 'That's odd, I spoke to Heidi myself.' (6) 'Ah,' Werner said, 'that explains it, Heidi does not take messages; she does not even work in this department.'

(7) The meeting, which was to settle the terms of the next stage of the consultancy project, dragged on and on, going over all the finest details. (8) X grew impatient. 'Let's cut to the issue, shall we? This could take all day.' The atmosphere grew even cooler. (9) X tried to lighten the atmosphere with a joke. Werner did not even smile. 'Can't we tie this up here?' X pleaded. (10) The manager looked shocked. 'I cannot make that level of decision. I will have to report to my Director.'

(11) 'We have experienced some difficulty with your company's performance, Dr X. I think you were given a report on the lack of precision in the initial findings, I might even say the lack of grasp of how important parts of our systems work. We would have expected this to be addressed and responded to in detail before proceeding to negotiate on the next phase.'

(12) 'But your overall assessment of our work was "satisfactory", wasn't it, and implementing the recommendations has brought cost savings, just as we said it would?' X replied. Werner responded, 'That is true, but that could have been mere good luck. It is difficult for us to have confidence for the future when you do not seem to have put in the work to really understand our operations in depth.'

X tried to defend his own and his colleagues' work. (They had followed the time-saving consultancy 'formula' successfully applied in many American and European companies – but he was not going to tell Werner Schmidt that.)

(13) However, the manager had every detail of the consultancy's promotional brochure at his fingertips, and firmly but politely refuted X's arguments point by point. X ended by subsiding into silence.

The responses of X's German client can be explained as follows:

(1) Entering a German manager's office without waiting to be invited in is a breach of manners and an invasion of the strong German sense of privacy. To enter without knocking would be unthinkable.

(2) Business attire in Germany is formal – suits, not smart sweaters.

(3) Manners are also formal – titles are used, first names are not, greetings are formal.

(4) Germans' spatial comfort distance is even greater than most North Europeans'.

(5) Punctuality is very important in German culture. Time is one of the 'principal ways of organizing life'.

(6) Most large German organisations are hierarchical and highly departmentalised. There is little lateral communication between departments.

(7) Germans see command of detail as one of their strengths, linked to their belief that they are more efficient than other people.

(8) The German manager may take impatience over a thorough examination of the project as a sign of lack of seriousness and thoroughness in the consultant's organisation.

(9) Germans regard jokes as inappropriate while doing business. In addition, like that of many nations, Germans' sense of humour is quite specific – X's joke may not have seemed funny to the manager.

(10) Unlike the French, Germans are willing to make decisions in meetings, but hierarchy sets firm limits on the discretion of individual managers at different levels.

(11) Germans regard open criticism of weaknesses as acceptable, even helpful. They regard themselves as having very high standards of performance and are critical when others seem to have lower

Box 7.1 *(cont'd)*

standards. They expect apologies and, in a business context, compensation, for failures.

(12) Germans require their business partners to be as thorough as they are themselves.

(13) Germans' method of arguing relies on absolute command of the facts – it can be very powerful.

Source: Based on the author's research

concerned. Institutional responses to the consequent needs of the individuals whom they send abroad to work are inadequate – training and preparation systems are generally poor.

In the words of Belay, 'Physical interconnectedness and interdependence among cultures and nations has reached a much higher level of development than the awareness and competency required from both individuals and institutions to handle this new reality positively.'[1] Working successfully internationally depends on having the necessary coping skills, resolving ethical issues that may arise in a foreign culture and dealing with the negative emotions aroused by the foreign culture.

Ability to cope in another culture

Coping on foreign assignments means being able to establish interpersonal relations with people from the host culture, communicate effectively and deal with psychological stress.[2] Ability to cope in another culture is affected by knowledge of the culture and its language, stereotypes of and attitudes towards people in the other culture, being able to suspend evaluation of other people's behaviour and understanding the self as a cultural being (i.e., being aware of one's own cultural identity).

■ Knowledge of the host culture and its language can be gained in several ways. These include reading books or articles, watching TV programmes or films, talking to people who have had extended contact with people from the other culture or talking directly to people from the other culture. Other ways of gaining information are by observing the members of the other culture interacting among themselves and by observing their behaviour when interacting with them. One of the best ways to learn about people in other cultures is to study their language. 'Without understanding some of the host language, it is not possible to understand their behaviour.'[3] This does not necessarily mean speaking the language fluently; however, the more of the language is understood, the more of the culture can be understood. Also, host nationals usually take making an effort to speak the language as a positive sign. It increases their desire to get acquainted. Two major factors that affect the amount and type of knowledge people obtain about other cultures are their motivation to adjust to living in the other culture and the nature of the contacts they have with people in the culture.

Knowledge of the host culture is needed to work out how people in the culture interpret and evaluate their own behaviour. For example, in Western countries, people greet each other with a handshake (and there are rules for what constitutes an appropriate handshake). In Japan, people generally do not shake hands. Rather, they bow (and there are rules as to what constitutes an appropriate bow). Though they are different behaviours, both shaking hands and bowing perform the same function, greeting another person. In another case, people may engage in the same behaviour, but use different rules. To illustrate, people may shake hands, but the rules for shaking hands appropriately may differ – in some cultures two hands are used. Knowing specific similarities and differences such as these is essential for knowing in detail how to behave. Knowledge of general cultural similarities and differences, such as whether another culture is collectivist or individualist, particularist or universalist, is also vital: it is needed for accurately interpreting the behaviour of people in another country.

■ Appropriate attitudes are needed to work effectively abroad. 'Once there is respect for different points of view as equally valid, there can develop a genuine desire to create new ways of working together. So long as individuals only accept the validity of their own view of the world, international working becomes a battle to get the French to follow the systems or to explain again to the Chinese that you are working to a deadline.'[4] The culture's own way of working probably represents the best way of doing things within a particular cultural context.

Respect towards the other culture is one necessary attitude; another is respect for the individuals with whom one interacts. These two attitudes can sometimes be lacking in, for instance, expatriates working in the former Soviet countries; the obvious deficiencies of some of the systems which operate (such as those referred to in Boxes 7.2 and 7.3) are translated into a broad disrespect for the entire culture and all its people, as in, 'They have no initiative,' or, 'They can all be bribed.' Such attitudes communicate themselves to the people among whom the expatriate is living and working. Naturally, they elicit responses that make the expatriate's life more difficult and thus more stressful.

It is also important to be willing to change one's own attitudes, sometimes in quite fundamental areas. One example is attitudes towards what constitutes success or failure; for instance, in the situation quoted in Box 7.2, the conference, seen as a

---

Box 7.2

A conference in Hungary, jointly organised by UK and Hungarian staff, had the following features:

Ninety-three invitations were sent out, only six replies were received by the start of the conference, and 72 people attended. The Hungarian staff said, 'Hungarian people have a bad habit: they do not reply to invitations.'

The conference was intended as a participative workshop. The Hungarian staff, in charge of on-the-ground arrangements, scheduled six presentations an hour for four hours, with no time allowed for questions. This was to be followed by a one hour 'discussion period'. The venue was the most formal room in the city's largest hotel; the seating was arranged round tables forming a huge hollow square. When the discussion period arrived (an hour later than scheduled) it was impossible to rearrange the room for group work, and, in plenary, discussion was stilted and consisted only of questions and comments addressed to the Chair.

The conference was ended sharply at six o'clock because, a Hungarian said, 'Hungarians always want to rush off home.'

The UK organiser felt the workshop had been 'hijacked' and had failed to fulfil its main purpose, which was networking. However, it had been impossible to insist on other arrangements, because the local people were obviously trying so hard according to their own preconceptions.

Source: Author's research

failure by the UK organiser, was regarded as a success by the Hungarians, who understood its purpose not as networking (reasonably enough, since that had not been explicitly stated) but as informing. The participants had learnt about the programme with which the conference was concerned; they had demonstrated their interest by seizing on all the brochures and by making follow-up enquiries by telephone.

- Describing others' behaviour before evaluating generally leads to understanding; evaluating prematurely leads to misunderstanding. There is a 'natural' human tendency to evaluate others' behaviour. Such evaluation, however, is generally based on an individual's own cultural standards. Using personal cultural standards to evaluate others' behaviour often makes it harder to understand them fully. To understand others, what is needed is first to describe what is observed; next, to look at alternative interpretations of the behaviour and then to try to work out which interpretation is most appropriate in the other culture. (To do this the knowledge gained about the other culture is needed.) Only then is it possible to evaluate the behaviour. Even then, unless it is necessary to decide whether or not to act similarly, it is better not to judge. Suspending judgement of others until the cultural logic behind their behaviour is understood is critical to making good decisions on how to react and behave towards them in various situations.
- Self-awareness overcomes the dangers of cultural self-imprisonment, which were pointed out in Chapter 5. Cultural self-awareness means being aware that usual approaches may be inappropriate.

A review of the literature suggested that cultural knowledge, cross-cultural understanding and a number of intercultural behavioural skills and situational variables are important for good intercultural relations.[5] Sojourners and short-stay international visitors alike should focus on three areas of objectives:

1. Behaviour objectives: to act in accordance with another culture's norms, or to create new 'third culture' patterns which incorporate elements of both home and host cultures.
2. Skills objectives, including communication and group process skills and skills of coping with cultural differences. Some personal qualities, such as openness, flexibility, a sense of humour and pluralistic values and attitudes are also helpful.
3. Knowledge objectives, which should be focused on the following:
   - Realistic expectations of the target culture(s), of which the most important are those that involve different attributions or interpretations of behaviour.
   - Information about roles and role relationships. This may be more useful than information about, for instance, economic, political and educational systems.
   - What problems to expect. Anticipating problems of the kind quoted in Box 7.3 comes with experience; other people's reported experiences can also be relevant, provided that the possibility of bias is borne in mind.

In an overseas host culture, there is a need both for specific knowledge of the kinds given in Boxes 7.2 and 7.3, and the more general understanding of cultural difference and similarity derived from the kinds of analysis presented in Chapters 2, 3 and 4.

Resolving ethical issues

There can be a dilemma over how far to accommodate to another culture when issues of principle are involved. For instance, although Japanese women are often highly

Box 7.3

'The settlement of our hotel bill was predictably exciting, since they tried to charge us $10 more than the quote for the room, and a dollar each for unsuccessful phone calls (which constitute an estimated 90 per cent of calls in Central Asia). The manager refused to take any responsibility for the error in the price quoted by the reception clerk, and when we insisted, he asked if he should punish the clerk by making her pay the extra $20! Appalling, of course, but this was classic Soviet policy, in which every employee was held personally responsible for errors in his [sic] work. This led to such practices as employing an extra staff person in a five-teacher English faculty, just to keep watch over and be responsible for the equipment and furniture of the faculty office and classrooms (a true example from Samarkand), and the absolute refusal of most employees to even consider performing the duties of an absent co-worker, which could expose them to additional liability.'

Source: Correspondence with a US aid worker in Uzbekistan; author's research

Box 7.4

'To transfer ... Chinese incumbent managers to lower or other positions, BGB (a UK/Chinese joint venture) can use the tactic of 'luring the tiger out of the mountain'. Once the 'Tigers' are out of their lairs, they will become less powerful. For example, a training program can be offered to them and while they are out studying or even sightseeing, a small non-production unit ... can be set up. After their return, they suddenly realise that they have been sent to the newly created unit. Though they will not be so pleased with the arrangement, they may feel it much better than involuntarily being put under the leadership of a newcomer.'

Source: Wang, W. (1996) 'Management development in Sino-foreign joint ventures', *London Business School*, Unpublished MBA Dissertation

educated, they are not widely accepted in the higher echelons of the corporate world. To send a woman, however senior, to negotiate in Japan is likely to prejudice the outcome. Yet for many Western organisations it is unthinkable to deny a woman such an assignment just on the grounds of her gender. Readers might wish to consider whether they would regard as ethical the solution advocated in Box 7.4 for a demotion situation.

In cases such as these, changing one's own attitudes, however desirable from the point of view of intercultural communication, may present not only psychological problems but also ethical or philosophical ones. One of the most difficult aspects of sojourning for work is trying to behave ethically when in another culture, particularly if that culture has values which are different from one's own. An 'honest' business person in a culture where bribes are routine, a teetotaller whose Russian hosts bring out a bottle of vodka to celebrate his/her arrival, or a vegetarian for whom they bring out caviar – such instances create real tensions between the need to be polite and the ethical need to adhere to one's own values. In addition, the elements of culture are interconnected; if someone thinks one element of culture should be resisted or changed, they need to consider whether it can be changed or resisted in isolation.

Dealing with negative emotions provoked by overseas encounters

Negative emotions are usually heightened when intercultural encounters occur outside one's own country as part of an international assignment or sojourn. Anxiety and stress are natural reactions to interacting intensively with members of other cultures or to living in another culture. Everyone experiences them to some degree. How well someone adjusts depends on how they cope with the stress and anxiety, not on whether they experience them. Anxiety and stress, therefore, are not 'bad' in and of themselves. In fact, anxiety provoked by unexpected reactions can serve as a cue that something is not right, and so stimulate ideas about how to adjust. There are many ways to cope with the anxiety and stress. 'Fighting' the other culture and looking down on its members, or 'taking flight' and interacting only with other members of one's own culture are both harmful. The most successful way to cope is to try to be flexible. This means adjusting behaviour to the situation by first observing the way things are done in the culture, keeping in mind that all members of the host culture do not behave in the same way. There can be tremendous variation in acceptable behaviour within a culture. These variations may occur because of education, age, social status, gender or individual differences. Armed with knowledge of how things are done in the host culture, new behaviours can be tried out; then the degree to which they were successful and enjoyable should be reflected on. Based upon reflection, a decision is made on whether or not to continue the new behaviour or try something different.

Equally, the same ways of coping used in the home culture to deal with anxiety and stress can generally be used in another culture. Ways that help include formal and informal relaxation techniques, exercise, talking to a friend about the problems, temporarily leaving the stressful situation, using humour and ensuring that you have at least one 'comfort zone' – one area of life which is continuous with your previous existence. Taking tranquillisers or other drugs, drinking too much coffee or coke or eating, smoking and drinking alcohol too often usually do more harm than good. Creativity in solving adjustment problems is also valuable.

> How people deal with working internationally ranges from functional ways such as adjusting behaviour to the situation to dysfunctional ways such as 'fighting' the other culture. Knowledge of the other culture, having appropriate attitudes, such as respect towards the other culture, describing others' behaviour before evaluating it, self-awareness, resolving ethical issues such as how far to accommodate to another culture and coping with negative emotions are all needed for success in working internationally.

7.2 SOJOURNING

Sojourners are people who:

- Grew up in (had their 'primary socialisation' in) one culture and moved, temporarily, but for at least a month, into another,
- Depend to some extent on the host environment for meeting their personal and social needs, and
- Are engaged in firsthand, continuous experiences with the host environment.

The real difficulties inherent in being a sojourner are demonstrated by studies that have shown that 16 to 50 per cent of US expatriates fail on foreign assignments.

Box 7.5

It takes about a month, anywhere in the world, before people begin to accept you. During that time, you wonder what on earth made you go there and how you're going to stand it. Then it gets better. I was asked at 7pm one Saturday in Scarsdale, New York, where, if I could have my pick, I'd like to be at this time. I said Magnetogorsk, in the bar. It's the unpredictability – anything could happen, but the most likely is that someone will do this to you (here he pressed the skin under his jaw), which means a party with the vodka flowing and the talk the liveliest on earth.

Source: Interview with an international executive: author's research

(Failing is defined as returning to the home country before the assignment is completed successfully – therefore not counting those who fail to perform satisfactorily but still stay on.) European and Japanese expatriates do better: 59 per cent of a European sample of organisations reported rates below 5 per cent, 38 per cent rates of 6 to 10 per cent and 3 per cent rates between 11 and 15 per cent. A study found that 70 per cent of US expatriates were sent abroad without any cross-cultural training. 90 per cent of their families also received no training, although the inability of the partner to adapt to the foreign environment is a very important cause of expatriate failure. Most of the US companies that did offer training provided only brief environmental summaries and some cultural and language preparation. Of the correspondents in the study's Western European sample 69 per cent sponsored training programmes to prepare candidates for foreign assignments. (The level was about the same in Japan.) Mostly, though, training was only for people sent outside Europe or the US, plus Eastern Europe.[6]

Another factor that may have contributed to poor adjustment is that, across many countries, job knowledge and technical or managerial ability appear to be most used for selecting international assignees. This means that little attention is paid to being able to cope in an 'alien' culture. Research that sheds some light on what these factors might be studied 338 international assignees from 26 diverse countries and 45 organisations, assigned to 43 diverse countries and performing diverse jobs. International assignees were defined as individuals posted from their home office to a host country subsidiary or branch. Five factors were identified by the international assignees themselves, in the following descending order of importance:

1. Family situation.
2. Flexibility/adaptability.
3. Job knowledge and motivation.
4. Relational skills.
5. Extra-cultural openness.

Importance ratings were not influenced by job type (managerial/non-managerial status) but they were by organisation type; in general, service organisation personnel attached more importance to relational and psychosocial factors, perhaps because they have more contact with the local community and host country nationals. These five factors accounted for over half the variance. Family situation was consistently important across all conditions.[7]

Culture shock

Part of the reason for the difficulties of international sojourners is expressed in the term 'culture shock'. This refers to feelings of anxiety and tension owing to loss of familiar customs and social interactions. Put differently, culture shock is a 'cumulative and debilitating state of disorientation, one that builds slowly from each experience in which the sufferer encounters contrary ways of perceiving, doing and valuing things'.[8] 'Culture shock' can appear in a number of guises, varying from mild to severe homesickness, feeling frustrated to suffering alienation and isolation. These feelings can be brought on by a number of things including the language barrier, loneliness, difficulty in penetrating the host society, not knowing how to react in a difficult situation and always being the centre of attention.

Adjusting to a relatively similar culture is often as difficult as adjusting to a 'distant' one. This may be because expatriates do not expect differences in relatively similar cultures.[9] However, Canadian research showed that people who admitted to higher levels of culture shock were the same people who were more effective on the assignment. It also found that the importance of personal variables may outweigh the situation – that is, that selection may outweigh training and social support. For example, of two individuals, one found the same situation constraining, the other liberating.[10]

The main characteristics consistently listed as negative factors for cultural adjustment include:

- National origin and perceived discrimination: in the USA, for instance, sojourners from African or Asian countries have more adjustment problems than Europeans do.
- Psychological depression.
- External locus of control.

The last two characteristics, depression and external locus of control, point to 'personality' factors. Canadian research also showed that personal variables were related to speed of adjustment: 'caringness' negatively, but self-centredness, self-monitoring, adroitness and low security-consciousness positively.[11]

Common symptoms of culture shock that have been identified include irritability, loneliness, depression and rigidity. Parallel symptoms to these have been described in the 'learned helplessness' literature. Therefore, one author suggests, the application of reformulated learned helplessness to cultural adjustment can contribute to understanding culture shock.[12] Learned helplessness is a person's belief that what happens to them and the outcomes of what they do are independent of what they do and how they do it; people suffering from learned helplessness attribute negative events internally, stably and globally ('global' here means that the cause is believed to operate on a large number of things, not just one). If people suffering from learned helplessness have a bad experience, they will tend to think it is caused by them, that the cause is long-lasting and unchangeable and that the cause will make other things bad, too. An individual's use of stable/unstable, global/specific, and internal/external attributions can affect his or her adjustment to a new culture. Figure 7.1 gives a flow chart of the possible relationship between learned helplessness and culture shock.

Culture shock and the need for a painful process of cultural adjustment have been described as 'universal aspects'.[13] Individuals are commonly disoriented when undergoing a transitional experience and the accompanying stress. Realising that what they are undergoing is 'normal' helps many individuals to tolerate stress.

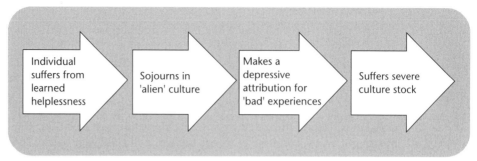

Figure 7.1   *Learned helplessness and culture shock*

Sojourner adjustment/adaptation

Despite problems of culture shock, most sojourners do eventually adjust to the point where they are coping and effective. How do they do it? Can the process be speeded up? One approach is to identify a series of stages that are usually gone through in the process of adjustment. In one such model the stages are:

1. Fascination. In the early days 'buffers' such as getting set up with work, accommodation, etc. prevent real contact with the host culture.
2. Hostility and aggression. As the buffers reduce, contact occurs and often leads to anger towards everything and sometimes everyone in the host culture. This is a critical point where the shock can develop into rejecting the host culture or accepting it and adjusting to the new surroundings.
3. Acceptance. The person then accepts the host culture as much as they can. This is never total but is sufficient to make life comfortable.
4. Adaptation. In spite of difficulties a person does his or her best to adjust to the new culture and refuses to give in to culture shock.

Motivation to adapt is the most important factor in how quickly individuals pass through these stages. Motivation to adapt depends partly on expected length of stay – the longer, the higher the motivation. Support programmes can ease the difficulties of sojourners when they first arrive. In the longer term, however, adaptation must occur primarily in the individual, not in the host society. In view of the importance of motivation, it is encouraging that a survey of expatriate managers on assignment to 59 countries, revealed that the majority of expatriates viewed their international assignment as an opportunity for personal and professional development and career advancement, despite perceived deficits in corporate career management systems and a widespread scepticism that the assignment will help their careers.[14]

According to Ady sojourner adjustment is a relatively short-term, individual and time-based process that is conceptually distinct from cultural or ethnic assimilation, adaptation or intercultural communicative competence. Ady argued that adjustment occurs, not 'globally' but in specific domains. There are many domains, but they can be grouped into three classes:

■ Task domains (employment and daily structuring tasks).
■ Social support domains (friendships, interaction with host nationals).
■ Ecology domains (physical aspects of the new environment).

In each separate domain, adjustment occurs as a function of the sojourner's judgement of how well s/he is meeting the demands of the environment and how well the environment is meeting his/her needs; total adjustment is a function of adjustment in all three domains. Figure 7.2 shows the model.

Ady put forward four axioms concerned with sojourner adjustment:

1. It is multidimensional.
2. It varies across domains and over time; some happen more quickly than others.
3. It is experienced by sojourners as happening through a series of crises.
4. It is experienced by sojourners as non-gestalt.[15]

Ady also contended that adjustment is highly salient to sojourners. While it is going on, the problems and solutions associated with it are often central in the sojourner's consciousness.

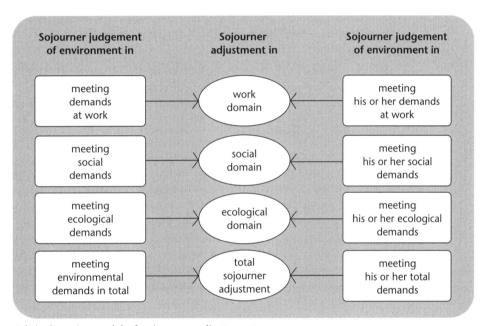

Figure 7.2   *Ady's domain model of sojourner adjustment*

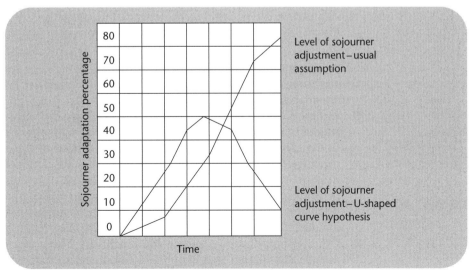

Figure 7.3   *Sojourner adjustment over time: U-shaped curve hypothesis*

There is a pessimistic model of sojourner adjustment, represented by a u-shaped-curve as illustrated in Figure 7.3, which hypothesises that after an initial 'honeymoon' stage sojourners often become frustrated with day-to-day living and retreat to the stability and comfort of home-culture friendships. Strom reported a study which, he argued, tends to support this hypothesis. Fifty-eight pairs of students, of whom half were from abroad and studying in an ESL (English as a Second Language) programme and half were home-country students in a university intercultural communication class, met for ten weeks in a cultural partners programme. During the programme, they conversed in English and were encouraged to make friends. The ESL students were tested at weeks two and ten for English proficiency, intercultural communication competence, interest in learning about culturally different others, interest in making friends with culturally different others, their number of cross-cultural acquaintances, number of cross-cultural friends and homophily. The overall impact of the cultural partners programme, Strom reported, appeared negligible:

- The intercultural communication skills of ESL students did not improve.
- Their desire to learn about other cultures did not increase.
- The only increase in intercultural friendships was with their programme partners.
- The university students were not perceived as having become better intercultural communicators either.[16]

There are several possible explanations for these findings: one is that the time spent together was too short, another that the students were reacting to unmet expectations (the programme had been explained to them as a social exercise). However, a third explanation, Strom suggested, is that the findings go to confirm the U-curve adjustment hypothesis. He concluded, 'Competence is a transactionally created phenomenon between unique communicators in specific contexts and not easily defined as an enduring trait across contexts.' This view implies that people cannot acquire a transferable skill for adjusting to new cultural environments, but must repeat the learning process and curve with each new sojourn.

Conversely, a more optimistic model of sojourner adaptation proposes that human beings have an inherent drive to adapt and grow; that adaptation to one's social environment occurs through communication and that adaptation is a complex and dynamic process.[17]

The process involves at least the following elements:

1. Unlearning some old cultural habits.
2. Learning new responses.
3. A stress-adaptation-growth dynamic:
   - In new environments, people find that they have difficulty in coping. They suffer from 'information overload', uncertainty about others' expectations, difficulty in interpreting others' communication and so on. These disequilibrating experiences are stressful. An initial response to stress, for many individuals, is to resort to defence mechanisms, such as selective attention, self-deception, denial, avoidance, withdrawal, hostility, cynicism and compulsively altruistic behaviour. Fortunately, these responses, which are not helpful to adapting, are temporary in most cases.
   - Other responses to the new environment are adaptation responses. They include assimilation (acting on the environment so that aspects of it may be

adjusted to their internal needs) and accommodation (responding to the environment by adjusting to the external realities). These occur through learning elements of the new culture and unlearning elements of the 'old'.

■ Adaptation responses lead to growth – in particular to an increased ability to adapt to further environmental changes. As they gain experience at making the transition to a new host environment, people get better at it.

As they begin to adapt successfully, sojourners show increased functional fitness (they can perform more effectively, both at work and in living), improved psychological health (they start to feel more cheerful), which is directly related to an increased ability to communicate, and an expanded and more flexible sense of themselves as people (they begin to have an intercultural identity).

However, sojourners go through the processes of intercultural adaptation at different rates – some adapt quickly, others more slowly, a few not at all. There are reasons for these differential rates. Some differences are related to the individual, but many, research suggests, are more closely related to the host environment: some countries and organisations are easier to fit into than others. Figure 7.4 shows the main influences.

A sojourner's ethnic identity is a key factor in their individual predisposition to adapt successfully. A strong ethnic identity tends to mean that adjustment initially

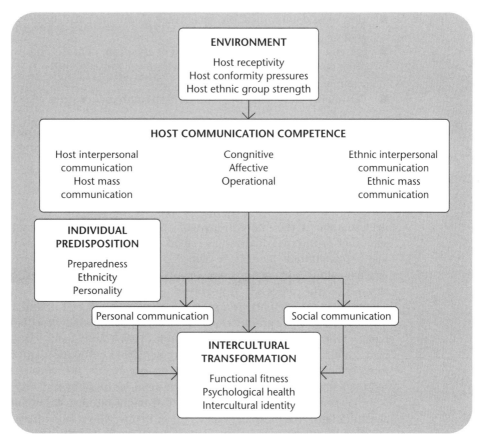

Figure 7.4   *Factors affecting individuals' rates of intercultural adaptation*

Box 7.6

A study of 52 international female managers who had worked in Asia found that they were overwhelmingly successful. Most of these women were the first female expatriates to be sent abroad to the role; only 10 per cent followed another woman into the international position. Therefore, no rules or role models existed. The decision process leading a company to send a female manager to Asia could be described as one of mutual education between management and the employee. The following is a quote by a US female manager based in Hong Kong: 'It doesn't make any difference if you are blue, green, purple, or a frog. If you have the best product at the best price, they'll buy.' US female expatriates were viewed first as Gaijinî (foreigners), then as women.

Source: Adler, N.J. (1994) 'Competitive frontiers: women managing across borders', in Adler, N.J. and Izraeli, D.N. (eds) *Competitive Frontiers: Women Managers in a Global Economy*, Cambridge, MA: Blackwell

occurs quite rapidly but then declines – there is a U-shaped curve; a weak ethnic identity is more likely to produce a slow but steady increase in adjustment.

Some empirical support for this stress-adaptation-growth model of sojourner adaptation can be found, as follows:

- Host mass communication, such as television, has been shown to help sojourners adapt.
- Extreme stress reactions in the form of escapism, neurosis and psychosis are most often seen among those whose native culture radically differs from that of the host community.
- Personality factors like openness and strength reduce stress reactions.

Finally, there is evidence that many employees seek out co-workers most like themselves as a way to reduce culture shock. The support of such groups helps some newcomers on the job and can promote self-esteem.[18]

Acculturation

Acculturation is the establishment of an 'intercultural identity' for an immigrant, sojourner or international assignee who successfully integrates into a new environment. Intercultural identity is achieved when an individual grows beyond their original culture and encompasses a new culture, gaining additional insight into both cultures in the process.[19] It involves understanding the norms and values, and adopting salient reference groups of the host society. Acculturation and acquiring an intercultural identity presuppose that the visitor's simplified view of the host society is replaced with a more realistic, more complex view. Competence in the language of the host country, being highly motivated to achieve acculturation and having access to interpersonal and mass communication experiences are the three factors which have most bearing on gaining more realistic perceptions of the host country.

It has been argued that additional stress might result in faster and more effective acculturation.[20] For example, Canadians in Kenya 'who would ultimately be the most effective in adapting to a new culture underwent the most intense culture shock during the transition period.' When stress is extreme, 'human plasticity' is activated to form the person more fully into a more complete intercultural identity: in longer stays (those of immigrants for instance), initial high stress levels result in more complete acculturation, an earlier adoption of an intercultural identity and lower stress levels eventually.

Evidence to support the acculturation model has been found.[21] Studies of international students showed that those students with the most host-national contact also showed the most adaptation, that 'psychological stress is found in individuals who attempt to integrate' and that longer stays resulted in more acculturation. It was also found that language ability was correlated to feeling at ease and satisfied with an international student experience. Evidence that initial stress can lead to eventual acculturation was found in studies of the spouses of international students. Amongst such spouses, stress was widespread. 'Initial feelings of sadness, loneliness, self-doubt, confusion, and frustration were present in their descriptions of the first weeks and months of the sojourn.'[22] Language difficulties made this initial stress worse. However, a 'positive change of mood usually happened within the first 3–6 months from arrival,' thus confirming the view that in time 'strangers become increasingly proficient in managing their life activities in the host society'.[23]

Conversely, there is some evidence that successful exchange student experiences are more related to expectations than to acculturation. Sojourners have consistently reported that expectations were met or positively violated. This may mean that the value of stress to acculturation has been overstated, as well as the value of acculturation to a successful experience. 'The notion of self-fulfilling prophecy accounts for the similarity between expectations and fulfilment of these expectations.'[24]

In Anxiety/Uncertainty Management theory, anxiety and the resulting stress is expected to drive sojourning individuals towards uncertainty reduction and eventual acculturation in the new culture. However, Witte considered that culture shock results in acculturation only when acculturation into the new milieu appears to be manageable. If the danger in a fear-provoking situation appears to be manageable, individuals' preferred adaptive response is to take action to reduce the danger. If the danger in a fear-provoking situation seems to be too large to handle, however, or danger reduction strategies are absent, fear reduction takes over and the danger is ignored or rationalised away. Such responses to new cultures would result in maladaptive seclusion, and not result in acculturation of the individual or the society.[25]

Learning how to learn from in-country experiences

There is a model, based on the concept of a 'learning cycle', of what sojourners need to do to learn from in-country experience.[26] The core model, shown in Figure 7.5, proposes that people who learn effectively from experience go through a recurrent cycle of concrete experience, reflective observation, abstract conceptualisation and active experimentation. For example, the first time native English-speaking sojourners enter a discussion in English with someone for whom it is a second language, they might speak very slowly, using simple words and sentence structures. If the local person's response uses more sophisticated words and phrases and is spoken more quickly than expected, the sojourners might reflect that this indicates that they are more fluent in English than anticipated and that a slow, emphatic style might have been somewhat insulting – this would be reflective observation. The sojourners might go on to think that in general it would be better to obtain as much information as possible about other people's level of English language competence before giving away their expectations – this would be abstract conceptualisation. Next time they met a 'stranger' for

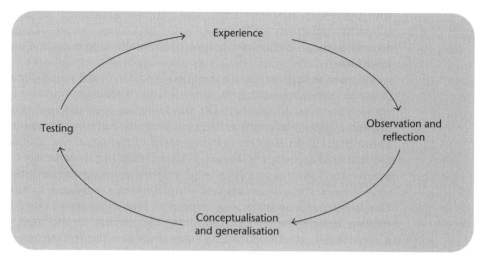

Figure 7.5   *Kolb's model for learning from experience*

a discussion in English, they might try to ask one or two open questions initially, to encourage the stranger to speak, thus giving themselves the opportunity to listen and gauge the other's language competence before themselves saying much – this would be active experimentation.

Research based on the model has shown that the process of learning from experience can be speeded up and more can be learnt by actively engaging in this cycle: seeking more experience, reflecting on it more, generalising from it more and testing the resulting 'model' more. There are, however, some cautions that users of the model need to bear in mind, especially if they are using it as a vehicle to understand different others:

■ *Concrete experience.* People with different backgrounds, such as those from other cultures, are likely to have had quite different experiences.
■ *Reflective observation.* Due to the variety of behaviour patterns, artefacts and institutions in different cultures, people from different societies are likely to acquire different bodies of knowledge and to make different assumptions about what is true.
■ *Abstract conceptualisation.* Since people from different cultures have different cognitive frameworks, there is a risk of using inappropriate frameworks in cross-cultural situations or of focusing on irrelevant information, while ignoring important cues, resulting in incorrect interpretations.
■ *Active experimentation.* Since cultures differ in behavioural patterns, cross-cultural situations may be misdiagnosed, resulting in inappropriate responses. Alternatively situations may seem unfamiliar and confusing, in which case sojourners may not know how to respond. Even when they know what to do, new behaviours may be difficult to perform smoothly.

These rather negative points can be made positive aids to learning from in-country experience, though, by regarding them as areas to which learners need to give particular attention. In this way they will enhance awareness of areas where intercultural misunderstanding can occur. Unrewarding or punishing experiences of any kind, as behaviourist learning theory teaches, can lead people to avoid or suppress the kind of behaviour which they associate with the negative reinforcement. For example, people who suffer embarrassment in an intercultural encounter because of ignorance of cultural norms may have a tendency to reduce exposure in future. This tendency, according to the learning cycle model, will reduce their speed and eventual level of intercultural orientation. One way to overcome this is by increasing knowledge in the areas where embarrassment is likely; another is to pursue a conversational strategy designed to minimise exposure to embarrassment; a third is to 'condition' the self to such embarrassment as an inevitable and productive element in gaining intercultural understanding: the arousal created by embarrassment will, according to cognitive learning theory, enhance the ability to learn.

Training for international assignments and sojourns

Clearly, the better prepared sojourners are for their visit to a country with a markedly different culture from their own, the more likely they are, other things being equal, to succeed in adjustment, adaptation or acculturation. The evidence on expatriate failure and distress therefore makes sojourner training of great concern. To date most training has concentrated on cultural content: how the host culture differs from the sojourner's home culture, especially on the surface. In cultural awareness models the emphasis is on cultural insight, with individual awareness an expected by-product. One type is the 'Contrast home culture' model, which aims to assist in recognising the sojourner-to-be's own culture's values as a first step in relating across cultures and so focuses primarily on cultural filters. Usually the contrasting culture is not intended to be seen as any specific one. So-called orientation models of sojourner adjustment have been criticised for failing to help sojourners learn and adapt once in the host country. The assumption underlying orientation models is that adaptation is primarily an intellectual process. In fact, though, emotional and behavioural adjustments give sojourners most difficulty. 'If the trainee has only learned specific bits of data and generalizations about a culture, his [sic] everyday experience with individual members of that culture will quickly invalidate a major portion of the content knowledge he has received. ... This difference between teaching for knowledge and teaching for performance and adaptation comprises the fundamental criticism of this model.'[27] Once they arrive in the host country,

■ Trainees will be experiencing a new environment and will need to understand approaches to deriving information from new sources; they will need to categorise the information in new ways, internalise it and use it to accomplish new goals or solve new problems.

■ They will be shifting their learning environment from the classroom to an experiential environment, that of existence in another culture.

■ The experiential learning environment will be intrinsically learner-centred (i.e., it will require adjustment from the learner).

■ Sojourners will be in an environment where:
  □ All cultural cues are ambiguous, if not intimidating.
  □ Their language skills may not be adequate to meet their needs.
  □ They are deprived of the ordinary reinforcement routinely received in the home culture.

Simulation or area training models try to allow for these considerations. They rely on reproducing situations and conditions that closely duplicate the actual overseas site and assignment. However, the drawback of these models is their cost. Opportunities to participate in a ten-week intensive residential training programme abroad are few. Another attempt is the self-awareness model, which is based on the principle that sojourners who understand themselves better will understand their culture better and consequently be more effective abroad: 'Cultural self-awareness stands as an important prerequisite component to learning the other culture's world view.' These models use T-group and role-play training methods. However, a T-group is an American invention, built on the American values of openness, equality, individuality and directness. For individuals from non-American cultural backgrounds, T-groups can be too challenging and so unhelpful. Another variant, 'sensitivity groups', are 'in all probability … counterproductive in intercultural training.'[28]

Sojourners cannot be trained to know everything they need about the target culture. Much will have to be learned from experience on arrival. Sojourners need to recognise that 'cultural diversity is not an intellectual endeavour but laden with values, beliefs and interpersonal complexities.' Sojourner training should enable trainees to develop intercultural skills to the level where they can use them independently.[29] Intercultural communication workshops may best achieve this objective. They focus on communication in a context of value differences. These workshops usually feature a small group experience with members of at least two different cultures, led by trained facilitators. The workshop becomes a laboratory in which members observe themselves.

Dealing with roles and responsibilities in an unfamiliar work environment

There is evidence that the work context usually provides lower levels of culture shock and an easier adjustment for the expatriate than private life. There is an 'international culture' of work which creates continuity between countries. Nevertheless, as earlier chapters of this book have shown, organisational cultures and the behaviour and expectations of colleagues, superiors and subordinates do vary cross-culturally, and the pressure may be exacerbated by the need to adjust quickly. Working successfully internationally depends on the relationships that the individual forms. A survey of 232 expatriates found that those who became involved with local businesses and communities felt less role ambiguity and had higher job satisfaction and more influence within their own companies than those who did not. Their influence was based on their ability to relay local information and identify opportunities that met the needs of their company. Local experience and the diversity of social networks available affected the extent of expatriates' boundary spanning, but having previous international work experience did not have much effect.[30]

Another study examined instrumental and expressive ties among 457 managers in a multinational enterprise (MNE). Instrumental ties arise in the performance of work and facilitate the transfer of physical, informational or financial resources. Expressive ties provide friendship and social support. The study demonstrated that managers form strong expressive ties with peers who are from culturally closer countries and from the same status group. However, strong instrumental ties appeared to be maintained by managers with different rather than similar background characteristics. This may be because expatriate managers make a conscious effort to overcome the barriers of their cultural background and status and to work extensively with local staff. Most interactions among managers in MNEs have both instrumental and expressive aspects. For example, formal vertical reporting relationships are often complemented by informal coaching and mentoring, while friendships and informal collegiality can lead to successful teamwork in formally appointed groups.[31]

Sojourning, which means medium-term residence in and, usually, working or studying in, a foreign country, makes high demands on individuals' ability to cope. Many international 'assignees' actually fail and return home. Selection that ignores cultural adaptation potential and poor preparation and training are widely blamed for this problem.

Nearly all sojourners experience culture shock. The problem is less, though, for people who speak the host country language competently, who have sojourned before and who do not suffer from learned helplessness. To deal with culture shock, it helps to understand that it is normal. To adjust and adapt to a new culture, it helps to recognise that stress can lead to adaptation and growth. The techniques for coping with stress and for experiential learning can be used to facilitate adaptation. Training and preparation need to be appropriate and effective. The work context partially reduces the effect of sojourning but may increase other pressures. Forming links to local businesses and communities provides expatriates with more job satisfaction and influence, though most obtain their social support from people from similar backgrounds. Task relationships, however, are often strongest with people from the host country.

7.3 SUMMARY

Working internationally calls for coping skills and behavioural adjustments as well as the cultural awareness and intercultural communication skills described in previous chapters. Sojourners usually suffer from culture shock; there are a number of models of how to achieve adaptation, acculturation and the ability to work effectively in a foreign environment.

QUESTIONS AND EXERCISES

1. Describe four factors that influence ability to cope in another culture.
2. Give examples of the following kinds of knowledge needed by sojourners and short-stay visitors to another country: (a) realistic expectations of the target culture, (b) information about roles and role relationships and (c) what problems to expect.
3. Give examples of two ethical issues that may create intercultural difficulties for people working on foreign assignments, and discuss how they may be overcome.
4. List six functional mechanisms for coping with anxiety and stress induced by intensive exposure to another culture.
5. Give your own intercultural example of the application of Kolb's learning model to learning from in-country experiences.
6. How can international assignees overcome the tendency to avoid intercultural experiences following an unrewarding or punishing experience?
7. How would you implement the text's recommendation that it is valuable to seek some degree of match between an individual's culture and the culture of the country to which they are assigned?
8. (a) What is 'learned helplessness'? (b) How does it relate to culture shock? (c) What are the implications of this relationship/analogy for overcoming culture shock?
9. Describe the four stages of a sojourner adaptation model.
10. Discuss the contention that sojourner adjustment is a relatively short-term, individual and time-based process that is conceptually distinct from cultural or ethnic assimilation, adaptation and intercultural communicative competence.

11. Discuss the contention that sojourner adjustment occurs in different domains in different ways and at different times.
12. Discuss the contention that during sojourner adjustment, the problems and solutions associated with it are often central in the sojourner's consciousness.
13. Discuss the contention that people cannot acquire a generic skill of adjusting to new cultural environments, but must repeat the learning process and curve with each new sojourn.
14. Explain the 'stress-adaptation-growth dynamic' theory of sojourner adaptation.
15. Which is more realistic, the U-shaped curve hypothesis or the 'stress-adaptation-growth dynamic' theory of sojourner adaptation? Give your reasons.
16. What are the outcomes of successful sojourner adaptation?
17. How does a sojourner's ethnic group identity strength affect his or her sojourner adaptation?
18. Explain in your own words the meaning of 'acculturation'.
19. The material in the text on acculturation identifies from the literature seven independent variables as leading to successful sojourner adjustment. These are: host country language competence, motivation, access to interpersonal and mass communication experiences, stress, expectations, anxiety and attributional confidence. Draw a diagram to show the relations among these variables. How would your own set differ, if at all, from these?
20. Bennett gives a set of four challenges faced by 'learners' in a host country. What are they?
21. Complete the following questionnaire, which assesses readiness for overseas location.

	Strongly agree	Agree	Neither agree nor disagree	Disagree	Strongly disagree
1. I look forward to meeting and getting to know some of the people in a foreign country					
2. I am willing to learn about the history, geography, arts, sports or politics of the foreign country					
3. I will try to learn the language					
4. I am willing to leave behind friends and family, and to reach out to make new relationships					
5. I am capable of giving up my job or my role as spouse/parent without great resentment or stress					

	Strongly agree	Agree	Neither agree nor disagree	Disagree	Strongly disagree
6. I am willing to leave behind the identity I have established in my community or job to go where no one knows of my accomplishments, interests, talents or foibles					
7. I am in good health and physically able to live overseas					
8. I am emotionally strong					
9. I truly want to go on this assignment					

URL: http://www.adm.uwaterloo.ca/infoiso/dest/settle/culture.html

NOTES AND REFERENCES

1. Belay, G. (1993) 'Toward a paradigm shift for intercultural and international communication: new research directions', *Communication Yearbook*, **16**: 437–57.
2. Gudykunst, W.B. (1988) 'Uncertainty and anxiety', in Kim, Y.Y. and Gudykunst, W.B. (eds) *Theories in Intercultural Communication*, Newbury Park, CA: Sage.
3. Gudykunst, W.B. (1988) op. cit.
4. Tayeb, M.H. (1996) *The Management of a Multicultural Workforce*, Chichester: John Wiley.
5. Dinges, N. (1983) 'Intercultural competence', in Landis, D. and Brislin, R.W. (eds) *Handbook of Intercultural Training, Vol. 1*, New York: Pergamon Press.
6. Baumgarten, K. (1995) 'Training and development of international staff', in Harzing, A.-W. and Ruysseveldt, J.V. (eds) *International Human Resource Management*, London: Sage.
7. Arthur, W. Jr. and Bennett, W. Jr. (1995) 'The International assignee: the relative importance of factors perceived to contribute to success', *Personnel Psychology*, **48**: 99–114.
8. Schreiber, E.J. (1996) 'Muddles and huddles: facilitating a multicultural workforce through team management theory', *The Journal of Business Communication*, **33**: 459–73.
9. Shenkar, O. (2001) 'Cultural distance revisited: towards a more rigorous conceptualization and measurement of cultural differences', *Journal of International Business Studies*, **32**(3): 519–35.
10. Kealey, D.J. (1989) 'A study of cross-cultural effectiveness: theoretical issues, practical applications', *International Journal of Intercultural Relations*, **13**: 387–428.
11. Ibid.
12. Reinicke, M.J. (1986) 'Cultural adjustment of international students in the U.S.: A re-evaluation using reformulated learned helplessness' *(ERIC Document Reproduction Service No. ED 274 939. URL: http://www.flstw.edu/pderic.html*
13. Martin, J. (1986) 'Training issues in cross-cultural orientation', *International Journal of Intercultural Relations* **10**: 103–16.
14. Günter, K.S., Miller, K.N. and Tung, R.L. (2002) 'Toward the boundaryless career: a closer look at the expatriate career concept and the perceived implications of an international assignment', *Journal of World Business*, **37**(3): 216–27.

15. Ady, J.C. (1995) 'Toward a differential demand model of sojourner adjustment', in Kim, Y.Y. (ed.) *Intercultural Communication Theory (International and Intercultural Communication Annual) XIX*, Thousand Oaks, CA: Sage.
16. Strom, W.A. (1994) 'The effects of a conversational partners program on ESL and university students', *Howard Journal of Communications*, **5**(1 and 2): 138–56.
17. Kim, Y.Y. (1988) *Communication and Cross-cultural Adaptation: An Integrative Theory*, Philadelphia: Multi-Lingual Matters.
18. Schreiber, E.J. (1996) op. cit.
19. Kim, Y.Y. (1992) 'Development of intercultural identity', Paper presented at the annual conference of the International Communication Association, Miami FL.
20. Ibid.
21. Ward, C. and Kennedy, A. (1993) 'Psychological and socio-cultural adjustment during cross-cultural transitions: a comparison of secondary students overseas and at home', *International Journal of Psychology*, **28**(2): 129–47.
22. De Verthelyi, R.F. (1995) 'International student's spouses: invisible sojourners in the culture shock literature', *International Journal of Intercultural Relations*, **19**: 387–411.
23. Kim, Y.Y. (1988) 'Facilitating immigrant adaptation: the role of communication', in Albrecht, T. and Adelman, M. (eds) *Communicating Social Support*: pp. 192–211. Newbury Park, CA: Sage.
24. Martin, J.N., Bradford, L. and Rohrlich, B. (1995) 'Comparing pre-departure expectations and post-sojourn reports: a longitudinal study of U.S. students abroad', *International Journal of Intercultural Relations*, **19**: 87–110.
25. Witte, K. (1993) 'A theory of cognition and negative affect: extending Gudykunst and Hammer's theory of uncertainty and anxiety reduction', *International Journal of Intercultural Relations*, **17**: 197–215.
26. Hughes-Weiner, G. (1986) 'The "learning how to learn" approach to cross-cultural orientation', *International Journal of Intercultural Relations*, **10**: 485–505.
27. Bennett, J.M. (1986) 'Modes of cross-cultural training: conceptualising cross-cultural training as education', *International Journal of Intercultural Relations*, **10**: 117–34.
28. Ibid.
29. Martin, J. (1986) op. cit.
30. Au, K.Y. and Fukuda, J. (2002) 'Boundary spanning behaviors of expatriates', *Journal of World Business*, **37**(4): 285–96.
31. Manev, I.M. and Stevenson, W.B. (2001) 'Nationality, cultural distance, and expatriate status: effects on the managerial network in a multinational enterprise', *Journal of International Business Studies*, **32**(2): 285–303.

chapter eight

Culture and Work Activities

Chapter 2 introduced the idea that cultural differences may be reflected in aspects of work such as roles and norms, attitudes to groupwork, manager–subordinate relations and organisational cultures. This chapter explores cultural differences in specific work activities. It also examines ways of working interculturally and internationally. The work activities covered are selection interviewing (Section 8.1), negotiating (8.2), mediating (8.3), working in groups and teams (8.4), leadership and management (8.5) and working in international alliances (8.6). Performing these work activities effectively in an intercultural setting depends on all the knowledge, understanding and skills described in earlier chapters. The content of this chapter supplements but does not replace that material. Figure 8.1 depicts the relationship of this chapter to the earlier ones.

8.1 SELECTION INTERVIEWING

Statistics suggest that interviews are by far the most widely used tool for selecting job candidates, and are the only means for 85 to 90 per cent of companies. Although applicants' objective credentials, such as job experience or academic performance, often determine who is invited to interview, they are far less important for hiring decisions than performance in the interview itself.

Cultural differences in selection interviews

How interviewers are received and treated in any environment is affected by the cultural response set of that society.

■ Respondents in some cultures often discern what they perceive the interviewer wants to hear, and modify their answers to comply with this perception. This stems from various attitudes held by respondents, such as courtesy to guests (the interviewers), the desire to satisfy them so that they may leave happy, having collected the information they 'wanted', and/or a lack of trust in the interviewers. Biases also arise because the interviewee perceives the interviewer as higher in status and, in selection interviews, higher in power.

■ The assumption that the respondents are aware of the meaning and methods of questioning is often not realistic in countries where the tradition of interviewing is not well established. Therefore, the scope for misunderstanding about what is required and its purpose is wide.

■ In some countries, the presence of other person(s) during the interview affects the response of the interviewee, depending on who this person is.[1]

Different self-presentations may be related to a (sub)culture's 'social rules'. For instance, a series of findings have shown that Chinese applicants tend to defer to the interviewer (who is categorised as a superior) and to focus on the group or family, besides being averse to self-assertion.[2] Gallois and Callan pinpointed Indians' emphasis on qualifications and their modesty about skills and individual contributions. In contrast, North European interviewers tend to prefer an emphasis on work achievements and assertiveness. Indians emphasise 'self-worth' in terms of other people's opinions of them – diplomas are authentic credentials; they want to show they can fit in rather than make their mark.[3] Similarly, in selection interviews, East German interviewees avoided showing disagreement with the interviewer or assertiveness. They seemed to 'orient more to the asymmetry of the encounter, whereas West Germans (interviewers as well as interviewees) seemed to play it down'. For example,

	Interviewing (8.1)	Negotiating (8.2)	Mediating (8.3)	Working in groups and teams (8.4)	Leadership and management (8.5)	Working in international alliances (8.6)
Diversity awareness (Ch. 1)	✓	✓	✓	✓	✓	✓
Cultural knowledge and awareness (Ch. 2)	✓	✓	✓	✓	✓	✓
How culture affects communication (Ch. 3)	✓	✓	✓	✓	✓	✓
How culture affects behaviour (Ch. 4)	✓	✓	✓	✓	✓	✓
Barriers to intercultural communication (Ch. 5)	✓	✓	✓	✓	✓	✓
How to communicate effectively across cultures (Ch. 6)	✓	✓	✓	✓	✓	✓
Working abroad (Ch. 7)	?	?	?	?	✓	✓

Figure 8.1　　*The relationship of the sections of Chapter 8 to previous chapters*

Box 8.1

The diversity of a company's existing workforce shows its commitment to diversity, according to 16 per cent of respondents to a survey. One third of the respondents indicated that they eliminated a company from employment consideration because of lack of gender or ethnic diversity. Among Black job applicants, 44 per cent of those surveyed reported that they had eliminated employers from consideration because of their lack of ethnic diversity. 'Research shows that companies that are the most successful in this area use creative recruitment practices, supported by a strong track record of deployment and promotion of diversity within their organizations.'[a]

A survey found that UK business employers prefer people with South East or Home Counties accents, because they expect them to be more reliable. Most disliked were the accents of large urban areas like Liverpool, possibly because these are associated with urban deprivation.[b]

Sources: (a) Leonard, B. (2001) 'Diverse workforce tends to attract more female and minority job applicants', *HR Magazine*, April 2001
(b) BBC 11 o' clock News 29 September 2003 (Hamer, A., University of Liverpool)

Box 8.2

During a selection interview, an Asian woman collapsed in tears and said her fierce Moslem father would not approve of her getting career advancement and so she could not go through with it.

A Japanese candidate kept using a term the interviewer could not understand. When she asked, the word was 'role'. This led to an impassioned plea for help: 'I'm finding my communication skills are not succeeding, it's proving disastrous for my career.' She had an inspiration: she asked for a few demonstration words she chose to be spoken, and established he'd also learned basic French and German. So she explained how much of English is based on French and German, historically. She pointed out how therefore it is rich in very varied synonyms. He could try avoiding words with 'r' and 'l', which are 'traditionally' difficult for Japanese people to say. Instead he could use their synonyms. She demonstrated this by writing a list of synonyms for 'role', but with hard consonants – for instance, 'job', 'post', 'position', 'task', etc. This produced an equally impassioned, 'Thank you, thank you. You've changed my life.'

Source: Contributed by a recruitment consultant, author's research

one East German interviewee, asked if she ever had any argument with her boss, denied it, stating that the reason was: 'I am respectful.' This was interpreted by the interviewer as implying that she would not be able to handle conflict either with a manager or in a team. Yet, later in the interview, she gave an example of handling a conflict with a manager very effectively. Again, when an East German interviewee was asked by a West German interviewer to say what she could bring to the job, she answered in terms of thinking she would find the job very interesting. To describe what her colleagues would say they like about her, she answered impersonally: 'That's a good question; one has to be, as I said, like everyone else, be on time ... everybody has their clients, one is interested, wants to ring them all.' The researchers concluded, 'Eastern candidates display a tendency to shift to unspecified, generalized perspectives

Box 8.3

X was interviewing Czech applicants for a graduate-level entry post with the Prague subsidiary of an international business. The applicant was neatly dressed, polite and soft-spoken. The C V showed a record of high scholastic achievement, participation in sports and leadership in student affairs. However, when it came to the 'standard' selection interview questions, although the applicant listened carefully and seemed to understand them, X found it difficult to get the kinds of answers he was used to.

For example, in response to the question, 'What are your greatest strengths?' the candidate hesitated, laughed, blushed, then said, 'I'm not sure. I am very interested in working for your company because it has such a good reputation.' When X pressed, saying, 'Yes, but what could you bring to our company? Why should I give the job to you instead of someone else?' the interviewee said, 'I am hardworking and I would be a loyal worker, but, of course, I'm sure all the other applicants would, too'.

Asked about ambitions, the candidate replied, 'To have interesting work and to serve my country'. Asked about a hypothetical situation in which a factory production problem had led to a chaotic disruption of deliveries to customers, the candidate said, 'I would need more information before I could answer, really.' Pressed once more, the applicant described a process in which the situation would gradually be brought under control through careful rationalisation. Asked about the most important factors in business success, the candidate answered, 'Solving problems creatively, being concerned for the well-being of others, being flexible.'

Based on: Author's research

in a variety of contexts. The examples given illustrate that the subjective perspective is replaced by an unspecified impersonal one and requests for an individual perspective are answered with a generalized one referring to a higher authority.'[4]

Factors in intercultural selection interviewing effectiveness

In job interviews, equal opportunities and diversity approaches can conflict. It used to be considered that a standardised interview procedure, which eschewed discriminatory questions ('How would your husband feel about your doing this work?'), ensured equal and therefore fair treatment. It is now recognised that some candidates may, for reasons of local knowledge or cultural background, be less able than others to answer the same 'fair' questions. Something subtler is needed, if the organisation is actively seeking to achieve a diverse workforce. Both the questions and the evaluation of candidates' answers need to take differences in cultural background into account. This makes cultural awareness a priority requirement for intercultural selection interviewers, who should also be self-aware of their own tendencies to bias, stereotyping and monocultural blindness. Evidence suggests that interviewer assessments of similarity and job-related competence (person–job fit) are important factors in stimulating their overall liking and final evaluations of applicants, and that interviewees' self-presentation is the strongest influence on these assessments. From a study of 72 real taped interviews it was found that interviewers' perceptions of person–job fit were strongly influenced by candidates' self-promotion. Their non-verbal impression management influenced perceived similarity.[5] Since there are cultural differences in both non-verbal behaviour and the acceptability of self-promotion, these biases of selection interviewers can distort selection.

Interviewers influenced by their own cultural rules and identity may misjudge candidates. A more subtle bias can occur where interviewees do not conform to stereotypes. A British study found that when selection interviewers assessed matched samples of male and female career applicants, they judged them by different criteria according to their gender. The applicants were penalised if they did not conform to gender stereotypes. Focusing on successes was very important in assessing the men but almost ignored in assessing the women; women, but not men, who self-deprecatingly took responsibility for poor performance ('I should have worked harder.') were rated highly; men were favoured for giving long answers, women for short; women who gave sideways glances, looked at the floor, cocked their heads and nodded when the interviewer talked were preferred, whereas men who faced the interviewer head on did better. Loud voice was preferred in both genders – this was the only similarity. The researcher said she hoped that the research findings would help to prevent employers from 'taking against a talented woman just because she doesn't act demurely enough'.[6] Another study showed experimentally that even selection interviewers who avoid discriminating may be biased. White undergraduate experimental subjects who acted as selection interviewers appointed Black and White applicants in equal proportion. However, a week later they recalled the Black interviewees as giving less intelligent answers, although they had actually given the same answers.[7]

Earlier in this book, it was shown how violations of expectations may disproportionately influence responses to different others. This applies to both interviewers and candidates. In the case of candidates, their expectations in an interview are likely to be influenced by the normal approach taken in their home country. 'The recruitment process is largely determined by the conventions and legislation requirements of the country in which it takes place. In Greece, the culture of recruitment and selection seems to sanction a greater degree of inquisitiveness about personal circumstances, than in the UK. Questions may be asked about family background and origins, marriage – questions which would be technically illegal and to which candidates could exercise a "right to lie" elsewhere in the [European] Community.'[8]

In international interviews, the questioner must observe lexical equivalence (asking the questions so that they mean the same in two or more languages) and conceptual equivalence (the transfer of concepts from one culture to another). This requires a high degree of understanding and knowledge of the local language and culture.

> Intercultural selection interviewers should be aware of and allow for cultural differences in candidates' approach to being interviewed. This applies both to the questions asked and the evaluation of the answers.

8.2 NEGOTIATING

Cultural differences in negotiation

International business negotiations are characterised by two levels of differences beyond those found in domestic business negotiations: individual level differences (in negotiator priorities, preferences, perspectives and scripts) and societal level differences (in national endowments, preferences (tastes), legal, economic and political systems and government involvement).[9] Intercultural negotiations, whether international or not, are affected by cultural differences in negotiators' behaviour,

Box 8.4

Establishing joint ventures in China is a test of cross-cultural negotiation under conditions of uncertainty within a complex network of constraints. On one side is the huge Chinese company, heavily bureaucratic and focused on taking care of all dimensions of its employees' lives. On the other side is the Western enterprise focused on quality performance and financial effectiveness.

Source: Faure, G.O. (2000) 'Negotiations to set up joint ventures in China', *International Negotiation Journal Abstracts*, **5**(1). URL: interneg.org/interneg/reference/journals/ in/volumes/5/1

goals, communication patterns, perceptions, values and norms. Individualism-collectivism is an important dimension of these differences. For instance, North Americans negotiate by exchanging information, aiming to encourage the other side also to exchange information expeditiously; the Japanese, however, attempt to develop a smooth, harmonious relationship that will eventually facilitate consensual decision-making; exchanging information is secondary. Americans are concerned about time efficiency; this leads them to focus on points of disagreement in an attempt to resolve them. For the Japanese, taking time to create a relationship is seen as a sign of wisdom and sincerity; focusing on disagreements is disliked as undermining harmony. Americans do not value strong interpersonal relationships in business and rely on legal contracts to define future relationships; for the Japanese, legal contracts are not acceptable substitutes for interpersonal trust.[10] Americans and Japanese also tend to have a different view of the purpose of negotiations. Americans see the goal of negotiations as to produce a binding contract that creates specific rights and obligations. The Japanese see the goal of negotiations as to create a relationship between the two parties; the written contract is simply an expression of that relationship. What the Japanese see as a reasonable willingness to modify a contract to reflect changes in the parties' relationship, Americans see as a tendency to renege. The Japanese may perceive American insistence on adherence to the original terms of the contract as distrust.

Other negotiator differences are based in concepts of time, power distance or universalism/particularism. Negotiators such as North Americans and West Europeans, who hold monochronic concepts of time, are more likely to process issues sequentially and to negotiate in a highly organised fashion. In contrast, negotiators with polychronic conceptions of time, such as Asians, Africans, South Americans and Middle Easterners, are more likely to process issues simultaneously. They tend to ignore conversational turn-taking, instead speaking simultaneously and using frequent interruptions. North Americans have been shown to regard their option of ending a negotiation as a source of power, whereas Japanese think of power as based on roles (e.g., buyer versus seller).[11] 'Some cultures prefer to start from agreement on general principles, while others prefer to address each issue individually. Some cultures prefer to negotiate by "building up" from an initial minimum proposal; others prefer to "build-down" from a more comprehensive opening proposal. Cultural differences also show up in the preferred pacing of negotiations and in decision-making styles.'[12]

In addition to the general differences in values and norms that have been described earlier in this book, some specifically negotiation-related norms and values differ across cultures. These differences include:

- The extent to which cultures perceive negotiations to be strategic or synergistic.
- The criteria by which they select their negotiators (e.g., by seniority or technical expertise).
- The significance they attribute to relationship building.
- Their concern with formality and protocol.
- Their predisposition for type of persuasive argumentation (e.g., emotional or logical).
- Their basis for trust (either written laws or mutual respect among the parties involved).
- Their propensity to take risk.
- The value they ascribe to time.
- Their system to make final decisions on the negotiation matter (e.g., authoritative or consensual).
- Their predisposition towards written contracts or oral agreements as binding.[13]

Factors in intercultural negotiation effectiveness

When negotiations expose differences on culture-based norms and values, not only can conflict be triggered, but also the negotiators are likely to experience negative moods and emotions. On the other hand, when expectations in these areas match, they can lead to positive feelings helpful to the negotiation process.[14]

Despite these findings on cultural difference, it is important not to see negotiators' behaviour as culturally determined. Negotiations 'are affected not only by culture but by contextual constraints, such as negotiator personality, organizational culture, age, prior relationship, experience, presence of interpreters, intercultural competence of the negotiators, countries' legal and economic systems, and roles'.[15] Research in which negotiation interactions were coded for information sharing, offers and distributive tactics showed that the more collectivist the orientation of a negotiation dyad, the higher its joint profit. However, culture had no direct effect on competitiveness or information exchange; it did affect the level of fixed-pie errors (the tendency to assume that one side's gain must be the other side's loss). The strongest effect found, though, was that seller collectivism has larger and more consistent effects on communication behaviour and joint profit than buyer collectivism. (The researchers suggested that these results support the 'culture in context' perspective, described in Chapter 2. This perspective takes into account negotiator qualities, contextual and structural features of the negotiation, and mediating processes in addition to cultural values.)[16]

Negotiators have mental models of negotiations in terms of such dimensions as relationship versus task, co-operation versus winning and emotional versus intellectual appeals. These models, or frames, often mutually influence each other, converging during the interaction. In turn, the frames affect individual and joint monetary outcomes, as well as satisfaction with the outcomes. The other party's frame influences each negotiator's behaviour. One negotiator sends messages that communicate the frame. In return, the responding negotiator sends messages adopting, rejecting or modifying this frame. Then a short period of initial interaction solidifies the mental models of the negotiators, resulting in a script that carries through the negotiation. When the parties do not come to a common model of the interaction, the negotiation is much more likely to result in impasse or widely disparate payoffs than when a single model is shared, regardless of how the shared model defines the interaction. This

Box 8.5

Negotiations are central to the functioning and dynamic development of the European Union. Historically, force, equilibrium or hegemony have underscored regional integration schemes in Europe, but, in contrast, the European Union is a voluntarily agreed arrangement of sovereign or semi-sovereign states that solve their conflicts by means of non-coercive negotiations. Due to its complex structure, the EU encourages the formation of networks, and negotiation is the most important vehicle for establishing and keeping these networks in operation.

Source: Pfetsch, F.R. (1998) 'Negotiating the European Union: a negotiation-network approach', *International Negotiation Journal Abstracts*, **3**(3). URL: interneg. org/interneg/reference/journals/ in/volumes/ 3/3

makes communication that supports harmonisation of mental models a key factor in intercultural negotiation.[17]

In experimental research, intercultural negotiators usually achieve worse joint outcomes than intracultural negotiators. A combination of power struggle, focus on self-interest and insufficient information sharing may produce this effect. However, negotiators who are motivated to search for information, and are flexible about how that search is carried out, can reach high-quality outcomes in intercultural negotiations.[18] Again, while differences between cultural 'scripts' can create conflict over procedure, differences in preferences present opportunities for compromise. For example, cultures that differ in their perceptions of risk can create value by sharing risks and benefits proportionally but asymmetrically. (One side can assume more risk, and have a chance of gaining more benefit, than the other. Because of their different risk preferences, both sides gain from this.) Moreover, it can be effective to balance the cultural preferences of both sides. For instance, if one party's cultural preference is to develop relationships and the other's is to exchange information, they can follow a procedure which begins by developing relationships with others, then leads to exchanging information about the topics under negotiation. Balance might also be reached by recognising multicultural techniques of persuasion and also emphasising the role of concessions in achieving agreement. However, there is as yet no evidence that an individual negotiator can transcend his or her own cultural background.[19]

> There are cultural differences in negotiators' behaviour, goals, communication patterns, perceptions, values and norms. While these differences can lead to conflict, differences in preferences present opportunities for mutually satisfying procedures and outcomes. Communication, which makes harmonisation of mental models possible, is a key factor in intercultural negotiation.

8.3 MEDIATING

Mediation has been defined as follows: 'Efforts by parties external to an immediate conflict, with no advance commitment by the conflicting parties to accept the mediator's ideas, which seek to bring about a settlement or resolution acceptable to both sides.'[20] Third parties can get round misperceptions, perceptions of threat and miscommunication. Mediators aim to understand each party's perceptions of the other party and the situation.[21] A basic assumption of much literature on international conflict, mediation and social psychology is that the process of mediation can modify the stereotypes or images that conflicting parties hold of each other; this change, it is argued, facilitates settlement. Three case studies of international conflicts found support for this assumption. The conflicts studied were the Israeli–Egyptian conflict from 1973 to 1979, the conflict between Greek and Turkish Cypriots from 1979 to 1983 and the Iran–Iraq war from 1980 to 1985. In the one case (Egypt–Israel) where resolution was reached, images did change in a way that correlated with mediation efforts over time. In the two cases (Cyprus, Iran-Iraq) where no resolution was obtained, no image change occurred.

Factors in intercultural mediation effectiveness

In some (collectivist) cultures, third-party mediation is almost a standard approach to conflict resolution. Where that applies, using a mediator may be the best strategy for intercultural conflict resolution. Carnevale and Choi suggested that in this way culture could play a positive role in the mediation of international disputes. 'Cultural ties between the mediator and one or both of the disputants can facilitate mediation by, among other things, enhancing the mediator's acceptability to the parties, and enhancing the belief that the mediator can deliver concessions and agreements. Moreover, a mediator who is closer to one side than the other can be effective in mediation, especially when the mediator acts in an even-handed manner.'[22] Data from laboratory research on mediation, as well as anecdotal evidence, support this view. All mediators confront three issues: the matter of impartiality, how to deal with the emotional and psychological dimensions of conflict in the mediation process and how to ensure that mediation empowers the participants rather than disempowering them.

- Mediators must be and be seen to be impartial. Impartiality means giving equal respect to the parties involved and treating them with equal fairness. All the parties concerned need to trust the mediator. If one of the parties perceives the mediator as biased, they will probably withdraw or disrupt the process in some way. To be seen as impartial, mediators emphasise 'good process' and technical impartiality. This refers to the mediator's ability to treat all people with respect, manage the mediation process in a way that is fair and even-handed, listen deeply to what each party is saying, identify deeper emotions and needs, and, through the skill of paraphrasing, determine whether each party has been adequately understood by all.
- The emotional aspects of conflict can lead to conflicts being recycled. 'A mediation session produces an outcome. Both parties seem relieved and satisfied. A few months later, however, the same parties are in conflict again. Different issues appear on the agenda, but with strong indications that the conflict is deriving its energy from the same deep emotional storage tanks.'[23] Mediation should not be terminated once a superficial settlement is achieved. Solutions sought on the level of, for instance pay packages and disciplinary procedures, do not make anger go away. To deal with the emotional aspects of conflict, mediators need to be in touch with their own feelings and recognise their own prejudices. Training to be a mediator can therefore never be only about acquiring technical skills; it has at the same time also to be about personal growth and maturity.
- Mediation has the potential to create greater equality in power relationships. It can empower the relatively disempowered. (This fact, however, creates a dilemma, because it is precisely its potential to equalise relationships that raises suspicions in

people who have power.) The deepest form of empowerment takes place when the knowledge and skills necessary for constructive conflict resolution are transferred in a way that enhances participants' understanding.

Successful mediation does not always result in resolving conflict. Partial success may be recognised when there is a decrease in the level of conflict intensity and an increase in useful communications between the parties, or when there is 'de-escalation in the means of struggle, negotiations that move toward an agreed-upon settlement and a settlement that contributes to an enduring resolution'.[24]

Leading authorities on intercultural mediation advocate a non-directive approach. This approach assumes that the best solutions are produced when parties listen to each other in a new way, co-operate in generating options and jointly arrive at the preferred solution. There should be no form of coercion or manipulation by the mediators. The parties must solve their own problems, because in this way their self-respect is served and the outcome is more sustainable. The role of the mediator is therefore to be a facilitator of communication. The mediator's task is to enable the parties to listen to each other on a deeper level than their previous hostile attitudes allowed. A mediator must ensure that the parties have heard each other adequately, and that each has developed sufficient understanding of the other's perceptions, motivations and interests. The mediators rely heavily on their listening, paraphrasing and summarising skills, checking continuously whether people have been correctly understood. Improved listening then leads to better mutual understanding, which strengthens the drive to reach a solution that takes the interests of all parties into consideration. Non-directive mediation uses a basic procedure. This procedure includes the parties themselves establishing procedural ground rules, allowing ample time for digressions, ensuring uninterrupted time for each side to state their perceptions and feelings, and joint problem solving.

Non-directive mediation is highly appropriate in situations where parties need to co-operate in future because the level of interdependence is high, and especially where conflicts are fuelled by basic differences in values or worldviews. Under such conditions the emphasis of mediation on promoting mutual understanding and on improving relationships is to be preferred over approaches that rely on arbitration or coercion.

> In intercultural conflicts or negotiations, particularly where the parties will need to co-operate in future, mediators can get round misperceptions, perceptions of threat and miscommunication. Being and seeming impartial, dealing with emotions and empowering participants are key issues for mediators. To ensure that the parties understand one another, mediators need high levels of listening, paraphrasing and summarising skills.

8.4　WORKING IN GROUPS AND TEAMS

This section considers the effect of cultural difference and diversity both on decision-making (problem-solving) groups and on teams entrusted with carrying out a project or performing a function.

Cultural differences in groupwork

It is no surprise that the processes at work in complex work decision settings are influenced by cultural factors. Culture affects participants' experience of variable decision situations, how predictable the environment is and how great the level of power distance is. In turn these variables affect how group members approach decision-making. For example, in a complex decision task, German managers used different decision-making processes from Indian managers, even though the latter worked in modern technological industries. Specifically, though both groups performed equally well, the German managers achieved their results with comparatively few but 'strong' decisions. The Indian managers achieved their results with many small steps. The researchers commented that both the 'massive' German and the 'incremental' Indian approach appear to be effective in their respective economic environments. Highly unpredictable economic environments, such as those in India, mean it makes sense to start with some small steps, closely monitor the effects and then gradually increase the size of decisions in those avenues that have proved reliable. In a more predictable environment, such as the German, probable outcomes of decisions can be anticipated and there is less risk involved in making strong decisions. The German and Indian decision-making styles may also be related to cultural differences in power distance. 'Large power distance could be related to cautious and defensive decision making whereas small power distance should work in the direction of risk-taking and assertiveness.'[25]

Similarly, in different cultural contexts, different patterns of expectations arise concerning team roles, scope, membership and objectives. At a general level, it is true, most definitions of a team are likely to include what a team does and for whom it does it, the scope of its activity, who is on the team (roles), why (the nature of membership, especially whether voluntary or compulsory), and the reason why the team exists (its goals and objectives). However, the specific content of what people mean by teamwork varies across cultures. This can be revealed by the metaphors they use. For instance, if the national context is individualist, then sports or club metaphors are more likely to resonate than those that imply a broader activity scope. An emphasis on tight control in the culture means that a military or family metaphor is likely to resonate.[26]

Factors in intercultural groupwork effectiveness

Given such cultural differences in approaches to group decision-making and teamwork, it is not surprising that diversity affects group and teamwork outcomes. In the words of Polzer *et al.*, 'The effects of diversity on group functioning are notoriously difficult to predict because they depend on so many factors, including, for example, the particular mix of diversity dimensions present in the group, the way the group's tasks and broader context shape the salience of various diversity dimensions, and the extent to which the particular members of the group hold and use stereotypes associated with categorical diversity dimensions.'[27] A study found that different percentages of various diversity categories affected group effectiveness. The diversity categories were gender, ethnic minority and persons with disabilities. The measures of effectiveness were perceived commitment, overall effectiveness, satisfaction, cohesion, trust, equal opportunity climate, and quality. The gender and ethnic minority categories showed increases in perceived work-group effectiveness at the 11–30 per cent diversity level. This implies that a low level of diversity is not only tolerated but may even be welcomed. As the mix exceeded 30 per cent, however, perceptions of group effectiveness declined, except for groups with women, which showed a slightly higher level of effectiveness up to 50 per cent diversity. Apparently, as the proportion of a minority increases in a work group beyond 30 per cent (50 per cent for women), there is potential for tension and conflict. (The category of persons with disabilities was an exception in which perceived performance exhibited an almost linear decline as the percentage increased without the 'blip' that other diversity subgroups manifested at 11 to 30 per cent.)[28]

In terms of objective, as opposed to perceived, measures, there are recent findings that moderately strong demographic subgroups in teams fostered learning behaviour. 'Subgroup strength' was defined as the degree of overlap across multiple demographic characteristics. In other words, where teams included subgroups of individuals from similar backgrounds, team learning was enhanced.[29] Another study found that the effects of national diversity on business expansion decision-making by teams were to increase how long it took to reach the decisions, the number of options considered and the attractiveness of international expansion options. Homogeneous national teams (Canadian) ranked home expansion options significantly more attractive than nationally diverse teams did.[30]

Findings that diverse work groups sometimes do but sometimes do not outperform homogeneous work groups has led to theorising and research about why. One leading explanation is that, instead of using the workgroup itself as the relevant ingroup, members of diverse workgroups treat their demographically or functionally similar co-members as their ingroup and the other members of the workgroup as outgroups. This reasoning suggests that inducing group members 'to replace cross-cutting demographic or functional categories with the inclusive workgroup boundary as the basis for social categorization will reduce the detrimental effects of intergroup biases'.[31] Another approach is to induce group members to re-evaluate their beliefs and expectations about cultural diversity itself and its role in their workgroup.[32]

Effects of different types of diversity

Other analyses of the performance effects of diversity distinguish different types. One such differentiates values, cognitions and demeanours as types of nationality-based diversity that differentially affect group effectiveness according to the type of group task. The types of task are creative tasks such as generating strategies; computational tasks that are likely to involve rather clear-cut data collection, analysis and solution generation; and co-ordination tasks involving elaborate interaction among group members. Table 8.1 summarises this analysis.

Table 8.1 *Effects of type of diversity and type of group task on group effectiveness*

Type of diversity	Type of group task		
	Creative	Computational	Co-ordinative
Values	Positive	Neutral	Negative
Cognitions (knowledge and assumptions)	Positive	Positive up to the point where all the knowledge needed for the task is available; beyond that point, neutral	Positive up to the point where all the knowledge needed for the task is available, beyond that point, negative
Demeanours	Moderately negative	Weakly negative	Strongly negative

- When a group is engaged in a creative task, diversity of values can benefit group effectiveness. Different values may affect members' preferences for certain task solutions, or for certain group processes, and will cause them to interpret stimuli in ways that suit their value structures. The varied perspectives and enriched debate that comes from increased diversity will be helpful in generating and refining alternatives. Different knowledge, assumptions and schema can also enhance the group's effectiveness in creative tasks. The differing perspectives that come from different cultures will serve as resources for solving the unstructured, novel task at hand. For instance, '[once] we brought in an international team to discuss the design of a new allergy product. Due to extreme differences in opinion on what constitutes good medical practice, the team designed the product with maximum flexibility to suit the major demands of each country.'[33]

- When the group task is computational, increases in value diversity are unlikely to be related to group effectiveness. Diversity of knowledge and assumptions do support group effectiveness in computational tasks, but only up to the point at which all the knowledge explicitly required for the task resides within the group. Cognitive diversity beyond that 'required' amount does not affect group effectiveness either positively or negatively. 'For example, a task may require certain facts about conditions in three countries. With the addition of knowledgeable representatives from each of these countries, group effectiveness is likely to improve; but adding a representative from a fourth country brings no further benefit.'[34]

- When the task requires co-ordination, diversity of values will tend to be negatively related to group effectiveness. In such a task situation, fluid and reliable co-ordination is required; debates or tensions over why or how the group is approaching the task, which will tend to occur when values vary, will be counter-productive. In addition, disparate values create interpersonal strains and mistrust, which become damaging when the group is charged with a co-ordination task. Increases in cognitive diversity up to the point explicitly required by the task are beneficial, but beyond that point they become counter-productive, because they require more 'costly' co-ordination without any corresponding benefits.

Diversity of demeanours (which are various kinds of surface behaviour involving punctuality, conversational style, body language and so on) provides no important group benefits, but imposes potentially significant costs in terms of interpersonal strain and mistrust. The greater the diversity of demeanours, the lower the group's effectiveness will be. Such a negative relationship will be strongest for groups engaged in co-ordination tasks, since such groups require maximum ease of communication and reliability of interaction in order to perform successfully; the objective nature of computational tasks makes these the least adversely affected by surface diversity, with creative tasks in between.

Thus, where the task explicitly favours multinational inputs or where there are only as many nationalities or cultures represented as needed for the task, the benefits of diversity outweigh the costs. In other cases, the reverse will apply, as, for example, if a German company with substantial experience in an industry was attempting to replicate its recent success in Spain with an entry into Portugal. The management team could benefit from consisting of one or more Germans, Spaniards and Portuguese. Any additional nationalities would be beyond what is expressly needed for the task and would be a liability.[35]

A field study of diversity, conflict and performance in 92 work groups lent support to this idea that some types of diversity may be beneficial and others harmful to work groups. Informational diversity positively influenced group performance but value diversity decreased satisfaction, intent to remain and commitment to the group.

(Readers should note that in this study 'values' referred, not to cultural values, but to what group members thought the group's real task, goal, target or mission should be.) Values differences can lead to task conflict – disagreements about task content, such as over what kinds of advertising to undertake. They may also lead to process conflicts – disagreements about delegation and resource allocation. For instance, group members who value effectiveness (e.g., quality) are likely to have disagreements about resource allocation with group members who value efficiency (e.g., units produced). In addition, similarity in group members' goals and values enhances interpersonal relations within the group. Most importantly for this book, the study found that social category diversity (age and gender) positively influenced group members' satisfaction, intent to remain, perceived performance and commitment, even though it also resulted in increased conflict. This finding runs counter to both conventional wisdom and past research. One explanation seems to be that high performance leads to high morale and low task conflict rather than that low task conflict leads to high morale and high performance. Diverse groups performed better and perhaps, therefore, were more pleased with the group in which they were working. Thus, this study found that teams are more effective when their members have high information diversity and low value diversity, more efficient when their members have low value diversity and have higher morale (higher satisfaction, intent to remain and commitment) when their members have high social category diversity and low value diversity. 'It is the diversity associated with values, and not social category, that causes the biggest problems in and has the greatest potential for enhancing both workgroup performance and morale.'[36]

Informational diversity is more likely to lead to improved performance when tasks are non-routine. Again, social category diversity unexpectedly led to greater satisfaction and commitment when task interdependence was high than when it was low. It may actually be that social category diversity results in higher morale in interdependent tasks. Being able to work together successfully, even when the group is diverse with respect to age and gender composition, may result in greater morale because the group has overcome a serious challenge to its effectiveness. Further, these groups may have discovered that the social category differences were not good signals of value diversity.

Another study explored the relations among work group diversity, two kinds of conflict within the group (task and emotional) and task performance. (This study concerned non-routine tasks performed by relatively newly formed groups.) In task conflict, group members disagree about task issues, including goals, key decision areas, procedures and the appropriate choice for action. In emotional conflict, group members have interpersonal clashes characterised by anger, frustration and other negative feelings. 'We suggest that job-related types of diversity largely drive task conflict.'[37] Task conflict is positive for performance, fostering a deeper understanding of task issues and an exchange of information that facilitates problem-solving, decision-making, and the generation of ideas.

The study found that functional background diversity is the key driver of task conflict, while diversity in race, gender, age and tenure within the group were related to task conflict but not to a statistically significant degree. In contrast to task-related conflict, 'emotional conflict is shaped by a complex web of diversity types that increase emotional conflict based on stereotyping and decrease emotional conflict based on social comparison'. Dissimilarity in ethnicity and tenure increases emotional conflict and tends to encourage heated interactions in work groups. On the other hand, age dissimilarity decreases emotional conflict in work groups, probably because age similarity triggers social comparison. Age is a career-related attribute, so employees tend to measure their own career progress by looking at that of co-workers in their age cohort.

When age similarity in a group increases, these comparisons of career progress, which prompt jealous rivalry, often increase. This study found no effect of gender on emotional conflict in work groups, though other studies have found important effects of gender heterogeneity on work group outcomes, including reduced performance on cognitive tasks, reduced cross-gender support, and increased within-gender support.[38]

The study found no evidence that emotional conflict impaired performance. This may be because 'while relationship troubles cause great dissatisfaction, the conflicts may not influence work as much as expected, because the members involved in the conflicts choose to avoid working with those with whom they experience [emotional] conflict'.[39]

The work environment plays a significant part in determining how well diverse work groups function. An important aspect of that environment is the perspective on workforce diversity itself that predominates in their work group and with their manager. A study distinguished an integration-and-learning perspective (a positive attitude to including and learning from different others), an access-and-legitimacy perspective (different others should have equal rights), and a discrimination-and-fairness perspective (different others can be treated differently but with fairness). The study found that which of these perspectives predominated determined all the following:

- How well a diverse work group and its members functioned.
- How people expressed and managed tensions related to diversity.
- Whether members of minority groups felt respected and valued by their colleagues.
- How people interpreted the meaning of their racial identity at work.

Only the integration-and-learning perspective provided the rationale and guidance needed to achieve sustained benefits from diversity.[40]

The organisational culture is another environmental factor in how effective diverse work groups are. A study showed that diverse co-workers in organisations with collectivist cultures communicated more by memos and less by face-to-face interaction than either diverse co-workers in organisations with individualist cultures or non-diverse co-workers in any kind of organisation. Sending memos may be less effective than face-to-face meetings for conveying information and resolving problems. When people are more different from their co-workers they are more reluctant to interact in person, especially when the organisational culture promotes collectivist values. However, no more conflict was found between demographically different co-workers than between demographically similar ones. Also, in a culture that emphasised collective goals, demographically different co-workers were more likely to find conflict beneficial. Workers in individualist organisational cultures were both more likely to experience conflict (probably because their goals and values differed more from each other's) and to find it harmful.[41]

This study also showed that dissimilar people in collectivist cultures had the highest creative output. This finding suggests that creativity emerges from the combination of access to a larger set of novel ideas afforded by more diverse members and trust that novel ideas will be used for the benefit of the collective. Also, while similar people were significantly more productive in individualist than collectivist organisational cultures, dissimilar people were similarly productive across the two cultures. They were also more productive overall than similar co-workers, despite being less likely to interact. Part of the explanation here may be in terms of what the co-workers interacted about – task-related or social interaction. Dissimilar members may have focused more consistently on tasks, because they had fewer other topics in common to discuss.[42]

This study's findings on creativity are consistent with other research. 'Research on creativity in groups has generally supported the notion that heterogeneity along a variety of dimensions leads to original and high quality ideas and problem solutions.'[43] There are two mechanisms for this effect:

1. Different experiences lead to cross-fertilisation of perspectives and attitudes. This proposition has been supported by studies of gender, personality and attitude (but not ability) and groups whose membership changes over time (but not closed groups).
2. Ideational (creative) ability varies. In addition, the presence of individuals with high ideational ability has been shown to raise the creativity of a group as a whole.

It is also possible that creative thinking ability may be 'related to ethnicity'.[44] The argument here is that previous work in USA found that Asian Americans, Hispanics and African Americans are bicultural; many are bilingual or biglossal (able to switch languages freely during the course of one conversation). 'Based on the flexibility and divergent thinking associated with bilingualism and biculturalism, we might expect to see greater creativity in groups that have members from those backgrounds than in groups from the predominant Anglo culture, which is typically not bilingual or bicultural.' A study found that more ideas, more unique ideas and more ideas rated as effective and feasible came from ethnically diverse groups.

Ethnic differences are also associated with behavioural differences and these, too, affect group outcomes. Groups composed of people from collectivist ethnic backgrounds co-operated more on a choice-based dilemma task than groups composed of people from an individualist ethnic background. However, the findings of a 17-week longitudinal study into the interpersonal processes and performance of culturally homogeneous and culturally diverse groups (with at least two nationalities and three ethnic groups) were less clear-cut. Groups were controlled for age, gender, years of work experience and educational achievement. Initially, homogeneous groups scored higher on both process and performance effectiveness. 'A high degree of cultural diversity did appear to constrain process and performance among group members in newly formed groups (up to nine hours). . .. The diverse groups reported more difficulty in agreeing on what was important and in working together and more often had members who tried to be too controlling, which hindered member contributions.' Over time, though, both types of group showed improvement in process and performance and between-group differences diminished. By week 17, there were no differences in process or overall performance: heterogeneous groups scored higher on identifying problem perspectives and generating solutions; homogeneous groups scored higher on problem identification, choosing the most effective of the solutions generated by the group and justifying their choice.[45]

Team building

Various factors affect the ease of difficulty of building multicultural teams, including:

■ Status and its accompanying power differentials. This may be because of its effect on conflict. Groups that contain high status minorities tend to have less conflict than those with less powerful minority members.
■ The reward structure of the group. Basing rewards on the performance of individuals exacerbates competition along diversity lines within the group. Group-oriented

rewards, conversely, refocus group members towards group effectiveness instead of personal success.

■ The cultural environment of the organisation, including the degree of tolerance for diversity, is also significant.

■ The task competence of the subgroup members affects team building. More task-capable minorities may have higher perceived value in the group.

Interpersonal conflict can destroy a team. Poor communication, dominant/passive personality clashes, status and rank in the company, as well as cultural differences, can trigger interpersonal friction. Time shortages, power struggles and excessive ego investment, along with different styles and inequitable distribution of tasks create further problems. Team management theory addresses these conflicts by breaking down hierarchical structures to decentralise power. A team orientation 'validates all roles through group decision-making.' All members have input and participate in role allocation. A supportive rather than competitive atmosphere encourages participation and negotiation. Non-evaluative statements like 'Let me review what I believe we've discussed so far', and using the word 'we' rather than 'you' reinforce a democratic approach rather than a judgemental, hierarchical one. In this way, it is argued, team theory supports diversity in organisations. The basic characteristics of well-functioning teams include trust, a non-judgemental atmosphere, conflict resolution and negotiation skills, goal-setting abilities and pervasive individual responsibility. These are also the requirements for success in diversity management. 'Problems in the workplace arise from exclusion, distrust, and fear. Teams counter these difficulties by creating bonds through working together towards mutually beneficial ends. Therefore, teams play an important part in restructuring the role of the individual and others in the workplace.'[46,47]

Another approach to building better teams from diverse groups is to apply multicultural theory, which 'promotes mutual understanding and respect for ethnic, religious, gender, class, language, and age differences.' It also promotes equal access to economic power. Applying multicultural theory implies encouraging co-operative learning through interactive activities, such as team members answering worksheets, individuals researching issues and reporting to the group, or pairs of group members researching both sides of a problem. This fosters positive interdependence, individual accountability and face-to-face problem-solving. Other methods include:

■ Resolving problems through brainstorming techniques that allow for group resolution. These techniques should address the conflicts inherent in diversity.

■ Training group members to improve their ability to work effectively in diverse groups. For example, it has been suggested that special team-building training may be necessary, so that groups containing members with disabilities may be able to function more effectively. Such training may involve changing not only how the members react to their fellow members with disabilities but also how each person (including those with disabilities) reacts to each other person in terms of beliefs, reactions and job performance expectations.[48]

■ Techniques that increase interpersonal congruence enhance effectiveness in diverse groups. Interpersonal congruence measures the degree to which group members see others in the group as those others see themselves. People often see themselves differently from how others see them. This factor affects group effectiveness. A study showed that creative task performance, social integration and group identification were all higher and conflict was lower in diverse groups with high interpersonal congruence. When people expressed their 'unique' characteristics within the group during their first ten minutes of interaction, the high level of interpersonal congruence within the group was still benefiting group outcomes four months later.[49]

■ Negotiation and persuasion are key to managing intercultural team differences. Being able to design appropriate persuasive messages in decision-making contexts and influence others in ethical ways that recognise others' perspectives is crucial. In the team-based, post-modern organisation, 'adapting messages to one's listeners takes precedence over individual eloquence'.[50] In an intercultural situation, this requirement includes adapting to the cultural perspective of the other person. Research has shown that both cognitive complexity (differentiation) and having a broad definition of one's role are related to how much someone used listener-adapted persuasive messages.[51]

■ Time spent together may also influence how much national differences affect a group's functioning. Newly formed multi-national groups are likely to be the most vulnerable to the drawbacks of diversity, but, over time, if they survive and meet nominal performance thresholds, they develop more trust and rapport. Members come to respect and welcome the group's complementarities, overlooking (perhaps even relishing) differences in demeanour, values and so on. For this reason, training programmes for enhancing the effectiveness of multi-national groups are most needed in the early stages of the group's operation. Similarly, it is at the outset of the group's work together that multi-national group leaders must be the most vigilant about possible group breakdowns due to diversity.[52]

Finally, building teams out of diverse groups requires both identifying shared values among subgroups (e.g., high quality work or orientation towards serving the customer) and also acknowledging the unique contributions of individuals. In this way, team builders can maximise the advantages of diversity, such as enhanced perspective and broader approaches, but minimise its disadvantages such as subgroup focus, power differentials and distorted communications.

> Cultural differences affect preferred decision-making styles and expectations concerning teamwork. Thus, diversity affects group and team functioning and performance. However, the type of diversity and the nature of the group task influence what those effects will be. The work environment, especially attitudes to diversity, and the organisational culture also influence diversity's impact on group performance. Factors including status differentials and reward structures, and methods such as training, internal negotiation and brainstorming conflict-related problems can improve performance in diverse teams.

8.5 LEADERSHIP AND MANAGEMENT

This section contains a discussion of cultural and intercultural leadership and management. It also considers four more specific topics: giving feedback, mentoring, diversity leadership and international project management.

Cultural differences in leadership

There is widespread agreement that what is expected of leaders or managers, what they may and may not do, and the influence that they have, varies considerably as a result of culture. There have, though, been findings of both universality and culture-specificity of various leadership behaviours. For instance, one study found that managers in nations of different 'cultural-industrialized' standing were all involved in the same 44 skill activities;[53] another found no difference in ratings on attributes such as innovation and commitment among Chinese and non-Chinese managers working for a Hong Kong airline.[54] On the other hand, a comparison of preferences for participation of managers in six European countries and the USA found differences that correlated positively with power distance scores for the seven countries. (The inconsistency may perhaps be reconciled by the distinction between the general or universal functions that effective leaders must carry out and the specific ways in which these functions are performed.) Within Europe, differences in preferences, habits, languages and cultures, in other words its diversity, are recognised as the constraint within which firms (and individuals) 'must exploit European integration opportunities'.[55]

Empirical research 'seems to show that cultural forces influence many aspects of leadership'.[56] These aspects include what is typically required of holders of leadership positions, the degree to which leadership roles are filled by ascription or achievement, typical leader behaviour patterns, preferences for and expectations of leaders, and followers' and subordinates' reactions to different kinds of leader behaviour. Culture also affects how much managers rely on their own experience, what they expect from work teams, how far subordinates participate in decision-making and leaders' confidence in subordinates' decisions.

A survey of managers in 16 countries found that in individualist, low power distance nations, managers rely more heavily on their own experience and training than they do in collectivist, high power distance countries. Further studies show differences in how Japanese, British and American supervisors judge work teams. In Japan, supervisors judge as most effective those work teams that place more reliance on their peers; in USA, those that make more reference to superiors; and, in Great Britain, those that show greater self-reliance. A comparison of decision-making by British and Chinese managers found both the national culture and the type of decision affected the degree of subordinate participation and supervisor consultation. Another study found Chinese and several other East Asian groups (but not Japanese) more confident than Americans that their decisions were correct. This may be owing to a greater propensity to select the first adequate problem solution that is identified rather than to survey a range of alternatives before deciding. These differences may be explicable in terms of variations in individualism–collectivism.[57]

Smith *et al.* argued that 'sources of guidance' serve as an intermediate variable between cultural values and actual managerial behaviours. Sources of guidance include formal rules, unwritten rules, subordinates, specialists, co-workers, superiors, own experience and widespread beliefs. Participation-oriented guidance sources, such as subordinates, are most employed in nations characterised not only by high individualism but also by cultural autonomy, egalitarianism, low power distance, mastery and masculinity. These are more typical of the nations of Western Europe than North America. Conversely, reliance on superiors and rules is associated not only with collectivism but with cultural embeddedness, hierarchy, power distance, mastery and masculinity. Most of the nations of Africa are especially high on these cultural dimensions, rather than the Asian nations more typically discussed as exemplars of contrasting management practices.[58]

A comparison of management in six nations – UK, France, Germany, USA, Japan and an Arab country – found a number of differences.[59] These differences can be understood in terms of cultural dimensions, as follows:

■ British managers are willing to 'listen' to subordinates (being low in uncertainty avoidance) and addicted to 'old boy networks' (they are high in masculinity).
■ French managers are high in power distance (preserved through formality) and individualism (expressed through 'intellectualism').
■ North American managers are high on individualism and achievement, leading them to embrace a 'tough', results-oriented approach to manager–subordinate relations.
■ Japanese managers, though high on achievement, are strongly collectivist, which produces the 'nurturing father' type of manager.

Box 8.6

Research into the decision-making style and attitudes towards risk of Arab executives found evidence that culture and tradition are 'crucial in understanding management practices'. Arabs display moderate levels of individualism, although individuals seek group recognition of achievements, and peers' and superiors' approval takes precedence over individual material reward. Thus 'incentives, while important, should be given to individuals in the context of a group setting and recognition'. Arab managers prefer a 'pseudo-consultative' decision-making style – one which goes through the form of consulting with those affected but actually does not delegate or share power. This may be because Arabs are aware that Islam is egalitarian and emphasises social justice. However, 'the basic aspects of the reality of Arab politics and organizations are the personalized nature of authority, tribalism and fluidity, and alternating fission and fusion of group coalitions and alliances'. This means that an intimate and personal conduct of affairs is required and therefore precludes delegation from flourishing in practice. Most political and business leaders in contemporary Arab society assign relatives and clan members to senior positions in organisations and in government, even though this nepotism violates Islamic teaching. Arab executives are somewhat risk-averse, but do not believe that plans should always be adhered to and are not cautious in making decisions. They believe that rules are

man-made and should be treated with flexibility. In addition, enforcement of rules and regulations is usually contingent on the personality and power of the individuals who make them. The tendency not to be cautious in making decisions reflects a strong inner security that stems from religious beliefs. While Arabs are traditionally hopeful and optimistic, they nevertheless display a remarkable attachment to religious proclamations. It is customary for Arabs to utter the phrase 'Insha Allah' (God willing). Contrary to the popular Western perception, the phrase manifests humility rather than weakness or fatalism.[a]

Saudi managers, in both government and business, reported that their organisations were less rule-bound, used more non-merit criteria in personnel decisions, and were characterised by greater nepotism than did US managers from business and government. Saudi managers were therefore found to be more traditional and less bureaucratic than US managers. On the other hand, they reported greater goal clarity, usually a criterion of bureaucratic organisation.[b]

Sources: (a) Ali, A.J. (1993) Decision-making style, individualism and attitudes towards risk of Arab executives', *International Studies of Management & Organization*, **23**(3): 53–74

(b) Al-Aiban, K.M. and Pearce, J.L. (1993) 'The influence of values on management practices: a test in Saudi Arabia and the United States', *International Studies of Management & Organization*, **23**(3): 32–52

- German managers are high on uncertainty avoidance, shown in adherence to routines and procedures and in close control of subordinates who are seen as apprentices.
- Managers in Arab countries are intermediate on all dimensions except power distance, where they are high: the distance between manager and subordinate is maintained through the high value placed on loyalty and on avoiding interpersonal conflict.

Box 8.6 describes research findings on Arab and Saudi-Arabian leadership and management. Box 8.7 gives more examples of differences in leadership and management within Europe. However, although such differences are important, there are also similarities in how Europeans manage, by comparison with managers in other parts of the world. For instance, a model of a European style of management consists of four basic characteristics: an orientation towards people, a characteristic which is mainly based on the 'social market economy' system in Europe and European business systems; internal negotiation, which deals primarily with the nature of the social dialogue within firms across Europe; managing international diversity in environments and administration; and managing between extremes, which positions the European style of management between the North American and Japanese models.[60]

Some differences are related more closely to factors other than national culture: for instance, to gender or age. A thematic analysis study of 30 women managers found 'surprisingly strong and similar' perceptions that men's and women's leadership communication differs along the dimensions of closed/open and intimidating/supportive. The women managers judged masculine communication to be harmful, overpowering and ineffective, but saw themselves as isolated by their values and numbers. Their most common reported ways of handling this were rejection of masculine power, self-doubt and blame, striving for competence, confrontation, isolation and resignation.[61] In a study of Nordic management style, the least development-oriented managers were older than 50. Many factors influenced a task-oriented style. The most significant factor for task-oriented management behaviour was the manager's gender – women were more task-oriented than men. Region, the manager's age, functional tasks (e.g., production, marketing and other services) and line of business (manufacturing, service industries) also explained variations in task orientation.[62]

In a sample of Belgian managers, public-organisation managers were more conciliatory, tended to be more risk-averse and had a stronger belief in external control than the average business manager. The attitudes expressed by the Belgian managers also depended on both ethnicity and organisational affiliation.[63]

Despite evidence that women make good leaders, there are few at the top. The reason sometimes given for this is that' ... the top executives still have very old-fashioned ideas of what makes good management'. Top executives have an intensive focus on the bottom line and performance targets instead of on developing individual talents and good communication, although these are more likely to produce good organisational performance. Another common explanation is that minorities, including women, find it difficult to attain top leadership positions in organisations because they do not fit culturally prescribed organisational prototypes.

Cultural and subcultural differences in attitudes to leadership lead to differences in how specific managerial functions, such as performance appraisal, are performed. For example, in the UK, performance appraisal is characterised as a joint problem-solving activity with decentralised responsibility over how individual objectives may be met. From a cultural point of view, this is not surprising. In the UK, but also in Denmark,

Box 8.7

- Management in the UK is seen as essentially an interpersonal task, focusing on getting things done. Management is transferable from one function to another; likewise career moves. In rejecting elitism, people are seen as having primary importance as individuals. Personal experience, rather than experience codified in the national culture, forms the basis of effectiveness so that issues of motivation, leadership and group dynamics all form a central focus of management.

- French organisations are staffed by technical experts and managed by the application of rationality. They therefore see management as an intellectually (rather than interpersonally) demanding task; job advertisements reflect this by asking for qualities of 'reception, rigueur, and l'esprit de synthese' (i.e., powers of keen observation, rigour, analysis and synthesis). Less attention is paid to 'emission' (i.e., capacity to communicate and motivate). An elite group of French managers, with at least five years of university education at the Grandes Ecoles and Polytechniques, are collectively known as 'les cadres'. These cadres exercise legitimated authority over subordinates.

- German managers do not manage in general but are instead seen to manage something in particular. German and Swiss-German managers rely on formal authority and attach a high value to technical competence, functional expertise and rationality. Organisations are seen as a co-ordinated network of individuals who will make rational decisions based on their competence and knowledge. In contrast to France, management-by-objectives transferred successfully to Germany. This may be explained by the German preference for decentralisation, lower emphasis on hierarchy, and acceptance of formalisation of goals, time frames and measurement.

- A comparison with US culture found that Russian culture is lower in individualism, higher in power distance, uncertainty avoidance and Machiavellianism but similar in terms of masculinity (competitiveness) and dogmatism. Russians are open to ideas from outside. Younger Russians (business students) had values closer to US values than Russian managers had. Under present Russian conditions, in addition to horizontal and vertical relations, managers' so-called diagonal relations are also very important. These are the 'contacts of industrial managers with "informal" (and, sometimes, criminal) structures. For example, managers of large enterprises bribe government servants to obtain state credits. Managers of small enterprises pay "protection fees" to racketeers. These diagonal relations serve from the perspective of managers as catalysts which increase the efficiency of official "horizontal" and "vertical" contacts.'[a] 'However, the second "wave" of managerial revolution in Russia has started. Instead of technocrats with experience in bargaining with central ministries, younger businessmen more oriented to their relations with shareholders have been appointed as managing directors of industrial enterprises.'[b]

- In Hungary, under Communism, ideological values encouraged the status quo, opposed a future orientation, equated entrepreneurship with cheating and criminal activity, and were against the desire to change and improve performance. Leaders of high-performing organisations were typically not rewarded for their efforts as any profits they made were used to subsidise lower-performing organisations. Therefore, managers tended to restrict their efforts and avoid surpassing average performance. Hungarian managers tend to be authoritarian. A study found that Hungarian managers were 'friendly but not considerate, nor did they show regard for their subordinates as individuals or allow them to make decisions. Hungarian managers seem to be less sophisticated in planning routines, but nevertheless think and analyse carefully before making decisions.'[c]

- In Central and Eastern Europe more widely, there may be a cultural tendency to avoid responsibility. For many, the current situation represents the first time in their lives that they can control their future.

Box 8.7 (cont'd)

'A generalised belief of "nothing depends on me" makes the foreigner wonder if the people of the region are not in a pervasive state of learned helplessness. There is also a general distrust in management, a view that "what is up is bad" '. Low levels of trust in organisations compound this situation. Poor performance is often attributed to external factors. 'Attitudes regarding individual accountability are difficult to teach.'

■ Typical organisational practices in Sweden have been summarised by the term pragmatism, meaning the balancing of rituals with rational choices, the rituals thus acquiring instrumental uses and the rational choices or instruments expressing important values. A series of studies conducted in leading Swedish companies concluded that Swedish managers are very sensitive to fashions and to trends that affect the metaphors and labels used for organisational ideas and ideologies. There are definite rules for introducing change, and organisational change is strongly institutionalised. This provides room for new ideas at the same time that it protects organisations from extreme swings.^{d}

■ Early studies found that Greek preferences concerning management style reflected Greek culture, in particular acceptance of authority and co-operative behaviour within the ingroup, rejection of authority and extreme competitiveness with the outgroup.

However, more recent work suggests the Greek model of management 'is not differentiated from the Western model'. The differences that do exist are considered more closely related to lack of modernisation and are disappearing under the joint impact of the EU and globalisation. These are differences such as concentration of power and control in the hands of top management and a lack of modern systems to support strategic decisions.^{e}

Sources: (a) Hecht, L., Kovach, K. and Tongren, H.N. (1995) 'Recognizing cultural differences: key to successful U.S.–Russian enterprises', Public Personnel Management, 24: 1–18

(b) Elenkov, D.S. (1997) 'Differences and similarities in managerial values between US and Russian managers: an empirical study', International Studies of Management & Organization, 27(1): 85–106

(c) Kovach, R.C. Jr. (1994) 'Matching assumptions to environment in the transfer of management practices: performance appraisal in Hungary', International Studies of Management & Organization, 24(4): 83–100

(d) Czarniawska-Joerges, B. (1993) 'Swedish management: modern project, postmodern implementation', International Studies of Management & Organization, 23(1): 13–27

(e) Bourantas, D. and Papadakis, V. (1996) 'Greek management: diagnosis and prognosis', International Studies of Management & Organization, 26(2): 77–95

Box 8.8

A survey of 3,500 British managers, reported to the British Psychological Society conference by Professor Alimo-Metcalfe of Leeds University, found that, except at the highest echelons of companies, both men and women subordinate managers rated female bosses more highly than male. They were found to be rated more highly on the following factors, listed in order of how much more highly the women were rated: being decisive, focusing effort, being a good mentor, managing change, inspiring others, openness to ideas, encouraging change, networking, problem-solving, clear strategy, and being supportive of mistakes. On being a good delegator, accessible and honest/consistent, men and women scored equally.

Source: Rumbelow, H. (2003) 'Even men say women make the best bosses', The Times, 9 January 2003, p. 9

Sweden, Norway and the Netherlands, the national culture combines low power distance with low uncertainty avoidance. The low power distance means that the boss can be bypassed and rules bent so that the employee can get things done. The independence and self-realisation of the employee is an issue. The boss therefore may need to find out the detail of the subordinate's tasks. This is blended with low uncertainty avoidance, which is associated with a higher tolerance of risk and acceptance of dependencies in performance, a reliance on resourcefulness and adaptability in achieving goals and a tendency to reactive rather than proactive feedback. It is not surprising, therefore, that it is legitimate to make the performance-appraisal discussion a joint problem-solving activity. In contrast, in Germany, Switzerland, Austria and Finland, the appraisal discussion is shaped by a desire to routinise goal implementation. In these countries, while power distance is still low, giving the employee an equal say, uncertainty avoidance is high. This leads to aiming for long-term forward control of goals and performance and a preference for final bureaucratic check-offs by superiors. In countries such as Portugal, Greece, Turkey, France, Belgium, Italy and Spain, uncertainty avoidance is high, bringing with it the desire for forward control, but power distance is also high. Therefore, there is an additional preference for centralised control, and a one-way direction of communication is more acceptable, under the assumption that the boss knows best and so may predetermine the 'how' of performance. Performance is seen as a duty, not a self-fulfilling activity, and face-to-face conflict is unacceptable. In any event, the boss has privileges and can bend the rules. Finally, although subordinates may be afraid to commit themselves to performance, they also expect protection from 'above'.[64]

Factors in intercultural leadership effectiveness

Tensions between managers and subordinates can arise from (sub)cultural differences in work attitudes. A case study of teamwork and management in a French–Slovenian plant uncovered friction. 'The Slovenian model, with a short power distance and a collective orientation, met the French model, where the power distance is large and individualism is common.' Whereas in French management style, authority is legitimised by the hierarchical position itself, in Slovenian management style, authority belongs to the person who has the expertise. Thus, from the Slovenian point of view, the hierarchical authority should be constrained and the professionalism of the individuals stimulated. From the French point of view, the hierarchical structure should be strengthened in the plant (which would actually further reinforce the workers' inertia). However, in this case, the French management was able to take into account two main characteristics of Slovenian management, the need for equality and mutual aid. They discovered, first, that varying management styles in different countries are linked to each country's culture; second, that these management styles should be respected and not dismissed as an artefact of underdevelopment. Third, they came to understand that defining the fundamental cultural references of a nation helps to anticipate the work behaviour and reactions of individuals regarding new management procedures. The better these procedures correspond to such fundamental cultural references, the better the results.[65]

Such attitudinal differences can also lead to internal conflicts for non-Western managers who are trying to apply Western management methods. Two case studies in Russian organisations suggest that participation and empowerment, as introduced in the Western literature, do not work well in Russian organisations. Explanations are found in a series of factors linked to Russian national and organisational cultures: 'the practice of vesting authority in one man [sic], tightly coupled hierarchies, lack of knowledge sharing, anti-individualism and dependence.'[66] Studies of hotel staff in Canada and the People's Republic of China showed that high power distance reduces the effect of empowerment on job satisfaction.[67] Studies of Turkish managers show a discrepancy between their beliefs in favour of participative leadership and their relatively low beliefs in employees' capacity for leadership and initiative. This may be owing to a conflict between their training in Western management and human-relations ideology and the high value placed in traditional Turkish culture on a benev-olent autocratic style of leadership. 'A dominating style in handling differences with subordinates is widespread and is perceived to be an effective method by superiors and subordinates alike.' Expressing support for participative leadership may be seen as socially desirable rather than realistic. Another possibility is that managers have a genuine belief in participative practices, but are frustrated by employees' responses. The subordinates may not yet have embraced participative-management ideology. Change efforts which bring a more comprehensive perspective and which from the outset involve all interested parties may be the more appropriate strategy.[68]

When a superior and his or her subordinate have the same nationality, ethnicity and gender the quality of their relationship is often better. People who share the same demographic attributes often share beliefs and values, or at least assume that they do. People who perceive that they think alike are more likely to like one another, feel comfortable in each other's company and have more confidence in each other because they view each other as more predictable. In addition, similar backgrounds often lead to people having similar communication patterns and so communicating more effectively and with fewer misunderstandings. In the case of age similarity, however, while the above reasoning may apply, an alternative possibility is that people of similar ages will feel themselves to be in competition (this is an implication of social comparison theory) and so have less positive superior–subordinate relationships than people of different ages. 'Subordinates who are roughly equal to their supervisor in terms of age may be inclined to consider the adverse implications for their own personal career progress.'

These effects interact with cultural differences. The negative association between age similarity and good subordinate–superior relationships is likely to be stronger in high power distance cultures, like that of Mexico, where it is expected that higher status goes with age. Confirming this, a study found that age similarity had negative effects on superior–subordinate relationship quality in Mexico, but not in the USA. Again, the positive association between gender similarity and the quality of supervisor–subordinate relationships can be expected to be stronger in cultures, such as that of Mexico, whose stronger patriarchal and machismo elements make female superior–male subordinate relationships more problematic. Despite this, while gender similarity had a stronger positive impact on one dimension of relationship quality (trust) in Mexico, it had a stronger positive impact on a second dimension of relation-ship quality (leader–member exchange, which largely involves support and under-standing) in the USA. A possible explanation of this unexpected finding on leader–member exchange is that the measure was culturally biased: Mexican men would resist the idea that their relations with other men involve support and under-standing. The researchers concluded, 'Overall, demographic similarity influences the quality of relationships between supervisors and subordinates but that the precise type of influence is affected by culture.'[69]

How leaders function cannot be studied independently of the group-based social context that gives their roles and qualities expression. 'Leaders and followers are transformed and energized as partners in an emerging social self-categorical relationship.'[70] Leaders must be 'one of us', exemplify what makes 'us' better than 'them' and stand up for the group. However, although cross-cultural research emphasises that different cultural groups often have different conceptions of what leadership should entail, attributes associated with charismatic/transformational leadership may be universally endorsed as contributing to outstanding leadership. This hypothesis was tested in 60 cultures as part of the Global Leadership and Organizational Behavior Effectiveness (GLOBE) Research Program. The results supported the hypothesis that specific aspects of charismatic/transformational leadership are strongly and universally endorsed across cultures.[71]

Cross-cultural endorsement of charismatic leadership is less surprising when account is taken of research showing that workgroup collectivism is important for charismatic leadership to emerge. Communication plays an important role in this process. (This is consistent with the school of thought that leadership is located, observed and interpreted as a communication process.) A collectivist group may place a high value on interdependence, co-operation and sharing. Thus it may not only allow a leader who embodies these values to be more effective, but also respond to such a leader's call for teamwork and focus on collective goals. In collectivist teams, control is exercised through value consensus and not through impersonal rules. Value consensus-based control may be more appropriate than impersonal rules for a charismatic leader.[72] Moreover, collectivism and power distance are highly correlated. A collectivist group that is also high in power distance may provide opportunities for an individual to take independent action that is perceived as a successful attempt to change the status quo. In turn, this may lead to the individual being perceived as a natural leader, exhibiting charismatic behaviours and possessing charismatic qualities.[73]

While similar management practices 'could be effective in societies that seem different', they need to be examined for their interpretation in different countries. This is the essence of the Global Integration–Local Responsiveness framework where global integration emphasises consistency or standardisation and local responsiveness emphasises customisation or adaptation.[74] Managers' responsiveness relates to communication style, the content of communications and use of third parties for negative feedback.[75] Next discussed is intercultural management in relation to the specific roles of giving feedback, mentoring, taking responsibility for diversity and managing international projects.

Giving feedback

Employee input is essential for identifying employee strengths and weaknesses in the most effective manner, as they are often most aware of both aspects of their work performance. To get high power distance oriented employees to increase their upward input to their superiors, managers are recommended to ask open-ended questions that provide opportunities for voluntary answers, and to direct specific questions to an individual's area of expertise. In collectivist cultures, it is important specifically to invite the employee to respond with his/her ideas and perspectives so that harmony is preserved. To build a personal relationship and trust with subordinates calls for being polite and showing respect. Another way to build trust is to have events where managers can have friendly and informal dialogues with subordinates. In collectivist cultures, it is important to show respect to older people and those with long tenure in the company; in high power distance cultures, this applies to those with higher social status. Respect can be shown by a marked emphasis on politeness and decorum. For example, a written communication should ask such senior employees to 'consider' doing certain things and should 'request' them to do it. Saying 'You must,' or 'You are required,' is considered impolite. In addition, proper titles should be used when addressing older people.

It is important to match the verbal and non-verbal communication styles of other cultures. In collectivist cultures, verbal communication of work assignments, requirements and priorities should focus on how the employee relates to the group and the organisation overall. In addition, feedback and recognition should be provided that establishes rapport with family, friends and associates as well as other important ingroups of collectivist employees. Non-verbally, in high-context communication cultures, loud and direct oral communication is socially unacceptable. Similarly, argumentative voices and exaggerated hand gestures are frowned upon and often lead to miscommunication. Instead of making demands, it is often useful to ask, 'May I ask you a question?' or 'May I make a suggestion?' It is also important to be aware of non-verbal cues. For instance, body gestures are also more restrained than is typical in the West in order to demonstrate one's humility and respect for the other person.

In collectivist cultures critical feedback may be seen as a personal attack, especially if someone outside of one's work group delivers the feedback. For this reason managers should establish a trusting personal relationship with the subordinate before providing any negative performance feedback. Intercultural managers should also offer advice in a diplomatic and caring manner. Managers should consider beginning by apologising for having to conduct the session and use analogies and other indirect communication to illustrate performance concerns. Instead of direct or blunt feedback, they should use open-ended questions, silence, paraphrasing and reflecting feelings. They should seek to observe the reaction of employees closely and be willing to tolerate ambiguities as well as sometimes leaving things unsaid rather then spelling out everything clearly. Collectivist subordinates will read between the lines and understand what is being said.

An intercultural manager should also consider using a third party to convey any negative feedback, gain a sense of the underlying issues and obtain possible responses from the subordinate before personally giving negative feedback. The reason for this is that it is acceptable for employees in collectivist cultures to provide constructive feedback to another member of their work group when they have established a close and trusting relationship with each other. A trusted third party can act as a buffer to help minimise conflict, explore hidden fears and preserve the relationship, face and self-esteem of the individual and the group. In addition, a respected third party can more easily serve as a mentor or ask more junior workers to contribute their views. In addition to a respected peer from the employee's team, other potential third parties are a senior employee in the company or an employee with expertise in a particular area.[76]

Mentoring

Mentoring refers to a senior and experienced member of staff of an organisation providing information, advice and support for a junior person. The mentoring relationship is intended to last over an extended period. While mentoring may be particularly beneficial for women and members of minorities, by giving the kind of support that may help them overcome the obstacles caused by prejudice, there is evidence that in fact it is White males who are most often given the most practical help. A study found that, while women and members of ethnic minorities received about the same level of mentoring help as White males, it differed in type. The help given to White males was mostly instrumental (for instance, career advice or contacts) while that given to the minority groups was mostly socio-emotional. This was mainly because of who mentored whom. White male mentors gave the same kind of instrumental help to all kinds of mentorees, but mainly mentored White males. Women and members of ethnic minorities were more likely to be mentored by women or ethnic minority members, who gave predominantly socio-emotional help.[77]

There are cultural differences in the expectations of different ethnic groups in regard to mentoring. For instance, culturally, Asian mentor-like relationships differ from their Western counterparts in that they are much more formally hierarchical and they blur the distinction between family and social ties. Formal language and titles, deference and other forms of reverence are expected between junior and senior peers. Asian personnel may not seek guidance and nurturance actively; instead, they expect the person with the greater power to initiate this. Asian staff are likely to be concerned about not taking up too much of the mentor's time. As a result, they may quickly usher themselves out of the office. This fear of being a burden is detrimental to an effective mentoring relationship.[78]

Crosby argued that issues of trust, comfort and rapport are central to intercultural mentoring. 'Some people might more readily act as instrumental sponsors than as psychosocial confidants for someone who differs from them on important dimensions of identity. Similarly, junior people may feel more suspicious of and behave more awkwardly around senior people who differ from them than around senior people who resemble them. Because most senior people in organizations today are still White men, insisting on the close emotional bond between a mentor and a protégé as the only vehicle for career advancement may unwittingly serve to reinforce the old (White) boys' network.'[79]

Mentorees from some cultural or social backgrounds need to be taught the meaning and functions of assertiveness, encouraged to ask questions and express opinions. Similarly, mentors should be educated about the meanings of silence and learn not to interpret the absence of questions and suggestions to mean that neither problems nor ambitions exist. Mentors should not dismiss or trivialise a mentoree's emphasis on race, gender or class (e.g., by saying, 'You're focusing on class too much,' or, 'You're looking at this through a class lens'). Mentors should help mentorees to make contacts and to network. They may not know how to go about it (e.g., how to introduce themselves to important figures in the field, how to remind someone that they've met before). 'The oppressed learn their place very well; even the most independent of persons knows the line.'[80] Mentorees from lower social classes may not ask how to go about doing something that everyone assumes they know how to do. They will not necessarily ask, because it can be humiliating to have to ask what you 'should' already know, such as whether a gathering is in semi-formal or casual dress, how to make small talk with guest speakers or how to contact a senior manager. Mentors should be prepared to talk with mentorees about things that they assume other junior employees know.[81]

Diversity leadership

To be effective, diversity programmes must have support from the top, and managers need to set the tone for an open and receptive environment, which actively incorporates difference. To develop functional intercultural communication, managers must reward new approaches. 'By modelling bias-free language, both written and spoken, and by illustrating a genuine acceptance of different methods and manners, managers can create a work environment that will nurture and profit from diversity.'[82]

The starting point in all diversity training programmes is an analysis of the self. Most employees are unaware of their own biases, how they are formed and how they emerge in the workplace in overt and subtle ways. Thus, good multicultural managers should have an understanding of themselves, be able to communicate effectively through verbal and non-verbal messages, be respectful and empathetic and understand other cultures' 'sense of time, concept of work and basic beliefs'. Managers who lack some of these qualities can develop them through training programmes. In many ways, cultural awareness training is key. For example, managers need to learn what is offensive to other cultures in terms of grooming, dress and communication methods as well as understand that what is perceived as 'odd' behaviour is really just different.

A commitment to respecting difference is the first step. Training that provides an understanding of the values, beliefs, customs and preferences of other groups is much more likely to enhance cultural diversity. Effective training also improves skills in listening, interpersonal communication, conflict resolution and negotiation. It also explores ways to alter current assumptions and paradigms. Training methods to achieve these goals include consciousness-raising activities (to study how culture shapes perceptions as well as behaviour) and interactive activities such as role-playing, creating scenarios to illustrate stereotypes, analysing case studies and viewing films for discussion. Trainers must create an atmosphere of trust in order to handle the 'serious and deep cultural and personal conflicts, which must be voiced, acknowledged, and explored'.[83] To minimise tensions, managers should set guidelines, such as encouraging all responses, use 'I' statements, listen with respect, maintain confidentiality and avoid blaming. These guidelines resemble those for forming effective teams; consequently, companies that encourage teamwork should succeed in multicultural efforts.[84]

International project management

Case studies of international construction projects have revealed some of the major managerial issues in intercultural management. One project, to build a hospital in Saudi Arabia, was managed by a five-member team of three Swedes, one Arab and one Briton. The construction workers were Arabs and Pakistanis. In this project the main managerial issues were negotiation, conflict resolution, raising productivity and delay in raising funds. Another project, also in Saudi Arabia, was to construct a major harbour and road. The consulting engineers were from Britain and the USA, the project manager was Swedish and the workforce consisted of more than 1000 Thais and Pakistanis; the client was Arab. Important managerial issues were to optimise labour costs by learning how to evoke pride in the workers, to give multi-skill training and to create rivalry among work groups. In a third project, Swedish contractors undertaking construction of a hydropower plant in Thailand found that Thai workers in Thailand were less productive than those who work abroad. A fourth case showed that the 'democratic' Swedish approach to management did not work well in a project to construct a tunnel in Hong Kong with Chinese and Swedish management and mainly Chinese engineers.

The authors of the cases concluded that the impact of culture on project management is likely to be evident from the very early days of the project. This impact is felt even before the formal process starts. For example, a project manager stationed in the Middle East said, 'Social relations in the Middle East are very important; if not for anything else, it is vital for getting information. In order to know very early that a project is proceeding, you must have a network of relations to be informed … they must know you and trust you as a person first, and then trust your company. It is impossible to build such interpersonal relations without cultural awareness.' Other conclusions included the following: 'Effective management of cultural diversity at project level is an art. For example, negotiation with Arabs requires a degree of patience that few

Western project managers have ever had to practice. Many of the problems are solved informally, in social meetings, based on interpersonal relationships. A project manager in the Middle East said, "There exists a strong and direct positive relationship between project performance and the project management's interpersonal relations with other actors involved in the project ... delays can be avoided and much time and resources saved." ' Finally, the researchers noted, 'The problems associated with cultural differences between the Arabs and Swedes were found to be very sensitive. In addition to differences in religion and value and belief systems, the concepts of contract, time and planning as well as philosophies of business were found to be different in the parties' cultural context. Arabs prefer to do business based on interpersonal relationships, they do not plan for a long-term future; to them verbal and written agreements have equal value; and they are not aware of technical and practical problems. "They contract a project today and want it to be delivered yesterday", said a project manager.'[85]

Although some universal aspects to leadership have been found, culture affects both what is expected of leaders and their usual behaviour. Many of these effects can be linked to the cultural values described in Chapter 2. There are also subcultural influences, particularly of gender, on leadership behaviours. Cultural differences lead to differences in how specific managerial functions are performed.

Intercultural leaders must prevent differences from leading to superior–subordinate tension, by respect for subordinates' 'face'. Feedback should allow for subordinates' attitudes to criticism. Mentors should allow for (sub)cultural differences in the kind of support the mentoree needs and in their willingness to ask for help. Diversity leadership requires top managers both to act as models, particularly with regard to how they communicate, and to instigate and strongly support diversity training. International project managers need high levels of cultural adaptability. In particular, Westerners may need to pay more attention to interpersonal relationships than they do usually, and be prepared to revise their usual management methods.

8.6 WORKING IN INTERNATIONAL ALLIANCES

An alliance is commonly defined as any voluntarily initiated co-operative agreement between firms that involves exchange, sharing, or co-development; it can include contributions by partners of capital, technology or firm-specific assets. At one extreme are 50/50 joint ventures, at the other, short-term product marketing arrangements. Relationships between partners are a prominent issue in all co-operative alliances. The dynamics of these relationships become even more fundamental in a cross-cultural setting, in which international co-operative ventures encounter more opportunities (e.g., mutual learning, knowledge transfer, market entry) as well as greater challenges (e.g., institutional volatility, cultural barriers, property rights protection).[86]

Cultural differences affecting international alliances

In international business alliances, barriers to effective communication, and so to performance, result from underlying national and organisational cultural differences. Differences in the cultural backgrounds of partners cause problems in international joint ventures (IJVs) but, as one study has shown, some differences are more disruptive than others. Cultural distance in uncertainty avoidance and long-term orientation reduce the survival chances of IJVs more than cultural distance in individualism, power distance or masculinity. (Differences in masculinity/achievement orientation do have a significant, but smaller, negative impact on IJV's survival.) Differences in uncertainty avoidance and long-term orientation may cause particular problems because these differences, which translate into differences in how IJV partners perceive and adapt to opportunities and threats in their environment, are more difficult to resolve than differences along the other three dimensions. Perhaps cultural differences regarding power distance, individualism and masculinity are more easily resolved because they are mainly reflected in different attitudes towards the management of personnel. Firms can make explicit agreements about personnel management before entering the partnership.[87]

In a German–Japanese joint venture, it was found, the organisational culture that emerged from the 'negotiations', was affected by the meaning that those involved made of organisational events.[88] This meaning was culturally determined – that is, people's differing cultural backgrounds strongly influenced how they interpreted events. Most managerial research about mergers has assumed that cultural differences imply 'acculturative stress' (i.e., stress caused by the need to adjust to different others). A study of European mergers confirmed that acculturative stress influences performance in the merged firms. However, it also found cultural differences in which factors had most effect on performance. For the French, for example, the most important factor was personal and societal responsibility. (The French place a high premium on concern for the health and well-being of employees, the local community and society at large.) For the British, the most important factor was performance and reward. (In British culture, individuals are achievement-driven and ambitious, they accept responsibility for their own work and therefore expect clear and objective standards of evaluation based on personal performance.)[89] A qualitative study of West European–Russian joint ventures found that cultural differences can have a key impact on operations and that cultural and operational differences can produce difficulties 'specific to this kind of partnership'. For instance, the Western Europeans felt a stronger pressure to achieve set targets within a given time frame. 'In contrast, while Russians are conscious of a goal to be reached, they do not seem to feel the time pressure or to be diligent in taking steps to achieve that goal.' Similarly, the Russians were inclined to present problems that arose to the Western partner with no suggestions for solutions, rather than to take the initiative to solve them. One Western manager in a manufacturing joint venture explained how difficult it was to show people that they have to make their own decisions and assume certain responsibilities.

Russians' assumptions about a company and its functions may be 'drastically different' from West Europeans'. Until recently, in Russia, the function of a company was not to make a profit by supplying a good or service; instead it was to serve a centralised and planned economy by complying with production standards. As a result business practices still differ in areas including price-setting, investment policies, cost analysis and control, quality control, and understanding the organisational structure. For example, one Russian joint-venture partner initially considered that the more people were employed, the greater the profit would be, on the grounds that labour is not a cost component to be included in the profit-and-loss statement. Russians were unaware of the management processes, systems and style that govern how a Western company functions. One manager described an instance when a mechanic appeared in the middle of a meeting of the board of directors.[90]

Factors in international alliances' success

The success of international alliances depends on the ability of both companies to work together. Western business practices, such as goal-setting, performance monitoring, conflict resolution and information sharing need to be adapted. Special attention must be paid to trust building. 'Co-operation between organizations creates mutual dependence and requires trust in order to succeed. This comes down to trust between the individuals who are involved in the alliance. Uncertainty about partners' motives, and a lack of detailed knowledge about how they operate, requires that a basis for trust be found for co-operation to get under way in the first place.'[91] Legal contracts play no significant role in this process. Methods of decision-making, conflict resolution and good interpersonal relationships have an important impact. Experienced managers in Russia advocate decision-making by consensus, rather than by voting majority or asserting ownership rights.

Because the relations that really matter exist in the social fabric, the behavioural element of importance is the role of trust.[92] A study showed that trust enables strategic managerial action to overcome the influence of business and institutional environments in cross-border ventures.[93] Effective communication with international business partners is also key.[94] Direct contact is important in building the relationship. One manager in a Western European/Russian joint venture explained that he preferred to use his own poor Russian language rather than an interpreter. A good interface becomes very important. Russians 'appreciate a true friendship and distinguish this one from a mere forbearance born out of pure economic interests'. In an American/ Polish health care joint venture, there were four factors linked to success. These were high 'stakeholder strength' – that is, both parties' contributions were essential; reduced uncertainty because key decision-makers were acquainted through common business associations; a corporate culture that reflected religious affiliation (both parties were Roman Catholic organisations); and high trust, which in this case was also promoted by religious affiliation.[95] More generally, initiating and fostering expectations that the relationship will continue, flexibility and information exchange between the partner firms are factors positively related to both trust and market performance in international partnerships.

Interpersonal interactions to inculcate shared organisational beliefs also foster trust. A survey that included 12 Swedish cross-border mergers and acquisitions showed how national and cultural differences in mergers and acquisitions could best be overcome and the beliefs and values of the affected employees harmoniously integrated. It found these positive effects occurred when 'the buying firms rely on social controls. That is, by participating in such activities as introduction programs, training, cross-visits, retreats, celebrations and similar socialization rituals, employees will create, of their own volition, a joint organizational culture.'[96]

A study of 282 international co-operative ventures in China found that 'attachments' between boundary spanners within cross-cultural international co-operative ventures (ICVs) stimulated their performance and increased financial returns. Attachment means that the parties' attitudes towards one another are positive; it is probably a precondition of trust, but trust also requires the parties to accept vulnerability (risk) based on those positive attitudes. 'Reliance and risk are two necessary conditions for trust but not for attachment.' Thus the finding that attachment itself promoted the ICV's performance is useful. Without personal attachment between boundary-spanning managers, opportunism tends to occur in these arrangements; it is hard to control by formal governance mechanisms. Personal attachment helps to suppress opportunism, boost trust and so counter dissolution.[97] Attachment between individual boundary spanners in the ICVs was found to increase as their time working together (their overlap in tenure) increased. Other factors promoting attachment were goal congruity and low cultural distance between the parent firms; market disturbance and regulatory deterrence also seemed to operate as external pressures that increased cohesiveness.[98]

> Underlying cultural differences, especially in uncertainty avoidance and time orientation, can destroy international alliances such as joint ventures. Differences have been found in the interpretation of events, in the factors that stimulate acculturative stress, in the perceived functions of a company and in business practices. Trust-building and effective communication, especially among boundary-spanners, are key to overcoming these differences.

8.7 SUMMARY

This chapter has shown how cultural differences affect selection interviewing, negotiating, mediating, working in groups and teams, leadership and management and international alliances. It has also shown how skilled intercultural communication helps overcome the difficulties produced by these differences.

QUESTIONS AND EXERCISES

1. Explain in your own words the problems that may arise in some cultures in obtaining accurate factual information from interviews. How may these problems be overcome?
2. Give five examples of ways in which selection interviewers who are influenced by their own social rules and identity may misjudge candidates.
3. How might an interviewer who was low in cultural awareness interpret the responses of the selection candidate in Box 8.3? How might cultural knowledge lead the interviewer to interpret the responses differently?
4. Discuss the findings reported in the text about how gender stereotypes bias selection interviewers. How can this be prevented?
5. Show how the differences in Japanese and American negotiating styles reflect collectivist and individualist values, respectively.
6. Discuss the contention of Brett [Ref. 18] that goals, power and information-sharing are each linked to different cultural values.
7. Complete the questionnaire.

In my culture negotiators tend to:	Strongly agree	Agree	Neither agree nor disagree	Disagree	Strongly disagree
1. See the goal of negotiating as creating a relationship.					
2. Expect the negotiated terms of a contract to be strictly adhered to.					
3. Think a buyer has more power than a seller.					
4. Try to get as much information as possible from the other party without giving any away themselves.					
5. Deal with one issue at a time.					
6. Expect both sides to improve on their initial offers by making concessions.					
7. Aim to 'win'.					
8. Select negotiators by seniority.					

For guidance on how to score and interpret this questionnaire, see Appendix C

8. Discuss the reasons why intercultural negotiators usually achieve worse joint outcomes than intra-cultural negotiators. How may such problems be overcome?

9. Discuss the contention that 'a mediator who is closer [culturally] to one side than the other can be effective in mediation'.

10. Do you agree that 'Successful mediation does not always result in resolving conflict'? Give your reasons.

11. Why do leading authorities advocate a non-directive approach to mediation, and what are the implications of such an approach for how mediators should act?

12. With a colleague from a different culture, compare the meaning of 'teamwork' in your respective cultures.

13. Comment on the possible reasons for the research finding given on p. 302 that 'A high degree of cultural diversity did appear to constrain process and performance among group members in newly formed groups (etc.)'.

14. Discuss reasons why the potential for conflict in a workgroup might increase as the percentage of ethnic minority or male members increases beyond 30 per cent. What reasons might explain the fact that the relevant percentage for women is different?

15. Discuss the research finding that dissimilar people in workgroups in collectivist organisational cultures had the highest creative output.

16. What processes might explain the finding that over time diverse work groups become as productive as non-diverse groups?

17. The text states that differences in how Japanese, British and American supervisors judge work teams may be explicable in terms of variations in individualism–collectivism. How?

18. Draw up a list of national characteristics and factors that appear to influence variations in European styles of leadership and management, based on the material in Box 8.7 and the surrounding text.

19. Why might participation and empowerment, as advocated in Western literature, be counter-productive in some European countries?

20. Pelled [Ref. 99] found that age similarity had negative effects on work relationship quality in Mexico, but not in the United States. How can this finding be explained?

21. What explains the finding that charismatic leadership is associated with collectivist values in the followers?

22. What should the diversity training of managers aim to achieve?

23. What adjustments in attitudes, expectations and communication behaviours are likely to be needed by a Western project manager working on a project in the Middle East?

24. A study found that some differences in cultural values are more important than others for the survival of international joint ventures. Which differences were these and how can the findings be explained?

25. Summarise the research findings reported in the text on the effects on international joint ventures of cultural differences. How, in the light of these findings, can the prospects of success of international joint ventures be increased?

NOTES AND REFERENCES

1. Hatem, T. (1994) 'Egypt: exploring management in the Middle East', *International Studies of Management & Organization*, **24**(1/2): 116–36.

2. Wong, I.F.H. and Phooi-Ching, L. (2000) 'Chinese cultural values and performance at job interviews: a Singapore perspective', *Business Communication Quarterly*, **63**(1): 9–22.

3. Gallois, C. and Callan, V. (1998) *Communication and Culture; A Guide for Practice*, Chichester, UK: John Wiley.

4. Birkner, K. and Kern, F. (2000) 'Impression management in East and West German job interviews', in Spencer-Oatey, H. (ed.) *Culturally Speaking*: pp. 256–71, London: Continuum.

5. Kristof-Brown, A., Barrick, M.R. and Franke, M. (2002) 'Applicant impression management: dispositional influences and consequences for recruiter perceptions of fit and similarity', *Journal of Management*, **28**(1): 27–46.

6. Rumbelow, H. (2003) 'Feminine charm is still a career girl's best bet', The *Times*, 9 January, p. 9.

7. Frazer, R.A. and Wiersma, U.J. (2001) 'Prejudice versus discrimination in the employment interview: we may hire equally, but our memories harbour prejudice', *Human Relations*, **54**(2): 173–92.

8. Torrington, D. (1994) *International HRM: Think Globally, Act Locally*, Hemel Hempstead, Herts: Prentice-Hall.

9. Weiss, S.E. and Curhan, J.J. (1999) 'Adopting a dual lens approach for examining the dilemma of differences in international business negotiations', *International Negotiation Journal Abstracts*, **4**(1). URL: interneg.org/interneg/reference/journals/ in/volumes/4/1

10. Abramson, N.R., Lane, H.W., Nagai, H. and Takagi, H. (1993) 'A comparison of Canadian and Japanese cognitive styles: implications for management interaction', *Journal of International Business Studies*, **24**: 575–88.

11 Bazerman, M.H., Curhan, J.R., Moore, D.A. and Valley, K.L. (2000) 'Negotiation', *Annual Review of Psychology*, **51**: 279–314.

12. Salacuse, J. (1991) 'Making deals in strange places: a beginner's guide to international business negotiations', in Breslin, J.W. and Rubin, J.Z. (eds) *Negotiation Theory and Practice*: pp. 251–60, Cambridge, MA: The Program on Negotiation at Harvard Law School.

13. George, J.M., Gonzalez, J.A. and Jones, G.R. (1998) 'The role of affect in cross-cultural negotiations', *Journal of International Business Studies*, **29**(4): 749–72.

14. Ibid.

15. Cai, D.A., Wilson, S.R. and Drake, L.E. (2000) 'Culture in the context of intercultural negotiation: individualism–collectivism and paths to integrative agreements', *Human Communication Research*, **26**(4): 591–617.

16. Ibid.

17. Bazerman, M.H. *et al.* (2000) op. cit.

18. Brett, J.M. (2000) 'Culture and negotiation', *International Journal of Psychology*, **35**(2): 97–104.

19. Bazerman, M.H. *et al.* (2000) op. cit.

20. Zartman, W. and Touval, S. (1996) 'International mediation in the post-Cold War era', in Crocker, C., Hampson, F. and Aall, P. (eds) *Managing Global Chaos*: pp. 445–61 (p. 431), Washington, DC: United States Institute of Peace Press.

21. Ayres, W.R. (1997) 'Mediating international conflicts: is image change necessary?' *Journal of Peace Research*, **34**(3): 431–47.

22. Carnevale, P.J. and Choi, D.-W. (2000) 'Culture in the mediation of international disputes', *International Journal of Psychology*, **35**(2): 105–10.

23. Odendaal, A. (1998) 'Modelling mediation: evolving approaches to mediation in South Africa', *Online Journal of Peace and Conflict Resolution*, **1**(3). URL: http://www.trinstitute. Org/ojpcr/1 3tt2.htm

24. Ibid.

25. Strohschneider, S. (2002) 'Cultural factors in complex decision making', in Lonner, W.J., Dinnel, D.L., Hayes, S.A. and Sattler, D.N. (eds), *Online Readings in Psychology and Culture* (unit 15, chapter 8). URL: http://www.wwu.edu/~culture

26. Gibson, C.B. and Zellmer-Bruhn, M.E. (2001) 'Metaphors and meaning: an intercultural analysis of the concept of teamwork', *Administrative Science Quarterly*, **46**: 274–303.

27. Polzer, J.T., Milton, L.P. and Swann, W.B. (2002) 'Capitalizing on diversity: interpersonal congruence in small work groups', *Administrative Science Quarterly*, **47**(2): 296–324.

28. Dansby, M.R. and Knouse, S.B. (1999) 'Percentage of work-group diversity and work-group effectiveness', *Journal of Psychology*, **133**: 486–95.

29. Gibson, C.B. and Vermeulen, F. (2003) 'A healthy divide: subgroups as a stimulus for team learning behavior', *Administrative Science Quarterly*, **48**: 75–99.
30. Punnett, B.J. and Clemens, J. (1999) 'Cross-national diversity: implications for international expansion decisions', *Journal of World Business*, **34**(2): 128–38.
31. Polzer, J.T. *et al.* (2002) op. cit.
32. Ely, R.J. and Thomas, D.A. (2001) 'Cultural diversity at work: the effects of diversity perspectives on work group processes and outcomes', *Administrative Science Quarterly*, **46**: 229–73.
33. Adler, J. (1991) *International Dimensions of Organizational Behavior*, Belmont, CA: Kent.
34. Hambrick, D.C. (1998) 'When groups consist of multiple nationalities: towards a new understanding of the implications', *Organization Studies*, **19**(2): 181–206.
35. Ibid.
36. Jehn, K.A., Northcote, G.B. and Neale, M.A. (1999) 'Why differences make a difference: a field study of diversity, conflict and performance in workgroups', *Administrative Science Quarterly*, **44**: 741–63.
37. Pelled, L.H., Eisenhardt, K.M. and Xin, K.R. (1999) 'Exploring the black box: an analysis of work group diversity, conflict and performance', *Administrative Science Quarterly*, **44**: 1–28.
38. Pelled, L.H. (1996) 'Relational demography and perceptions of group conflict and performance: a field investigation', *International Journal of Conflict Management*, **7**: 230–46.
39. Jehn, K. and Weldon, E. (1992) 'A comparative study of managerial attitudes toward conflict in the United States and the People's Republic of China: issues of theory and measurement', Annual Meeting of the Academy of Management 1992, Las Vegas, NV.
40. Ely, R.J. (2001) op. cit.
41. Chatman, J., Polzer, J., Barsade, S. and Neale, M. (1998) 'Being different yet feeling similar: the influence of demographic composition and organizational culture on work processes and outcomes', *Administrative Science Quarterly*, **43**(3): 668–98.
42. Ibid.
43. McLeod, P.L. and Lobel, S.A. 'The effects of ethnic diversity on idea generation in small groups', *Academy of Management Best Papers Proceedings* **92**: 227–36.
44. Ibid.
45. Watson, W.E., Kumar, K. and Michaelson, L.K. (1993) 'Cultural diversity's impact on interaction process and performance: Comparing homogeneous and diverse task groups', *Academy of Management Journal*, **36**(3): 590–602.
46. Schreiber, E.J. (1996) 'Muddles and huddles: facilitating a multicultural workforce through team management theory', *The Journal of Business Communication*, **33**: 459–73.
47. Hirschhorn, L. (1991) *Managing in the New Team Environment: Skills, Tools and Methods*: p. 54, Lincoln, NE: Author's Choice Press.
48. Dansby, M.R. (1999) op. cit.
49. Polzer, J.T. (2002) op. cit.
50. Coopman, S.J. and Applegate, J.L. (1997) 'Social-cognitive influences on the use of persuasive message strategies among health care team members', in Eisenberg, E. and Goodall, H. (eds) *Organizational Communication: Balancing Creativity and Constraint*, 2nd edn, New York: St. Martin's Press.
51. Fine, M.G. (1995) *Building Successful Multicultural Organizations*, London: Quorum Books.
52. Hambrick, D.C. (1998) op. cit.
53. Lubatkin, M.H., Ndiaye, M. and Vengroff, R. (1997) 'The nature of managerial work in developing countries; a limited test of the universalist hypothesis', *Journal of International Business Strategy*, **28**(4): 711–33.
54. Furnham, A. and Stringfield, P. (1993) 'Personality and occupational behavior: Myers-Briggs Type indicator correlates of managerial practices in two cultures', *Human Relations*, **46**: 827–44.
55. Boone, P.F. and van Den Bosch, F.A.J. (1996) 'Discerning a key characteristic of a European style of management: managing the tension between integration opportunities and the constraining diversity in Europe', *International Studies of Management & Organization*, **26**(3): 109–27.
56. House, R., Wright, N. and Aditya, R.N. (1999) 'Cross cultural research on organizational leadership: a critical analysis and a proposed theory', *Working Paper of the Reginald H. Jones Center*, The Wharton School University of Pennsylvania WP 99-03A 48.

57. Bond, M.H. and Smith, P.B. (1996) 'Cross-cultural social and organizational psychology', *Annual Review of Psychology*, **47**: 205–35.
58. Smith, P.B., Trompenaars, F. and Dugan, S. (1995) 'The Rotter locus of control scale in 43 countries: a test of cultural relativity', *International Journal of Psychology*, **30**: 377–400.
59. Torrington, D. (1994) *International Human Resource Management*, Hemel Hempstead, England: Prentice-Hall.
60. Calori, R. and Lawrence, P. (1992) 'Diversity still remains – views of European managers', *Long Range Planning*, **25**(2): 33–43.
61. Sloan, D.K. and Krone, K.J. (2000) 'Women managers and gendered values', *Women's Studies in Communication*, **23**(1): 111–30.
62. Arvonen, J. and Lindell, M. (1996) 'The Nordic management style in a European context', *International Studies of Management & Organization*, **26**(3): 73–93.
63. Cummings, L.L., Harnett, D.L. and Stevens, O.J. (1971) 'Risk, fate, conciliation, and trust: an international study of attitudinal differences among executives', *Academy of Management Journal*, **14**: 285–304.
64. Sparrow, P.R. and Budhwar, P. (1998) 'Reappraising psychological contracting: lessons for the field of human-resource development from cross-cultural and occupational psychology research', *International Studies of Management & Organization*, **28**(4): 26–52.
65. Globokar, T. (1996) 'Intercultural management in Eastern Europe: an empirical study of a French–Slovenian plant', *International Studies of Management & Organization*, **26**(3): 47–60.
66. Michailova, S. (2002) 'When common sense becomes uncommon: participation and empowerment in Russian companies with Western participation', *Journal of World Business*, **37**(3): 180–87.
67. Hui, M.K., Au, K. and Fock, H. (2004) 'Empowerment effects across cultures', *Journal of International Business Studies*, **35**(1): 46–60.
68. Kozan, M.K. (1993) 'Cultural and industrialization level influences on leadership attitudes for Turkish managers', *International Studies of Management & Organization*, **23**(3): 7–18.
69. Pelled, L.H. (1996) op. cit.
70. Haslam, S.A. and Platow, M.J. (2001) 'Your wish is our command: the role of shared identity in translating a leader's vision into followers' action', in Hogg, M.A. and Terry, D.J. (eds) *Social Identity Processes in Organizational Contexts*: pp. 213–28, Philadelphia, PA: Psychology Press.
71. Hartog, D., House, R.J., Hanges, R.J., Ruiz-Quntanilla, S.A. and Dorfman, R.W. (1999) 'Culture specific and cross culturally generalizable implicit leadership theories: are attributes of charismatic/ transformational leadership universally endorsed?' *Leadership Quarterly*, **10**(2): 219–56.
72. Triandis, H.C. *et al.* (1993) 'An etic-emic analysis of individualism and collectivism', *Journal of Cross Cultural Psychology*, **24**: 366–83.
73. Pillai, R. and Meindl, J.R. (1998) 'Context and charisma: a "meso" level examination of the relationship of organic structure, collectivism, and crisis to charismatic leadership', *Journal of Management*, **24**(5): 643–71.
74. Anakwe, U.P., Anandarajan, M. and Igbaria, M. (2000) 'Management practices across cultures: role of support in technology usage', *Journal of International Business Studies*, **31**(4): 653–66.
75. Sparrow, P.R. (1998) op. cit.
76. Czaplewski, A.J., Milliman, J. and Taylor, S. (2002) 'Cross-cultural performance feedback in multinational enterprises: opportunity for organizational learning', *Human Resource Planning*, **25**(3): 29–43.
77. McGuire, G.M. (1999) 'Do race and sex affect employees' access to and help from mentors?: insights from the study of a large corporation', in Murrell, A.J., Crosby, F.J. and Ely, R.J. (eds) *Mentoring Dilemmas: Developmental Relationships within Multicultural Organizations*, Mahwah, NJ: Lawrence Erlbaum.
78. Goto, S. (1999) 'Asian Americans and developmental relationships' in Murrell, A.J., Crosby, F.J. and Ely, R.J. (eds) *Mentoring Dilemmas: Developmental Relationships within Multicultural Organizations*, Mahwah, NJ: Lawrence Erlbaum.
79. Crosby, F.J. (1999) 'The developing literature on developmental relationships', in Murrell, A.J., Crosby, F.J. and Ely, R.J. (eds) *Mentoring Dilemmas: Developmental Relationships within Multicultural Organizations*, Mahwah, NJ: Lawrence Erlbaum.

80. Hoyt, S.K. (1999) 'Mentoring with class: connections between social class and developmental relationships in the Academy', in Murrell, A.J., Crosby, F.J. and Ely, R.J. (eds) *Mentoring Dilemmas: Developmental Relationships within Multicultural Organizations*, Mahwah, NJ: Lawrence Erlbaum.
81. Hoyt, S.K. (1999) op. cit.
82. Fine, M.G. (1995) op. cit.
83. Ibid., p. 153.
84. Schreiber, E.J. (1996) op. cit.
85. Dadfar, H. and Gustavsson, P. (1992) 'Competition by effective management of cultural diversity: the case of international construction projects', *International Studies of Management & Organization*, **22**(4): 81–92.
86. Luo, Y. (2001) 'Antecedents and consequences of personal attachment in cross-cultural cooperative ventures', *Administrative Science Quarterly*, **46**(2): 177–202.
87. Barkema, H.G. and Vermeulen, F. (1997) 'What differences in the cultural backgrounds of partners are detrimental for international joint ventures?' *Journal of International Business Studies*, **28**(4): 845–69.
88. Brannen, M.Y. and Salk, J.E. (2000) 'Partnering across borders: negotiating organizational culture in a German–Japanese joint-venture', *Human Relations*, **53**(4): 451–7.
89. Very, P., Lubatkin, M. and Calori, R. (1996) 'A cross-national assessment of acculturative stress in recent European mergers', *International Studies of Management and Organization*, **26**(1): 59–86.
90. Abramov, M., Arino, A., Rykounina, I., Skorobogatykh, I. and Vila, J. (1997) 'Partner selection and trust building in West European–Russian joint ventures: a Western perspective', *International Studies of Management & Organization*, **27**(1): 19–38.
91. Aulakh, P.S., Kotabe, M. and Sahay, A. (1996) 'Trust and performance in cross-border marketing partnerships: a behavioral approach', *Journal of International Business Studies*, **27**(5): 1005–32.
92. Child, J., Chung, L. and Davies, H. (2003) 'The performance of cross-border units in China: a test of natural selection, strategic choice and contingency theories', *Journal of International Business Studies*, **34**(3): 242–54.
93. Griffith, D.A. (2002) 'The role of communication competencies in international business relationship development', *Journal of World Business*, **37**(4): 256–65.
94. Child, J. *et al.* (2003) op. cit.
95. Byers, K.M. and Lyles, M.A. (1994) 'An examination of a health care international joint venture in Poland', *International Studies of Management & Organization*, **24**(4): 31–47.
96. Larsson, R. and Lubatkin, M. (2001) 'Achieving acculturation in mergers and acquisitions: an international case survey', *Human Relations*, **54**(12): 1573–609.
97. Inkpen, A.C. and Beamish, P.W. (1997) 'Knowledge, bargaining power, and the instability of international joint ventures', *Academy of Management Review*, **22**: 177–202.
98. Luo, Y. (2001) op. cit.
99. Pelled, L.H. (1996) op. cit.

Appendices

appendix A

European Diversity Data

A.1 GROWTH OF TRADE

By value indexed at 100 in 1990, world exports of merchandise increased from 2 in 1950 to 183 in 2000, dipping to 175 in 2001. Europe shared in this growth. Western Europe's merchandise exports grew by an average annual 5.9 per cent over the period 1995 to 2000, only falling back by 1 per cent in 2001; merchandise exports of Central and Eastern Europe, the Baltic states and CIS grew by an average annual 8.4 per cent between 1995 and 2001, despite a dip in 1999. Sixty-seven per cent of Western Europe's merchandise trade is within the region and 6 per cent is with the rest of Europe; for Central and Eastern Europe, the Baltic states and CIS, 27 per cent is intra-regional and 55 per cent with Western Europe. World exports of commercial services grew by 77 per cent between 1991 and 2000, with a small drop to 75 per cent in 2001; Europe's share of this trade was 51 per cent in 1990 and though it had fallen to only 46 per cent of this total by 2001, it had nevertheless grown by 58 per cent over the period. Statistics for exports of commercial services for Central and Eastern Europe, the Baltic States and CIS are only available since 1998, and they show a 6 per cent growth by 2001.

A.2 STOCKS OF FOREIGN POPULATION

The total recorded stock of foreign population living in European countries in 1997 was almost 21 million people (out of a total population of 810 million). The foreign population thus appears to constitute some 2.5 per cent of the aggregate population of Europe. The greater part of this foreign stock was resident in Western Europe. In Eastern Europe, the country with the highest percentage of foreign nationals in 1997 was Slovenia, with 2.1 per cent; of the 147 million population of the Russian Federation, only 0.1 per cent was recorded as foreign nationals. It is important to bear in mind, however, that the amount of interethnic and intercultural communication is a function of the ethnic mix of the national population as well as foreign residents; ethnic mix is much higher in Russia than many other countries (see Table A.1).

Table A.1 *Percentage of minority group members and foreign residents in various European countries*

Country	Pop'n millions	Ethnic groups	Religions	Languages	Foreign residents (%) 1990	Foreign residents (%) 1997
Austria	8	German 88%, Non-nationals 9.3% (includes Croatians, Slovenes, Hungarians, Czechs, Slovaks, Roma), Naturalised 2% (includes those who have lived in Austria at least three generations)	Roman Catholic 78%, Protestant 5%, Muslim and other 17%	German	5.9	9.1
Belgium	10.3	Flemish 58%, Walloon 31%, Mixed or other 11%	Roman Catholic 75%, Protestant or other 25%	Dutch 60%, French 40%, German less than 1%, Bilingual (Dutch and French)	9.1	8.9
Czech Republic	10.3	Czech 81.2%, Moravian 13.2%, Slovak 3.1%, Polish 0.6%, German 0.5%, Silesian 0.4%, Roma 0.3%, Hungarian 0.2%, Other 0.5% (1991)	Atheist 39.8%, Roman Catholic 39.2%, Protestant 4.6%, Orthodox 3%, Other 13.4%	Czech		
Denmark	5.4	Scandinavian, Inuit, Faroese, German, Turkish, Iranian, Somali	Evangelical Lutheran 95%, Other Protestant and Roman Catholic 3%, Muslim 2%	Danish, Faroese, Greenlandic (an Inuit dialect), German (small minority)	3.1	4.5
Estonia	1.4	Estonian 65.3%, Russian 28.1%, Ukrainian 2.5%, Belarusian 1.5%, Finnish 1%,	Evangelical Lutheran, Russian Orthodox, Estonian Orthodox, Baptist, Methodist, Seventh-Day Adventist,	Estonian (official), Russian, Ukrainian, Finnish, Other	n/a	n/a

		Roman Catholic, Pentecostal, Word of Life, Jewish	Other 1.6% (1998)		
Eire	4	Roman Catholic 91.6%, Church of Ireland 2.5%, Other 5.9% (1998)	Celtic, English	English, Irish (Gaelic) spoken mainly in areas along the western seaboard	0.8	3.1
Finland	5	Evangelical Lutheran 89%, Russian Orthodox 1%, None 9%, Other 1%	Finnish 93%, Swedish 6%, Sami 0.11%, Roma 0.12%, Tatar 0.02%	Finnish 94%, Swedish, 6% Small Lapp- and Russian- speaking minorities	0.5	1.6
France	60	Roman Catholic 83%–88%, Protestant 2%, Jewish 1%, Muslim 5%–10%, Unaffiliated 4%	Celtic and Latin with Teutonic, Slavic, North African, Indo-Chinese and Basque minorities	French, Rapidly declining regional dialects and languages (Provencal, Breton, Alsatian, Corsican, Catalan, Basque, Flemish)	6.3	6.3
Germany	83	Protestant 34%, Roman Catholic 34%, Muslim 3.7%, Unaffiliated or other 28.3%	German 91.5%, Turkish 2.4%, Other 6.1% (made up largely of Serbo-Croatian, Italian, Russian, Greek, Polish, Spanish)	German	8.2	8.9
Greece	11	Greek Orthodox 98%, Muslim 1.3%, Other 0.7%	Greek 98%, Other 2%	Greek 99% English, French	2.3	1.5
Hungary	10	Roman Catholic 67.5%, Calvinist 20%, Lutheran 5%, Atheist and other 7.5%	Hungarian 89.9%, Roma 4%, German 2.6%, Serb 2%, Slovak 0.8%, Romanian 0.7%	Hungarian 98.2%, Other 1.8%	n/a	n/a

cont'd

Table A.1   *(cont'd)*

Country	Pop'n millions	Ethnic groups	Religions	Languages	Foreign residents (%)	
					1990	1997
Italy	58	Italian (includes small clusters of German-, French-,and Slovene-Italians in the north and Albanian-Italians and Greek-Italians in the south)	Predominantly Roman Catholic with mature Protestant and Jewish communities and a growing Muslim immigrant community	Italian, German, French, Slovene	1.4	2.2
Latvia	2.4	Latvian 57.7%, Russian 29.6%, Belarusian 4.1%, Ukrainian 2.7%, Polish 2.5%, Lithuanian 1.4%, Other 2%	Lutheran, Roman Catholic, Russian Orthodox	Latvian, Lithuanian, Russian, Other		
Lithuania	3.6	Lithuanian 80.6%, Russian 8.7%, Polish 7%, Belarusian 1.6%, Other 2.1%	Roman Catholic (primarily), Lutheran, Russian Orthodox, Protestant, Evangelical Christian Baptist, Muslim, Jewish	Lithuanian, Polish, Russian		
Netherlands	16	Dutch 83%, Other 17% (of which 9% are non-Western origin mainly Turks, Moroccans, Antilleans, Surinamese and Indonesians) (1999 est.)	Roman Catholic 31%, Protestant 21%, Muslim 4.4%, Other 3.6%, Unaffiliated 40% (1998)	Dutch	4.6	4.5
Norway	4.5	Norwegian, Sami (20,000)	Evangelical Lutheran 86%, Other Protestant and Roman Catholic 3%,	Norwegian, Small Sami- and Finnish-speaking	3.4	3.6

Poland	39	Polish 97.6%, German 1.3%, Ukrainian 0.6%, Belarusian 0.5% (1990 est.)	Roman Catholic 95% (about 75% practising), Eastern Orthodox, Protestant, and other 5%	Polish	n/a	n/a
Portugal	10	Homogeneous Mediterranean stock, Citizens of black African descent who immigrated to mainland during decolonisation number less than 100,000, Since 1990 East Europeans have entered Portugal	Roman Catholic 94%, Protestant	Portuguese	1.1	1.7
Russia	145	Russian 81.5%, Tatar 3.8%, Ukrainian 3%, Chuvash 1.2%, Bashkir 0.9%, Belarusian 0.8%, Moldavian 0.7%, Other 8.1%	Russian Orthodox, Muslim, Other	Russian, Other	n/a	0.1
Slovenia	2	Slovene 88%, Croat 3%, Serb 2%, Bosnian 1%, Yugoslav 0.6%, Hungarian 0.4%, Other 5% (1991)	Roman Catholic 70.8%, Lutheran 1%, Muslim 1%, Atheist 4.3%, Other 22.9%	Slovenian 91%, Serbo-Croatian 6%, Other 3%		
Spain	40	Composite of Mediterranean and Nordic types	Roman Catholic 94%, Other 6%	Castilian Spanish 74%, Catalan 17%, Galician 7%, Basque 2%	1.0	1.5
Sweden	9	Swedish Finnish and Sami minorities,	Lutheran 87%, Roman Catholic,	Swedish, Small Sami- and minorities	5.6	5.9

cont'd

Table A.1 *(cont'd)*

Country	Pop'n millions	Ethnic groups	Religions	Languages	Foreign residents (%) 1990	Foreign residents (%) 1997
		Foreign-born or first-generation immigrants: Finns, Yugoslavs, Danes, Norwegians, Greeks, Turks	Orthodox, Baptist, Muslim, Jewish, Buddhist	Finnish-speaking minorities		
Switzerland	7	German 65%, French 18%, Italian 10%, Romansch 1%, Other 6%	Roman Catholic 46.1%, Protestant 40%, Other 5%, None 8.9% (1990)	German 63.7%, French 19.2%, Italian 7.6%, Romansch 0.6%, Other 8.9%	16.3	19.4
United Kingdom	60	English 81.5%, Scottish 9.6%, Irish 2.4%, Welsh 1.9%, Ulster 1.8%, West Indian, Indian, Pakistani and other 2.8%	Anglican and Roman Catholic 66%, Muslim 2.5%, Presbyterian 1.3%, Methodist 1.2%, Sikh, Hindu, Jewish	English, Welsh (about 26% of the population of Wales),Scottish form of Gaelic (about 60,000 in Scotland)	3.3	3.5
Turkey	67	Turkish 80%, Kurdish 20%	Muslim 99.8% (mostly Sunni), Other 0.2% (mostly Christians and Jews)	Turkish, Kurdish, Arabic, Armenian, Greek	n/a	0.2
United States	281	White 77.1%, Black 12.9%, Asian 4.2%, Amerindian and Alaska native 1.5%, Native Hawaiian and other Pacific islander 0.3%, Other 4% (2000)*	Protestant 56%, Roman Catholic 28%, Jewish 2%, Other 4%, None 10% (1989)	English, Spanish (spoken by a sizeable minority)		

| World | 6,233 | Christians 32.88% (of which Roman Catholics 17.39%, Protestants 5.62%, Orthodox 3.54%, Anglicans 1.31%), Muslims 19.54%, Hindus 13.34%, Buddhists 5.92%, Sikhs 0.38%, Jews 0.24%, Other religions 12.6%, Non-religious 12.63%, Atheists 2.47% (2000 est.) | Chinese, Mandarin 14.37%, Hindi 6.02%, English 5.61%, Spanish 5.59%, Bengali 3.4%, Portuguese 2.63%, Russian 2.75%, Japanese 2.06%, German, Standard 1.64%, Korean 1.28%, French 1.27% (2000 est.) | n/a | n/a |

Note: * a separate listing for Hispanic is not included because the US Census Bureau considers Hispanic to mean a person of Latin American descent (including persons of Cuban, Mexican or Puerto Rican origin) living in the US who may be of any race or ethnic group (White, Black, Asian, etc.)

Source: World Factbook 2002 (CIA). Stock of foreign population as a percentage of total population in selected European countries, 1980–97 (%): Council of Europe, Social Cohesion Committee

Immigration in 1992 into the nine EU countries able to provide data was substantial and diverse, including 400,000 former Yugoslavians, 130,000 Poles, 110,000 Romanians, 90,000 Turks and 75,000 Russians.

A.3 LABOUR MARKET POSITION OF ETHNIC MINORITIES IN THE NETHERLANDS

Out of a total population of 16 million, the Netherlands population in 2001 included 320,000 Turks, 273,000 Moroccans, 309,000 Surinamese, 117,000 Antilleans and 179,000 refugees, not counting refugees from the former Yugoslavia. The labour market position of some of these groups is shown in Table A.2. While it is clear that these minorities suffer labour market disadvantages, it is also clear that they are a significant element in the workforce.

Except for Turks, the relative disadvantage in comparison with Dutch of all ethnic minority groups in terms of percentage in work fell between 1991 and 1998: for example the percentage working increased by 15 percentage points for the Surinamese against 8 percentage points for the Dutch. All groups also experienced a substantial reduction in unemployment levels during those years, again outweighing the reduction for the Dutch. Despite this, as Table A.2 shows, the level of unemployment among these minority groups remained high.

A.4 LABOUR MARKET POSITION OF ETHNIC MINORITIES IN THE UK

At the 2001 Census, 87 per cent of the population of England and Wales described themselves as White British, 1.2 per cent as White Irish, 2 per cent as Pakistani, 2 per cent as Indian, 0.5 per cent as Bangladeshi, 1.1 per cent as Black Caribbean, 0.9 per cent as African, 0.2 per cent as from other Black groups, and 1 per cent of mixed ethnicity. Around half of all the members of the ethnic minority groups listed earlier were born in England or Wales. In England, they made up 9 per cent of the total population, an increase from 6 per cent in 1991. Nearly half (45 per cent) of the total minority ethnic population lived in the London region, where they comprised 29 per cent of all residents; another concentration was in the West Midlands, where they made up 13 per cent of the population.

According to the UK Labour Force Survey, in 2001 the unemployment rate for people from ethnic minorities (median 14 per cent for men and 10 per cent for women) was

Table A.2   *Labour market position of Turks, Moroccans, Surinamese, Antillians and Dutch in the Netherlands in 1998 (%)*

	Labour market participation (% 15–64 age group)	Working (% of labour market participants)	Registered unemployed (% of labour market participants)
Turks	47	37	18
Moroccans	44	34	20
Surinamese	66	58	10
Antilleans	62	53	13
Dutch	69	65	4

Note: Columns 2 and 3 do not add to 100%, because of 'not working' labour market participants

Table A.3   *Managerial responsibility of employees: by gender and ethnic group, Spring 2000 (%) Great Britain*

	White	Black	Indian	Pakistani/ Bangladeshi	Other	All employees
Males						
Managers	23	13	17	12	21	23
Foremen	12	12	8	7	11	12
Not managers, foremen or supervisors	65	76	75	81	68	65
Females						
Managers	14	12	10	—	12	14
Foremen [sic]	11	14	13	—	13	11
Not managers, foremen or supervisors	74	75	77	82	76	74

Source: Labour Force Survey, UK Office for National Statistics

more than double the rate for White people (5 per cent and 4 per cent respectively). On the plus side, members of the ethnic minorities experienced lower rates of part-time employment, with its usual connotations of poor pay, lack of security, pensions, sick pay and holiday pay, at 21 per cent and 26 per cent respectively, though these figures are strongly influenced by the lower rate of part-time employment of ethnic minority women (33 per cent against 46 per cent for white women); 10 per cent of ethnic minority men were in part-time employment against 7 per cent of White men.

In 1995, average hourly earnings of full-time employees from ethnic minorities were about 92 per cent of those of White employees. However, the overall figures disguise some significant differences: 49 per cent of all Pakistani and Bangladeshi workers earned less than £4.50 (7.2 euros) per hour compared with 31 per cent of White workers and 21 per cent of Black workers.

Obtaining qualifications helped both ethnic minority and White employees: in 2001 the median employment rate gap between those with higher qualifications and those with none was 35 and 38 percentage points for ethnic minority men and women respectively, against 32 and 37 percentage points for their White equivalents. However, cultural factors, such as the tendency for women in some groups to neither seek qualifications nor work must have an influence, while higher qualifications still do not give ethnic minority members the same advantage as Whites: the median employment rates for ethnic minority men with higher qualifications was 83.5 per cent against 90 per cent for their White equivalents (but for Indians it was 91 per cent); for women the corresponding figures are 75 per cent and 85 per cent respectively.

There are various explanations given for the evident employment disadvantage of members of ethnic minorities:

■ Employers commonly claim that such workers have 'communication difficulties'; there is some truth in it as regards some small groups such as older Asian women in Coventry, but the disadvantage also applies to the much larger and growing part of the population which was born and educated in the UK.

- Employers also claim that ethnic minority members have skill or education deficits. However, several studies have shown that when qualifications are controlled for, ethnic minority workers are still more likely to be unemployed or at lower job levels. There is also evidence that discrimination blocks ethnic minority young people at the earlier training stage.

A.5　GENDER AND POSITIONS OF POWER

In both Eastern and Western Europe women are under-represented in positions of power; however, the comparative position varies between the two regions in respect of senior positions in the public and private sector and in representational roles. In Eastern Europe, women have done better in the private sector but worse in public administration; in representational assemblies, the 1987 position in which there were more women in parliaments in the East was reversed following the end of communism there. Indeed it has shown an absolute decline, while in Western Europe women improved their position. In the UK, the 1997 election increased women's representation in parliament by more than one hundred Members of Parliament.

A.6　ETHNICITY/GENDER INTERACTIVE EFFECTS

Ethnicity and gender can be expected to produce combined effects on the employment positions of ethnic minority women, though there is some debate about whether the combination tends to make for 'double jeopardy' or to be mutually compensatory. In the UK, ethnic minority women are less likely to be unemployed than their male equivalents, though to a lesser degree than White women are in comparison with their male counterparts. They are less likely to be in part-time employment than White women (33 per cent against 46 per cent) though more than three times as likely as ethnic minority men (10 per cent) and nearly five times as likely as White men (7 per cent). Most of the difference in earnings of ethnic minority workers compared to White is due to different pay rates for White and ethnic minority men. Earnings of women from ethnic minorities were on average roughly the same as those of White women.

A.7　PEOPLE WITH DISABILITIES

A UK study showed that of men with a long term illness or disability affecting their daily lives, 18 per cent were senior managers, 27 per cent were first-tier managers,

Table A.4　*Percentage of women's share in the main professional categories, Eastern and Western Europe 1990*

	Eastern Europe	Western Europe
Professionals and technicians	56	50
Administrative and management personnel	33	18
Office clerks and similar positions	73	63
Sales force	66	48
Production and transport operators and manual workers	27	16

Source: Women's Indicators and Statistics Database (United Nations)

23 per cent were field workers, 27 per cent were residential workers, 5 per cent were home care workers (base 22). Of women, 1 per cent were senior managers, 12 per cent were first-tier managers, 16 per cent were field workers, 26 per cent were residential workers, 45 per cent were home care workers (base 148). These figures show that the careers of people with disabilities are not always adversely affected.[1] They are, however, disproportionately likely to suffer unemployment, as Figure 1.3, for eight EU countries, illustrated.

A study of 21 countries found that labour market participation rates of people with disabilities were relatively high in Sweden, New Zealand, Germany and France, below average in Ireland, Poland, Greece and Italy, while Great Britain, Australia, Finland, Norway and Austria are amongst those in between. Sweden, Finland, Norway and the English-speaking countries have high levels of labour market training for people with disabilities, in the case of the Nordic countries generally with long-term wage subsidies; market participation does not, however, correlate very closely with the availability of such programmes.

A.8   OLDER PEOPLE IN THE WORKFORCE

Sixty-two per cent of British men and 45 per cent of women in the 50-plus age group are at work. These are well above average EU figures, but still far below those for younger people. About 25 per cent of the UK population in 2006 is projected to be aged between 45 and 65, compared with 22.7 per cent in 1996 and this figure is set to continue rising. In February 1996 figures were published which claimed that the number of workers aged over 49 unable to find employment within two years or more had doubled since 1990. There is evidence that discrimination is part of the cause. However, a combination of demography and law are expected to reduce age discrimination across the EU, as the following extract suggests:

> The UK government, supposedly obeying an EU directive, but really because it is worried by the growing pensions burden, is to ban age discrimination.
>
> The ban will be wide. It will cover recruitment, training (including entry to higher education), promotion, pay, job-retention and – not least – retirement. In principle, enforced retirement at a given age will be banned; but the government is open to the idea that some employers could 'objectively' justify a fixed age, and/or that any employer could lawfully push workers out at 70.[2]

NOTES AND REFERENCES

1. McLean, J. (2002) 'Employees with long term illnesses or disabilities in the UK social services workforce', *Disability and Society*, **18**(1): 51–70.
2. 'Times up for ageism', *The Economist*, 5 July 2003, p. 32.

Culture and Mediated Work Communication

Telephone conversations, letters, electronic mail (e-mail), fax messages, text messaging on mobile phones, computer conferencing and voice mail are all examples of mediated interpersonal communication. Their growing use at work raises important questions about their direct and indirect effects on communication and relationships, especially when the users are from different (sub)cultures.

Media can be ranged along a continuum of 'social presence'. This is a matter of how well different media overcome various constraints of time and distance, transmit the social symbolic and non-verbal cues of human communication and convey ambiguous information.[1] Media high in social presence produce representations of objects, events and people that look and sound like the real thing, create a sense that two or more participants are physically together, and provide immediacy and intimacy, which are two important features of face-to-face communication. Face-to-face communication has the richest level of social presence, followed by audio-visual, audio and written communication in that order. However, it has been shown that computer users respond socially to their computers. For instance, they follow social rules concerning politeness and gender stereotypes, and evaluate a computer's performance in a tutoring task more favourably when another computer praises the tutor computer than when it praises itself.

A medium's social presence is determined by its formal and content features and by characteristics of the medium user. Media features include the number of human senses for which a medium provides stimulation, the quality of its visual display, and whether it uses stereoscopic images, subjective camera shots and changes of viewpoint and sound quality. Interactivity is another important media feature for presence. Major aspects of interactivity include the number of inputs from the user to which the medium responds, its speed of response ('real time' is ideal) and how closely the type of medium response corresponds to the type of user input. Characteristics of the media user that can affect social presence include his or her willingness to suspend disbelief and amount of prior experience with the medium. (Prior use of the medium reduces the amount of social presence experienced.)

High social presence has been found to enhance performance on tasks which are wide ranging, complex and uncertain, such as tele-operations, where operators need to be able to extend their adaptive responses to another physical environment. Research subjects who watched a 15-minute infomercial in a visually immersive setting (cinema) experienced higher presence than those who watched it in a visually non-immersive setting (at-home television). They also expressed more confidence in their brand choices, showing that higher social presence can influence attitudes. Again, memory of images may be enhanced by high presence, though memory of the source of the images may be impaired.

Not surprisingly, there is as yet little concrete information on how (sub)cultural differences affect mediated communication. In theory, because communication media like e-mail lack social context cues and participants may have a feeling of anonymity, people of lower social status may participate more equally than they do face-to-face. However, findings do not support this contention. In on-line discussions, research found, men sent longer and more frequent messages than women, and Whites sent more messages than other cultural groups. Moreover men were more willing to adopt the technology than women and Whites were more willing than other cultural groups. Men presented more dominating behaviour on-line. The researcher concluded that on-line discussions parallel face-to-face interaction in respect of participation by different groups.[2] Another researcher found that in a setting of participants with diverse linguistic backgrounds (an arbitrarily selected 6.5 hour chat session which elicited 3092 contributions from 185 participants), the dominance of English was very strong. This feature may reduce participation by people with limited English language competence.[3]

In a work context, it has been argued that culture can influence the success or failure of intercultural virtual teams. For example, decisions on what data to store in a database could depend on the degree of uncertainty avoidance of a culture, while who gets access to the data could depend on the culture's power distance level.

Mediated communication creates the following opportunities and problems for intercultural communication at work:

- People often experience an extended range of human contacts through electronic communication. Many of these additional contacts may be with people from different (sub)cultures. An example is the now common experience of European consumers interacting with staff of call centres in India.
- Forms of social interaction change. New rules must be established, covering, for instance, what to disclose and what to conceal. Users must also re-align working relationships. People can participate and withdraw from different encounters intermittently. Electronic mediation affects greetings, feedback, turn management and sequencing, all of which this book has shown to be culturally influenced. These changes alter the availability of techniques for improving intercultural communication; for instance, it has been shown that feedback is more necessary for successful intercultural communication but in electronic communication the rate for feedback words is lower than in ordinary spoken interaction. Again, although in electronic communication considerable effort is expended on communication management, conversations nevertheless lack the 'orderliness' of comparable conversations face-to-face or by telephone.
- Users can and must adopt changed roles – new identities and senses of appropriate social standing. The need to manage personal and cultural identities is changed. In some cases, participants can, by not revealing their identities, avoid being stereotyped or victims of prejudice.
- Power structures change in favour of employees who hold new skills or have control of information needed to perform work or receive its benefits. With changed power structures come changed expectations about language, deference and privilege.

NOTES AND REFERENCES

1. Rice, R.E. (1992) 'Task analyzability, use of new medium and effectiveness: a multi-site exploration of media richness', *Organization Science*, **3**(4): 475–500.
2. Stewart, C.M., Shields, S.F. and Sen, N. (2002) 'A Study of cultural and gender differences in Listservs', *Electronic Journal of Communication*, **8**(398). URL: http://www.cios.org/www/ejc/v8n398.htm
3. Allwood, J. and Schroeder, R. (2000) 'Intercultural communication in a virtual environment', *Intercultural Communication*, **4**. URL: http://www.immi.se/intercultural/nr4/allwood.htm

appendix C

Scoring and Interpretation of Questionnaires

CHAPTER TWO

Q24 Questionnaire on own culture

For questions 1, 2, 4, 6, 7, 8, 10, 11, 13, 15, 16, 17 and 19, score 1 for 'Strongly agree', 2 for 'Agree', 3 for 'Neither agree nor disagree', 4 for 'Disagree' and 5 for 'Strongly disagree'.

For questions 3, 5, 9, 12, 14, 18 and 20, score 5 for 'Strongly agree', 4 for 'Agree', 3 for 'Neither agree nor disagree', 2 for 'Disagree' and 1 for 'Strongly disagree'.

Questions 1 to 5 score universalism versus particularism: add your scores for the four questions; scores of 20 or above indicate a strongly universalistic culture; scores of 15 to 19 a moderately universalistic culture; scores of 5 or below a strongly particularistic culture; scores of 6 to 10 a moderately particularistic culture; scores between 10 and 15 are indeterminate.

Questions 6 and 7 score Trompenaars' version of individualism versus collectivism: add your scores for the two questions; scores of 7 and over indicate an individualistic culture; scores of 4 and below a collectivist culture; scores of 5 or 6 are indeterminate.

Questions 8, 9 and 10 score neutrality versus emotionalism: add your scores for the three questions; scores of 10 or above indicate a culture high in 'emotionalism'; scores of 5 or below one high in neutrality; scores between 6 and 9 are indeterminate.

Questions 11 and 12 score specificity versus diffuseness: add your scores for the two questions; scores of 7 and over indicate a specific culture; scores of 4 and below a diffuse culture; scores of 5 or 6 are indeterminate.

Questions 13 to 15 score achievement versus ascription as the basis for status: add your scores for the three questions; scores of 10 or above indicate an 'achievement' culture; scores of 5 or below indicate an ascription culture; scores between 6 and 9 are indeterminate.

Questions 16, 17 and 18 score the value placed on time: add your scores for the three questions; scores of 5 and below indicate a culture which values time highly; scores of 10 and above a less time-conscious culture; scores of 6 to 9 are indeterminate.

Questions 19 and 20 score past versus future orientation: add your scores for the two questions; scores of 4 and below indicate a past-orientated culture; scores of 7 and above a future-orientated culture; scores of 5 or 6 are indeterminate.

CHAPTER THREE

Q14 For all questions, score 5 for 'Strongly agree', 4 for 'Agree', 3 for 'Neither agree nor disagree', 2 for 'Disagree' and 1 for 'Strongly disagree'.

This questionnaire scores collectivistic high-context communication (CHCC) – individualistic low-context communication (ILCC). Scores above 32 indicate strong CHCC, scores 25 to 32 indicate moderate CHCC, scores below 9 indicate strong ILCC, scores of 9 to 16 indicate moderate ILCC, scores of 17 to 32 are indeterminate.

Q18 For all questions, score 5 for 'Strongly agree', 4 for 'Agree', 3 for 'Neither agree nor disagree', 2 for 'Disagree' and 1 for 'Strongly disagree'.

This questionnaire scores different approaches to compliance gaining with subordinates, and is based on the research described in that subsection of this chapter.

Questions 1 and 2 score the main methods used by US managers, reasoning and friendliness. Add your scores for the two questions. Scores of 7 or above indicate agreement with their approach, scores of 3 and below disagreement, scores of 4 to 6 are neutral.

Questions 3 and 4 score the methods used by Japanese managers in permanent employment. Add your scores for the two questions. Scores of 7 or above indicate agreement with their approach, scores of 3 and below disagreement, scores of 4 to 6 are neutral.

Q19 For questions 1, 4, 6, 7 and 8, score 5 for 'Strongly agree', 4 for 'Agree', 3 for 'Neither agree nor disagree', 2 for 'Disagree' and 1 for 'Strongly disagree'.

For questions 2, 3 and 5, score 1 for 'Strongly agree', 2 for 'Agree', 3 for 'Neither agree nor disagree', 4 for 'Disagree' and 5 for 'Strongly disagree'.

Add your scores for all questions. Your culture strongly favours a harmonising, collectivist kind of conflict management if your score is 33 or above, moderately favours it if your score is 25 to 32; scores of 8 or below and 9 to 16 indicate a culture that strongly or moderately favours a competitive, problem-solving individualist kind of conflict management; scores between 17 and 24 are indeterminate.

Q22 For questions 1, 2 and 6, score 5 for 'Strongly agree', 4 for 'Agree', 3 for 'Neither agree nor disagree', 2 for 'Disagree' and 1 for 'Strongly disagree'.

For questions 3, 4, 5 and 7, score 1 for 'Strongly agree', 2 for 'Agree', 3 for 'Neither agree nor disagree', 4 for 'Disagree' and 5 for 'Strongly disagree'.

This questionnaire scores a culture's tendency to high- or low-context communication: Add your scores for all seven questions; scores above 21 indicate a culture that favours low-context communication, to a greater or lesser extent according to the score; scores below 15 indicate a culture that favours high-context communication, similarly to a greater or lesser extent according to the score; scores between 15 and 21 are indeterminate.

CHAPTER FOUR

Q8 For all questions except Q3, score 5 for 'Strongly agree', 4 for 'Agree', 3 for 'Neither agree nor disagree', 2 for 'Disagree' and 1 for 'Strongly disagree'; Q3 is inverse scored. This questionnaire scores different types of communication apprehension (CA).

Add your scores for questions 1 to 5: scores above 20 and 16 to 20 indicate very high and moderately high CA; below 6 and 6 to 10 very low and moderately low CA; 11 to 15 are indeterminate.

Questions 6 to 9 score different kinds of CA: 6 with people of the opposite sex, 7 with people with disabilities, 8 with foreigners, 9 with people from other ethnic groups. For each of these questions, scores of 4 or 5 indicate high CA, 1 or 2 low CA and 3 is indeterminate.

Q19 For questions 1, 4, 9 and 10, score 5 for 'Strongly agree', 4 for 'Agree', 3 for 'Neither agree nor disagree', 2 for 'Disagree' and 1 for 'Strongly disagree'.

For questions 2, 3, 5, 6, 7 and 8, score 1 for 'Strongly agree', 2 for 'Agree', 3 for 'Neither agree nor disagree', 4 for 'Disagree' and 5 for 'Strongly disagree'.

This questionnaire scores self-construals through their effect on communication. Add your scores for all ten questions; scores above 40 indicate strong interdependent self-construals (InterSCs); scores of 31 to 40 indicate moderately strong InterSCs; scores below 11 indicate strong independent self-construals (IndSCs); scores from 11 to 20 indicate moderately strong IndSCs; scores between 21 and 30 are indeterminate.

CHAPTER FIVE

Q20 For questions 1, 3, 4, 6 and 7, score 5 for 'Strongly agree', 4 for 'Agree', 3 for 'Neither agree nor disagree', 2 for 'Disagree' and 1 for 'Strongly disagree'.

For questions 2, 5, 8, 9 and 10, score 1 for 'Strongly agree', 2 for 'Agree', 3 for 'Neither agree nor disagree', 4 for 'Disagree' and 5 for 'Strongly disagree'.

This questionnaire scores communication apprehension/confidence from a different angle from the questionnaire in Chapter 4. Add your scores for all questions. Scores above 40 indicate very low communication apprehension (CA): this can be too low for effectiveness – see the comment on anxiety/uncertainty management on p.397; scores of 31 to 40 indicate moderately low CA; scores below 11 indicate extremely high CA; scores of 11 to 20 indicate moderately high CA; scores of 21 to 30 are indeterminate.

CHAPTER SIX

Q10 Questions 2, 4, 6, 8, 10, 12, 14, 16: score 5 for 'Strongly agree', 4 for 'Agree', 3 for 'Neither agree nor disagree', 2 for 'Disagree' and 1 for 'Strongly disagree'.

Questions 1, 3, 5, 7, 9, 11, 13 and 15, score 1 for 'Strongly agree', 2 for 'Agree', 3 for 'Neither agree nor disagree', 4 for 'Disagree' and 5 for 'Strongly disagree'.

This questionnaire scores tolerance for ambiguity. Scores above 70 indicate high tolerance for ambiguity; scores below 50 indicate low tolerance for ambiguity.

Q24 For all questions, score 5 for 'Strongly agree', 4 for 'Agree', 3 for 'Neither agree nor disagree', 2 for 'Disagree' and 1 for 'Strongly disagree'.

This questionnaire scores states and traits associated with intercultural effectiveness (IE). Item 1 scores mindfulness; item 2 empathy; 3 to 6 tolerance for ambiguity; 7 cultural relativism; 8 attributional confidence; 9 and 10 ethnolinguistic identity strength; and 11 and 12 are obvious.

For an overall measure of intercultural effectiveness, add your scores for all items except Item 11. Scores of 44 and above indicate high IE, 33 to 43 moderately high IE, below 11 very low IE, 12 to 23 moderately low IE, between 24 and 32 are indeterminate. Equivalent interpretation can be made of the scores on individual or groups of items.

CHAPTER EIGHT

Q7 Questions 2, 4, 5, 6, and 7: score 5 for 'Strongly agree', 4 for 'Agree', 3 for 'Neither agree nor disagree', 2 for 'Disagree' and 1 for 'Strongly disagree'.

Questions 1, 3 and 8, score 1 for 'Strongly agree', 2 for Agree', 3 for 'Neither agree nor disagree', 4 for 'Disagree' and 5 for 'Strongly disagree'.

This questionnaire scores Western-style versus non-Western-style negotiating approaches. Scores above 32 indicate a strong cultural tendency to negotiate in a Western style (WSN); scores of 25 to 32 indicate moderate WSN; scores below 9 indicate a strong cultural tendency to negotiate in a non-Western style (NWSN); scores of 9 to 16 indicate moderate NWSN; scores of 17 to 24 are indeterminate.

Scores on the individual items are also revealing.

Glossary of Terms as Used in this Book

Accommodation

Process of adapting communication to make it more similar to or more different from an interlocutor's.

Achievement-ascription

Cultural value dimension which contrasts determining people's status from their achievements versus determining it from their position resulting from external factors such as inherited wealth.

Ageism

Prejudice or discrimination on the grounds of age.

Anxiety

Fear of aspects of a communication episode, including its outcome.

Apprehension

Fear of communicating experienced beforehand.

Attribution theory

A set of theories about how people decide what mainly caused (or is causing) another person's action.

Authoritarianism

Orientation or belief system of high deference to those in authority; often associated with a rigid value system and prejudice against deviants. An individual trait, not a cultural value.

Biculturalism

Ability to orient oneself fully to more than one culture.

Co-cultures

Groups within a nation or culture (ethnic or religious, for example) treated as equivalents, not main and subordinate.

Collectivism

Cultural value that prioritises the group to which a person belongs over the individual him- or her-self.

Communication

Message exchange between two or more people.

Conforming/varied ideation

Suppression of divergent points of view and convergence towards normative views in decision-making, versus its opposite.

Context

Those aspects of the environment of an encounter that are present in the minds of participants and may influence them; a context may be physical, social (such as the participants' work roles), relate to its purpose or other aspects such as past encounters.

Convergence	Process of adjusting communication style to be more like an interlocutor's.
Conversational constraints	Concerns which influence a communicator's choice of conversational strategy – for example, for clarity or minimising imposition.
Cultural distance	The extent to which two cultures differ, based on an assumption that this can be measured.
Cultural identity	That part of an individual's social identity that is based on his or her membership of one or more cultures.
Cultural relativism	The belief that all cultures are equally valid and that any culture's values and practices must in principle be understood from the point of view of its members.
Culture	Socially constructed set of actions, ideas and objects that people share as members of an enduring, communicatively interacting social group; in this book 'culture' is generally applied only to whole social systems. The term 'subculture' is used for parts of social systems.
Demographic profile	An individual's description in terms of ethnicity, age, gender, (dis)ability level, sexual orientation, nationality, education and socio-economic status.
Discourses	All forms of social interaction, spoken or written, treated as constructing and performing reality, not just reflecting it. Different social groups, such as doctors, use different discourses.
Discrimination	Any situation in which a group or individual is treated unfavourably on the basis of arbitrary grounds, especially prejudice.
Divergence	Process of adjusting communication style to be less like an interlocutor's.
Diversity	Presence of, or stakeholding by, a range of groups of people differentiated by their demographic profile.
Elaborated code	Communication style which explicitly verbalises much of the message; it assumes little shared knowledge with the receiver.
Embeddedness–autonomy	Cultural value related to individualism–collectivism and autonomy/conservatism, but also contrasts openness to change with maintaining the status quo.
Ethical relativism	The claim that there is no culture-free, universal morality and therefore no way of ranking moral views and practices as more or less right, at least across cultures.
Ethics	Moral systems.
Ethnic minority	Ethnic group, which, for reasons of relative numbers or history, often has subordinate status within a society.
Ethnicity	Membership of a population whose members believe that in some sense they share common descent and a common cultural heritage or tradition, and who are so regarded by others.
Ethnocentrism	Belief that one's own culture or ethnic group is superior to others.

Face
Social value people assume for themselves, the image they try to project. Positive face is based on the need for others' approval; negative face on the need to be independent of others and their approval.

Face-threatening acts
Speech acts that threaten the positive or negative 'face' of either the speaker or the hearer of a communication.

Facework
Communication strategies and actions aimed at meeting the communicator's 'face' needs.

Femininity
Cultural value that prioritises modesty, compromise and co-operative success over assertiveness, competition and aggressive success.

Gendering of organisations
Process by which a 'masculine' (or, rarely) 'feminine' culture is created within an organisation.

Globalisation
Processes, facilitated by modern technology and communications, by which economic and business activity, employing capitalist means and values, are alleged to be becoming global and to drive out traditional cultures and values.

Grounding
Process by which people establish and continuously update their shared understanding in conversations.

Harassment
Vexing by repeated attacks, which may be verbal and/or non-explicit.

Heterogeneity, of work groups
Work group composition that is mixed in terms of demographic profile.

Hierarchy–egalitarianism
Cultural value system which contrasts a belief that people are equal with one that elevates some individuals to a right to greater power and status. In addition to equality, egalitarianism implies that people recognise one another as moral equals who share basic interests as human beings.

High-context communication
Culturally endorsed communication style that assumes high levels of shared knowledge and so uses elliptical speech.

Human capital
A society's resources in terms both of its population's economic and social abilities and skills but also of its institutions (civil society).

Humanism/materialism
Cultural value system that contrasts prioritising relationships and caring with prioritising material success.

Individualism
Cultural value that prioritises the individual him- or her-self over the group to which he or she belongs.

Ingroup favouritism
The tendency of members of groups to favour the group to which they belong over other groups in allocating desired resources.

Intercultural communication
Communication between members of two or more cultures, especially, but not only, when their cultural memberships are salient.

Intergroup bias
Prejudice in favour of any group to which the bias-holder belongs or aspires.

Intergroup communication	Communication between members of two or more groups, especially, but not only, when their group memberships are salient.
Interlocutor	Participant in a dialogue or conversation.
Interpersonal communication	Communication between two or more participants, usually, here, face-to-face.
Kinesics	Analyses of human movement.
Learned helplessness	Theory that some people suffer from a sense of helplessness, learned from negative experiences.
Locus of control	An individual's generalised expectations regarding the forces that determine rewards and punishments. 'Internal' locus of control is usually contrasted with 'external', with implications for the individual's other attitudes and behaviour.
Low-context communication	Culturally endorsed communication style that assumes low levels of shared knowledge and so uses verbally explicit speech.
Marginalised groups	Within co-cultural communication theory, social groups that are excluded from full participation in their society.
Masculinity	Cultural value which prioritises assertiveness, competition and aggressive success over modesty, compromise and co-operative success.
Mastery-harmony	Cultural value dimension that contrasts prioritising controlling one's environment with prioritising harmonising with it. Mastery is similar to masculinity but does not imply selfishness; harmony is related to uncertainty avoidance but does not imply an emphasis on controlling ambiguity.
Micro-inequities	Low-level discrimination practised against individuals or groups.
Micropractices	Elements of communication that convey meaning through tiny signs; usually referred to as excluding some groups from full participation.
Monochronic/polychronic time	Cultural value dimension contrasting a preference for doing one thing at a time with a preference for undertaking multiple activities simultaneously.
Neutrality–emotionalism	Cultural value dimension contrasting a preference for an appearance of emotional neutrality with a preference for open display of emotions.
New racism	Prejudice that argues for the social and cultural relevance of biologically rooted characteristics and distinguishes groups of people from one another hierarchically on this basis.
Organisational culture	A set of values and practices supposedly embedded in an organisation; often in reality inculcated by top management.
Persistent injustice effect	Rejection of excuses or apologies by people who have suffered persistent injustice.

Politeness	Facework adjusted to the perceived amount of face-threat involved in a communication.
Power distance	Cultural value dimension which contrasts acceptance that power is distributed unequally with its opposite.
Protestant work ethic	Belief system that stresses successful outcomes for anyone who works hard, and attributes failure to personal factors such as lack of effort and weakness of character.
Proxemics	Analysis of human spatial distance preferences.
Rapport management	Management of relationships during communication.
Restricted code	Communication style which uses limited syntax and vocabulary, but relies extensively on non-verbal behaviour; it assumes a context of knowledge shared with the receiver.
Rhetorical sensitivity	Tendency to adapt messages to audiences.
Self-construal	Mental representation of the self, derived, at least in part, reflexively – that is, by interpreting how others seem, from their communication, to perceive the self.
Self-monitoring	Trait of self-observation and analysis.
Semiotics	Study of signs and symbols.
Social accounts	Explanations, apologies and excuses.
Social dominance orientation	Belief in and support for a natural hierarchy among individuals and groups.
Social loafing	Tendency to work less hard in a group than individually, partly because effort is less likely to bring personal reward.
Specificity-diffuseness	Cultural value dimension of people's sense of what is in the public and private domains of life and of how separate these different domains should be.
Speech acts	Communications treated as performing a function, such as promising, requesting or informing.
Stakeholder approach	An attitude of organisations and institutions that gives weight to the interests of all groups affected by their actions, not, for instance, just shareholders of a company.
Stereotypes	Stable set of beliefs or preconceived ideas that the members of a group share about the characteristics of a group of people.
Subculture	Socially constructed set of actions, ideations and objects that people share as members of an enduring, communicatively interacting social group which is not a whole social system. Applies to gender, social class and so on.
Subjective culture	A society's 'characteristic way of perceiving its social environment'; emphasises psychological constructs.
Topic-comment structure	Order in which a message is given – context first, then main point or vice-versa.
Uncertainty	Inability to predict what strangers' attitudes, feelings, beliefs, values and behaviour will be or explain why they behave in the way they do.

Uncertainty avoidance

Cultural value dimension which refers to the extent to which a culture prefers to avoid ambiguity and to the way in which it resolves uncertainty.

Universalism/particularism

Cultural value dimension that contrasts a preference for drawing general principles versus a preference for the anecdotal or itemised.

Values

'Concepts or beliefs that pertain to desirable end states or behaviors, transcend specific situations, guide selection or evaluation of behavior and events and are ordered by relative importance' or, broad tendencies to prefer certain states of affairs to others.

Further Reading

PART I   CULTURE AND COMMUNICATION AT WORK

Deetz, S. (1995) *Transforming Communication, Transforming Business: Building Responsive and Responsible Worksplaces*, Cresskill, NJ: Hampton Press.

Alvesson, M. and Billing, Y.D. (1997) *Understanding Gender and Organization*, London: Sage.

Buchanan, D. and Huczynski, A. (2003) *Organizational Behaviour, An Introductory Text*, 5th edn, Harlow, Essex: Pearson Education.

Cohn, S.I. (2000) *Race and Gender Discrimination at Work*, Boulder, CO: Westview Press.

Harrison, L.E. and Huntington, S.P. (eds) (2000) *Culture Matters*, New York: Basic Books.

Hofstede, G. and Hofstede, G.J. (2004) *Cultures and Organizations: Software of the Mind: Intercultural Cooperation and Its Importance for Survival*, New York: McGraw-Hill.

Huntington, S.P. (1997) *The Clash of Civilizations and the Remaking of World Order*, London: Simon and Schuster.

Amos, J. (2001) *Cultural Navigation Guide to Europe, Asia and Latin America*, Los Angeles, CA: Interlingua Publications.

Thompson, N. (2003) *Communication and Language: A Handbook of Theory and Practice*, Basingstoke: Palgrave Macmillan.

Littlejohn, S.W. (2001) *Theories of Human Communication*, 5th edn, Belmont, CA: Wadsworth.

Lewis, R.D. (1999) *When Cultures Collide: Managing Successfully Across Cultures*, 2nd edn, London: Nicholas Brealey.

Braithwaite, D.O. and Thompson , T.L. (eds) (2000) *Handbook of Communication and People with Disabilities: Research and Application*, New York: Lawrence Erlbaum.

Adler, N.J. (2001) *International Dimensions of Organizational Behavior*, 4th edn, Cincinnati, OH: South-Western College Publishing.

Brislin, R. (1999) *Understanding Culture's Influence on Behavior*, Stamford, CT: Thomson Learning.

Argyle, M. (2000) *Psychology and Religion: An Introduction*, London: Routledge.

Manstead, A.S.R. and Hewstone, M. (eds) (1996) *The Blackwell Encyclopaedia of Social Psychology*, Oxford: Blackwell.

PART II   INTERCULTURAL COMMUNICATION AT WORK

Bennett, M.J. (ed.) (1998) *Basic Concepts of Intercultural Communication: Selected Readings*, Maine: Intercultural Press.

Chen, G.-M. and Starosta, W.J. (1998) *Foundations of Intercultural Communication,* Boston, MA: Allyn and Bacon.

Chaney, L.H. and Martin, J.S. (2003) *Intercultural Business Communication,* 3rd edn, Prentice-Hall.

Guirdham, M. (2003) *Interactive Behaviour at Work,* 3rd edn, Harlow, Essex: Pearson Education.

Casmir, F.L. (ed.) (1997) *Ethics in Intercultural and International Communication,* Mahwah, NJ: Lawrence Erlbaum Associates.

Ting-Toomey, S. and Oetzel, J.G. (2001) *Managing Intercultural Conflict Effectively,* Thousand Oaks, CA: Sage.

PART III   EXTENSIONS AND APPLICATIONS

Brislin, R.W. (1996) *Intercultural Interactions: A Practical Guide,* 2nd edn, Beverley Hills, CA: Sage Publications.

Kohls, S. (2001) *The Art of Crossing Cultures,* London: Nicholas Brealey.

Schneider, S.C. and Barsoux, J.-L. (2003) *Managing Across Cultures,* Harlow, Essex: Pearson Education.

Bartlett, C.A. and Ghoshal, S. (2002) *Managing Across Borders, The Transnational Solution,* Cambridge, MA: Harvard Business School Press.

Hickson, D.J. and Pugh, D. (2002) *Management Worldwide: Distinctive Styles Amid Globalization,* Harmondsworth: Penguin Business.

Riccucci, N.M. (2002) *Managing Diversity in Public Sector Workforces,* NY: Westview Press.

Murrell, A.J., Crosby, F.J. and Ely, A.J. (eds) (1999) *Mentoring Dilemmas: Developmental Relationships within Multicultural Organizations,* Hillsdale, NJ: Lawrence Erlbaum.

APPENDIX B

Herring, S.C. (ed.) (1996) *Computer-Mediated Communication: Linguistic, Social and Cross-Cultural Perspectives,* Amsterdam: J. Benjamins Pub.

Index

3M